Domesticating Neo-Liberalism

RGS-IBG Book Series

Published

Domesticating Neo-Liberalism: Spaces of Economic Practice and Social Reproduction in Post-Socialist Cities
Alison Stenning, Adrian Smith, Alena Rochovská and Dariusz Świątek

Swept Up Lives? Re-envisioning the Homeless City
Paul Cloke, Jon May and Sarah Johnsen

Aerial Life: Spaces, Mobilities, Affects
Peter Adey

Millionaire Migrants: Trans-Pacific Life Lines
David Ley

State, Science and the Skies: Governmentalities of the British Atmosphere
Mark Whitehead

Complex Locations: Women's geographical work in the UK 1850–1970
Avril Maddrell

Value Chain Struggles: Institutions and Governance in the Plantation Districts of South India
Jeff Neilson and Bill Pritchard

Queer Visibilities: Space, Identity and Interaction in Cape Town
Andrew Tucker

Arsenic Pollution: A Global Synthesis
Peter Ravenscroft, Hugh Brammer and Keith Richards

Resistance, Space and Political Identities: The Making of Counter-Global Networks
David Featherstone

Mental Health and Social Space: Towards Inclusionary Geographies?
Hester Parr

Climate and Society in Colonial Mexico: A Study in Vulnerability
Georgina H. Endfield

Geochemical Sediments and Landscapes
Edited by David J. Nash and Sue J. McLaren

Driving Spaces: A Cultural-Historical Geography of England's M1 Motorway
Peter Merriman

Badlands of the Republic: Space, Politics and Urban Policy
Mustafa Dikeç

Geomorphology of Upland Peat: Erosion, Form and Landscape Change
Martin Evans and Jeff Warburton

Spaces of Colonialism: Delhi's Urban Governmentalities
Stephen Legg

People/States/Territories
Rhys Jones

Publics and the City
Kurt Iveson

After the Three Italies: Wealth, Inequality and Industrial Change
Mick Dunford and Lidia Greco

Putting Workfare in Place
Peter Sunley, Ron Martin and Corinne Nativel

Domicile and Diaspora
Alison Blunt

Geographies and Moralities
Edited by Roger Lee and David M. Smith

Military Geographies
Rachel Woodward

A New Deal for Transport?
Edited by Iain Docherty and Jon Shaw

Geographies of British Modernity
Edited by David Gilbert, David Matless and Brian Short

Lost Geographies of Power
John Allen

Globalizing South China
Carolyn L. Cartier

Geomorphological Processes and Landscape Change: Britain in the Last 1000 Years
Edited by David L. Higgitt and E. Mark Lee

Forthcoming

Globalizing Responsibility: The Political Rationalities of Ethical Consumption
Clive Barnett, Paul Cloke, Nick Clarke & Alice Malpass

Spatial Politics: Essays for Doreen Massey
Edited by David Featherstone and Joe Painter

The Improvised State: Sovereignty, Performance and Agency in Dayton Bosnia
Alex Jeffrey

In the Nature of Landscape: Cultural Geography on the Norfolk Broads
David Matless

Learning the City: Translocal Assemblages and Urban Politics
Colin McFarlane

Fashioning Globalization: New Zealand Design, Working Women and the 'New Economy'
Maureen Molloy and Wendy Larner

Domesticating Neo-Liberalism

Spaces of Economic Practice and Social Reproduction in Post-Socialist Cities

Alison Stenning, Adrian Smith,
Alena Rochovská and Dariusz Świątek

WILEY-BLACKWELL

A John Wiley & Sons, Ltd., Publication

This edition first published 2010

© 2010 Alison Stenning, Adrian Smith, Alena Rochovská and Dariusz Świątek

Blackwell Publishing was acquired by John Wiley & Sons in February 2007. Blackwell's publishing program has been merged with Wiley's global Scientific, Technical, and Medical business to form Wiley-Blackwell.

Registered Office
John Wiley & Sons Ltd, The Atrium, Southern Gate, Chichester, West Sussex, PO19 8SQ, United Kingdom

Editorial Offices
350 Main Street, Malden, MA 02148-5020, USA
9600 Garsington Road, Oxford, OX4 2DQ, UK
The Atrium, Southern Gate, Chichester, West Sussex, PO19 8SQ, UK

For details of our global editorial offices, for customer services, and for information about how to apply for permission to reuse the copyright material in this book please see our website at www.wiley.com/wiley-blackwell.

The right of Alison Stenning, Adrian Smith, Alena Rochovská and Dariusz Świątek to be identified as the author of this work has been asserted in accordance with the UK Copyright, Designs and Patents Act 1988.

Library of Congress Cataloging-in-Publication Data is available for this book.

ISBN 978-1-4051-6991-2 (hardback)
ISBN 978-1-4051-6990-5 (paperback)

A catalogue record for this book is available from the British Library.

Set in 10/12pt Plantin by SPi Publisher Services, Pondicherry, India
Printed and bound in Malaysia by Vivar Printing Sdn Bhd

1   2010

Contents

List of Plates, Figures and Tables		vi
Series Editor's Preface		ix
Preface and Acknowledgements		x
1	Domesticating Neo-Liberalism and the Spaces of Post-Socialism	1
2	Neo-Liberalism and Post-Socialist Transformations	33
3	Domesticating Economies: Diverse Economic Practices, Households and Social Reproduction	58
4	Work: Employment, Unemployment and the Negotiation of Labour Markets	81
5	Housing: Markets, Assets and Social Reproduction	112
6	Land and Food: Production, Consumption and Leisure	144
7	Care: Family, Social Networks and the State	175
8	Conclusions	219
Appendix I:	*Summary Information on Interviewed Households*	238
Appendix II:	*Semi-Structured Interviews with Key Informants*	250
Notes		258
Bibliography		267
Index		295

Plates, Figures and Tables

PLATES

1.1	Haanova, Petržalka	22
1.2	Gessayova, Petržalka	23
1.3	Lúky-sever, Petržalka	24
1.4	Osiedle Willowe, Nowa Huta	24
1.5	Osiedle Górali, Nowa Huta	25
1.6	Osiedle Przy Arce, Nowa Huta	26
1.7	Osiedle Dywizjonu 303, Nowa Huta	27
1.8	Osiedle Oświecenia, Nowa Huta	28
4.1	A steelworker at Arcelor Mittal, Nowa Huta	88
5.1	New private housing development in Petržalka	118
5.2	Balcony renovations in Nowa Huta	130
6.1	Vegetable plot on an allotment in Nowa Huta	146
6.2	Workers' allotment garden, Nowa Huta	147
6.3	Allotment garden and small cottage, Petržalka	147
6.4	Carrefour Hypermarket in Nowa Huta	163
6.5	Tomex, a market in Nowa Huta	166
7.1	Pensioners talk in Nowa Huta	202
7.2	Towarzystwo Solidarnej Pomocy (Mutual Assistance Association), Nowa Huta	214

FIGURES

1.1	Income inequality in Central and Eastern Europe, 1989 and 2006 (Gini coefficient)	9
1.2	Map of Nowa Huta	14

1.3 Map of Petržalka   15
2.1 State expenditure on social assistance for those in 'material
     deprivation', Slovakia 1997–2004   54
3.1 The economy as iceberg   66
3.2 A diverse economy   67
4.1 Sectoral employment change, Bratislava and Kraków   87
4.2 Occupational profile of household members relative to
     poverty risk levels, Petržalka and Nowa Huta   92

TABLES

1.1 Poverty risk in East Central Europe   8
1.2 Population of Nowa Huta, Kraków and Poland, 1950–2002   16
1.3 Population of Petržalka, Bratislava and Slovakia, 1950–2001   17
1.4 'Risk of poverty' and social exclusion in Nowa Huta
     and Petržalka   18
1.5 Surveyed neighbourhoods in Nowa Huta   20
1.6 Surveyed neighbourhoods in Petržalka   21
2.1 Flat tax rates on personal incomes in East Central Europe   52
4.1 Average monthly gross wages in Poland and Slovakia   83
4.2 Employment structure of households in Nowa Huta and
     Petržalka relative to 'at risk' of poverty levels   91
4.3 Average equivalized monthly income for households with
     different employment structures in Nowa Huta and Petržalka   93
4.4 Gender and occupational structure in Nowa Huta
     and Petržalka   93
4.5 Average proportion of income derived from
     various sources   98
5.1 Means of acquisition of current apartment, by income category   120
5.2 Tenure status of surveyed households   121
5.3 Average apartment prices in selected central European
     cities, 2004   122
5.4 Average apartment sale prices in Petržalka and Nowa Huta   123
5.5 Surveyed neighbourhoods in Petržalka   123
5.6 Surveyed neighbourhoods in Nowa Huta   124
5.7 Total living space   125
5.8 Living space per person in Petržalka and Nowa Huta   126
5.9 Average proportion of household expenditure on housing
     by income groups   139
6.1 Access to land by income categories   150
6.2 Gender of the main household members with responsibility
     for working on land   151

6.3	Generational structure of household members working on household plots	151
6.4	Primary purpose of having access to land	154
6.5	Average proportion of household expenditure on food, leisure and savings	156
6.6	Average household provisioning of vegetables and fruit	156
6.7	Average proportion of household expenditure on various items by income groups relative to median income	170
7.1	Household composition in Petržalka and Nowa Huta	180
7.2	Domestic work: gender of primary responsible household member	183
7.3	Percentage of households engaging non-household members in routine tasks	187
7.4	Frequency of family help	188
7.5	Help given and received from family, friends, neighbours, colleagues and organizations	189
7.6	Households with some level of contact with neighbours, by neighbourhood	203
7.7	Forms of neighbourly support	204
7.8	Average proportion of income derived from various sources	207
7.9	Households receiving state or local authority assistance in previous 12 months	209
7.10	Households receiving school assistance in previous 12 months	209

Series Editor's Preface

The RGS-IBG Book Series only publishes work of the highest international standing. Its emphasis is on distinctive new developments in human and physical geography, although it is also open to contributions from cognate disciplines whose interests overlap with those of geographers. The Series places strong emphasis on theoretically informed and empirically strong texts. Reflecting the vibrant and diverse theoretical and empirical agendas that characterize the contemporary discipline, contributions are expected to inform, challenge and stimulate the reader. Overall, the RGS-IBG Book Series seeks to promote scholarly publications that leave an intellectual mark and change the way readers think about particular issues, methods or theories.

For details on how to submit a proposal please visit:
www.rgsbookseries.com.

Kevin Ward
University of Manchester, UK

Joanna Bullard
Loughborough University, UK

RGS-IBG Book Series Editors

Preface and Acknowledgements

This book is the product of a research project funded by the UK's Economic and Social Research Council entitled *Social Exclusion, Spaces of Household Economic Practice and Post-Socialism* (RES-00023-0695). This project has generated a range of publications (many of which are listed in the bibliography) and we have altered author order over this range of publications to achieve some balance between the two primary investigators (Adrian Smith and Alison Stenning). *Domesticating Neo-Liberalism* has been primarily written jointly by Adrian and Alison, with very important input from Alena and Dariusz in terms of data collection, analysis and interpretation. In that sense it is very much a joint endeavour.

Research of the kind discussed in this book inevitably results in the accumulation of a whole series of debts and gratitudes to those who so freely gave of their time to allow us to develop the understandings discussed here. We are first and foremost truly appreciative of the time and space that all of our respondents and informants in Nowa Huta, Petržalka and beyond provided, often at times when they had many other pressures on their lives, as we document in *Domesticating Neo-Liberalism*. The kindness shown by our informants and respondents marks one of the key elements, as we note in the book, of everyday life in Nowa Huta and Petržalka, namely a deep-seated economy of generosity.

Throughout the timeframe of the research we benefited from the careful and thoughtful comments of an advisory group who helped us in the design and implementation of the research and our interpretation of the material that was being generated. In particular, we would like to thank Bernardína Bodnárová and Anton Michálek in Bratislava, Alena Ledeneva in London, and Claire Wallace in Vienna and then Aberdeen. We are also grateful to Paweł Buczkowicz, Karol Janas, Tomasz Padło, Małgorzata Sadowniczyk, Anna Świątek and Beata Zawilska in Nowa Huta and Peter Brezovský,

Slavomír Brezovský, Zuzana Zajacová and Anton Sorád in Bratislava for assistance in carrying out the household survey, in transcribing interviews and in assisting with data entry.

A large number of colleagues across Europe and beyond provided ideas, comments and discussion of our work in research workshops, conference sessions and more informally. As a team, we would particularly like to thank: Bob Begg, Stefan Bouzarovski, Mike Bradshaw, Andy Cook, Kathie Gibson, Julie Graham, Jane Hardy, Kathrin Hörschelmann, Deema Kaneff, Wendy Larner, Roger Lee, Sallie Marston, Linda McDowell, Pete North, Marianna Pavlovskaya, Jamie Peck, John Pickles, Frances Pine, Al Rainnie, John Round, Martin Sokol, Adam Swain, Adam Tickell and Judit Timár. Versions of some of the chapters of this book were presented at academic conferences and in departmental seminars. We are grateful to all those who provided their comments and ideas.

Ed Oliver produced the maps and we are very grateful to him for responding in the calm and patient manner he always does to our many requests for changes and alterations.

Sections of Chapter Four have been published previously in Smith, A., Stenning, A., Rochovská, A. and Świątek, D. (2008) 'The emergence of a working poor: Labour markets, neoliberalisation and diverse economies in post-socialist cities', *Antipode*, 40 (2): 283–311, which has been reprinted as Smith, A., Stenning, A., Rochovská, A. and Świątek, D. (2008) 'The emergence of a working poor: Labour markets, neoliberalisation and diverse economies in post-socialist cities', in Smith, A., Stenning, A. and Willis, K. (eds) (2008) *Social Justice and Neo-Liberalism: Global Perspectives* (London: Zed, pp. 164–198). We are very grateful to Wiley-Blackwell and Zed Books for permission to use parts of this material here. We are also very grateful to Julie Graham, Kathie Gibson and the Community Economies Collective for permission to reproduce Figure 3.1, which is attributed to Ken Byrne. All the photographs that appear, including on the front cover, are the work of the project team.

Kevin Ward has been a wonderfully patient and supportive RGS-IBG book series editor; Jacqueline Scott at Wiley-Blackwell has provided first rate editorial input; and we are very grateful to the reviewers of the initial proposal and of the draft manuscript for their help in clarifying issues and pushing us to be sharper in our analysis.

In addition, Adrian would personally like to thank Milan Buček, Roman Džambazovič, Juraj Janto, Rudolf Pástor, Leo Singer, Peter Spišiak, and Zuzana Kusá for their help and collaboration, as well as Angela Baxter, Alex, Dom and Theo for all their love and support. Alison would like to thank her Polish and UK colleagues (especially Mariusz Czepczyński, Stuart Dawley, Bolesław Domański, Helen Jarvis, Nina Laurie, Jane Pollard and Aneta Słowik) and her PhD students for their ongoing support, interest and ideas. In Nowa Huta, she owes a huge debt of thanks to Danuta Szymońska and Kasia Danecka-Zapała for their interest in her work, their ongoing encouragement and, above all, their friendship. She also thanks her mother, Elisabeth Banks, for a careful proofread, and other help along the way. Finally, at home, Fergus Campbell has lived with her everyday domestications and she thanks him with all her heart.

Chapter One

Domesticating Neo-Liberalism and the Spaces of Post-Socialism

Domesticating Neo-Liberalism

In February 2004, three months before Slovakia was due to join the European Union, the Slovak government mobilized 20,000 extra police and 1,000 soldiers to quell a revolt by members of the Roma community in the east of the country. The revolt involved, primarily, the looting of basic provisions from food stores and was a reaction to the dramatic scaling back of the social welfare system. As the then Minister for Labour, the Family and Social Affairs and architect of a radical overhaul of the social assistance system, L'udovít Kaník, was quoted as saying 'Cuts in benefits are needed to end a culture of dependence among Roma' (Burgermeister, 2004). This series of events emerged out of a much larger-scale state initiative, which originated in the political economy of the collapse of state socialism in 1989 and intensified after the 1998 election of a centre-right coalition government, to dramatically overhaul the nature of political and economic life, modelled strongly on neo-liberal principles (Smith & Rochovská, 2007; Fisher, et al., 2007). The events of February 2004 represented, then, part of a popular reaction against neo-liberalism, which culminated in the election – after eight years of neo-liberal policies – of a more centre-left coalition government in June 2006.

Three years after these events in Slovakia, in the summer of 2007, 'Poland ... witnessed one of the biggest waves of social protests in health-care in many years' (Czarzasty, 2007) – the so-called 'white protests' – as thousands of Polish nurses and doctors expressed in different ways their own discontent with the neo-liberalization of Poland's health care sector. After weeks of strikes (*Warsaw Voice*, 20 June 2007), a demonstration outside the Prime Minister's chancellery suffered a disproportionate response from the authorities as nurses, doctors and their supporters were attacked by riot police. Refused a meeting with the Prime Minister, four of the nurses' leaders launched a sit-in of the chancellery and some 1,500 of their supporters camped out in solidarity in nearby Lazienki Park, creating the so-called 'White Village', a 'tent city' with kitchens, lectures, clinics and its own newspaper, which was maintained for over four weeks, with the support of miners, steelworkers and others who shared the nurses' concerns. These protests emerged against a backdrop of repeated strikes and protests (Stenning & Hardy, 2005) through which nurses, in particular, contested ongoing reforms to the health sector. Their particular concerns were 'inadequate financial expenditure on the public healthcare system in general and ... insufficient pay levels in particular' (Czarzasty 2007), which their leaders argued resulted from the commercialization of the health service, and the creation of health care funds which introduced internal markets into health care provision. These – and the chronic underfunding which ensued – were, in turn, the result of pressures to reduce government debt, in the hope of Poland's entry into the Eurozone. In contrasting ways, then, the nurses' protests of summer 2007 echoed the earlier contestation of neo-liberalization in Slovakia, and a growing wave of concern about its effects across East Central Europe (ECE).

The key elements of the reforms contested by the Slovak Roma and the Polish health care workers – benefits cuts, attacks on 'dependence', public sector rationalization, fiscal austerity – sit at the heart of the project of neo-liberalism. Indeed, the 'transition' from communism to capitalism in ECE represents perhaps one of the boldest experiments with neo-liberal ideas in the world today, demonstrating vividly the policies and practices associated with this market-led ideology.[1] The project of neo-liberalism (or neo-liberalization), as we discuss in more detail in Chapter Two, rests on a theory of political economy which promotes markets, enterprise and private property, restructures regulation into more limited forms, and reduces the role of the public sector and welfare (Harvey, 2005; Peck & Tickell, 2002; Larner, 2003; J. Clarke, 2004). But it is more than a political-economic project; neo-liberalization is a social project too. It is predicated on a rejection of 'society' and on a promotion of the individual – most particularly, the entrepreneurial self (du Gay, 1996) – and of an idealized notion of the family. Neo-liberalism remakes the familial spaces of the household and of social reproduction as it remakes the economy. In all of these ways, the neo-liberal projects adopted and struggled over around the world have very real and often negative consequences, especially for the poor, the socially excluded and the marginalized (Smith et al., 2008a).

Domesticating Neo-Liberalism examines the remaking of household economic practices and social reproduction in Poland and Slovakia in the context of these neo-liberal transformations. In short, it asks how Polish and Slovak households work to ensure that their basic needs for income, housing, food and care are met as wider political economies are neo-liberalized. Through this focus, *Domesticating Neo-Liberalism* seeks to understand how the processes of neo-liberalization are promoted, received, lived, negotiated and resisted in Poland and Slovakia.

In order to explore the articulations between everyday economic practices, social reproduction and the construction of neo-liberal worlds, we take inspiration from Creed's (1998) argument that state socialism could only be understood within the context of its *domestication*, as it was negotiated, constituted and made possible through the practices of everyday life and social reproduction. For Creed, domestication involves envisioning 'big' political-economic projects not simply as 'out there' and all-powerful, but as always already particular, domestic, and local phenomena too.

Building on Creed (1998) and others who work with the notion of domestication (see Chapter Three), we intertwine two versions of domestication. On the one hand, we explore the ways in which politicians, academics, think tanks and social institutions at the national, regional and international scales have 'domesticated' the dissemination of neo-liberal policies in Poland and Slovakia in ways which query the idea of neo-liberalism as a singular, top-down political-economic project. This perspective builds on accounts of neo-liberalism that characterize it as a geographically differentiated, locally complex process (invariably called 'neo-liberalization') (Barnett, 2005; Castree, 2006; Harvey, 2005; Larner, 2003; Leitner et al., 2007; Smith et al., 2008; Ward & England, 2007).

On the other hand, we read neo-liberalism as a process that is domesticated not only by the actions of national elites but also by the everyday economic practices of individuals, households and communities. This interpretation follows Creed (1998) more closely and presents domestication as an everyday and ongoing set of practices that at times destabilizes neo-liberalism but at other times articulates the neo-liberal with its others. As a result, domestication entails much more than explicit attempts at resistance, as Creed (1998: 3) explains in the context of socialism:

> By simply doing what they could to improve their difficult circumstances, without any grand design of resistance, villagers forced concessions from central planners and administrators that eventually transformed an oppressive, intrusive system into a tolerable one. In short, through their mundane actions villagers domesticated the socialist revolution.

In *Domesticating Neo-Liberalism*, this second reading itself folds in three key claims. We argue that a focus on the mundane practices of economic life enables a detailed understanding of how neo-liberalism is understood, negotiated, contested and made tolerable in homes, communities and workplaces; how neo-liberalism is lived in articulation with a host of economic, political and social others; and how those practices are themselves involved in the remaking of neo-liberalism.

Domesticating Neo-Liberalism, then, connects two interrelated concerns. Empirically, we are concerned to document and explain the 'violence of the economy' (Pickles, 2004b; see also Žižek, 2006, 2008) in post-socialist East Central Europe and to build an account of the ways in which Polish and Slovak households have negotiated – or domesticated – the dislocations and exclusions that have emerged since 1989. Conceptually, we seek to employ these analyses of 'domestication' to think again about neo-liberalism in general and its post-socialist form in particular, by considering how neo-liberalism has been made and remade in Poland and Slovakia, at a variety of scales from national policy debates, through the work of think tanks, firms and charities, to the household and individual.

The research for this book took place in 2005 and 2006, before the global economic crisis of 2008/9, which has begun to transform neo-liberalism and the landscape of global economic policy-making in important ways. As we discuss more fully in the concluding chapter, the extent and nature of these transformations and their impact on both national political economies and everyday economic practices in Poland and Slovakia remains an open question.

Post-Socialism

In the Polish and Slovak contexts, which form the focus of *Domesticating Neo-Liberalism*, these analyses of both the particular policy circuits and environments as well as the lived experiences of neo-liberalism demonstrate the importance of both the legacies of socialism and the particular political economies of the post-1989 period. Thus, we also explore the particularities of post-socialist neo-liberalism, seeking to understand the difference that post-socialism makes to the processes of neo-liberalization.

Since the collapse of state socialism, debates about post-socialism have been centred in large part on the discursive power and political economy of neo-liberalism. While the early debates revolved around the distinction between 'shock therapy' and 'gradualism' (Sachs, 1990; Popov, 2000, 2007; see also Chapter Two), the perceived 'failure' of the state to effectively manage political-economic life refracted earlier concerns over state intervention and the likelihood for some that it would lead to a 'road to serfdom' (Hayek, 1994; for a critical review, see Peck, 2008). Different models of economic transformation emerged across the region, but each was committed in various ways to neo-liberalism: to the primacy of market relations; to the establishment of the social relations of capitalism based on private production, appropriation and redistribution of the economic and social surplus; to re-configurations of property ownership relations and class power; to a transformation of the state in the support of the development of market economies and capitalist social relations; and to the establishment of an ethic and subjectivity of individual responsibility. This 'transition culture' (Kennedy, 2002) left little space for debate or for alternatives. Policy prescriptions were frequently teleological, modernizing and reductionist (see Chapter Two) and placed an overwhelming emphasis on the changes that needed to be implemented for the post-socialist states to reach the 'standards and performance norms of advanced industrial economies' (EBRD, 1996: 11–12; see also Smith, 2002b; Stenning & Bradshaw, 1999). To meet these norms, four 'pillars' were identified – privatization, stabilization, liberalization and internationalization – whose correct and successful implementation would lead, it was argued, to the emergence of a market economy. This orthodox prescription sits within the wider notion of the 'Washington Consensus' (Williamson, 1990; Stiglitz, 2002), derived from the policies of international financial institutions, such as the World Bank, the International Monetary Fund (IMF) and the European Bank for Reconstruction and Development (EBRD). In these ways, the 'transition to capitalism' in ECE has been experienced as a thoroughly neo-liberalizing process. However, as we explore here in detail, the neo-liberal transition has been articulated with a host of 'others', economic and social relations which were not reducible to the market but were connected to it in complex ways (Smith & Stenning, 2006; Smith & Rochovská, 2007).

As the 1990s progressed, and as the policy focus shifted away from establishing the building blocks of market capitalism across the region, the possibility of wider geo-political and geo-economic integration with the European Union (EU) further consolidated a commitment to the primacy of capitalist and neo-liberal social relations (Gowan, 1995; Rainnie et al., 2002a; Smith, 2002b). The EU had, of course, by this time – following the introduction of the single currency, the extension of the single market and the Lisbon agenda on competitiveness – become thoroughly committed to a neo-liberal framework, despite the attempt to balance this with a continuing commitment to social cohesion. The prospect of EU membership and the imposition of the *aquis communautaire* (the European Community's complete legislative framework) enabled a process of West–East policy transfer. In this way, policies to secure the primacy of the market and the legal basis for competition policy were adopted across the candidate countries as the basis for approval of their accession to the Union. Such was the power of this discursive and material framing of neo-liberal transformation in the run-up to EU enlargement that several commentators argued that accession represented the effective end of 'post-socialism' as the countries of the region became 'normalized' into the European family of nations (for a critique, see Stenning & Hörschelmann, 2008).

The notion of domestication, and the attention we draw to other sets of social relations that articulate with neo-liberalism, echo a conceptualization of post-socialism which is marked by a diversity of social forms, by continuity and change, and by an appreciation of the ways in which 'actually existing' state socialism continues to reverberate through the cultural and political economy of ECE (Stenning & Hörschelmann, 2008). As Hann et al. (2002: 10) suggest, 'the everyday moral communities of socialism have been undermined but not replaced', such that the experiences of post-socialism continue to be distinctively shaped by 'the socialist past and narratives of the past' (Hemment, 2003). The narratives and legacies of the past – including those that hark back to the era before socialism – articulate with contemporary processes of globalization and neo-liberalization. They do so in their particular incarnation as 'transition', but also in their other more universal manifestations, with the passage of European Union enlargement and with wider experiences of restructuring and development, with which post-socialism shares both discursive and material features (Pickles & Smith, 1998; Stenning & Bradshaw, 1999).

Everyday Life in Post-Socialist Poland and Slovakia

As this account of post-socialist transformation suggests, the collapse of communism in ECE in 1989 heralded a set of political, economic, social and cultural transformations which radically remade the landscapes of everyday life. In the spheres of work and labour markets, home and housing, community and social networks, and consumption, amongst others, the lives of post-socialist citizens shifted dramatically. These everyday transformations have attracted increasing attention in studies of post-socialism, as geographers, sociologists and anthropologists seek to document and understand the lived experiences of post-1989 transformations (Burawoy & Verdery, 1999; Bridger & Pine, 1998; Shevchenko, 2009). In part this reflects a renewed interest in the everyday across the social sciences (Bennett & Watson, 2002; Moran, 2005; see also Chapter Three), but it also reflects the particularities of post-socialism. Not only was the 'transition to capitalism' in East Central Europe and the former Soviet Union one of the boldest projects of social, political and economic reform of recent times, but the very nature of the political economy of state socialism meant that many of the spheres of everyday life were particularly interconnected, and thus their transformation particularly complex.

Domesticating Neo-Liberalism focuses on the spheres of work, housing, food, and care, all of which have been dramatically transformed in the years since 1989. In the sphere of work, redundancy and unemployment have been coupled with the emergence of new forms of work in new sectors of the economy, and with the remaking of pay and conditions across the labour market. In housing, the rapid development of markets has promoted owner occupation, and has fed the construction of new forms of residential space, the stigmatization of socialized housing and the polarization of housing outcomes. Through the home, housing transformations have been connected to wider transformations in relationships and family life, as marital, sexual and domestic politics have shifted, and phenomena such as alcoholism, homelessness and depression have grown and/or become more visible. These shifts themselves have remade social networks, communities, and institutions, positively and negatively, as some have been eroded by poverty and inequality and others have emerged from new opportunities and new connections. Rising poverty and inequality have also structured access to post-socialist spheres of consumption, marked above all by the diversification of retail provision as large transnational corporations enter the market alongside a multiplication of domestic retailers, marking out a complex geography of provision.

Together, these transformations have radically remade the everyday lives of post-socialist citizens and their geographies. The complexity of these everyday transformations has been increasingly recognized,[2] but much of this work has focused on the question of 'survival strategies'. In *Domesticating Neo-Liberalism*, as we discuss in more detail in Chapter Three, we shift the focus away from survival towards social reproduction. The focus on survival strategies, we argue, delimits the breadth and complexity of household economic practices; it suggests that such practices are responsive acts, constructed in conditions of austerity to achieve survival, rejecting the possibility that such practices may be planned, creative, rooted in family and community cultures, and oriented towards pleasure, thriving and flourishing. In focusing instead on social reproduction, we echo the necessity of economy – that is, as Lee (2006) has argued, economic practices must be 'life-sustaining' – but expand our focus to reflect a recognition that social reproduction demands the satisfaction of more than material basic needs, to include care, comfort, pleasure and community.

One of the concerns, however, that the literature on survival strategies does highlight is that of growing poverty in post-socialism. While poverty was relatively 'hidden' prior to the collapse of state socialism (Golinowska, 2000; Tarkowska, 1999), in many of the new EU member states levels of poverty (defined in relation to the standard of 60% of national median income) remain close to, or above, the EU average (Table 1.1). Poland stands out as having among the highest levels of poverty and the geography of poverty at the sub-national level in both Poland and Slovakia is very uneven, with many geographically concentrated 'pockets' of immiserised peoples (Michálek 2004, 2005; Rochovská, 2004; Kusá & Džambazovič, 2006;

Table 1.1   Poverty risk in East Central Europe (% of households below 60% of median income)

	Risk of poverty after social transfers	Risk of poverty before social transfers	Risk of poverty for those in work
EU25	16	23	8
EU15	16	22	7
Bulgaria	14	–	–
Czech Republic	10	16	3
Estonia	18	28	8
Latvia	23	35	11
Lithuania	20	30	10
Hungary	16	25	7
Poland	19	28	13
Romania	19	–	–
Slovenia	12	15	5
Slovakia	12	18	6

Source: Extracted from Eurostat online database 2007

Džambazovič, 2007; Tarkowska, 1999; Warzywoda-Kruszyńska, 1999). In both Poland and Slovakia, high concentrations of poverty are found in rural regions dominated by former state and collective farms, on the eastern and western borders, and in urban regions experiencing industrial decline (Danglová, 1998; Smith, 1998; Stenning et al., 2007; Stenning, 2005a).

Patterns of poverty are uneven not only spatially but also socially. In institutional (Alam et al., 2005) and academic accounts of poverty in post-socialism, the most vulnerable groups are regularly identified as children and young people, women, pensioners, minority ethnic households, those living in households headed by people out of work (as a result of unemployment, disability or ill-health) and by those with low levels of education. Yet whilst poverty levels amongst many of these groups are disturbingly high, increasingly large numbers of those living in poverty fit none of these categories; these are the working poor – a new phenomenon in ECE (which we explore in more detail in Chapter Four).

The costs of 'transition' can be measured not only in rising poverty, but also in increasing inequality. Before 1989, many of the countries of ECE (and the former Soviet Union) recorded some of the lowest levels of income inequality in the world. Since 1989, however, indicators suggest that there has been a rapid increase in inequality (see Figure 1.1).[3] This rising income inequality is a result partly of 'top-end' shifts as the decompression of wages, the rewarding of entrepreneurship, the appearance of some well-paid jobs

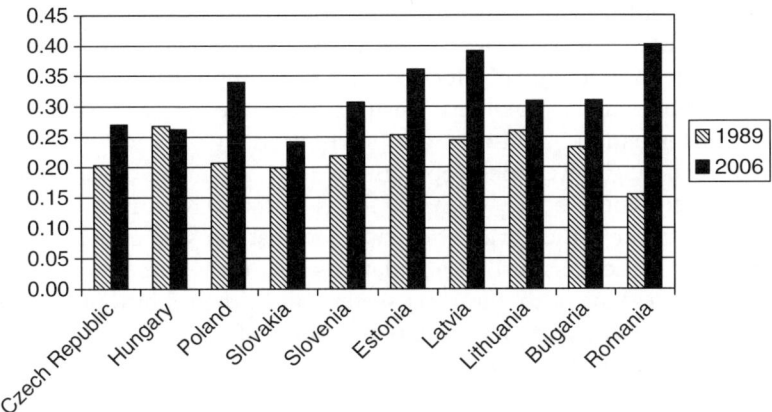

Notes : 2005 data: Czech Republic, Estonia; 2004 data: Latvia, Lithuania

Figure 1.1 Income inequality in Central and Eastern Europe, 1989 and 2006 (Gini coefficient)
Source: Elaborated from UNICEF TRANSMONEE database

in global corporations and the 'windfalls' of post-socialist privatizations enable the emergence of the wealthy and even 'super-rich' in ECE. However, it is the simultaneous negative shifts at the 'bottom' end of the income continuum which account for most of the polarization of income; job loss, wage decline and arrears, and the reliance of some on informal labour markets have led to marked impoverishment for many. Income inequality is, moreover, reinforced by the erosion of other material assets (such as housing, land and equipment), by the poverty of social networks, by the absence of opportunity (for work, education, consumption and leisure), and by exclusion from mainstream spaces and institutions. Inequalities reflect asymmetries of both economic and socio-cultural power and draw attention to the ways in which the neo-liberal commitment to individualized responsibility both rests on and remakes gender, class, generation, and ethnicity.[4]

The uneven experience of post-socialist neo-liberalization suggests that the domestication of post-1989 transformations will play out in particular ways in large cities. Much of the research on poverty and inequality in post-socialism has been focused on marginal, rural regions, and has avoided serious analyses of these issues in diverse, dynamic urban centres. As the emergence of in-work poverty suggests, however, these are important issues in large urban spaces too. Although poverty in cities tends to remain hidden within the overall context of economic growth, inequality has become increasingly visible as employment, income and access to work have become more and more polarized, not least because cities have been at the forefront of post-socialist transformations (Andrusz et al., 1996; Bodnár, 2001; Stenning,

2004). This centrality is connected to positive transformations, such as high rates of economic growth, low levels of unemployment, and increasingly diversified economies (in production and consumption), at least until the 2008 economic crisis. But these positive indicators are also suggestive of rapid transformation – and thus the need for adaptation and negotiation – and conceal the uneven development of post-socialism. These questions become all the more acute when the focus shifts away from the globalized city centres towards the peripheral, state socialist housing estates where the majority of post-socialist urban populations live. These large estates became an essential element of the housing system and urban fabric of societies in ECE, home to largely in-migrating populations of relatively young families, often with roots in rural society. During state socialism, as we discuss in more detail in Chapter Five, the estates tended to be socially mixed, housing both working- and middle-class households, but since the collapse of communism there has been an expectation that they would become increasingly divided, echoing patterns in Western European cities (Sýkora, 2000). *Domesticating Neo-Liberalism* interrogates this idea in detail, focusing as it does on the remaking of everyday life in such districts since 1989.

Transforming Post-Socialist Cities and Neighbourhoods: Kraków and Bratislava

The empirical focus of this book, then, is the everyday economic practices of individuals, households and communities in two districts in two large cities: Nowa Huta in Kraków, Poland, and Petržalka in Bratislava, Slovakia. By focusing on these two districts in two cities in two countries, we examine the differentiated practices of domesticating neo-liberalism at a variety of scales, attentive to the specificities of place and to articulations with wider urban, national and international cultures and political economies. In this context, the comparison between Poland and Slovakia is not the book's primary analytic; instead we seek to explore the many ways in which geography makes a difference, from the scale of the household, through the housing block and neighbourhood, to the city and beyond. As we discuss in Chapter Three, the idea of practices and the concept of domestication explicitly focus on the weaving together of places and scales in the everyday. Our research design, explored below, was constructed explicitly to enable us to develop each of these comparative aspects and was structured in and around certain neighbourhoods in the two districts in the two cities. Because the particular geographies of our case studies are critical to understanding the differential experiences of post-socialist neo-liberalization, and its domestication, what follows provides an introduction to the cities, districts and neighbourhoods.

Bratislava and Kraków

In many ways, Bratislava and Kraków represent some fairly typical post-socialist urban transformations. Both cities have been radically remade since 1989 and are now fully inserted into global circuits of capital, travel, culture and politics. Beyond the visible symbols of capitalism, ubiquitous not only in their city centres but in their neighbourhoods too, the two cities' economies have been liberalized and internationalized, with impacts on patterns of ownership, on the shape of local labour markets, and on patterns and levels of growth in the economy. As a result of both Bratislava and Kraków being at the heart of their countries' economic dynamism, unemployment rates stood at just 2% and 7% respectively in 2007, compared to national rates of between 8% and 11%.[5] Alongside the restructuring of labour markets, the cities have experienced significant housing market transformations (Chapter Five) and expanded and increasingly differentiated retail provision (Chapter Six; see also Stenning et al., 2009), which have added to the costs of living for households and individuals within both cities. Kraków and Bratislava are increasingly recognized as high-cost cities; in 2006, Bratislava was ranked higher than Prague, Warsaw and Budapest in an index of city living costs[6] and Kraków was identified as having the highest increase in property prices in Europe (Royal Institute of Chartered Surveyors, 2007). In this context, as in other large post-socialist cities, labour market segmentation, the emergence of 'bad jobs' (which offer low pay and insecure conditions) and rising living costs raise critical questions about the connection between employment, a living wage and the ability to secure household social reproduction.

For all their similarities, however, Bratislava and Kraków have distinct histories and geographies, which play a significant role in shaping their contemporary economies. Kraków was capital of Poland from 1038 to 1596, when the seat of the Polish monarchs was moved to Warsaw (Carter, 1994). It remained a key city throughout Poland's early modern and modern history, even during the Partitions (1772–1918), when Poland was occupied by the Prussians, Russians and Austrians and disappeared as a territorial entity from the map of Europe. Indeed, from 1815 to 1846, Kraków was established as a free city by the Congress of Vienna and became a hub both of Polish intellectual and political life and of economic liberalism. During this period, and under the later Grand Duchy of Kraków when the city continued to be afforded more economic, political and cultural freedom than the rest of occupied Poland, Kraków attracted traders, immigrants, entrepreneurs, artists and activists from across the occupied territories. In all this time, Kraków was also the capital of the wider region, Małopolska (or Little Poland). As a result of this history, the city is endowed with a range of historic national monuments and a wealth of cultural, architectural, and intellectual resources. It also inherited, on independence in 1918, an economy largely oriented to trade and science, rather than to industry. Although some industries did exist in pre-war Kraków (including, for example, tobacco, pharmaceuticals and confectionary), the major dynamic of industrial growth in the city was the construction of socialism after World War II, and in particular the establishment of the Lenin Steelworks and Nowa Huta, to the east of the historic city centre (Hardy and Rainnie, 1996; Pounds et al., 1985). In some ways, this phase of industrial development can be seen as a detour in Kraków's economic history; since 1989, the focus of much economic activity has returned to historic spheres, incarnated in post-socialism through an expansion of tourism, a boom in retail and commercial services, and high levels of foreign investment in high-tech sectors (such as software engineering) and in research and development. In 2008, Kraków overtook Łódź to become Poland's second largest city,[7] with a population of 756,441,[8] and a total of approximately 1,200,000 in the conurbation as a whole (OECD, 2008b: 51).

During the majority of the twentieth century, Bratislava occupied a key role in both Czechoslovakia and as capital of the independent Slovak Republic during the Second World War, returning to that role following the division of Czechoslovakia in 1993. Prior to this, Pressburg, as Bratislava was then known (or Pozsony in Hungarian), was the capital of the Hungarian monarchy between the 1500s and 1783 when – following Turkish invasion of the Hungarian Empire – the capital city was relocated there. As such, despite its relatively small size for a capital city (the current population is nearly 430,000), the city has been a political, economic and cultural centre for many centuries and continues to play a key role as the political and economic core of today's independent Slovakia. The economic dominance of the Slovak capital is underlined by the fact that its GDP per capita placed it in 2006 at 149% of the EU27 average, among the highest for the new EU Member States (see also Dunford & Smith, 2000).[9] The sectorally diverse nature of the city's economy has been underlined by the growth of tertiary sectors over the past 15 years, particularly in finance and information technology-related activity (see Chapter Four), and Bratislava has become home to the headquarters of many of the country's foreign investors. Industrial activity remains important; its overall significance has declined relatively, but major foreign investment projects in the automotive sector, centred on Volkswagen, as well as the major oil refinery Slovnaft, are based in the city and remain key employers (Sokol, 2007). Alongside industrial and service sector activity, Bratislava's centrality in political and administrative structures also means that employment in central government and public administration is important. The city boasts five major higher education institutions and large parts of the population have high levels of educational attainment. In addition to these features, Bratislava has also seen its geographical location become a major factor in the city's transformation over the past 20 years. It is the only capital city to border another state (Austria) and Bratislava is only 60 km from Vienna, with both cities being considered as part of the 'golden triangle' of Vienna–Bratislava–Györ (Smith, 1998). This location has meant that Bratislava has been the main regional focus for foreign investment in Slovakia, with 68% of FDI located in the city region in 2007,[10] and significant pressure for land, property and commercial development has resulted, as we discuss in later chapters.

Nowa Huta and Petržalka

Within these cities, patterns of economic transformation have been differentiated, as the processes of post-socialist transformation have played out unevenly in homes and communities. The focus of this book is on two particular districts of Kraków and Bratislava – Nowa Huta and Petržalka (Figures 1.2 and 1.3). Petržalka is one of 17 urban districts of Bratislava and Nowa Huta comprises five of Kraków's 18 urban districts (Nowa Huta, Bieńczyce, Mistrzejowice, Czyżyny and Wzgórza Krzesławickie). Petržalka is the largest district of Bratislava in terms of both its area and population and, like Nowa Huta, is one of the largest housing estates in Central Europe. In 2005, Petržalka was home to 115,000 residents, comprising 27% of the population of the capital. Nowa Huta houses 220,000 people, a similar proportion of Kraków's population. The two districts are located on the periphery of their respective cities and were largely constructed at the height of state socialist urbanization. However, notwithstanding their commonalities, Nowa Huta and Petržalka possessed different starting points in their experience of post-socialist transformation. Petržalka forms part of the diverse urban economy of a capital city, characterized by a range of employment opportunities across different economic sectors. Nowa Huta, by contrast, was constructed on the edge of Kraków to serve a single workplace (the Lenin Steelworks), locked into the industrial economy but closely connected to the persistent peasant economy. Both districts are currently experiencing a re-articulation of their relationship with the wider cities in which they are located.

Nowa Huta was created as a settlement primarily housing workers for the newly built steelworks from the late 1940s (Stenning, 2000). The first three- and four-storey brick-built blocks of flats were constructed in 1949 on the area of three villages – Mogiła, Pleszów and Krzesławice. Initially the district provided accommodation for construction workers employed to build the then Lenin Steelworks, who migrated from mainly rural and old industrial areas of Poland. As late as 1970, 74% of Nowa Huta's population were of 'peasant' origin (Stenning, 2000). Once the steelworks opened, Nowa

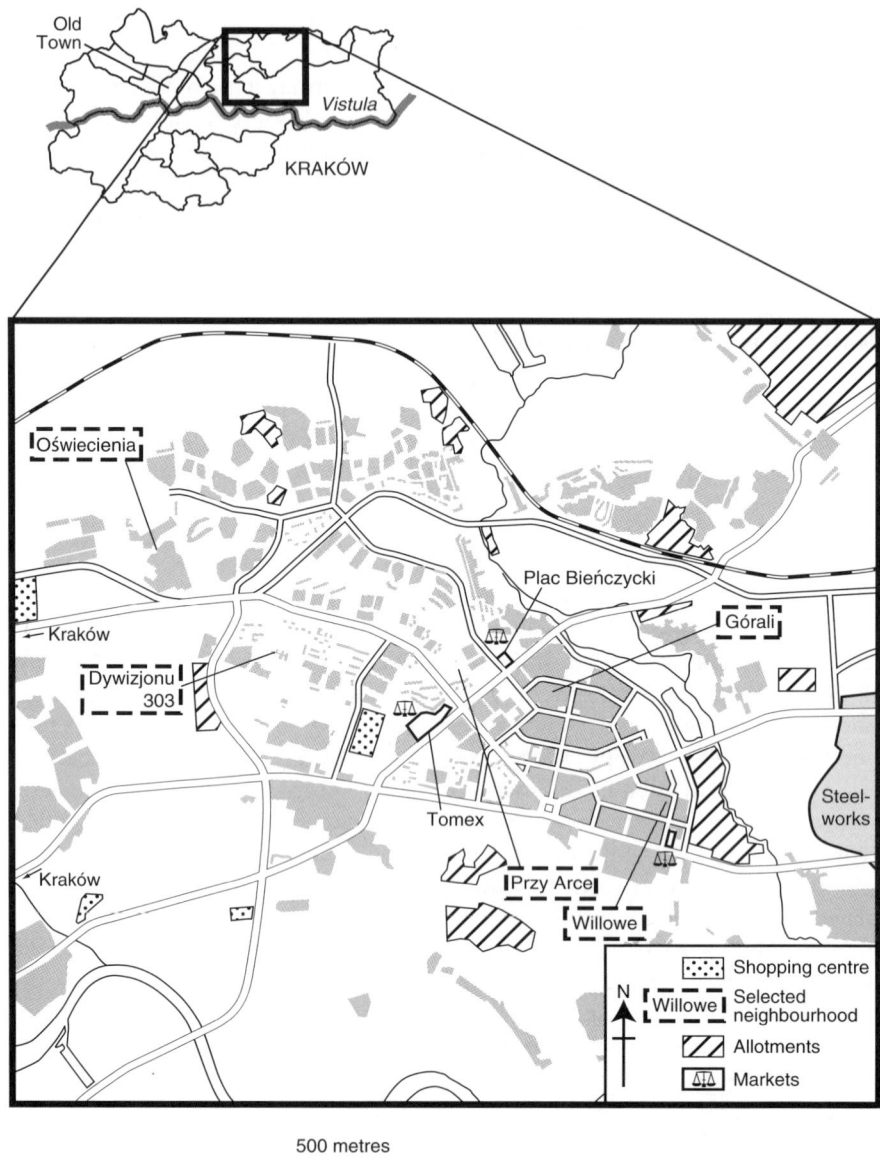

Figure 1.2   Map of Nowa Huta

Huta provided accommodation for new workers and increasing demand for
accommodation, particularly in the 1960s, led to a further expansion of
Nowa Huta towards the north and the villages of Bieńczyce and Mistrzejowice
(Table 1.2). A third phase of development rested on the introduction of

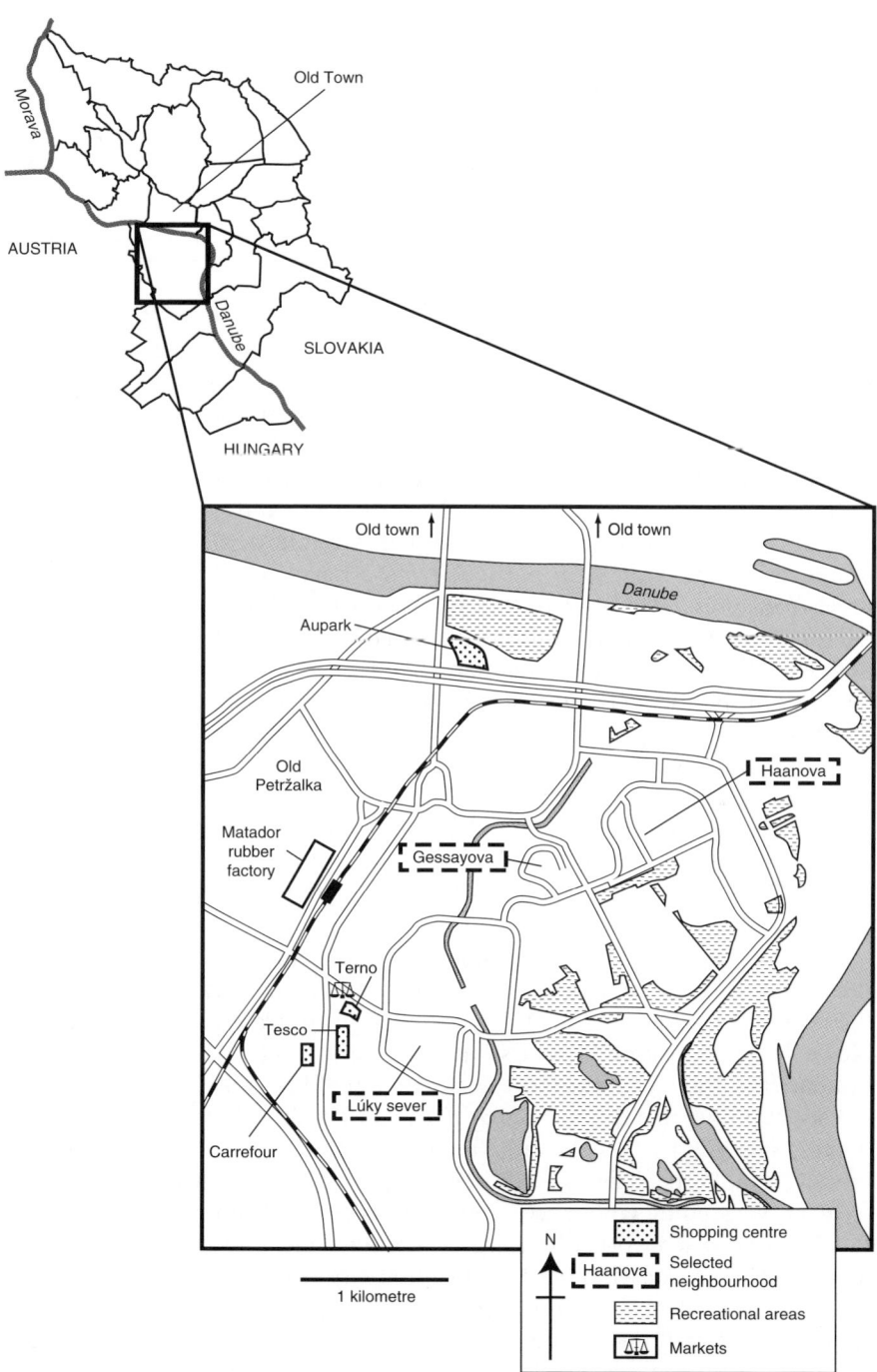

Figure 1.3 Map of Petržalka

Table 1.2   Population of Nowa Huta, Kraków and Poland, 1950–2002

	1950	1960	1970	1978	1988	2002
Poland	25,008,000	29,776,000	32,642,000	35,061,000	37,879,000	38,218,531
Kraków	343,600	481,300	588,000	693,600	746,600	738,544
Nowa Huta	18,800	101,900	164,548	207,467	222,558	216,027

Source: Polish National Censuses 1950, 1960, 1970, 1978, 1988, 2002 (NB: figures for some years are rounded)

panel-built high-rise blocks, which were still under construction until the late 1990s. Nowa Huta was originally planned for 100,000 residents but between 1950 and 1985 the population of Nowa Huta actually increased to 223,000, and growth there accounted for much of Kraków's overall demographic and territorial growth (Soja, 1990). Nowa Huta's population was, for many years, younger, more male, less educated, and more dependent on industrial employment than the rest of Kraków, but demographic and economic shifts since 1989, in particular, have narrowed the gap. The Lenin Steelworks employed over 40,000 workers at their height, the majority of whom lived in Nowa Huta, and, like many major industrial enterprises under socialism, the steelworks supported a range of social and cultural facilities in the town (B. Domański, 1997; Stenning, 2000). The rhythm of life in Nowa Huta was shaped by the rhythms of the steelworks and many were drawn to the new town in search of the work that might offer stability and security for their families (Stenning, 2005c). There were, however, other important employers, including not only the extensive public sector (health, education, administration) but also other industrial enterprises, such as ZPT Kraków, a major cigarette factory now owned by Philip Morris (Hardy & Rainnie, 1996).

Petržalka, by contrast, was for many centuries an independent, rural settlement outside of the city of Bratislava, and divided from the main city by the natural boundary of the Danube River to its north and east. Similarly to Nowa Huta, but some 20 years later, the rural character of Petržalka was dramatically transformed by the construction of low- and high-rise housing blocks, resulting in a dramatic growth of population (Table 1.3) (for further details, see Mládek, 1994, and Mládek et al., 1998). In the same way as Nowa Huta, Petržalka was established to provide mass housing for workers to meet burgeoning labour requirements in the city. But unlike Nowa Huta, Petržalka provided worker housing for a much wider employment base – the diverse economy of what became a capital city region. The construction of Petržalka was (like Nowa Huta and other Central European cities) designed to try to deal with the significant under-investment in housing under state socialism, what Szelényi (1983) has called under-urbanization. Between the

Table 1.3   Population of Petržalka, Bratislava and Slovakia, 1950–2001

	1950	1961	1970	1980	1991	2001
Slovakia	3,486,000	4,174,046	4,537,290	4,991,168	5,274,335	5,379,455
Bratislava	209,397	241,796	305,932	380,259	442,197	428,672
Petržalka	15,966	12,666	14,056	48,755	128,251	117,227

Source: Slovak National Censuses 1950, 1960, 1970, 1978, 1988, 2002

1970s and 1980s, 36,498 flats were built, and the resident population increased to nearly 130,000, largely as a result of significant in-migration from elsewhere in Bratislava, but also from across what was then Czechoslovakia. The new residents were generally characterized as having a high level of economic activity, good levels of education and qualifications (more than half of inhabitants had secondary- and university-level education), and a relatively young age structure (70% of residents were in economically active age groups and only 5% were in 'post-productive' age groups). Through this process of urban development Petržalka has been transformed into a high-density urban district, with a relatively young population, many of whom commute to work in other parts of Bratislava. This has created a distinct set of transport, employment and social connections with the wider city and partially limited the development of social and retail infrastructure within the district itself (Miškolci & Mládek, 1994; Mládek, 1994; Mládek et al., 1998).

While both Nowa Huta and Petržalka saw different periods of population growth – the main periods of expansion occurring about 20 years earlier in Nowa Huta – both districts continued to see a growth in population until the last decade of twentieth century, when the first signs of population loss were evident (the population of Petržalka reduced by 11,000 and that of Nowa Huta by 6,500) (Tables 1.2 and 1.3). Both districts are also witnessing an overall ageing of the population and these demographic shifts have taken place alongside wider social and economic developments. These are documented in more detail in Chapters Four to Seven, but recent years have seen a diversification of land use and population in both Nowa Huta and Petržalka. In Petržalka, the 1990s saw a dynamic construction boom with development of new, private housing blocks, office space, shopping centres and hypermarkets. Once known as the dormitory housing estate for the wider city of Bratislava, Petržalka has today been transformed into a much more multi-functional space. Petržalka's location as part of the capital city and its proximity to the border with Austria have meant that pressures for growth have been somewhat more significant than in Nowa Huta, but Kraków's booming economy – and available space – have fed major changes in Nowa Huta too. Many new hypermarkets have been

Table 1.4   'Risk of poverty' and social exclusion in Nowa Huta and Petržalka

		Below 60% median	61–100% median	101–140% median	Above 140% median
% of survey households by median income category	Nowa Huta	10	18	25	48
	Petržalka	15	36	19	30

Note: Rounded figures may add up to more than 100
Source: Household survey

constructed in Nowa Huta and vast new estates of private housing have also been developed. Much of this development has taken place on Nowa Huta's western and north-western edges, eroding the belt of land which lay undeveloped between Nowa Huta and Kraków for 50 years.

The social situation of households and poverty in Nowa Huta and Petržalka

In Chapters Four to Seven we focus on the range of social and economic practices developed and adopted by individuals and households in Nowa Huta and Petržalka. These attempts to sustain social reproduction in neoliberalizing cities are, of course, situated in a context of increasing poverty and inequality in the two districts as the uneven social and economic transformations impact on resident households. Using equivalized household per capita income relative to regional median income levels, 10% of surveyed households in Nowa Huta and 15% of those in Petržalka fell below the 'at risk of poverty' level (Table 1.4).[11] In total, 28% of surveyed households in Nowa Huta and 51% of those in Petržalka received incomes placing them below the regional median income. At the same time, over 40% of surveyed households in Nowa Huta and 30% of Petržalka households received incomes placing them above 140% of the median, reflecting the growing polarization of household income in the two cities.

Looking at overall household structure and levels of social exclusion in Nowa Huta, approximately half of adult-only households (one adult, 44%; two adults, 55%) were concentrated in the highest income category of 140% of the median income, while the worst income situation was found in single-parent households, with 60% of these surveyed households falling below 60% of the median income, echoing national patterns. The proportion of surveyed households which were 'at risk' of poverty was much lower for households without children. Levels of educational attainment were also very closely connected to risk of poverty: households comprised of university graduates were far more likely to appear in the wealthier categories and those with a basic education or less were concentrated in the very low income category.

In Petržalka, there was a clear connection between the likelihood of surveyed households being at risk of poverty and the number of children present: 36% of surveyed households without children were found below the median income, whilst 79% of surveyed households with children were below this level. The proportion of surveyed households which were 'at risk' of poverty was much lower for households without children. For example, around 40% of all surveyed households with just one or two adult members were concentrated in the highest income category. All single-parent households with children were below the median income. For households with children, higher levels of poverty risk were found in households with younger children; older dependent children were likely to be university-level students, who may also have been working and contributing to household income. There was also a positive relationship between education level and the extent of 'risk of poverty' among households: surveyed individuals with higher education were more likely to be living in households with the highest incomes.

Neighbourhoods

Within Nowa Huta and Petržalka, *Domesticating Neo-Liberalism* focuses on the economic practices and social reproduction of households in particular neighbourhoods chosen to reflect a range of socio-economic characteristics and to enable us to capture the diversity of economic life. Neighbourhoods were selected on the basis of a range of criteria, including relative levels of poverty and social exclusion (judged from preliminary analysis of census data in Petržalka, data on housing debt in Nowa Huta and detailed field observation), location and accessibility in relation to the main city, period of construction and types of blocks. In choosing the neighbourhoods in each community, we also considered issues such as the history of the neighbourhood, flat and block size, as well as proximity to markets, allotment gardens and public transport. Within each neighbourhood, individual housing blocks – which were the primary unit through which we accessed respondents – were again chosen to reflect the range of socio-economic situations, including levels of poverty, block size, and demographic composition (see Tables 1.5 and 1.6).

Petržalka is divided into 24 main neighbourhoods. The three neighbourhoods that were selected for this research each have a similar population

Table 1.5 Surveyed neighbourhoods in Nowa Huta

	Nowa Huta			Willowe/Górali		Przy Arce		Dywizjonu 303		Oświecenia	
	2002 census	Survey	%	Survey	%	Survey	%	Survey	%	Survey	%
Population	216027	611		147		139		155		170	
Economically active	140411 (65.0%)	304	50	60	41	72	52	75	48	97	57
Unemployment rate	18.3	42	14	19	32	12	17	3	4	8	8
% with university education	11.3	101	4	6	4	18	13	36	23	41	24
Period of construction				1947–1950		late 1960s		1970s		1970s/80s/90s	
Type of construction				Brick built, mostly low-storey. Smaller apartments		Large panel-built blocks, 8–12 storey with multiple stairways		Large panel-built blocks, 8–12 storey with multiple stairways		Large, multi-storey blocks, some single-family homes	
Location				'Old' Nowa Huta, closer to steelworks		Good communications, close to major markets		Closer to Krakow and close to major markets/ hypermarkets		Closer to Kraków, further from steelworks, good communications and close to major hypermarkets	

Source: Polish National Census, 2002; field observations and household survey

Table 1.6 Surveyed neighbourhoods in Petržalka

	Petržalka	Gessayova			Haanova			Lúky-sever		
	2001 census	2001 census	Survey	%	2001 census	Survey	%	2001 census	Survey	%
Population	117,227	4,548	140		4,532	183		5,361	183	
Economically active	71,127 (61%)	2,755 (61%)	91	65	2,976 (65.7%)	117	64	3,312 (61.8%)	118	65
Unemployment rate	10.6	12.2	9	10	10.1	8	7	11.4	24	20
% with university education	16.7	14.2	20	14	18.9	24	13	16.0	25	14
Period of construction		1971–80			1971–80			1981–90		
Type of construction		Single, wall-like 12-storey block			Many 4-storey blocks			Mixed		
Location		Close to the city centre			Close to the city centre			Quite distant from the city centre		

Source: Slovak census, 2001, field observations and household survey

Plate 1.1   Haanova, Petržalka

size, but reflect a range of social status positions. The **Haanova** neighbour-hood, with a population just over 4,500, is located close to the city centre, just south of the River Danube, and has the most positive social characteristics among the three neighbourhoods in Petržalka (Plate 1.1). Unemployment rates were the lowest among all neighbourhoods in the district (10%)[12] and the proportion of the population with a university degree was 19%, which was the highest level for the whole of Petržalka. Haanova was one of the earliest developments of Petržalka in the 1970s and is dominated by smaller, four-storey blocks, which have more green space between them than in other parts of the district. Haanova is also close to the centre of Petržalka with good public transport connections.

The **Gessayova** neighbourhood, by contrast, is an area with a much poorer social structure (Plate 1.2). Like Haanova, Gessayova is located close to the city centre, and has a population of just over 4,500, but the built form and the social characteristics of the neighbourhood are very different. The unemployment rate was among the highest for Petržalka (12%); the area had the lowest proportion of population with university education (14%); and a relatively large young population (the highest in Petržalka at 12% of the total population of the neighbourhood). The neighbourhood

Plate 1.2   Gessayova, Petržalka

comprises a single, wall-like 12-storey block of apartments, a large proportion of which are small, one-bedroom flats that have experienced some
rapid changes in ownership.

The **Lúky-sever** neighbourhood was selected as an 'average' Petržalka
neighbourhood incorporating a range of both middle-status and poorer
residents (Plate 1.3). The population in the neighbourhood was almost
5,400 and the unemployment rate was 11%. The housing structure consists
mainly of blocks typically ranging from four to twelve floors, with the majority being eight-storey buildings. Lúky-sever is located further from the city
centre and, like many neighbourhoods to the south of Petržalka, was built
most recently (between 1981 and 1990). It is closest to the main centre of
hypermarket development on the western arterial road of Petržalka and one
of the main outdoor markets is very close.

In similar ways to Petržalka, the four neighbourhoods (*osiedla* in Polish) in
Nowa Huta represent contrasting socio-economic fortunes. Osiedle **Willowe**
and Osiedle **Górali** are two neighbourhoods located in so-called old Nowa
Huta (Plates 1.4 and 1.5). Willowe is one of the two oldest neighbourhoods,
located at the easternmost edge of Nowa Huta and constructed in the late
1940s for the first workers who were employed to build the steelworks. It

Plate 1.3   Lúky-sever, Petržalka

Plate 1.4   Osiedle Willowe, Nowa Huta

Plate 1.5   Osiedle Górali, Nowa Huta

consists of small brick-built blocks (three or four storeys) built around play-grounds and other green space, and is adjacent to Nowa Huta's two major allotments sites. The population is around 2,000 to 2,500, living in approxi-mately 30 blocks and smaller (one- or two-room) flats predominate. The population here is older than the Nowa Huta average, with many resident since the 1950s. Not only does that mean that fewer are economically active, but also that social networks are more deeply rooted. Because of the smaller apartment size, households tend to be smaller. **Górali** is located fairly cen-trally, on the northern edge of old Nowa Huta, close to the first post-1960 developments. It is home to some of Nowa Huta's key cultural institutions (including Ośrodek Kultury im. Norwida, which leads the Partnerstwo Inicjatyw Nowohuckich [Partnership of Initiatives for Nowa Huta] and man-aged the EU-funded EQUAL project Nowa Huta Nowa Szansa). The neigh-bourhood dates from the late 1950s and has a mix of smaller blocks built around courtyards and a few taller (though not high-rise) blocks. Much of the area is slightly more run down than other parts of old Nowa Huta, and one part of the neighbourhood is home to a 'blok interwencyjny' (intervention block) which houses some particularly poor families. There is also a soup kitchen within the neighbourhood, but this serves people from beyond Górali too.

Plate 1.6   Osiedle Przy Arce, Nowa Huta

Osiedle **Przy Arce** is located in the geographical centre of Nowa Huta (Plate 1.6). It is a neighbourhood of large housing blocks dating from the late 1960s and is adjacent to Nowa Huta's first church (Arka Pana), from which it takes its name. There are about 20 blocks in total in the neighbourhood, two of which are so-called *mrówkowiec*,[13] and it has a total population of over 5,000. Przy Arce is a fairly 'average' neighbourhood in terms of its social and economic status, but the size of the blocks and the location mark it out as more unusual. The church, Arka Pana, was the centre of 'underground' activity during the Solidarity and martial law years and was the focus of a network of social support activities, providing food, money etc. for the families of imprisoned activists (Kenney, 2003), and remains a major community centre. Przy Arce also lies between two major outdoor markets – Tomex and Plac Bieńczycki – which are sites of both major employment and 'unofficial' sellers (of food, clothes (new and second-hand), home equipment, flowers, etc.) and it is adjacent to a major transport hub with trams and buses running across Nowa Huta and Kraków.

Osiedle **Dywizjonu 303** is on the western edge of Nowa Huta, and is closer to Kraków than the other neighbourhoods (Plate 1.7). The neighbourhood dates from the 1970s, and comprises mostly panel-built high-rise

Plate 1.7   Osiedle Dywizjonu 303, Nowa Huta

blocks. It is dissected by a defunct Second World War runway and adjacent to a park established on the site of the old airport. Dywizjonu 303 has a population of approximately 8,000 and consists of both high-rise and low-rise long blocks. There is a high proportion of families with many children, a significant Roma population, and high, if variable, levels of rent arrears. It is generally seen as a relatively poor neighbourhood, and though it has a few small shops, it is relatively under-serviced. It does, nevertheless, have reasonable access to hypermarkets and good links to Kraków city centre.

Osiedle **Oświecenia** is located in the north-western corner of Nowa Huta, to the north of Osiedle Dywizjonu 303, and dates from the latest period of the district's development (from the late 1970s and through the 1980s), when much new housing was built through cooperatives (see Chapter Five) (Plate 1.8). The neighbourhood is seen as relatively affluent, with a good physical location (it is located on a hill and the old town of Kraków is visible from most of the flats) and 'desirable' in the housing market. Flats are generally larger than those in some of the other districts, comprising three or four rooms. The neighbourhood is also close to Kraków and it has been the site of significant new development – both residential and commercial – since 1989; it is located immediately adjacent to one of

Plate 1.8   Osiedle Oświecenia, Nowa Huta

Kraków's major retail/leisure developments comprising a Geant, Obi, a multiplex cinema and an aqua-park.

A Note on Method

These neighbourhoods provided the main empirical site for our research. However, the neighbourhoods were also part of a nested geography of spaces that frame the research approach at a variety of scales: neighbourhood, housing district, city and nation. In the chapters that follow, we draw out both the commonalities and differences arising at these different scales, both in relation to how neo-liberalization has been pursued and how the everyday economic practices of households and individuals have been reconfigured to negotiate these differentiated experiences of transformation.

Understanding the complexity of forms of household practices and social reproduction in Petržalka and Nowa Huta required the deployment of a multi-method approach, which involved five main elements: analysis of available data on poverty and social exclusion; a questionnaire survey of 350 households undertaken across the Nowa Huta and Petržalka neighbourhoods; semi-structured, in-depth, follow-up interviews with 64 households in the neighbourhoods (Appendix 1); multi-sited ethnographies of a range of household and community economic practices and sites across Petržalka and Nowa Huta; and semi-structured interviews with close to 90 key informants in relevant institutions (Appendix 2). The majority of the qualitative and ethnographic work was undertaken during the late autumn and winter of 2005 and the spring of 2006.

While resources and accurate population records prevented the undertaking of a fully random representative sample survey of households, our approach was to select 'representative' neighbourhoods using the criteria already discussed. Within each neighbourhood, individual housing blocks were chosen to reflect the range of socio-economic situations, including levels of poverty, block size, and demographic composition (Tables 1.5 and 1.6). Within each selected block, households were surveyed randomly, ensuring that responses were received from at least two or three households in each staircase in each selected block. Thus, while the questionnaire survey research did not aim to provide a *statistically representative* profile of households, the research undertaken does provide a *structured purposive sample* of households from different neighbourhoods and housing blocks to enable an understanding of a range of socio-economic situations *and* the extent to which intra-neighbourhood and intra-block interactions existed and were important in the everyday economic practices of households. In Petržalka, the sample represents between 3% and 4% of the population of the selected neighbourhoods and the profile of surveyed residents was broadly the same as that in the 2001 census (Table 1.6). The absence of localized population census data for Nowa Huta limits the ability to make similar comparisons with the wider population, but given that the same sampling strategy was undertaken in both housing districts, the sampled population is likely to be broadly similar to the total population of each area. The questionnaires explored a wide range of economic practices and resulted in a body of empirical material which covers, amongst other issues, household incomes and expenditures, housing, employment, care work and consumption.

After initial analysis of the questionnaire data, households were identified for follow-up, in-depth interviews. A number of intersecting criteria were used to identify such households, starting with household income, to ensure a range of household material positions, but also including household size, employment status and location. Interviews lasted between 45 minutes and 2 hours and were conducted in Polish and Slovak, often with more than one household member present. All interviews were recorded and transcribed in Polish and Slovak, and later coded using a common coding frame, reflecting both the research questions and the experiences from interviews. The interviews explored in detail the changing shape of the household, paying attention to the process of household formation, the importance of location and the size and shape of the home itself. The focus of each interview then switched to patterns of domestic work within the household, paying attention to gender and generational distinctions, to the role of friends and other family members in the domestic life of the household, and to the processes of decision-making. The links between the interviewed household and other households, of family, friends and neighbours, within and beyond the home location were also explored, as were the levels of acquaintance and assistance within these social networks and we paid particular attention to their geography. The sensitive topic of informal access to goods and services was also discussed. Other sections of the interviews focused on household activities, including the use of land for domestic food production and employment trajectories, including not only the 'main job' but also additional work, seasonal work and work overseas. These sections also explored the various state and social benefits accessed by the households. In the final section of each interview, household income, expenditure, and consumption practices were explored.

This questionnaire and interview work was complemented by broader ethnographic research, including observations in street markets, soup kitchens, homeless hostels, pensioners' clubs, allotments, playgrounds and other key community sites in the neighbourhoods. This work was coupled with 90 semi-structured interviews, carried out with key informants in a range of local, city and national state institutions and non-governmental organizations, to explore issues of social exclusion, policy measures, institutional responses and the identification of neighbourhoods. Towards the end of the data collection phase, a series of meetings and workshops were held with individuals and organizations in Nowa Huta and Petržalka to feedback and discuss preliminary findings. These discussions fed, in particular, into the exploration of public policy ideas in Nowa Huta and Petržalka, some of which we return to in Chapter Eight.

Plan of the Book

Understanding the changing fortunes of these individuals and households and how they attempt to create the conditions for their social reproduction in the context of rapidly changing economic circumstances and neo-liberalizing policy contexts is the key focus of *Domesticating Neo-Liberalism*. In the next two chapters we explore in more detail the key conceptual ideas relating to neo-liberalism and its formation in Poland and Slovakia, and to the frameworks of domestication, economic practices and social reproduction. Chapters Four, Five, Six and Seven examine four sets of economic practices (in work and employment; in housing; in food procurement and the use of land; and in care) with which households seek to domesticate neo-liberalism and ensure their social reproduction.

To a certain extent, Chapters Four, Five, Six and Seven can be read on their own; each begins with a contextual introduction, outlining how the set of practices in question can be understood and highlighting the key transformations since 1989. Together, however, they form a more complete picture of the range of practices that households develop. In each of these four chapters, we establish the forms of neo-liberalization encountered by households and the diverse economic practices they employ to domesticate those transformations. We focus not only on the ways in which households negotiate and contest neo-liberalism but also on the ways they attempt to make it more tolerable. In each chapter, we seek to understand the histories of those practices, their articulations with other spheres and other practices, their geographies (both scales and spatialities), and the ways in which those geographies make a difference to the practices themselves, and to tease out important comparisons between the Nowa Huta and Petržalka cases, and between neighbourhoods and blocks within the two districts. Thus, as we discuss in more detail in Chapter Three, diversities, articulations, histories, geographies, contestations and, ultimately, domestications shape the analyses in these four chapters.

We begin, in Chapter Four, with a focus on employment, unemployment and the restructuring of labour markets. Notwithstanding our focus on the diversity of household economic practices and on the value of spheres beyond work, we stress, echoing Burawoy et al. (2000) and S. Clarke (2002), the critical importance of employment in the attempt to secure household social reproduction. For this reason, our exploration of work and households' negotiation of neo-liberalizing labour markets is the starting point for our analyses. In Chapter Five, we shift our attention to housing practices. Housing is the sphere in which market transformations are quite literally brought home, or domesticated. Housing sits at the heart of households' economic practices since it not only offers shelter and, for some, the potential for investment and income generation, but it also enables or constrains the potential to increase the size of the household and thus diversify both sources of income and of domestic labour and care. Chapter Six shifts the focus to food provisioning practices and the role that access to land, to economies of exchange, and to retail plays in domesticating the neo-liberalization of consumption.[14] In this chapter, we explore the importance of land to the domestic production of food, the transformations which threaten households' ability to produce food, the role of exchange and gift of food amongst households, and the ways in which households negotiate the rapid transformation of the food retail sector. Chapter Seven explores the place of care and caring practices within and between households in Nowa Huta and Petržalka, a set of practices that in many ways underpins work, housing and consumption. This chapter documents and explores the place of family, kinship and friendship networks, of charitable organizations, and of the restructured welfare state in providing everyday support – for example, emotional, financial, practical – to households. The final chapter returns to the question of diversities, articulations, histories, geographies and contestations highlighted in each of the four preceding chapters, pulling these together to restate the central concerns of *Domesticating Neo-Liberalism*. Through these analyses, the concluding chapter connects back to our key concerns, drawing conclusions about the ways in which Polish and Slovak households have negotiated – or domesticated – the neo-liberal transformations of post-socialism and employing these analyses of 'domestication' to think again about neo-liberalism in general and its post-socialist form in particular.

Chapter Two

Neo-Liberalism and Post-Socialist Transformations

Theorizing Neo-Liberalism

Definitions, emergence and central tenets

In his critical account of global neo-liberalism, Harvey (2005: 2) argued that:

> Neoliberalism is in the first instance a theory of political economic practices that proposes that human well-being can best be advanced by liberating individual entrepreneurial freedoms and skills within an institutional framework characterized by strong private property rights, free markets, and free trade.

Such a conception of political-economic change has its 'prehistories' (Peck, 2008) that lead back to the twentieth-century thinking of the Austrian liberal political economists Friedrich August von Hayek (1994) and Ludwig von Mises (1996) and to debates over the possibilities for state intervention in economic life (Lange, 1994; Friedman & Friedman, 1990). It is not our purpose here to provide a historiography of neo-liberal ideas; rather we focus upon the central tenets of what has become widely recognized as the political economy of neo-liberalism (Peck & Tickell, 2002; Tickell & Peck, 2003) and relate these to ongoing post-socialist transformations. These tenets have been steadily institutionalized through wide-ranging, global networks of political intervention and economic policy and have come to be seen – not unproblematically – as one of the dominant projects of contemporary capitalism.

The first tenet of neo-liberalism is the claim that the market is the only and most effective way to organize human existence and should be extended to as many spheres of life as is possible. There should be freedom for capital, goods and services, with limited direct governmental intervention. Private owners of capital and entrepreneurs should be left to self-regulate their market activities. Markets are seen to lead ultimately to an equalization of social outcomes as wealth famously 'trickles down' from rich to poor. It is the role of government, therefore, to remove impediments to capital mobility, and the state should be charged only with setting the regulatory context within which the market can most freely operate and upholding the rule of law. The promotion of markets connects to state deregulation of the economy and the pursuit of an agenda of privatization, all of which have been central planks of the various post-socialist reform agendas pursued since the collapse of communism (Smith & Pickles, 1998; Stenning & Bradshaw, 1999). The creation of private property rights through mass privatization and through the development of new private firms has been dramatic. Yet, as many have recognized, the particular ways in which private property has been created have often involved, worked through, and been embedded within already existing constellations of power and control in the economy, what Stark (1996) has called 'recombinant property' (see also Grabher & Stark, 1997; Smith, 1998). A further tenet is that the state should do all it can to reduce public expenditure. Not only does this follow the monetarist agenda of fiscal austerity, but it is also part of withdrawing the state, as far as possible, from direct intervention in society. However, as many critics of neo-liberalism have pointed out, despite the rhetoric of state withdrawal, most neo-liberal states have in fact restructured activity towards *de facto* subsidies of the private sector, enhancing the wealth of the most affluent through tax cuts. In the context of the 2008/9 global financial crisis, state intervention, of enormous proportions, is back on the agenda and seen, in part, as a way of mitigating the economic and social consequences of a finance-led neo-liberal development model.

A final tenet relates less to how the economy – and by extension the whole of society – is governed and more to a moral stance promoting individualism and individual responsibility for health, wealth and welfare. This is what McCarthy (2006) has called the individualizing 'ontology of neo-liberalism', which rests on both political and moral economies and on the production of neo-liberal subjects and citizens (K. Mitchell, 2006; Ong, 2006) who are 'entrepreneurial, self-responsible individuals' (Larner, 2003: 511; see also du Gay, 1996). In the particular post-socialist context, the promotion of neo-liberal subjectivities relies on a rejection of the caricatured citizen of state socialism, who was happy to depend on the state for work, consumption, leisure and health care, and who finds the challenges of the market debilitating (Weiner, 2005;

Junghans, 2001). So apparently antithetical is the enterprising neoliberal subject to the inherited subjectivities of socialism that the process of 'adaptation' forced onto post-socialist subjects is extreme and rapid (Yurchak, 2003).

Perspectives on neo-liberalism

In theorizing neo-liberalism it is important to make a distinction between different conceptual approaches to understanding the neo-liberal project. The first way in which neo-liberalism has been theorized is by seeing it as an all-powerful global and hegemonic project – the direct outcome of the policies of global economic institutions such as the International Monetary Fund, the World Bank and the World Trade Organization, aligned to wider imperial power in the post-Cold War world of the United States of America. Harvey (2005), for example, has reminded us about the all-embracing power of neo-liberal ideas and the ways in which they constitute, in a thoroughly penetrative way, the world in which we live. He argues that:

> Neoliberalism has ... become hegemonic as a mode of discourse. It has per-vasive effects on ways of thought to the point where it has become incorpo-rated into the common-sense way many of us interpret, live in and understand the world (Harvey, 2005: 3).

As Ward and England (2007: 11) argue,

> [i]n this work political (and indeed cultural) dominance is exercised through the formation of class-based alliances – elite actors, institutions, and other representatives of capital – at a variety of spatial scales, who produce and cir-culate a coherent program of ideas and images about the world, its problems, and how these are best solved.

This version of neo-liberalism offers a powerful critique of market utopias and their alignment to the imperial interests of global powers (see also Gowan, 1995). It highlights the discursive power of neo-liberal agendas and their incorporation into 'common-sense' understandings of the econ-omy, such that, amongst politicians, policy makers and the public, 'there is no alternative'. This reading also represents neo-liberalism as a class project, which results in a reinforcing, even an exacerbation, of class inequalities globally, nationally and locally (Smith, 2000). This, in turn, acknowledges the 'fundamental systemic violence of capitalism' (Žižek, 2008: 11; see also Escobar, 2004), a violence unleashed by destructive forces of neo-liberalism (Bourdieu, 1998). However, there is also a danger that this perspective presents too hegemonic a version of neo-liberalism, painting it as a universal project, constructed 'out there' by global institutions and the agents of multinational capital (Gibson-Graham, 1996). It fails to consider how neo-liberal power is contested and is constituted through a range of other social relations and everyday practices.

A second approach envisions neo-liberalism as a geographically differentiated, locally complex process, invariably called 'neo-liberalization' (England & Ward, 2007). Neo-liberalism touches down in different ways in different places, but these 'variegations' are not 'unruly and unpatterned' (Brenner et al., 2010: 36); the resemblances and differentiations of 'variegated' neo-liberal forms reflect the uneven development and regulation of processes of neo-liberalization and 'their continued collision with, and tendential reworking of, inherited institutional landscapes' (Brenner et al., 2010: 4). In this reading, neo-liberalization involves a set of processes in which market rules extend into ever increasing spheres of life, but are always constituted by contingent circumstances and in the context of local institutional forms and structures. These might be specific forms of state apparatus, local labour market institutions, or struggles over the exercise of power. Neo-liberalism is a hybrid; it 'never acts alone' (Castree, 2006: 4) as 'neoliberal practices always … exist in a more-than-neoliberal context' (Castree, 2006: 3). This approach has tended to fire the imagination of geographers because of its focus on the uneven geographical development of neo-liberalization and on the local remaking of the neo-liberal project. In particular, the emphasis has been on understanding how 'the origins of neoliberalism cannot be reduced to the mere exporting of policies and programs from the US "diffusion centres" of New York and Washington' (Ward & England, 2007: 6). Peck's (2008: 4) 'zigzagging prehistories' of neo-liberalism 'serve as timely reminders of the contradictory, contingent, and *constructed* nature of the neoliberal present, its produced and contextually embedded form, and its inescapable impurity' (emphasis in original). In some ways, this attention to national differentiations in the processes of neo-liberalization echoes debates about the 'varieties of capitalism' (Hall & Soskice, 2001; Peck & Theodore, 2007) and the turn to context and particularity is helpful in moving our understandings of neo-liberalism away from that of an undifferentiated, global, hegemonic project. However, like the 'varieties of capitalism' approach, this perspective tends to focus on national differentiations and on institutional sources of variation and fails to deal adequately with the ways in which neo-liberalism is constituted at other scales and in other spaces. To complement this perspective, then, others have drawn on Foucault's notions of governmentality to understand the importance of the 'multiple and contradictory aspects of neoliberal spaces, techniques, and subjects' (Larner, 2003: 509) and to analyse the diverse practices of 'acting subjects' (Larner, 2003: 511). This perspective adds to political economy approaches to explore neo-liberalism as 'a system of meaning that constitutes institutions, practices and identities in contradictory and disjunctive ways' (Larner, 2000: 12). It enables both analyses of neo-liberalism at everyday scales and in everyday spaces, such as 'workplaces, educational institutions and health and welfare agencies' (Larner, 2000: 13), as well as in the national centres of economic policy and practice, and a consideration of the role of the everyday practices of individuals, households and communities in mediating and remaking the processes of neo-liberalization.

For some, however, these theorizations of neo-liberalism are lacking precisely because they cannot 'account for how top-down initiatives "take" in everyday situations' (Barnett, 2005: 9). For Barnett, the overwhelming focus in studies of neo-liberalism on institutions, bureaucracies and policy networks means that too little attention is paid to wider conceptualizations of social relations. In particular, they 'manage to reduce the understanding of social relations to a residual effect of hegemonic projects ... [and] ... pay little attention to the pro-active role of socio-cultural processes in provoking changes in modes of governance, policy, and regulation' (Barnett, 2005: 10). For Barnett, this means that instead of seeing neo-liberalism as a set of processes driving social change, we should seek a more contextual analysis of long-term 'populist tendencies' and 'much longer rhythms of socio-cultural change that emanate from the bottom-up' (Barnett, 2005: 10). However, it is also possible to see in this critique the necessity of developing a perspective on neo-liberalism that allows for the full incorporation of everyday social and economic practices.

As we suggested in Chapter One, in *Domesticating Neo-Liberalism*, we support a theorization of neo-liberalism as a process, neo-liberalization, which is geographically and historically differentiated, hybrid, constructed at a variety of scales – from the global to the everyday – and enacted not only by economists, bureaucrats, entrepreneurs and politicians, but also by 'ordinary' people in their daily lives. We therefore acknowledge and explore the varying national and urban engagements with neo-liberalism in the Polish and Slovak case studies that formed the focus of our research, but we also take on the challenge of producing an understanding of neo-liberalization which takes seriously the diversity of everyday social relations and seeks to account for the negotiation, adaptation, contestation and adoption of neo-liberal policies and practices in everyday life. These, for us, are the central commitments of the idea of domesticating neo-liberalism.

Neo-Liberalization and Domestic Economic Policies in Post-Socialism

To elaborate this perspective, we can begin by drawing attention to the ways in which neo-liberal transitions in post-socialism have been domesticated through the flows and networks of economic knowledge (Swain, 2006; Bohle & Neunhöffer, 2005; see also T. Mitchell, 2002, 2005 for wider discussions of neo-liberal economic knowledges). Bockman and Eyal (2002) have argued, for example, that it is impossible to see neo-liberalism as something that was either new to East Central Europe after the collapse of communism or something that was simply imposed on it from outside through the policy frameworks of multilateral financial institutions. Through a careful and illuminating account of the interactions, largely through international conferences, between East European 'reform' economists and Western liberal economists during the 1980s and through a consideration of the political and academic marginalization of reformist economists in the East, they argue that:

> it is impossible to divide this transnational dialogue into an active, Western "author" of neoliberal ideas and policies and a passive, East European "recipient". Neoliberalism was not simply disseminated from West to East, but was made possible and constructed through the dialogue and exchanges that took place within this transnational network (Bockman & Eyal, 2002: 311).

They contend that we have to see the origins of neo-liberal economic ideas in the context of struggles over economic knowledge in the twentieth century. The influence of Hayekian and von Misesian theories of the market and economic individualism on contemporary neo-liberal theory can only be understood within the context of earlier debates over the possibilities for socialist economic planning in the 1920s and 1930s and – in the view of these liberal economists – the impossibility of state regulation and planning (Hayek, 1994). Fundamentally, these were debates over the realm of state intervention and planning (from the Polish reform economist, Oskar Lange (see below), to Keynesian intervention in Western Europe) that had their roots in the attempt to make planned socialism work, and as such liberal economic ideas were already constituted through 'resistance' to the communist experience of East Central Europe. As Timothy Mitchell (2002, 2005) has emphasized in other contexts, the way that economic knowledge is constructed is fundamental to understanding the boundaries of what is possible in economic practice. The work of economics contributes to the making of the economy and to the discursive ways in which 'economy' and its organization – through the pursuit of markets and commodification – becomes an object of intervention and action (see also Lee et al., 2008).

The debates over socialist economic calculation thus became constitutive of a mode of economic practice – through resistance to state intervention and the perceived eradication of individual liberty under actually existing state socialism – that became known as neo-liberalism. In this way, neo-liberalism was 'domesticated' in ECE from the outset.

Neo-liberalism was domesticated further, across ECE, as local think tanks, academics, policy makers, political parties and trade unions, among others, developed neo-liberal policies and programmes in the context of post-1989 reforms and of public reactions to those reforms. Although, as we have suggested, most of the post-socialist states of ECE embarked on programmes of reform that engaged fully with wider narratives of neo-liberalism, they did not produce identical programmes. Bohle and Greskovits (2007), for example, identify three 'variants' of capitalism in ECE, which share much but are also marked by significant differences, whilst Drahokoupil (2007) explores both divergence and convergence in the forms of capitalism developed in ECE. Key differences exist, in particular, in the varying commitment to social cohesion and solidarity, but also in the detail of the policies developed, and these differences reflect national variations in, for example, inherited political legacies, social protest, (in)stability in electoral politics, national identity and culture, industrial relations, relationships to the EU and the role of transnational corporations (see also Bradshaw & Stenning, 2001).

These two processes – the longstanding development of neo-liberal ideas in ECE and the 'domestic' variation of contemporary neo-liberalization in the region – form the focus of our first take on the domestication of neo-liberalism in Poland and Slovakia. In what follows, we explore how neo-liberal policies have been domesticated in Poland and Slovakia and argue that these processes of domestication destabilize the idea of neo-liberalism as a singular, top-down, political-economic project. Twenty years after the collapse of communism in Poland and Slovakia, it is clear to see that the experience of post-socialist transformation has been contested and highly uneven. The power of neo-liberal fundamentalism in shaping the post-socialist transformations of these two societies has waxed and waned, although throughout this period there has been at the core a commitment to throw off the perceived 'shackles' of communism and central planning to replace them with a commitment to privatization, economic liberalization and global, market-led engagement. After 15 years of transformation, these tendencies were reinforced by accession to the European Union, a process which intensified the neo-liberalization of the Polish and Slovak economies (Shields, 2007).

This section charts these neo-liberal trajectories and argues that any account of the experience of neo-liberalization in Poland and Slovakia has to attend to the ways in which these political economies were not simply imposed from outside, but were embedded within the fabric of policy and academic thinking in the two countries. As we have suggested, neo-liberalization has been pursued in different ways in Poland and Slovakia over the two decades since the fall of state socialism and, in the final section of this chapter, we compare and contrast the varied commitments to neo-liberalization in the two countries as context for later analyses.

Neo-Liberalism and the Polish Political Economy

Poland's neo-liberal reforms have taken on a mythical form in the context of East Central European transformations. The reform plan – the Balcerowicz Plan – launched on 1 January 1990 by the then finance minister, Leszek Balcerowicz, came to be seen as the archetypal 'shock therapy' programme and was to be copied in various ways across the region and beyond. Yet, the engagement with neo-liberal thought in Poland can be traced, at least, to the academic work of reform economists in the 1970s (Bockman & Eyal, 2002; Bohle & Neunhöffer, 2005). These young economists, in an environment of greater openness, were drawn to Western economic analyses as a means of interpreting the problems of socialism, seeing the work of Hayek, von Mises and Friedman as an important counter to the Keynesian, etatist approaches. For Balcerowicz, the so-called socialist calculation debate of the 1930s was central to the development of his ideas. This debate over the role of pricing and the consequent inefficiency of socialist economies drew in a number of key economists of the time, including not only Hayek and von Mises, but also – as we have already noted – the 'market socialist' Oskar Lange.[1] Balcerowicz (2000) explained that he 'studied the socialist economic system and knew that it was basically flawed because it deprived people of economic freedom, which is one of the other fundamental freedoms, private property, the right to set up enterprise'. He continued to note that, 'against this background, people like Hayek or von Mises or then Friedman, but especially Hayek and von Mises, came to me as people who were not mistaken' (Balcerowicz, 2000).

The young liberal economists who emerged through the 1970s and 1980s and worked with Balcerowicz in informal seminars and networks included many who were to appear repeatedly in government or as advisers to government after 1989. These included Robert Gwiazdowski who founded the Polish Adam Smith Center in 1989, Marek Dąbrowski, later deputy in the Ministry of Finance and founder, with other liberal economists including Leszek Balcerowicz and his wife Ewa, of the think tank CASE, and Stefan Kawalec, one of Balcerowicz's chief advisers. This group, in more or less coordinated actions, promoted the ideas of Hayek and Friedman during the last decades of socialism, often through samizdat (illegal, underground) publications.

Despite the fact that Poland's dominant opposition movement, Solidarity, was a trade union with its roots in industrial workplaces, as opposition towards the communist state grew the movement's liberal intellectual advisers strengthened their position (Ost, 2005) and began to develop and promote their neo-liberal plans for the reform of the Polish economy. Much of what later became the Balcerowicz Plan was already in place before 1989, if underground and disseminated amongst a small intellectual elite. Indeed, Balcerowicz noted in interview that 'we worked on the Polish program ... for 12 years before it was actually launched. We were arriving at successive solutions, and I think such directions as privatization, convertibility of currency, stabilization, they were worked out here' (Balcerowicz, 2000).

In this context, it is clear that Poland's neo-liberalism was – at least in part – home-grown. As Kochanowicz et al. (2005: 91) argued, '[i]n spite of the important role played by foreign advisers including Jeffrey Sachs and representatives of international financial institutions, the Polish stabilization and liberalization reform package was a Polish product.' Yet, in 1989, when the socialist government did concede power to the opposition, key external actors were critical for the plan's success. Balcerowicz (2000) notes that the approval of the British-based Polish economists Stanisław Gomułka of the London School of Economics and Political Science and Jacek Rostowski of the School of Slavonic and East European Studies at the University of London was critical for the development of the reform plans, but most influential of all was Jeffrey Sachs, then from Harvard University's Institute for International Development (HIID).

Sachs first arrived in Poland, on the invitation of the outgoing socialist government, on the day the 1989 round table agreement was signed (Sachs, 2000). He returned later with his colleague David Lipton to begin discussions with the leaders of Solidarity. As Sachs explains:

> We went on for a few hours like this. I was exhausted and the room was filled with smoke and he [Jacek Kuroń, a Solidarity leader who went on to become Minister for Labour and Social Policy in the first Solidarity government] said, "Okay, clear." Our friend was translating, he said, "Clear, write up the plan." And we got up, I said, "Well, this will be a great honor. Doctor Lipton and I are leaving tomorrow evening or the next day and we'll send you something just as soon as we can." "No. Tomorrow morning I need the plan." And I laughed and he said, "I'm absolutely serious, I need this written down now." And we looked at each other and our friend, who was the business manager of the Gazeta Wyborcza, which was the embryonic newspaper at the time.... He said, "We'll go back to the office and we'll write something." And Lipton and I went back and we wrote up a plan that night, from about 10:00 in the evening until I don't know if it was 3:00 or 4:00 in the morning. [We] delivered it the next morning ...

In this account, the plan that was to transform Poland – for better and for worse – was devised in just six hours.

Of course, these ideas about Poland's political economic transformation were not uncontested. In the 1980s, there had been some discussion of alternatives. Indeed, market socialism and worker self-management had been central planks of Solidarity's early economic proposals (Hyclak, 1987; Rainnie & Hardy, 1995) and had a strong Polish heritage (Lange, 1957). Yet, as a result both of the communist regime taking on and discrediting ideas around worker self-management and of the increasing likelihood of regime change, the strength of these alternative proposals was much reduced. Market socialism was seen as an acceptable alternative in limited circumstances, but once it became clear that Solidarity would be able to form a government and shape economic policy, the attachment to socialism was shed altogether. This rejection within Solidarity of any alternative to the market grew through the 1980s such that by 1989, all 'third roads' had been all but dismissed in favour of wholehearted marketization (Slay, 2000). As Kochanowicz et al. (2005: 46) argue:

> there were few people in Poland at the beginning of transition who were able to go beyond sweeping slogans concerning a "Third Way", a "socialist (or social) market economy" or a labor-managed economy and formulate a consistent and detailed reform package which could have served as an alternative to the Balcerowicz team's program.

For Kochanowicz (1997), there were a number of key ingredients that led to the dominance of Balcerowicz's ideas over others. The vision of the young Polish liberal economists and their preparedness for regime change was critical. They had ideas and had developed these in formal and informal groups, networks, and, latterly, think tanks (see also Ost, 2005; Bohle & Neunhöffer, 2005) in the years preceding the launch of the Balcerowicz Plan. In contrast, notwithstanding earlier plans, by 1989 the promotion of alternatives was weak and uncoordinated. The liberal economists also had the backing of the World Bank, the IMF, Jeffrey Sachs and other influential transnational actors (Smolar, 2006) and this international influence not only restrained their policy choices but also confirmed their legitimacy to many. Once a reform plan had been devised by Balcerowicz's team with the support of the Solidarity leadership, it was taken for granted that Solidarity and its millions of rank-and-file members would accept the plan. As Ost (2005: 56) suggests '[t]he plan was introduced as Solidarity's economic reforms, the solution for which people had been waiting.' In this way, the liberal economists benefited from the 'extraordinary politics' (Kochanowicz, 1997: 1458, citing Balcerowicz) of the immediate 1989 period, a honeymoon period when 'the new, freely elected government enjoyed a credit of trust, enabling it to push through very radical reforms' (Kochanowicz, 1997: 1458). Finally, as explored below, the presence of a strong safety net tempered many, though far from all, of the costs of market-led transition.

It was in this context, that a plan conceived over decades and supposedly finalized on one night was so convincingly implemented. Indeed, the strong position of Balcerowicz's team explains to a considerable extent how and why the planned reforms could be implemented so quickly. Much has been written on the Balcerowicz Plan, not least by Balcerowicz and Sachs (Balcerowicz, 1995, 2000; Sachs, 1990, 2000; Sachs & Lipton, 1990; Lipton & Sachs, 1990; see also Slay, 2000; Gomułka, 1998), such that it is necessary only to summarize the key points.

The Balcerowicz Plan rested on the commitment, outlined in Sach's famous *Economist* article 'What is to be done?',[2] that 'Eastern Europe must take a swift, dramatic leap to private ownership and a market system' (Sachs, 1990: 23). In delineating 'shock therapy', Sachs continued:

> There should be four simultaneous parts to a programme of rapid market transformation. First, let prices find market-clearing levels, in part based on free trade with the West. Second, set the private sector free by removing bureaucratic restrictions. Third, bring the state sector under control, by privatisation and by imposing tougher disciplines on such state firms as remain. Fourth, maintain overall macroeconomic stability through restrictive credit and balanced budgets (Sachs, 1990: 23).

These four pillars (which came to be identified as liberalization, internationalization, privatization and stabilization) were converted in a series of government legislation approved by the Polish *sejm* (parliament) and signed into law by the Polish president on 31 December 1989. The acts facilitated bankruptcy of inefficient enterprises, tightened monetary control, ended preferential subsidies for state-owned enterprises (SOEs), taxed excessive wage increases in SOEs (the so-called *popiwek*), restructured the tax system, legalized foreign investment, abolished the state monopoly on foreign trade and increased the exchangeability of the złoty, created a uniform customs rate, restructured job centres, and established guidelines for large lay-offs and guarantees for unemployment benefit and severance pay. Crucially, the programme of acts was also approved by the IMF in December 1989, creating a stabilization fund of US$1 billion, additional stand-by credit and subsequent support from the World Bank. As Sachs is keen to note, the plan also enabled him to push Western governments to accept the cancellation of many Polish debts[3] (which in 1989 equalled 65% of Polish GDP), without which the potential 'success' of shock therapy would have been severely circumscribed.

As the details of the plan suggest, Balcerowicz and his team were committed to a neo-liberal understanding of the economy. They championed entrepreneurialism, free trade, private property, markets, reductions in government spending and critiqued the welfare state, state ownership and intervention, and industrial policy (Ost, 2005; Kochanowicz, 1997). Theirs was a conceptualization of the economy founded on spontaneous market development and on 'real' capitalism, unfettered by the state, cronyism or any half-hearted marketization. It was above all a vision that prioritized the narrowly defined economic over all other considerations.

All that remained of opposition to radical and rapid marketization within Solidarity were a few marginalized voices, such as that of Tadeusz Kowalik, and of the strong social protectionism of Jacek Kuroń, who was, importantly, to become Solidarity's first Minister for Labour and Social Policy. Kuroń described himself as the anaesthetist of shock therapy (Kowalik, 2001; see also Belka, 2001) since his warnings of the social – and thus political – cost of the Balcerowicz Plan meant that social transfers stood at a much higher level during this period than Balcerowicz and Sachs might have wished. Social transfers accounted for an average of nearly 18% of GDP from 1990 to 1997 (Keane & Prasad, 2002: 325). However, within the neo-liberal model, social transfers were seen as a transitional measure which mitigated the costs of an imperfectly working market economy (Brown, 2007), costs which would be avoided if more reform could make the market work as it should. In this context, pressures grew for these protectionist measures to be cut as the reforms progressed. In 1998, Stanisław Gomułka, one of the architects of reform, argued that such a high level of social transfers 'helped to reduce the social cost of reform, but is inhibiting Poland's ability to sustain rapid growth' (1998: 166). From the mid to late 1990s, the increase in social transfers ceased and social inequalities became more visible (Keane & Prasad, 2002).

This notwithstanding, Balcerowicz (2000) has claimed that shock therapy produced only *relative* losers: all, he argued, were better off than under socialism. Others disagree. Grzegorz Kolodko, who was to become finance minister in the mid-1990s, described Balcerowicz's plan as 'shock without therapy' (2005) whilst Tadeusz Kowalik has repeatedly drawn attention to what he sees as the 'ugly face of transition' (Kowalik, 2001, 2006, 2007). For Kowalik, Balcerowicz's programme and the Poland it created has been marred by rising poverty, the emergence of unemployment, increasing disparities in income and living standards, declining working conditions in the expanding private sector, the loss of trade unions, a housing crisis, agricultural decline and a crisis of the welfare state.

Beyond these social costs, a further impact of the Balcerowicz Plan has been on the shaping of economic and social policy debates throughout the past 20 years. The Solidarity government lost the 1993 election,

thereby beginning a process that has continued since in which no incumbent government has ever won a general election, with the pendulum
swinging from post-communist to post-Solidarity parties each time until
the 2007 election.

Under the post-communist governments of Pawlak, Oleksy and
Cimosiewicz from 1993 to 1997, Kolodko primarily fulfilled the role of
finance minster. Kolodko is recognized as a critic of neo-liberalism in
Poland, arguing for more therapy with the shock (Kolodko, 2005) and
during this period launched his 'Strategy for Poland'.[4] This strategy focused
on reducing the social costs of reform, getting the institutions right and
shifted reform policy from a 'shock therapy' approach to a more gradual
one (Kolodko and Nuti, 1997). The SLD government (1993–6) is also seen
as one more favourable to labour (Ost, 2005) since it abolished the unpop-
ular *popiwek*, committed to regular public sector pay increases, established
a Tripartite Commission, legislated for compulsory enterprise social funds
and passed a range of other labour-friendly legislation. Yet, for all these
commitments, Kolodko continued to profess a belief in 'financial and
economic fundamentals':

> Here I do not differ from IMF orthodoxy or a classical mainstream liberal
> approach. Fiscal balance has to be restored, current account has to be sustain-
> able, inflation has to be brought down, liberalization has to proceed vis-à-vis
> prices and trade, and privatization has to be completed (Kolodko, 1998: 2).

As Ost confirms, '[i]n general macroeconomic policy, the government differed little from previous ones … Its neoliberal wing controlled the finance
and privatization ministries, pushing to limit expenditures and speed privatization' (2005: 81; see also Kochanowicz, 1997). Even Kolodko himself
notes the convergence of his policies with those of Balcerowicz, citing
Balcerowicz who 'admits that the SLD's economic policies and goals
expressed … are virtually indistinguishable from those of [Balcerowicz's
party] UW' (Kolodko & Nuti, 1997: 25). This convergence is confirmed by
the appointment of Marek Belka, a Chicago-trained economist who completed a PhD on the work on Milton Friedman in 1986,[5] to replace Kolodko
at the finance ministry.

The election of Electoral Action Solidarity (Akcja Wyborcza Solidarność,
AWS) in 1997 brought Leszek Balcerowicz back to the Finance Ministry
where he launched what has been referred to as the 'second Balcerowicz
plan' (Blazyca, 1999). This plan was 'based on a determined tax-cutting[6]
effort, a fast-declining state budget deficit, economic "de-bureaucratization"
with a final de-coupling of the state from the economy' (Blazyca, 1999: 812)
with a view to promoting enterprise and inward investment, and thus
growth, but also ignoring growing social and geographical inequalities.

The success with which Balcerowicz managed to achieve this second plan was tempered by pressures within Solidarity to maintain social spending in the face of rising unemployment.

The change of government in 2001, with the re-election of SLD under Leszek Miller, brought first Marek Belka and then Grzegorz Kolodko back to the Finance Ministry. Balcerowicz was, however, during this time president of the National Bank of Poland, and thus continued to play a major fiscal role. There were few fundamental changes to economic policy, although Kolodko did pursue a somewhat more interventionist approach to enterprise restructuring and investment. Reflecting the shift towards interventionism within this SLD administration, the Minister for Economy, Labour and Social Policy, Jerzy Hausner, was a key actor and deputy prime minister. Hausner undertook to implement a major programme of reform, which became known as the Hausner Plan and was eventually passed, in a watered-down state, in 2004. Like many of the government programmes that had preceded it, the Hausner Plan was targeted at cutting government spending, with a focus on administrative and welfare budgets, in part motivated by pressures to cut the public finance deficit and achieve fiscal stability in the run-up to EU enlargement. In the welfare sphere, the key actions were restrictions on inflationary adjustments for pensions, restricted access to early-retirement pensions and incapacity benefits, and a reduction of unemployment benefits in relation to the minimum wage. Whilst the goal of fiscal discipline appeared to be paramount in Hausner's plan, Hausner himself claimed that it was in part an attempt to better target benefits to the poor and was coupled with actions to alleviate unemployment through the reform of the labour code and his earlier 'Entrepreneurship, Development, Work' programme (Chancellery of the Prime Minister, 2002). Hausner was clear that this was not simply a financial issue and signalled the need for an economic policy beyond a fiscal one: 'If we get the finances right and the economy wrong, we will have social revolts and everything else will be lost' (quoted in Wagstyl, 2005; see also Millard, 2006; Cienski, 2003, 2004a, 2004b).

A number of commentators have drawn attention to the absence of radical change from government to government. For Shields, in Poland, '[t]he politics of neoliberalism are increasingly characterized by the convergence of policy platforms among apparently competing parties' (2007: 170; see also Smolar, 2006; Steele, 2005). Particular questions are raised in the sphere of social policy. Brown (2007) argues that throughout the transition period there has been a passive approach to social policy, and to dealing with unemployment specifically, which reflects an apparently contradictory attachment to both protectionism and neo-liberalism. From this perspective, the role of social policy is to react to the economic policy dictates of the Ministry of Finance, a position well illustrated by Kuroń's social policy outlined above. Whilst on the one hand, this position highlights the assumed primacy of the economy, it also underlines the widespread commitment to protectionism and solidarity (small 's'). In his electoral analyses, Szczerbiak (2007) draws attention to the persistent support of Poles for policies of intervention and solidarity notwithstanding the faith in the market (see also Bohle & Greskovits, 2007). This is summed up by the call by social policy expert Kolarska-Bobińska (Kolarska-Bobińska & Rymsza, 2007: 2) to 'combine solidarity with liberalism'.

The centrality of these dual commitments is clearly played through in contemporary Polish politics. The 2005 parliamentary and presidential elections were shaped by a mooted divide between social and liberal positions,[7] with the Kaczyński twins, leading Prawo i Sprawiedliwość (PiS, Law and Justice), characterizing Donald Tusk's Platforma Obywatelska (PO, Civic Platform) as the party for winners and claiming themselves to be pro-poor and increasingly protectionist (Szczerbiak, 2007; Millard, 2007). PiS rejected Balcerowicz – then still president of the national bank – both in personal and policy terms and, despite the role that the Kaczyński twins had played in Solidarity's early 1990s government, sought to turn their back on the pro-market perspectives of Balcerowicz, and Tusk. During the campaign, PiS became increasingly suspicious of marketization and globalization and promoted an increasingly strong Polish state (Steele, 2005).

PiS won the 2005 election, but for all their rhetorical campaign rejection of neo-liberal models, they had little to offer as an alternative. For some left critics, the dominant feature of PiS's economic policy was its absence. Kochanowicz, for example, argued that the 'leaders of PiS have never had much interest in the economy, nor does the party have many (if any) people with expertise in economics' (2007: 3). The first PiS prime minister, Kazimierz Marcinkiewicz, commissioned Poland's Adam Smith Center to review the country's economic challenges and suggest a policy programme. Its key recommendations were for 'further flexibilization of the labor market flexibility, a reduction of labor costs, taxes and social spending' (Kowalik, 2007: 276). PiS appointed as its finance minister Zyta Gilowska, a neo-liberal economist previously associated with the 'liberal' Platforma Obywatelska and key proponent of the flat tax concept. Thus, apart from the introduction of the so-called '*becikowe*' (a one-off payment for all new parents) and some other minor policy shifts, economic policy remained largely neo-liberal (Kowalik, 2007; see also Kochanowicz, 2007) and characterized by a marked failure to get to grips with unemployment.

In part as a result of their policy inaction, but more particularly as a result of coalition in-fighting, PiS called new parliamentary elections in the autumn of 2007. They lost dramatically and Platforma Obywatelska's Donald Tusk became prime minister. What is striking in Tusk's government is the strength with which it has restated a neo-liberal agenda. In speeches and interviews since the election, Tusk, his British-born finance minister Jacek Rostowski (who was a central player in Balcerowicz's team) and Adam Szejnfeld, his deputy Minister of Economy, have made clear their economic priorities. These include reducing government spending, pushing forward with further privatizations, reforming the tax system (including scrapping capital gains tax on investments and stock market gains and promoting again a single flat tax), taking 'a machete' to regulation (Cienski & Wagstyl, 2007c) and freeing entrepreneurs (see also, Cienski & Wagstyl, 2007a, 2007b; Tezy Tuska, *Gazeta Wyborcza*, 24 February 2008; Tusk 2007). Like Slovakia in the early 2000s, their oft-cited model for economic growth is Ireland and their commitments deeply neo-liberal. For Tusk, 'economic freedoms and private ownership' are central to economic growth (*Financial Times*, 30 November 2007).[8]

As the analysis above suggests, policy reforms have been remarkably constant, notwithstanding occasional shifts in emphasis from government to government, with overwhelming attention being paid to privatization, reducing government spending, promoting enterprise and remaking the labour market, all policies set in train by the early initiatives of Balcerowicz and his team. In almost all major policy spheres successive governments have taken on and developed existing or planned policies. It was not until the late 1990s that Polish governments (first the SLD/PSL coalition, then AWS government from 1997) turned their attention to reform of the public sector and public administration, the so-called 'second wave' of reforms (Kolarska-Bobińska, 2000; see also Stenning & Hardy, 2005). This second wave consisted of interlinked reforms all founded on a move to decentralize, to rationalize and to introduce the market into public institutions.

In the health sector, the primary feature of reform has been the separation of the management and financing of health care and the introduction of a compulsory insurance premium (collected through income tax), initially paid to new regional health funds (*kasa chorych*) (Tymowska, 2001), but later to a re-centralized National Health Fund (Narodowy Fundusz Zdrowia, NFZ) with regional branches. The health funds in turn sign renewable contracts with service providers (i.e. hospitals, clinics and doctors) who are therefore under pressure to compete for contracts by offering high-quality, low-cost health services. This move introduced market mechanisms into the management and financing of health care (McMenamin & Timonen, 2002) and was predicated on the diversification of health care providers, including new private providers.

In the sphere of welfare, following the increase in social transfers in the early 1990s, the trend has been declining spending and increased targeting, such that both the numbers receiving benefits and the level of benefits received has fallen. For example, in the late 1990s, just 23% of unemployed

Poles received unemployment benefit (Cazes & Nesporova, 2004). After years of relatively generous and fairly accessible early retirement and disability pensions, more recent policies – starting with the Hausner Plan – have attempted to limit these benefits. With respect to pensions, the model – as in Slovakia and elsewhere in the region – has been Jose Pinera's Chilean reforms, introduced to Poland by the Adam Smith Center think tank and promoted by Marek Belka during his term as finance minister (see also the following discussion of Slovakia). Pinera's model shifted the focus to the private sector and in Poland led to the introduction of a three-pillar system based on pension fund accounts managed by private providers (Duszczyk & Wiśniewski, 2006). Since the reforms were introduced in 1999, alliances between Western and Polish financial institutions (such as Citibank, Commercial Union, Allianz, Credit Lyonnais) have become the dominant providers.

In addition to a tendency to reduce social transfers, the emphasis in the sphere of labour market interventions has increasingly also been on 'active' social policies which include some form of work or training as a requirement for the receipt of benefits. As Tusk (2007) proclaimed in his 'maiden speech', 'social policy … will be active and will activate people'. These reforms of benefits have sat alongside amendments to the Labour Code, predicated on 'the belief that by easing the burden for entrepreneurs the government hopes to speed up economic growth and by this to increase the number of available jobs' (Surdej, 2004: 34). Hausner's reforms were focused on the introduction of more flexible labour laws which eased health and safety burdens for employers and have made it easier for employers to hire and fire. Such a focus works against employment and is coupled with an overwhelming emphasis on enterprise, an emphasis that is central to Tusk's agenda to support creativity and innovation within which 'we must a give a chance to those who do not expect money from the state' (Tusk, 2007).

The last word on Poland's neo-liberal reforms should perhaps be left to Balcerowicz. Writing an obituary for Milton Friedman on his death in 2006, Balcerowicz (2006) wrote: 'I live in a Poland that is now free, and I consider Milton Friedman to be one of the main intellectual architects of my country's liberty.'

Neo-Liberalism and the Slovak Political Economy

In Slovakia, the trajectory of neo-liberalism has been equally as variegated as that in Poland although the specifics differ in some important ways. In the years immediately after the collapse of the communist state in 1989, the federal state of the then Czechoslovakia was committed to pursuing a relatively rapid programme of liberalization (although not as radical as that in Poland). This was coupled with a moralistic stance – held strongly by the then federal president, Václav Havel – towards the de-militarization of the economy and the ending of weapons production. This sector had been a mainstay of the Czechoslovak economy, and especially of certain regions in Slovakia which were almost wholly dependent on employment and economic activity in large armaments factories (see Smith, 1994, 1998).

However, the establishment of a neo-liberal trajectory following the collapse of state socialism in Czechoslovakia was not achieved overnight; nor was it without conflict over a number of discourses of development (Smith, 1998). The two main competing models that emerged in Czechoslovakia involved the neo-liberal shock therapy variant of Václav Klaus and the social market economy variant developed by more reform-minded economists such as Valtr Komárek (Myant, 1993). As in Poland, Komárek's reform-orientated programme had a long tradition associated with the reform economists of the 1960s, particularly Oto Šik. This programme reflected an attempt to find a specific Czechoslovak road out of state socialism which, while recognizing the centrality of marketization, reflected the concerns of the 1960s reformers for a more socialized economy. Although Komárek was deputy prime minister in the 'government of national understanding' prior to the 1990 election, he became increasingly marginalized in the policy debate as Klaus consolidated his position as finance minister. The neo-liberal discourse won out and the transformation programme, as implemented in January 1991, involved a belief in the superiority of the free market and a concern to block inflationary pressures through fiscal austerity. The state remained central to regulating this process of transformation, but what had changed was the nature of that state and its inability to wield direct economic power through ownership of the means of production.

One of the main consequences of the commitment to end weapons production and its negative impacts on the Slovak economy (Smith, 1994, 1998), when combined with the neo-liberal stance of Klaus' federal government, was the rise of a nationalist-populist political agenda in Slovakia. This ultimately resulted in the collapse of the federal state in 1993. A nationalist-populist government in newly independent Slovakia under the premiership of Vladimír Mečiar attempted the creation of a market economy in which vested political interests retained economic control (Carpenter, 1997; Smith 1998; Haughton 2001, 2002; Mesežnikov & Gyárfášová, 2008). In some ways resembling a form of statist capitalism, the resulting clientelist political economy set limits to the rolling out of neo-liberalism, although there remained a widespread commitment to private property ownership and market mechanisms, as long as these were controlled through the 'right' channels (Smith 1998). The Mečiar government's antipathy towards EU membership and 'Westernization' also led to relative international isolation until 1998 when an opposition coalition of centre-left and rightist parties won the election and set the country on a much more right-of-centre trajectory, not least embracing a much more neo-liberalizing agenda, especially following the re-election of the government of Mikuláš Dzurinda in 2002. On its election, and over the years until the Dzurinda government's defeat by a more left-of-centre and nationalist coalition in 2006, a radical neo-liberalizing agenda was implemented (Fisher et al., 2007; Smith & Rochovská, 2007). The new government was fully committed to being included in the first wave of EU enlargement and to what became a radical neo-liberal project of reform.[9] Dzurinda surrounded himself with a group of radical, reform-minded economists. Many of these reformers had been politically marginalized under the Mečiar government, and had developed close links to a number of external institutions such as the Bratislava-based Friedrich Hayek Foundation and the MESA10 think-tank that was founded in 1993 by the economist Ivan Mikloš, who became finance minister during Dzurinda's second term in office. This group was determined to transform Slovakia towards a 'neo-liberal market paradise under the Tatra mountains' through a series of radical reforms (Smith and Rochovská, 2007).

For the proponents of the neo-liberal project, the new Slovak government after 1998 was remarkably successful. Indeed, Slovakia's neo-liberal shift became a role model for other neo-liberalizing states. For example, following a visit to Slovakia, the editor-in-chief of *Forbes* business magazine proclaimed that the country had become an 'investors' paradise'. The country, he argued, was 'set to become the world's next Hong Kong or Ireland, i.e. a small place that's an economic powerhouse' (Forbes, 2003). Forbes went on to claim that, '[i]f Slovakia remains on its reform path, it could become the domino that pushes the rest of the EU, particularly "Old European" nations Germany and France, toward a more free-enterprise, entrepreneurial era. That would be good news for everyone.'

For the Dzurinda government, markets and individual responsibility were seen to be the way of solving many of the economic and social problems of the country – not least the second highest unemployment rate in the European Union (13.4% in 2006) and high levels of social exclusion. For example, the *National Action Plan on Social Inclusion 2004–2006 for the Slovak Republic* argued that: 'the social strategy of the Slovak Republic focuses on strengthening the role of the individual and his/her self-support by means of a system of social protection that strengthens and motivates his/her participation in the labour market' (Slovak Ministry of Labour, Social Affairs and Family, 2004). Labour market participation, under the government's slogan

Table 2.1   Flat tax rates on personal incomes in East Central Europe

Country	Tax rate	Year introduced
Estonia	26	1994
Lithuania	33	1994
Latvia	25	1995
Russia	13	2001
Serbia	14	2003
Ukraine	13	2004
Slovakia	19	2004
Georgia	12	2005
Romania	16	2005

Source: *Economist* 2005

'work pays', and an emphasis on individual responsibility were therefore key motifs of the neo-liberal reform agenda. In order to stimulate this process of individualization and the expansion of market relations, a number of reforms were enacted.

One of the most important changes involved the adoption of a new Labour Code in 2003. The revised code involved several key features liberalizing the labour market, including lowering the costs of making workers redundant, establishing more flexible overtime and working hours for employees, greater flexibility in the use of fixed-term and part-time contracts and weakening the power of trade unions in the workplace (see Goliaš & Kičina, 2007; Jurajda & Mathernová, 2004).

In addition to labour market reform, the key change, which received international acclaim, was the 2004 introduction of a flat tax regime of 19% on income, corporate and value-added tax to reduce the 'tax burden' on individuals. This included a significant reduction in corporation tax from 45% in 1993 to 19% in 2004 (Goliaš & Kičina, 2005) and took place in the context of the development of flat tax systems in many post-socialist states (*Economist*, 2005) (Table 2.1). The new tax system involved the creation of public acceptance for reduced personal income tax through a 'tax freedom day', promoted by radical economists, including Finance Minister Ivan Mikloš and those associated with the Slovak Taxpayers Association (effectively part of the Bratislava-based Hayek Foundation).[10] The tax reform has – like that in the United States (Harvey, 2005), although very different in its scope and proportions – involved a significant redistribution of wealth towards the rich and corporations (Goliaš and Kičina, 2005).

The third area of neo-liberal reform, which also received international attention and paralleled that in Poland, focused on pensions. In the context of increasing concern over the costs of sustaining a pay-as-you-go state-funded system, a new pension system was introduced in 2004. This system involved an increased retirement age of 62 for all (previously it was 60 for men and between 53 and 57 for women), and a new 'three pillar', largely privatized pension system.[11] The new system, like that in Poland, was based to a large extent on the neo-liberal Chilean model and was directly influenced by a variety of agencies of neo-liberalism, such as the Hayek Foundation, who were recruited by the Minister of Labour, Social Affairs and the Family to design the new system. The Hayek Foundation was heavily influenced by the architect of the Chilean reform, José Pinera, co-chair of the right-wing think-tank Cato Institute's Project on Social Security Choice and founder of the International Center for Pension Reform. The reform process was centred on the expansion of the market into the pension system and is likely over time to create significant differentiation of pension outcomes for different social classes depending on ability to pay. Indeed, as one of the architects of the new system commented when asked about the possibility of increasing income inequality among pensioners under the reformed system: 'Economists do not know the word "justice".'[12]

A further area of reform involved a thoroughgoing transformation of the social welfare and benefits system. A central component of these reforms was the attempt to reduce high unemployment levels by creating 'incentives' for people to work rather than receive benefits under the government slogan 'work pays', and the implementation of reductions in state expenditure on benefits. For example, in 2001 about half of those in receipt of social assistance benefits (about 162,000 people) who fell below social subsistence level were 'reclassified'. As a result they were no longer eligible to receive benefits. In addition, benefits to those still receiving them were halved between 2002 and 2004 alongside an overall fall in state expenditure on social assistance (Figure 2.1). Those losing the right to benefits were largely people who were not prepared to do 'public work', the long-term unemployed, those voluntarily leaving work, and those refusing to undertake retraining or other Labour Office programmes (Jurajda & Mathernová, 2004; Brook & Leibfritz, 2005).

The retrenchment of state social assistance effectively impoverished large numbers of people. Basic benefit levels became insufficient to sustain a livelihood and, even when supplemented by payments to 'reward' participation in active labour market programmes, the total benefit level still placed an individual below the official state poverty line (for fuller details, see Smith & Rochovská, 2007). As a consequence, the poor had little option but to resort to work in the informal economy, the significance of which stimulated a

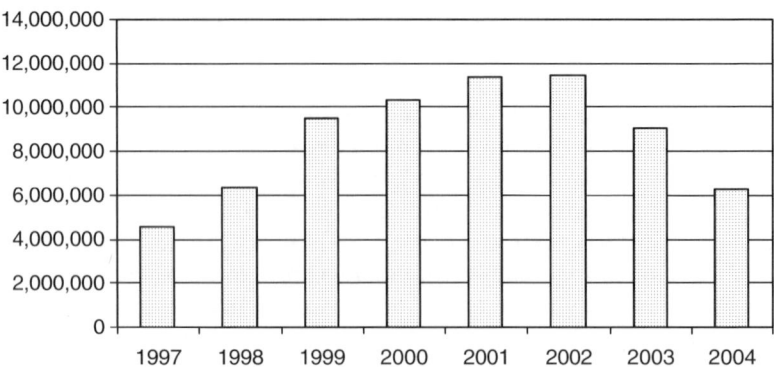

Figure 2.1   State expenditure on social assistance for those in 'material deprivation', Slovakia 1997–2004 (Slovak koruna)
Source: Data provided by Slovak Ministry of Labour, Social Affairs and Family

campaign by the government against what it labelled as 'black work' in 2005. But informal employment opportunities both in the market and non-market economy have, at the same time, enabled neo-liberal welfare reform to take place in locations where such opportunities exist. Recourse to such informal income sources has enabled basic social reproduction to be achieved, even with the loss of state benefits. This is not to argue that this retrenchment is a positive dynamic, but rather to recognize how alternative forms of employment have partly enabled the implementation of neo-liberal reform. Where few informal opportunities exist, the real material limits of the reform become all too apparent, as the example of the Roma revolt in Chapter One attests. This is not to suggest that the informal economy provides a solution to neo-liberalism, and should be expanded. Rather, it is to recognize the important role that informal economic opportunities provide in the maintenance of some level of social reproduction, and this is an issue we return to in later chapters.

Finally, there has been an ongoing process of marketization and reform in the health care system, which has significantly increased the financial costs of medicine and has most negatively impacted on the elderly and the poor. In 2004, a series of reforms involved increasing the level of health service co-payments, introducing commercial health insurance and privatizing health insurance companies. Consequently, household expenditure on medical services and medicines increased (Nemec, 2005). According to one survey, 69% of pensioners said that they do not have enough money for medicine, and 53% of the disabled said they could not afford the price of medicine (Sme, 2006). Furthermore, between 2002 and 2003 visits to doctors declined by 10%, and use of emergency services fell by 13% (Slovak Embassy, 2004).

By 2006, in the run-up to the national elections, there was increasing dissatisfaction with this reform trajectory, particularly among the poorest and most vulnerable sections of society. Increasing inequality and dramatic increases in relative poverty across ECE, but particularly in Slovakia, have affected especially vulnerable groups such as children and the Roma (UNICEF Innocenti Research Centre, 2005; Rainnie et al., 2002b; Vašečka et al., 2003). This dissatisfaction was manifest in increasing support for centrist and left-of-centre political parties, such as the social democratic SMER party which ultimately won the 2006 elections in coalition with the nationalist Slovak National Party and Mečiar's HZDS (Haughton and Rybář, 2008). Indeed, SMER fought the election on a platform of a return to a welfare state, ensuring societal prosperity and of 'righting the wrongs' of earlier privatizations. However, as several reports have noted, the extent to which the new government's legislative agenda profoundly transformed the radical reforms of the Dzurinda government, despite changes such as an increase in the minimum wage, has been limited (see, for example, Goliaš & Kičina, 2007). For example, the 2007 changes to the Labour Code, whilst 'somewhat tighten[ing] employment protection legislation' (OECD, 2007: 6) by making amendments which allow for greater protection of workers' rights, leaves most of the radical steps introduced in 2003 'untouched' (Goliaš & Kičina, 2007: 4). Those changes that have been made, however, 'would not harm employment and would promote equity' (OECD, 2007: 6), suggesting that earlier commitments to neo-liberalizing the labour market have been tempered by other commitments to social concerns.

Comparing Polish and Slovak Neo-liberalization

The processes of neo-liberalization in Poland and Slovakia reflect domestic contexts, commitments and compromises so that whilst the experience of neo-liberalism is in many ways shared, it is also distinct. This distinctiveness points to the ways in which neo-liberalization has become domesticated in the two countries.

As we have seen (and explore in more detail in Chapters Four, Five, Six and Seven), in spheres such as pensions, labour markets and housing, Polish and Slovak policies have been remarkably similar and have borrowed heavily from global models of neo-liberal reform (such as Pinera's Chilean pension reform and US–UK 'work first' commitments). Despite the fact that both countries have been marked by repeated electoral shifts, as the pendulum has swung from left to right and as incumbent governments have tended to fail to be re-elected, there has been an extraordinary consistency in economic policy. Across both countries, the convergence – among both the post-communist left and the newer right-wing parties – around pro-market policies has been marked. Few within the political mainstream of either country have promoted policies that contest the foundations of neo-liberalism. These commonalities point to some of the key contexts of post-socialist neo-liberalism: unstable electoral politics, the widespread discrediting of left alternatives, and the influence of external policy frameworks in the context of both aid for reform programmes and, more recently, EU accession.

The two countries have also been characterized by a common, if varying, commitment to social cohesion and to policies which mediated the costs of transition and reflected earlier debates about social market or reform socialism in the 1960s and 1970s. In Slovakia, however, these social commitments were stronger in the early phases of reform, immediately post-1989, whereas in Poland they emerged more fully in the early to mid 1990s after a period of rapid and dramatic neo-liberal reform. This contrasting timing was reflected in the early 2000s too, as Slovakia, under Mikuláš Dzurinda, embraced a particularly neo-liberalizing agenda just as in Poland the post-communist SLD was demonstrating a commitment to intervention alongside more neo-liberal policies. Both of these agendas were implemented in the context of rising unemployment and highlight clearly the plurality of post-socialist neo-liberalisms. At times the process of neo-liberalization has seemed more concerted in Slovakia, and it is perhaps true to say that the Polish commitment to social cohesion and to solidarity has been more persistent.

The particular growth of unemployment in both Poland and Slovakia in the early 2000s points to a further similarity between the two states: both have faced profound social and regional inequalities, evidenced by persistent poverty and long-term unemployment, and both have seen the development of visible protests against neo-liberalism and illiberal, reactionary alternatives to mainstream democratic politics. The ways in which individuals and households in Slovakia and Poland have negotiated these persistent socio-economic dislocations is at the heart of *Domesticating Neo-Liberalism* and we return to the question of political responses to these dislocations in our conclusions in Chapter Eight.

Conclusions

As we have suggested, we tend towards a theorization of neo-liberalism which acknowledges the discursive and material strength of its ideas and practices but which also draws attention to its contingent, contradictory and uneven implementation. In this chapter, we have employed our first 'take' on domestication to develop this perspective, arguing that Polish and

Slovak processes of neo-liberalization have been shaped by the very particular ways in which neo-liberal ideas developed before 1989 in domestic theoretical and political circuits and by the construction of particular policy programmes which reflect the two countries' political, social and cultural contexts and legacies. Together these domestications lead to an understanding of Polish and Slovak neo-liberalizations as both entangled with global geographies of neo-liberalism and differentiated and contested in particularly Polish and Slovak ways. In both the Slovak and Polish versions of neo-liberalism, we have identified a dominant and persistent promotion of markets and a set of inconsistencies and contestations that problematize and temper the implementation of neo-liberal reforms.

These analyses have begun to identify some of the ways in which processes of neo-liberalization have been domesticated in Poland and Slovakia and to tease out the similarities and particularities between the two cases. However, as we have suggested, accounts of neo-liberalization which focus on the national institutional, technocratic and political contexts are limited. Attention must also be paid to the everyday domestications of neo-liberalism and the ways in which neo-liberal policies and programmes are understood, negotiated, mediated and contested by individuals, households and communities as they construct their everyday economies and seek to achieve social reproduction. This focus on economic practices, domestication and social reproduction is central to the following chapter, which explores these ideas in more conceptual detail.

Chapter Three

Domesticating Economies: Diverse Economic Practices, Households and Social Reproduction

Introduction

In Chapter One we highlighted the need to 'domesticate' neo-liberalism in two ways: firstly, through a careful analysis of the ways in which national, international and transnational institutions and processes mediate the dissemination of neo-liberal policies in different times and different places (a theme which forms the focus of discussions in Chapter Two); and, secondly, through a focus on the mundane practices of economic life, which enables not only a detailed understanding of how neo-liberalism is lived in articulation with a host of economic, political and social others, but also how those practices are themselves constitutive of neo-liberalism. This chapter focuses in more detail on the concepts and frameworks we employ in *Domesticating Neo-Liberalism* to explore and analyse the latter.

The most common approach to studying everyday economic practices and social reproduction in the post-socialist world (and beyond) has been within a framework of household survival strategies (see, for critical treatments, Bridger & Pine, 1998; Wallace, 2002; Clarke, 1999; Meurs, 2002). This focus on household survival strategies is problematic for a number of reasons: firstly, it often assumes that the household is a relatively coherent economic unit which sits at the centre of everyday economies; secondly, it prioritizes survival over any other socio-economic goal; and, thirdly, it often presumes that everyday economic practices are strategic. In this chapter, and throughout *Domesticating Neo-Liberalism*, we seek to develop an alternative framework that enables a fuller exploration of everyday economies of individuals, households and communities in post-socialist East Central Europe.

In place of strategies, we think about practices, arguing that such a perspective enables an exploration of economic activities which is not constrained by any notion of strategic action. In this way, whilst acknowledging the often careful and intelligent development of economic practices, we explore a range of other potential, sometimes irrational, motivations for economic activity and the limits on 'strategic' economic action. This approach values two particular sets of interconnections: through a consideration of both material inequalities and moral rationalities, it explores the interplay between everyday economies and, for example, class, gender, generation and geography; and through an exploration of diverse practices, it analyses how economies articulate and how, in particular, the economies of neo-liberalism both necessitate and erode other economic spaces and practices. The 'practice turn' also encourages a view of the economy as embedded in the multiscalar spaces of everyday life and this challenges us to explore the household and its geographies in more detail. This, in turn, replaces the idea of the household as self-contained and harmonious with a representation of the complex spaces, practices and relations that come together in the household. To pursue this we employ the notion of 'domestication', a process which, we argue below, promotes a perspective of the household as connected and populated by diverse subjects engaged in sometimes conflictual processes of negotiation and adaptation. Finally, in place of survival, we focus on social reproduction, asking how individuals, households and communities seek to sustain themselves and each other. Our emphasis is not only – though importantly – on material sustenance (housing, clothing, feeding and so on) but also on the sustenance of social and emotional values and relationships. In this way, we ask whether the everyday economies explored here might enable not only survival (and sometimes barely that) but also a thriving and a flourishing.

Practices and Everyday Economic Lives

The idea of practices is one that appears frequently in social science literatures to explore the 'ongoing mix of human activities that make up the richness of everyday social life' (Painter, 2000: 242) and the 'apparently insignificant activities of everyday life' (Simonsen, 2007: 168). A theory of practice attends, in the simplest terms, to what people do and seeks to understand why and how they do what they do. Following Bourdieu, 'practice happens (although ... it would be incorrect to suggest that Bourdieu thinks that it *just* happens)' (Jenkins, 2002: 70). The attempt to understand *how* practices happen, how actors make sense of their worlds, get a 'feel for the game' (Bourdieu, 1990: 61) and 'decide' how to act, often in unacknowledged ways, forms the focus of studies of practices. In this light, anything can be a practice and theorists acknowledge the ubiquity of practices. Simonsen (2007: 169) notes, for example, that 'social life is plied by a series of human practices', exemplified by 'such practices as negotiation practices, political practices, cooking practices, banking practices, recreation practices, religious practices, and educational practices' (Schatzki, 2002: 70). In the attempt to value and understand everyday life, to ensure that 'everyday practices, "ways of operating" or doing things, no longer appear as merely the obscure background of social activity' (de Certeau, 1984: xi), apparently mundane activities such as shopping, working, caring, balancing household budgets and cooking (see de Certeau et al., 1998) come to be seen as meaningful and often innovative practices which are key to the negotiation of economic life and to the process of social reproduction.

For some, the notion of practices is one which connects to the politics of the other and to the spaces carved out by 'subaltern' actors to counter 'the strategies of instituted power' (de Certeau, 1984: 23).[1] Thus, practice is seen to be marked by 'its particularity and its peculiar tenacity in the face of powerful forces from "above"' (Highmore, 2002: 12) and enables us to 'trace out the ruses of other interests and desires that are neither determined nor captured by the systems in which they develop' (de Certeau, 1984: xviii). Inherent in many acts of 'making do' is a desire to re-use, remake or even subvert the products, representations and activities imposed by the powerful, established order. Thus, in the context of neo-liberalization, practices might be seen as the ways in which individuals, households, and communities contest and subvert the market agendas of powerful actors. Yet this desire to subvert is, we would argue, only one of the motivations embodied within everyday practice, and indeed many practices are intentionally or accidentally orientated towards supporting the status quo. Indeed, one of the paradoxes we explore here is the ways in which practices that appear to reflect alternative or subaltern rationalities might in fact enable neo-liberalism. Nevertheless, the logic of creating everyday, subaltern spaces within the dominant system is one of diversification and pluralization. The notion of practices works against an assumption of singularity and highlights ' "indirect" and "errant" trajectories' (de Certeau, 1984: xviii) which reflect multiple logics and are often contradictory. As Kaplan and Ross (1987: 3) suggest, practices reflect, at the very least, 'a conjunction of habit, desire and accident'. In this multiplicity, attention needs to be paid to the articulations and disarticulations that come into play in practice.

In part, then, the study of practices is focused on drawing attention to the multiplicity of mundane, everyday activities, often taken for granted or passed over in accounts of macro-scale transformation, such as neo-liberalization, but it also involves a particular perspective on those activities. Schatzki (1998: 244) theorizes practice as 'a series of actions that are governed by practical intelligibility and performed in interconnected, local settings', stressing both the skills and knowledges and the articulations embedded in practice. This perspective is echoed in Simonsen's (2001: 44) use of Heidegger to depict ' "Being-in-the-world" ... [as] an everyday skilful coping or engagement with an environment'. The analysis of practices seeks to understand how people 'make do' by drawing on their own agency within wider structures and tends to seek the answer to this question in a space between determinism and autonomy. As Jenkins (2002: 70) suggests:

> This can be interpreted – in part – as a restatement of Marx's adage that, although men [sic] make their own history, they do not do so in circumstances of their own choosing. It is also, however, a comment upon the fact that actors do not just *confront* their current circumstances. They are an integral part of those circumstances. Within them they have grown up, learning and acquiring a set of practical cultural competences ...

These perspectives suggest that practices incorporate both intelligent reflection and the employment of a range of often tacit and undervalued skills. Practices are ways of 'making do' which draw on embodied experience and knowledge, networks, power and resources, and inherited ways of being, and are learnt. They are not always 'rational' in a received or singular sense (Schatzki, 1996). Not only may practices sometimes appear 'irrational' but they also draw on a range of 'culturally defined and historically variable rationalities' (Jenkins, 2002: 73) and, as a result, have both temporalities (related not only to history, but to lifecourse and the rhythms of everyday life) and spatialities (connected to what Schatzki (1988) calls settings (see below), but also to mobilities and so on).

The spatiality of practices forms a particular focus of this book and thus deserves additional attention. 'Practice is located in space' (Jenkins, 2002: 69) and Schatzki's notion of 'setting' explores this in two ways. First, practices 'constitute the spatiality of human existence' (1998: 246) since they are often oriented 'toward and in response to the people, events and objects encountered in settings' (Schatzki, 1998: 246). Second, the 'particular rules, paradigms, ideas and so on' which are encountered in settings are a factor in determining what makes sense to people to do. In the first account, practices are constitutive of places since they not only rest on but also shape the interconnections of co-existent 'people, events and objects'. Practices both rest on and build, for example, social networks, collective identities, communities and common traditions. In this way, places are produced by the coming together of diverse practices, as Simonsen (2007: 179; see also Massey, 1993) suggests:

> [s]patial entities (places, cities etc.) then become loci of encounters, outcomes of multiple becomings. They are meeting points, moments or conjunctures

where social practices and trajectories meet up with moving and fixed materialities and form configurations that are continuously under transformation and negotiation.

For de Certeau et al. (1998: 3), the articulation between practices and neighbourhood is intimate. Indeed, 'living in the neighborhood' is defined by the 'structure of activities punctuated by spaces and relationships' such that the task they set themselves is 'elucidating the cultural practices of city dwellers in the very space of their neighborhood' (de Certeau et al., 1998: 7). The attention paid here to the 'very space of the neighborhood' emphasizes the need to account for the impact of the geography of the neighbourhood – and by implication other everyday spaces – on the shaping of practices. As we explore in much more detail below (and in Smith & Stenning, 2006), practices take place in a series of 'nested geographies', in households, workplaces, institutions, shops, restaurants, and in many other spaces between and beyond these. Thus, the nested geography of these sites (their built form, accessibility, proximity, interrelationships, cultures and so on) are important factors in an analysis of practices.

In the second sense explored by Schatzki, the particularity of situated rules, knowledges and customs shapes what have become known, in other literatures, as moral rationalities. Moral rationalities are defined as 'collective negotiations and understandings about what is morally right and socially acceptable' (Duncan & Edward, 1997: 30) and are seen to be both gendered and classed – and so connected to the making and remaking of subjectivities – and 'geographically and historically articulated' (Duncan, 2005: 73). For example, geographical patterns of economy and employment reflect not only the presence or absence of jobs and infrastructures but are also shaped by ideas about what ought to be done (Duncan & Smith, 2002). Whilst research in this field has focused primarily on the gendering of moral rationalities (that is, 'what men and women ought to do' (Duncan & Smith, 2002: 24)), it is also clear that geography is articulated with class, race and generation in shaping what makes sense (Duncan, 2005). The articulation of material patterns and moral rationalities echoes Schatzki's theorization of the 'realm of the setting' (1998: 247). For Schatzki, the setting both encourages co-located actors to respond to events experienced in common and incorporates the physicality of the place (e.g. the location of shops or access to the telephone system), which enables and constrains particular actions. In both of these takes, the spaces of everyday life are seen to be the point at which 'objective material and administrative constraints' and 'the *murmuring* of the everyday' meet (de Certeau et al., 1998: 7).

A key question that arises in this discussion of the spatiality of practice is that of scale. It may be assumed that a focus on practices implies a privileging of the local, of the micro, placed-based geographies of everyday lives. But not only may practices themselves stretch across long distances and tie diverse spaces together (migrant workers and the role of remittances in household social reproduction is an obvious example), but the experiences, environments and embodiments which come to make up daily practice may also be constructed and enacted at multiple scales. Indeed, Highmore (2002: 14) notes that 'the everyday takes us in directions that are both local and global, or to put it another way, both micro-cultural and macro-cultural'. For Neilson and Simonsen (2003: 919), everyday practices counter common hierarchical perspectives through an exploration of the ways in which such practices 'weave places (and scales) together'. This articulation of multiple scales suggests that 'conventional bipolar perspectives relating "the local" to "the global" are too narrow and overlook the multiple, intersecting scales through which everyday life is constituted' (Rankin, 2003: 723). This perspective leads to the conceptualization of domestication, which we explore in more detail below.

The Limits to Practices: Assets and Power

For Bourdieu and other writers in his legacy, the power of a practice perspective lies in its attempt to transcend many of the dualisms common in contemporary social science (Bourdieu, 1977, 1990; Jenkins, 2002). Bourdieu's attention to the articulations present in practices and his attempt to theorize between determinism and autonomy work to both mediate social structures and subjective, individual actions and to highlight the relations between common dualisms. Practices emerge from the negotiation of subjective needs or desires with the constraining presence (or absence) of structures, customs, resources and so on. This recognition of the interplay of structure and agency emphasizes the need to see practices as contextual and relational, and to recognize the limits to practices. Particular geographies, inequalities of power and uneven access to assets and resources all play a role in enabling or constraining the success of particular practices. A practice perspective centres the analytical focus on understanding how these spheres are articulated: 'While acknowledging that all social actors seek to exercise control over their conditions of livelihood, practice theory begins with the premise that power is unevenly distributed …' (Rankin, 2003: 713). Yet, even with such an uneven distribution of power constraining the range of possible action that can be deployed, people 'can still utilize the resources available to them in a host of inventive and creative ways' (Gardiner, 2000: 170).

Bourdieu's analysis of practices is coupled with a focus on 'capitals', such that the 'mix of activities and ways of acting tend to encompass distinctive deployments of different forms of capital' (Bridge, 2004: 59).[2] Assets of various forms (such as property, social networks, skills) are key building blocks of an individual's or household's repertoire of practices and are deployed in varying attempts to ensure social reproduction. Indeed, the ways in which actors accumulate, manage, exchange, deplete and squander assets can be seen as some of the most important practices of social reproduction. Yet, as the broader discussion of practices above has highlighted, the employment of assets cannot be seen in isolation. An individual's, a household's or a community's assets work in combination. Some assets – such as land, for example – are useless without the social and other material assets needed to reach and work the land. In contrast, other asset reserves reinforce each other: a household with a much stronger set of social networks may be much more likely to know where and how to access its due citizenship assets or employment opportunities to enhance its income.

Access to assets and the capacity to employ them are enabled or constrained by factors both endogenous and exogenous to the household and individual, including socio-economic status, embodied subjectivities, norms and traditions, and by wider political economic imperatives or structures. We can see, for example, how labour markets, uneven development, geography and the built environment can complicate the identification and use of assets (Beall & Kanji, 1999). More intangibly, Simonsen (2007: 172) draws attention to 'the social and bodily forces that both constrain and enable practices' and 'the indispensable relationships among practice, body and space' (Simonsen, 2007: 175), such that class, gender, generation and other subjectivities influence the assets and other resources that individuals and households can employ, and the spaces they occupy and move through, in their everyday economic lives.

To summarize the conceptual framework thus far, practices are the everyday actions in which households, individuals and communities engage to 'make do' and 'get by' in everyday life. Practices result from the articulation (or disarticulation) of agency, geography, experience, subjectivities, and assets, all employed within the wider context of political-economic structures and power relations. These different elements in combination serve to enable or constrain the available array of practices and each must be considered in any analysis of practices. Practices are entwined with each other, reflect multiple, often 'irrational' and contradictory, motivations, and have both temporalities and spatialities. They both reflect and construct geographies, and weave together multiple scales in the everyday.

Economic Practices and the Diverse Economy

The 'practice turn' has increasingly influenced economic geography such that it is now common within the sub-discipline to see 'the economy' as a set of relational and cultural practices (James et al., 2007; Murphy, 2008) and to explore the economy as performed and practised by firms, governments, international lending agencies and academic experts (Thrift & Olds, 1996; Mitchell, 2002, 2008; Swain, 2006; Lee et al., 2008). In *Domesticating Neo-liberalism*, however, the focus extends beyond the formal institutions of economic life to explore the ways in which the practices of 'everyday' individuals, households and communities – especially in peripheral spaces – have a role in 'performing' the economy (Nagar et al., 2002; Rankin, 2003; Lee et al., 2008). This perspective is one that is increasingly common in development studies, economic sociology and economic geography and encourages a de-centred view of 'the economy', as transformed, negotiated, mediated and lived everyday. These attempts to re-vision 'the economy' are inspired by a range of interrelated theoretical frameworks – for example, feminism, non-essentialist Marxism, post-colonialism, post-structuralism, post-development, post-socialism – and have sought to challenge the way we research and theorize 'the economic' by exploring the geographical construction and performance of 'the economy' and the articulations between 'the economy' and its others.

The desire to see the economy differently is a longstanding project with roots in feminist and socialist-feminist attempts to bring to the fore other sites of the economy – most particularly the household – and to envision the 'whole economy'.[3] The whole economy is seen as comprising not just the partial economy of commodity flows and monetary exchange or of gross domestic product (GDP), but also the social and informal economy and the natural resource base. For Gibson-Graham (1996) and the Community Economies Collective, the metaphor of an iceberg (Figure 3.1) works well to depict the diversity of economic life and to argue that 'what we know as the "economy" is like the tip of an iceberg … below the waterline are many sites and activities which produce and transact values, goods and services'. Not only does this depiction better represent the complexity of the economy, but it also suggests that the activities of communities, households, cooperatives, volunteers, street traders, illegal markets and barter exchanges ensure that the 'official' economy stays afloat. This leads Gibson-Graham (1996) to explore the capitalo-centrism of orthodox accounts of the economy – both from neoclassical and some more classical Marxist perspectives – which, for different reasons, overplayed the importance of *capitalist* economic processes. The de-centring of the economy in this way allows for a more open conceptualization of economic practices, one which is not reducible to the inexorable power of capitalism. Echoing the 'practice turn', this approach seeks to identify the many capitalist and non-capitalist economic forms that co-exist with the 'dominant' economy but have often been obliterated from view. At best, these other economies are represented in terms of their relationship to capital; at worst, they are derided as some relic of the past or as some corrupt and inefficient practice. There is a constant desire to subsume 'diverse forms, practices, and

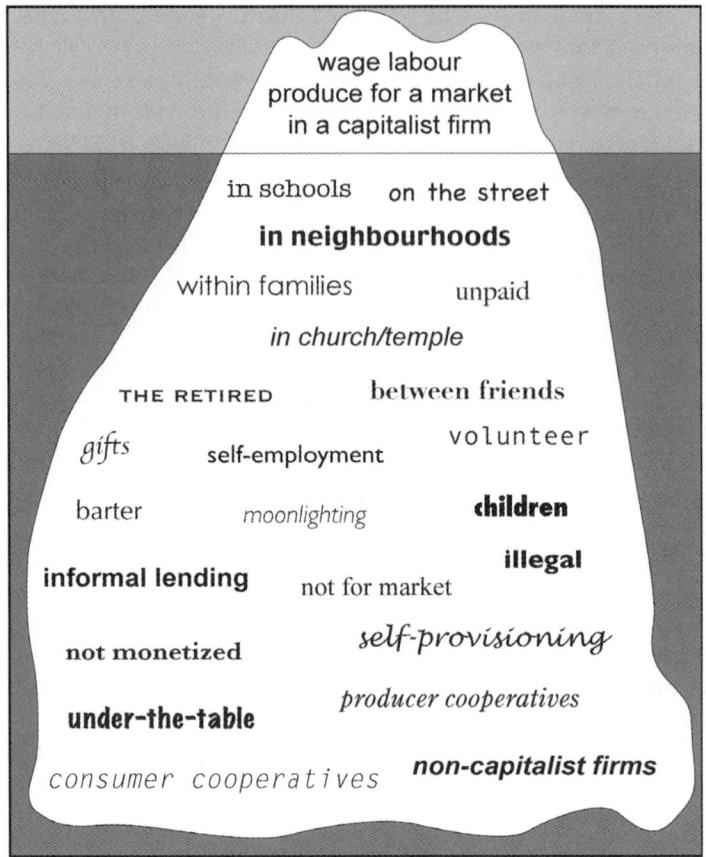

Figure 3.1 The economy as iceberg
Source: Ken Byrne/Community Economies Collective (www.communityeconomies.org/info.php)

understandings of life into universalist political-theoretical categories' (Chakrabarty, 2000: 17). In contrast, Chakrabarty (2000: 63) draws attention to all manner of practices that do not 'belong to capital's life process', conceptualizing these diverse economies as History 1 and History 2. History 1 is precisely the kind of history that sees global capitalism as encroaching on the 'non-capitalist'; History 2, however, evokes the range of practices that 'inhere in capital and yet interrupt and punctuate the run of capital's own logic' (Chakrabarty, 2000: 64). Chakrabarty thus raises an important question concerning the ways in which political economic forms articulate:[4]

> History 1 and History 2, considered together, destroy the usual topological distinction of the outside and the inside that marks debates about whether or not the whole world can be properly said to have fallen under the sway of

Transactions	Labour	Organizational Form
MARKET	WAGE	CAPITALIST
ALTERNATIVE MARKET Sale of public goods Ethical "fair-trade" markets Local trading systems Alternative currencies Underground market Co-op exchange Barter Informal market	ALTERNATIVE PAID Self-employed Cooperative Indentured Reciprocal labour In-kind Work for welfare	ALTERNATIVE CAPITALIST State enterprise Green capitalist Socially responsible firm Nonprofit
NON-MARKET Household flows Gift giving Indigenous exchange State allocations State appropriations Gleaning Hunting, fishing, gathering Theft, poaching	UNPAID Housework Family care Neighbourhood work Volunteer Self-provisioning labour Slave labour	NON-CAPITALIST Communal Independent Feudal Slave

Figure 3.2 A diverse economy
Source: Gibson-Graham, 2006

capital. Difference, in this account, is not something external to capital. Nor is it something subsumed into capital. It lives in intimate and plural relationships to capital, ranging from opposition to neutrality (Chakrabarty, 2000: 65–66).

In this sense, History 2 is not necessarily 'precapitalist', 'feudal' or 'outside', but always already constitutive of the economic relations that we know of as capitalism.

These varied relationships to capital are theorized by Gibson-Graham's (2006) differentiation of economic practices into those involving market relations, those involving non-market relationships and those involving alternative market relations (Figure 3.2) (see also Gibson-Graham, 1996, Community Economies Collective, 2001). Economic relations through the market are those invariably involving capitalist social relations and are structured through monetary transactions such as the wage form. As such they involve capitalist class processes and the production, appropriation and exchange of surplus value. Non-market relations are those structured through other forms of economic interaction involving, for example, the exchange of use values through non-monetary means, which might include forms of reciprocal exchange of goods for labour, forms of barter and various forms of care work. Alternative market relations are those that are rendered through market transactions but which are constituted by different forms of equivalence than those of commodity economies of capitalism. Such relations might range from alternative currencies to 'illegal' market transactions, and may be structured around cooperative forms of organization or forms of indentured or quasi-indentured labour.

As this theorization suggests, the different relationships which constitute an economy vary in space and time, as the extent of the market ebbs and flows and as economic practices such as the production of food, the expression of care and the acquisition of shelter are enacted in varying economic spheres. Neo-liberalization, as we discuss in Chapters One and Two, rests centrally on the extension of the market into ever-increasing spheres of economic life, reflecting the commitment that it is the most efficient form of economic organization. For this reason, understanding market relations is critical to understanding the economies of neo-liberal times. Yet, the framework presented here emphasizes the co-existence of other economic relations and the articulation between market and non-market relations, even at a time of rapid marketization, and these articulations form a key focus of our analyses.

Economic Practices and (Post-)Socialism

Dominant accounts of socialism – in the West and in the East – promoted a vision of a singular economy, either in the ideology of communism or in the service of a totalitarian perspective, both of which obliterated alternative economies for political reasons. The sphere of everyday life was all but absent in accounts of socialism until the late 1970s and 1980s, when the system's failings highlighted the multiple spaces of survival and negotiation (Sik, 1994). Since the fall of communism, revisionist historians have sought to explore the 'limits of dictatorship' and document the everyday lives and cultures – of adaptation, resistance, acceptance and ignorance – of ordinary people within the spaces of socialism (Fitzpatrick, 2001; Horváth, 2005; Pittaway 2005; see also Stenning, 2010).

Within the economy, appreciation of the centrality of diverse economic practices in the formulation of state socialism has been increasingly important since the 1980s (for more on this, see Smith & Stenning, 2006). To acknowledge the plurality of economic life within late socialism, the Hungarian sociologist Endre Sik (1994) highlighted the 'multicoloured' economies of socialism, a notion developed by Lomnitz and Sheinbaum (2002: 10) in their metaphor of the 'rainbow economy':

> In the Soviet system, total welfare in the family was the sum of what could be obtained from a multiplicity of "second" economies that Katsenelinboigen (1978, quoted by Rose 2000: 37) has aptly characterized as a "rainbow-coloured" system, since methods for producing or getting goods and services shaded into each other; they were interdependent rather than separate. The three primary "colours" of the rainbow system were the official or modern economy, relying on legal, large-scale formal organizations such as state enterprises or pensions from the ministry; an uncivil or anti-modern economy in which individuals earned cash outside the reach of the national plan or by breaking rules about the allocation of goods and services; and social or pre-modern economies in which goods and services were produced within households and informal networks without any money changing hands.

Central to the notion of a 'rainbow' or 'multicoloured' economy was the articulation between the different parts of the economy and different forms of economic practice. Thus, the economy was no longer seen as singular or made up of distinct spheres. Instead, in the context of a formal economy increasingly characterized by shortage, the diversity – and articulation – of economic practices was increasingly acknowledged. It was recognized that households engaged in informal work, the production of food, and barter and other networks to access goods and services otherwise inaccessible. Informal and additional work was undertaken across the economy, often dependent on the spaces, skills, client bases and equipment available and developed within the primary workplace (Kalleberg & Stark, 1993). For some, secondary working was condoned or even encouraged by the formal employer as workers were permitted to produce goods or services after normal working hours (Medgyesi, 2002). In less legal scenarios, workers saw the workplace as a source either of additional covert earnings (Birdsall, 2000) or for acquiring socialist property for personal use or reappropriation (Grossman, 1977). The resources and skills available through the workplace were also critical components of the networks of reciprocal exchange which enabled further access to scarce goods. It is precisely these various ways in which household and domestic economies articulated with wider political economies that led Creed (1998) to argue that state socialism was domesticated.

Within a context of economic shortage, individuals and households developed all kinds of complex ways of negotiating access to scarce goods, based upon networks of reciprocal exchange. Ledeneva's (1998) discussion of *blat* in the Soviet Union is perhaps the most comprehensive treatment, although work in Poland on *załatwić sprawy* and on *blizki* in Bulgaria points to similar sets of relations (Wedel, 1986, 1992; Begg & Pickles, 1998; Cellarius, 2004). According to Ledeneva (1998: 39), *blat* is a 'distinctive form of non-monetary exchange, a kind of barter based on personal relationship ... It worked where money did not.' For Wedel (1986, 1992) and others, the 'arranging of matters' (goods, access, information, services) became essential under the shortage economy of late socialism when formal supply channels simply did not work. *Załatwić sprawy* ('to arrange things') was an accepted[5] and everyday practice founded on the networks of friends and family who made up one's *środowisko* or circle. Such practices were wholly engaged with the formal economy, relying as they did on the position and status of family, friends and acquaintances in the formal economy and the access they had to goods, services, information or influence. Frequently too, these networks of reciprocity incorporated what is variously known as the 'economy of jars' (Smollet, 1989), the economy of 'organic exchange' (Caldwell, 2004a) or the 'dacha economy' (Clarke, 2002), that involved the household production of food on allotments, in gardens or on rural land, which we return to in more detail in Chapter Six. In the first instance, the private production of food enabled households to spend less of their finite resources in the increasingly empty shops but also offered entrance to a wider 'economy of regard' (Lee, 2000) involving the exchange of food products and the occasional process of commodification as domestically produced food became increasingly visible on the streets and in informal markets (Caldwell, 2004a; Cellarius, 2004; Smith, 2002a).

The persistence and development of these practices in the context of post-socialism has been the focus of a rich set of literatures examining various aspects of 'survival strategies' and 'informal' economies in post-socialism (Arnstberg & Boren, 2003; Bridger & Pine, 1998; Caldwell, 2004a; Cellarius, 2004; Clarke, 1999, 2002; Pavlovskaya, 2004; Pickup & White, 2003; Round, 2006b; Round et al., 2008; Seabright, 2000; Sik, 1995; Smith, 2000, 2002a, 2002b; Williams & Round, 2007). This work explores the ways in which the diverse economic practices of socialism have enabled individuals and households to negotiate the ongoing transformations, and also the ways in which the practices themselves have been transformed by marketization, commodification and the partial rolling back of the state – in short, by neo-liberalization. In the sphere of labour, for example, the 'forced flexibilization' of the workforce has caused workers to increasingly engage in flexible and multiple employment strategies to ensure an adequate income. This has often involved employing dual job strategies through which workers maintain income security and access to a range of in-kind benefits through their primary employment, high levels of remuneration, and access to wider social (capital) networks through secondary, informal employment (see Chapter Four). More widely, Ledeneva (1998) has argued that *blat*-like relationships continue, albeit in mutated forms, including the closing of the circles of mutual help around immediate household and family kin networks, a partial commodification of *blat* relationships, the gradual break up of personal networks initially established through *blat*, and their translation to new institutions and new spaces. It is argued that, since the collapse of state socialism, the role of 'black' and 'grey' economies has continued, intensified and even developed into new forms; these new forms articulate in quite complex ways with the market and, in many cases, are actually constitutive of market relations. The emergence of protection rackets, for example, has enabled street and market traders to continue activity in particular places.

The set of economic practices that have perhaps generated the most attention in the literature on post-socialist 'survival strategies' has been connected to domestic food production and self-provisioning (see Caldwell, 2004a; Cellarius, 2004; Clarke, 2002; Meurs, 2002; Seeth et al., 1998; Smith, 2000, 2002a, 2002b; Smollet, 1989). Household food production has become a *relatively* more significant part of household economies since 1989 as formal incomes declined during the 1990s (Meurs, 2002; Cellarius, 2004), but there has been considerable debate about whether or not the production and exchange of food are part of a set of survival strategies developed by households to cope with austerity, or whether such practices are best seen within a wider context of a cultural-economy of life in the region (Smith & Stenning, 2006; Smith, 2002a, 2002b).

Perhaps paradoxically in the context of neo-liberal discourses of state withdrawal, state benefits and transfers have often been identified as one of the most important 'legs' in any household's economy in post-socialism (Meurs, 2002). For poor families, in particular, social transfers are becoming an increasingly important part of family budgets and state benefits can be seen to enable economic practices in other spheres (Cellarius, 2004; Förster & Tóth, 2001; Kovacheva, 2002; Lokshin et al., 2000). As a result, 'the state is very much at the center of the strategies of poor households, even if it dispenses very little' (Burawoy et al., 2000: 47).

All of this work has, in various ways, underpinned a need to focus attention on the diversity of economic life in state socialism and post-socialism. Recognition of this diversity is, as we have already noted, part of an economic sensibility that recognizes the centrality of capitalist, market-based relations but that refuses to end the analysis at that point. It is a sensibility that recognizes how economic practices are intertwined and how, in this context, neo-liberal economies are always already domesticated. The value in documenting and analysing this diversity is twofold, and echoes the rationale of practice theory outlined above. Firstly, such an account better represents the complexity, enterprise and articulations of everyday economies, as a counter to monolithic notions of the economy, be they related to a totalitarian and top-down vision of communism or a singular and teleological notion of neo-liberal transitions to capitalism. Seeing the economy as diverse brings into view the multiple spaces, practices and resources engaged in the making of economies in the socialist and post-socialist world and sets a challenge to analyse and explain the sources and implications of such diversity. The very presence of multiple economies in socialism is part of the explanation for contemporary diversity since, as many have argued, post-socialism is built 'on and with the ruins of communism' (Stark & Bruszt, 1998, cited in Pickles 2004a: 87) such that 'social change is more like a process of appropriation grafting on, and reworking with already available resources, capacities and social relations than it is a break with the past' (Pickles, 2004a: 87). But the diversity of economic practices rests, as we will see, not simply on the experiences and inheritances of the past, but also on the knowledges, resources, relationships and negotiations of households and individuals in the present. Recognition of this active diversification of economic practices works to counter more problematic accounts of everyday post-socialism, especially within poor, working-class communities, where dominant tropes are of marginalization, failure to adapt and impoverishment in the world of post-socialist neo-liberalization (see Stenning, 2005a for a fuller elaboration). Teasing out the relationship between everyday economic practices with capitalism highlights the second value of an approach which documents diverse economies: such an approach aims to de-centre capitalism and points to the often very partial nature of dominant accounts of 'transition'. 'Transitions to capitalism' are that, but they are also much more (Pickles & Smith, 1998). Emergent capitalist relations in post-socialist societies should be seen as but one part of a 'disseminated' (Pickles, 2004b) or 'proliferative' (Leyshon & Lee, 2003) economy, constituted by a host of economic practices articulated with one another in dynamic and complex ways and in multiple sites and spaces. This recognition opens up our theorization of 'economy' in post-socialist societies and provides the focus for much of the analysis which follows.

Domestication

As we have suggested, we employ the notion of domestication to explore the negotiation and articulation of diverse economic practices in post-socialism. Our employment of this concept draws upon that developed by Creed in his *Domesticating Revolution* (1998). Creed's research explored the ways in which communism was negotiated and constituted through the practices of everyday life in one Bulgarian village and, on this basis, he developed an argument concerning how 'big' economic and social processes – such as the construction of state socialism – are always already local and domestic projects too. Such processes are always mediated through everyday practice, always made tolerable as best one can, through the lives of ordinary people. Creed (1998) argued that in their 'mundane' everyday economic practices, but without explicit acts of resistance, the Bulgarian villagers in his study transformed state socialism and made it more tolerable.

It is this notion of domestication that we seek to explore further in this book, and in this section we set out in more detail how we conceptualize domestication, drawing on a number of related literatures. Domestication, as a social science concept, has its roots in anthropological accounts of the taming of animals and the cultivation of plants as these were incorporated into the economies and thus homes of agricultural communities. Within this conceptualization, there is a notion of control and of appropriation, through which 'wild' objects were pacified and made safe, and an understanding of something external being incorporated into internal, intimate and private space. It is these features that have been explored as the concept has shifted into other realms.

Most prolifically, domestication has been taken up in social studies of technology to explore the 'taming' or domestication of technology (Silverstone, 2005; Lie and Sørensen, 1996). In this use of the concept, something from outside – new technology – 'comes to be naturalized and domesticated so as to make it less threatening and more manageable for its inhabitants' (Morley, 2003: 448). Domestication is seen as a set of practices (appropriation, objectification, incorporation, adaptation and conversion) to describe the introduction and integration of technology, physically and symbolically, into everyday routines. Domestication is the process of making familiar, owning, and the learning processes that are part of this. These processes incorporate both discursive (subjective) experiences (e.g. of identity and attitude) and also material practices (e.g. everyday routines) and suggest, within the process of domestication, a duality of imposition and adaptation.

The concept has also been developed in a post-colonial context where domestication is seen as an attempt to make particular social practices 'appear as commonsense as everyday reality' (Myers, 2006: 292). For Myers (2006), domestication is a colonial practice aimed at subordinating or subjugating subaltern social formations. In contrast, Owusu (1997) employs a more positive but still ambivalent interpretation of domestication such that it appears as a process that enables the imposition of global concepts, albeit in a way which appears less violent. Importantly, Owusu conceptualizes domestication as 'a dynamic and continuous process' and highlights not only how democracy transforms local practices but also how democracy itself is transformed and mediated by local beliefs, concerns and practices. De Boeck (1998) pushes this dynamism further to explore how domestication can be seen as a process which enables spaces for rethinking and reinvention and for articulations between dichotomous realms, practices and beliefs (such as past/present, foreign/domestic, modern/traditional).

As well as resonating with Creed's conception of domestication, these themes also run through the particular literatures on domestication in the post-socialist world (Caldwell, 2004b; Rulyova, 2007; Vann, 2005). In her study of domesticating the French fry, Caldwell explores the ways in which Muscovites 'draw[…] aspects of McDonald's into the intimate spaces of their everyday lives and personaliz[e] the public McDonald's experience' (2004b: 5) in order to make McDonald's 'locally meaningful' (Caldwell 2004b: 7). At the same time, McDonald's aims to remake itself as a local institution through an engagement in local political discourses and a campaign to make visible its local sources. For both Muscovites and McDonald's, in different ways, the aim is to routinize French fries and burgers, to make them 'seem natural and ordinary' (Caldwell 2004b: 8). Domestication, following Appadurai's exploration of the local, is 'a continuous process of creativity and adjustment' (Caldwell 2004b: 11) on the part of both the Muscovites and McDonald's, all of whom express 'agency and autonomy' in the process. Rulyova echoes Caldwell by arguing that domestication incorporates 'both universalizing and particularizing tendencies' (Robertson, 1997: 4, cited in Rulyova, 2007: 1367) and points to tensions which arise not just between the global and the local (and the national), but also 'between the centre and the periphery, between commercial/capitalist and traditional/folk practices, and between the collective and the individual' (Rulyova, 2007: 1368). Rulyova pushes this analysis further, however, to insist that domestication 'is an act of subversive glocalisation in which an imported global format is distorted to undermine itself and to create a glocalised product' (Rulyova, 2007: 1384).

In all of these literatures some common analytical strands can be identified. Firstly, domestication focuses on the articulation of the internal and the external. As such it is a relational concept and is 'dependent on the juxtaposition of inside and outside, and on its continuous negotiation' (Silverstone, 2005: 233) such that the focus of analysis is the ways in which one is remade by the other. In this way, domestication seeks to move beyond the duality of passive consumption versus resistance. It identifies ambivalences around questions of power and hegemony. For some, domestication is a subversive practice (echoing de Certeau); for others it is another form of hegemony. This ambivalence reflects the way in which the concept incorporates dualities of taming – of both being tamed and taming (see also Ruddick, 2004). Domestication can be seen as an active, empowered process for households to make familiar – make their own – and manage 'external' processes but also as a process by which households are tamed by hegemonic 'external forces' and/or encouraged to see 'external' ideas, commodities and processes as domestic and therefore acceptable.

In the majority of literatures, albeit in different ways, the internal/external dichotomy is represented by the local and the global, but domestication also problematizes the articulation between the domestic and the foreign, the private and the public, the past and present, and the traditional and the modern too. In exploring these articulations and rejecting a one-way process of imposition, domestication works to blur the boundaries of the two extremes and to remake scalar geographies by bringing the local and the global into confrontation and engagement. Domestication remakes spatialities and can be seen as an 'inverted territorialisation', 'inverting the process of the globalisation of the local' (de Boeck, 1998: 804). As Silverstone (2005: 233) suggests '[d]omestication bridges, a priori, the macro social and the micro social'. The echo here with practice theory and its attempts to transcend binaries leads us to our second point; that 'domestication is practice' (Silverstone, 2005: 231). For de Certeau, practices are ways of making things 'habitable' and, thus, domestication can be seen as the set of practices which enables households to adopt and adapt external policies, strategies and technologies within their everyday lives. As with practice more generally, domestication is founded on the employment of domestic values, assets, routines, patterns, hierarchies, relations and dynamics and is an iterative process, such that the ways in which a household domesticates the external must be seen as a continuous process of negotiation and of ever-changing combinations of assets, values and knowledges. Domestication is a learning process, focused on learning new practices and ways of being, both in order to make the external more familiar and manageable but also to feedback to spaces beyond the domestic. For these reasons, domestication is 'not necessarily harmonious, linear or complete' (Ward, 2005: 150) and the theorization of domestication works against rational, linear, monocausal, determined, and singular narratives of change (Silverstone, 2005). It is also a dialogic process since the act of domestication transforms the domestic and the 'thing' being domesticated, and this in turn both alters the context for future domestications and the nature of future 'things' to be domesticated.

The emphasis on relations and iterations, and the blurring of boundaries discussed above, leads us to our third point concerning the spaces of domestication. Domestication centres the household or the home, the domestic, and much attention has been paid in the literature to the space of the household and its characteristics. Yet, more recent work has problematized the focus on the household in two particular ways: firstly, by seeing the shape of the household as dynamic and complex, reflecting its changing composition and the changing health, employment, education, networks and lifecycles of its members (Bakardijeva, 2005); and, secondly, by extending analyses beyond the narrowly domestic to include broader everyday geographies and wider social networks (Lie and Sørensen, 1996; Morley, 2003; Bakardijeva, 2005). As Morley (2003: 436) notes, for reasons of both social and technological change, 'the home nowadays is not so much a local, particular or "self-enclosed" space'. In these ways, household activity has to be seen as part of a 'nested geography' through which everyday practices domesticate wider political economies (such as neo-liberalism) in the process of social reproduction (Smith & Stenning, 2006). This dynamic and complex geography of the household forms the focus of the following section.

Conceptualizing the Household

The household is a key site of economic practices, of assets, of domestication, but it is also critical to problematize this centrality by connecting the household to other spaces of economic and social life and by recognizing its internal differentiation. In the specific context of socialism and post-socialism, discussions of 'survival strategies' often assume that the household is *the* strategic site and decision-making unit (Bridger & Pine, 1998; Sik, 1988; Wallace, 2002). As Sik (1988: 527) argues 'the household is the unit of analysis because it is the household which defines economic goals, makes the decision necessary to achieve them, and has the power (to some extent) to organize the labour of its members'. The household was invariably seen as the idealized site of resistance and escape under state socialism, as a flexible unit able to cope with shortage under late socialism (Burawoy, 1999; Boym, 1994) and has, arguably, taken on a greater importance – both as a physical and economic asset and as a key economic unit – in post-socialism where the 'fulcrum of production and redistribution has moved from the factory to the household' (Burawoy et al., 2000: 43). As such, understandings of the diverse economies of post-socialism have become centred on the household with little consideration of either the wider constitutive and relational geographies or of the power relations expressed through these geographies. In opening up this centred geography, we highlight two key issues.

First, as many feminist scholars remind us, the idea of the household as a singular and harmonious space is countered by the power geometries (Massey, 1993) of gender in particular (Fraad et al., 1994; Pine, 2002; Wheelock & Oughton, 1996), but also of generation. Because the household involves the production, appropriation, and distribution of surplus labour it is 'a major site of class processes' (Gibson & Graham, 1992: 116) where the exploitative power of class and patriarchy come together. In the post-socialist context, such processes are refracted through the particular domestic and gender politics of actually existing post-socialism with an increasing recognition that women carried the 'double burden' of work and care during socialism (Ashwin, 2000; Einhorn, 1993; Gal & Kligman, 2000a, 2000b; Meurs, 1998). Domestic divisions of labour also derive from and create intergenerational inequalities, as the presence of multiple generations with differing abilities and responsibilities shapes the allocation of labour and resources within the household. Intergenerational relationships within households can be marked by, for example, deference, respect, exploitation, and neglect. All these influence the shape and dynamics of the household and raise questions about how households make everyday economic decisions. Whilst gender and generation are perhaps the strongest influences, the shape and the dynamics of the household and its divisions of labour – within and beyond the home – can also be destabilized by ill-health and disability, by fractious family relationships and by uneven skill-sets. Moreover, of course, different household members have different commitments to the household, and these are often reflected in their contribution to household economies. All of these concerns give lie to the idea of the household as a coherent economic unit.

Second, the household may not necessarily be *the* site at which economic practices are constituted, governed, and conceived. It is only sometimes the site where economic practices are enacted. Household networks stretch throughout communities and families and rest on a range of institutions in particular places (the workplace, the apartment block, the allotment, and the 'home' village) where relationships are created and offer a multiplicity of economic opportunities. Households are involved in a process of time-space coordination as they negotiate what Jarvis (2005: 135) calls the 'infrastructure of daily life' (see also Jarvis, 1999; Ward et al., 2007). Quite simply, where work is in relation to home, school, childcare, other people's work, bus stops, the shops, the doctors and so on has a real impact on the scope of everyday practices. The importance of these geographies testifies to the necessity of seeing the household as more than a single site, home to a co-located nuclear family. Family members 'operate in many different collective dimensions' (Folbre, 1994, cited in Wheelock & Oughton, 1996: 150) and household economic strategies reflect these different positions and economies. Thus, the household, as an economic unit, can be seen 'as a node in a multilayered web or the locus for a number of networks of relations: economic, social and technological' (Wheelock & Oughton, 1996: 156). As such, it offers less a centre and more one point of entry to complex and multiply located or nested geographies of diverse economic practices (Smith & Stenning, 2006).

Social Reproduction

Notwithstanding this extended conceptualization of the household, our concern in this book is on the ways in which the households at the core of our research attempt to ensure their social reproduction. Even after all the discussions of diversity and complexity above, we acknowledge the singularity of economic life in the sense that an economy that works is one which enables social reproduction and which is 'life-sustaining' (Lee, 2006). The discussions above highlight the need to understand the multiplicity of economic practices which come together in the process of social reproduction. This articulation – in particular between the sphere of work and those of housing, food, and care – shapes the structure of the next four chapters.

Social reproduction is '[a]t the most fundamental level ... about how we live' (Mitchell et al., 2003: 416); it is 'the fleshy, messy, and indeterminate stuff of everyday life' (Katz, 2001: 711). But it is not simply just what goes on from day to day: the practices of social reproduction are those which are 'involved in maintaining people both on a daily basis and inter-generationally' (Glenn, 1992: 1, cited in Kofman, 2006: 11). Social reproduction is what enables a household and its members to live another day, to sustain life, and thus is focused around providing basic needs, recognizing that such needs reflect not only material but also other values (Lee, 2006). In this definition, social reproduction involves all manner of practices from caring – emotionally, morally and physically – for children, older adults, other dependents and other family members; to the provisioning of food and clothing (through shopping, exchange or self-production, for example); to acquiring and maintaining adequate shelter; to education and socialization; to the nurturing of kin and community relationships; to the management of household budgets; and to other acts of love and responsibility. Many of these are aspects of economic life that have historically been feminized and were often taken for granted until feminist theorists argued for their theoretical importance (Marston, 2003).

Whilst the household tends to be the geographical focus of accounts of social reproduction, its actual geography tends to be more extended, complex and dynamic. Historically, social reproduction was associated with the private sphere of the home, but throughout the nineteenth and twentieth centuries in the more affluent economies of the world, and in particular East Central Europe and the Soviet Union, the state became increasingly involved in social reproduction, either through the provision of sites for social reproduction (such as nurseries and care homes) or through financial support (welfare and subsidy) (Marston, 2003). A range of other actors and spaces, including charities, churches and, increasingly, businesses have also engaged in the practices of social reproduction (Katz, 2001). More recently, processes of neo-liberalization have once more remade the geographies and relations of social reproduction, as the state has contracted out or withdrawn provision and as spheres of reproduction have been transnationalized (Katz, 2001; Kofman, 2006; Bakker, 2007).

The wider articulations of social reproduction are highlighted in the recognition – by feminist and Marxist scholars in particular – that the acts of social reproduction are crucially organized towards 'maintaining labour power' and reproducing 'the material conditions of daily existence that enable production to occur' (Marston, 2003: 176). Social reproduction produces workers, both physically and emotionally, and the productive economy rests on – and is subsidized by – the largely unpaid or low-paid labour of (predominantly) women in the sphere of social reproduction. Social reproduction is also identified as one of the spheres which 'regulates' the labour market (Peck, 1996; Helms & Cumbers, 2006) since it often shapes the types and patterns of work which are possible and the supply of labour for work. In all these ways, an analysis of economic transformation – transition, globalization, neo-liberalization – is impossible 'without addressing the restructuring of social reproduction' (Katz, 2001: 709).

The sphere of production is not, of course, the single most important influence on the sphere of reproduction. Other sets of social relations – most particularly those of gender – are critical in shaping the practices of social reproduction, such that we can understand 'social reproduction [as] a complex set of knowledges and practices that, while bound up with capitalist production, also reflect the bodily particularities of the times, places, and people within which and by whom they are enacted' (Marston, 2003: 176).

Conclusions

In *Domesticating Neo-Liberalism*, we draw on ideas of practice, domestication and social reproduction to explore and analyse the ways in which individuals, households and communities in Nowa Huta and Petržalka adopt and enact a multiplicity of economic activities in their attempts to achieve social reproduction in the context of neo-liberalization. In rooting our analyses in these literatures, we seek to highlight a number of key features that frame, more or less explicitly, the discussions in the following chapters. Firstly, we highlight *diversities* in a desire to explore how households pull together diverse economic practices and work to mediate the articulations between these diverse economies, and in doing so constitute a diverse economy of post-socialism. *Articulations* (and disarticulations) are explored not only within and between different spheres of the economy and of everyday life, but also within and between past, present and future economies. In this way, we argue that exploring the multiple *histories* of economic practices is critical for understanding the uneven legacies and inheritances – both enabling and constraining – of earlier political economies (most especially state socialism, but also earlier rural economies, and the path dependencies of 'transition' policies). The particular articulations of diverse economies and their historical antecedents draw attention to their uneven and dynamic *spatialities*. This focus highlights both the multiple and changing spaces and the scalar geographies of everyday economic life, and asks what difference these geographies make to households' attempts to achieve social reproduction. The difference that geography makes is drawn out in *comparisons* which seek to understand the differential economic practices of our research communities not only, as we suggest in Chapter One, at the national scale – that is, comparing and contrasting 'Polish' Nowa Huta with 'Slovak' Petržalka – but also at the urban scale, through comparative analyses of different neighbourhoods and blocks within the two housing districts. Together these analyses enable us to explore and account for differential and uneven *domestications* identified in the economic practices of households in Petržalka and Nowa Huta, domestications which not only enable households to make neo-liberalization tolerable, but also create the space for its remaking. Within these processes of domestication, there is some evidence of *contestations*, and we seek to highlight these when individuals, households and communities seem to be actively rejecting or resisting aspects of 'transition'. The central but uneven adoption and implementation of neo-liberalism in both Poland and Slovakia provides the context for all our analyses, and our final analytic framing draws attention to the way in which these *neo-liberalisms* shape, and are shaped by, the economic practices of households in Nowa Huta and Petržalka. In short, much of our analysis focuses on the ways in which the *domestication of neo-liberalism* in Slovakia and Poland challenges existing accounts of post-socialist transformation and produces more complex understandings of economic life 20 years after the end of state socialism.

Chapter Four

Work: Employment, Unemployment and the Negotiation of Labour Markets

Introduction: The Place of Work

During state socialism, work was at the heart of all households' economic practices. To work was not only a right but also a duty, and this had two major implications. Firstly, there was, to all intents and purposes, no choice in accepting the place of work in structuring most other spheres of life (Offe, 1996; Rainnie et al., 2002a). These states were constructed, at least in theory, as workers' states (Haraszti, 1977; Crowley & Ost, 2001) and those living in them were seen as worker-citizens, whose rights and value were founded on their 'work contribution in the creation of a new social reality' (B. Domański, 1997: 176). The workplace developed to become 'the main axis of organiza-tion of social life' (Ciechocińska, 1993: 32), such that social lives and access to education, health care, leisure, housing, and much more, rested on the employment status of household members. Secondly, full employment was the assumed state, which meant that workers generally experienced a very high level of employment security, tended to take on jobs for life, and, if they did move jobs, quickly found new work. While under-employment became a major issue, open unemployment was all but non-existent (and certainly not acknowledged) and the threat of job loss or plant closure was minimal.

The overwhelming centrality of work during state socialism means that shifts in the place, meaning and experience of work in post-socialist East Central Europe have been more marked than in the West, where the 'end of work' has attracted most academic attention (Bauman, 1998; Beck, 2000; Sennett, 1998; but see Stenning, 2005a, 2005c). Since the collapse of state socialism, there has been an extensive transformation of the nature of work and labour markets, a transformation which has had a profound impact on the ability of households to maintain employment security, to achieve social reproduction and to sustain the social relationships centred on work. In large urban labour markets, such as Kraków and Bratislava, in particular, these processes have led to relatively secure and singular employment in the state-owned economy giving way to much greater labour market segmentation and employment uncertainty. Labour shedding from former state-owned industries has been extensive as a result of de-industrialization (Smith, 2000), but industrial decline has been accompanied both by the growth of new forms of employment and by increasing non-participation (Rainnie et al., 2002a). As the neo-liberalization of the economy has proceeded apace, sectoral restructuring has been connected to an expansion of service sector activity, particularly in major cities such as Kraków and Bratislava, where it has created new jobs in both the highly paid finance and other intermediary sectors, alongside a raft of less secure and low-paid employment in lower status sectors. Many of these new growth sectors have been allied to changes in employment contracts and security, resulting in increasing insecurity in the labour market.

These transformations have exacerbated the segmentation of labour markets (Peck, 1996) across the region, creating several distinct labour markets characterized by very different pay, employment and status conditions, and reinforcing social divisions. In these contexts, this chapter examines the growing phenomenon of insecure, poor quality, contingent labour (Peck & Theodore, 2001) and the diversification of work among households in the two districts of Nowa Huta and Petržalka. We ask how households negotiate the segmentation of the labour market, the erosion of employment security, and the emergence of in-work poverty, and we explore the diverse working practices of those for whom formal employment does not provide a living wage. We assess the articulations between labour market participation and other spheres of economic life, including informal and illegal labour, household social networks, state benefits and the use of material assets (which we return to in contrasting ways in later chapters). In short, we explore how neo-liberalized work is domesticated, and articulated with a host of other economic practices, in the attempt to secure social reproduction. Through this, we also explore the ways in which labour market change leads those who would traditionally have been seen as workers into a diversity of class positions (Gibson & Graham, 1992) as their changing work practices remake the materialities and subjectivities of class (Stenning, 2005a, 2005c).

Transformation and the Neo-Liberalization of Labour Markets

While the experience of work and employment restructuring varies across the region, a number of common labour market trends are identifiable (Rainnie et al., 2002a). High levels of relatively secure employment under state socialism have given way to widespread official and/or hidden

Table 4.1   Average monthly gross wages in Poland and Slovakia (euros)

	Poland (2006)	Kraków (2006)	Slovakia (2005)	Bratislava (2005)
Average wages	652	600	485	700
Financial intermediation	1,254	971	947	1,049
Hotels and restaurants	501	384	360	428

Source: Calculated from data provided by the Slovak Statistical Office and the Polish Central Statistical Office

unemployment; 'jobs for life' have been replaced by increasing employment insecurity; and employee representation has weakened as political settlements shifted and trade unions declined. In addition, dependency on state-owned enterprises to provide not only a monetary wage but also social amenities in kind (the social wage (B. Domański, 1997)) has been replaced by greater differentials in the value of formal wages and, for the unemployed, reliance on low-value state benefits and on informal legal and illegal income-generating activities. What appeared previously as *relatively* singular labour markets, with a dominant state sector and some additional activities on the margin (Smith & Stenning, 2006), have become much more diverse and fragmented.

A number of interconnected processes have operated in the labour markets of the post-socialist world, and in Poland and Slovakia in particular. Post-socialist labour markets are characterized by a much more distinct set of segmentation processes than their state socialist predecessors (Pailhé, 2003), although segmentation did exist under the previous system (H. Domański, 1990). Labour market segmentation has occurred both between sectors and within them, leading to the emergence of a number of relatively distinct worlds of work. Segmentation between sectors is occurring as a result of the de-industrialization of the economies of the region and the attendant growth of financial, producer and basic service employment, particularly in major cities. But segmentation also involves an increased differentiation of the conditions of, and remuneration for, work within sectors, reflected in a polarization of income (Milanovic, 1999). Average monthly wage levels in Slovakia and Poland have become increasingly differentiated (Table 4.1). Financial intermediation is the highest paid sector, whilst the lowest paid work is found in the hotel and restaurant sector. Both activities are increasingly concentrated in major urban areas, including Kraków and Bratislava, leading to wage polarization in cities.[1]

Labour market segmentation has also been accompanied by a reconfiguration of gender and age differentials within the labour market. Women were often first to lose jobs and have found it more difficult to find new work, experiencing longer periods of unemployment than men (Hardy & Stenning, 2002; Pine, 1998). Generational differences have also emerged, at both ends of the age spectrum. Unemployment has been persistently high among young people, including graduates, such that many of the young unemployed have never held formal employment. In both Poland and Slovakia in 2005, the unemployment rate amongst 15- to 24-year-olds was approximately double the average rate (in Poland, 36.9% against 18.1%; in Slovakia, 30.1% against 15.9% (Eurostat, 2006b)). Large numbers of older workers (over 50) have also been laid off, more often through early retirement than redundancy (Cazes & Nesporova, 2003a; Surdej, 2004), and have found it difficult to re-enter the labour market (Junghans, 2001; Stenning, 2005a, 2010).

Post-socialist labour markets have also become increasingly precarious (Waite, 2008) as the commitment to full employment has given way to a range of neo-liberalizing tendencies including, *inter alia*, individualized employment relationships, the decline of collective representation, instability in working time and, in some cases, greater casualization. The uncertain legal status of temporary contracts, reflecting their relatively recent appearance in many central European labour markets,[2] has seen employers resort to the increasing use of civil law[3] and self-employment contracts, enabling them to avoid health and safety responsibilities, regular pay increases, and the payment of social contributions, and to fire staff more easily (EIROnline, 2002). Recent attempts to regulate temporary work and the appearance of global staffing agencies in the region (Coe et al., 2006) suggest that this form of contingent labour will become more significant. Moves to increase labour market flexibility have also been associated with instability of job tenure, particularly in the new service sectors, and considerable levels of 'multiple job holding'.

Non-participation, through labour market withdrawal and persistent unemployment, has increased (Cazes & Nesporova, 2003b), although this is regionally uneven, with some of the major cities – as we highlight below – managing unemployment with the creation of new, often poorly paid, jobs. Estimates vary but suggest that across the region around 19 million jobs were lost in the first decade of transition (Smith, 2000). More recently, the return to positive economic growth has led to greater degrees of employment creation, but most national economies in the region have been unable to create jobs sufficient in number and location to balance employment losses. Indeed, there has been a general failure to tackle serious problems of long-term unemployment, particularly in more marginal regions (Burns & Kowalski, 2004). In 2005, in Poland, Hungary, the Czech Republic and Slovakia, between 46% and 68% of the registered unemployed had been out of work for more than 12 months (OECD, 2006: 269). In most countries, unemployment benefits are limited to 6–12 months such that coverage rates are often as low as 25–30% of those unemployed (Cazes & Nesporova, 2003b:

116). The limiting of unemployment benefit is just one of the factors behind a marked growth in people leaving the workforce, either to become officially 'inactive' or to exchange non-existent unemployment benefits for pensions or incapacity benefit. Echoing experiences in old industrial regions in the United Kingdom (Beatty & Fothergill, 2002), withdrawal from the labour market has become a key feature of labour market dynamics across ECE.

Finally, persistently high levels of regionally concentrated unemployment have provided a context for the neo-liberalization of labour market regulation and social welfare systems aimed at promoting flexibility (Jurajda & Mathernová, 2004; Smith & Rochovská, 2007; Surdej, 2004; see also Chapter Two). As a World Bank study has argued, 'EU countries may need to err on the side of greater [labour market] flexibility and lower [employment] security. This may be the case for newer EU members in particular, because they have much poorer business environments, lower employment rates, and far greater disparities in employment' (Rashid et al., 2005: 59). The report goes on to argue that any employment, even in low-paid jobs, is worth while, not least because 'low paid workers are often secondary earners whose earnings complement incomes of other family members. If this is the case, low pay does not necessarily imply poverty' (Rashid et al., 2005: 64), although the authors offer no evidence to support this claim. High levels of unemployment at the national scale have therefore encouraged governments in the region to focus their attention on job creation without considering the quality of employment, in an echo of Western 'work first' policies (Peck & Theodore, 2000).

In Poland and Slovakia, the focus of labour market policy during and in the years preceding our research had been on reducing unemployment rates by cutting benefits, providing 'incentives' to work, and liberalizing labour markets through labour code reforms. This was most clearly captured in the 'work pays' slogan and liberalization programme of labour market and social welfare reform of the former Dzurinda government in Slovakia (Barancová, 2006; Fisher et al., 2007, Smith & Rochovská, 2007), and the Polish government's 2002 'Entrepreneurship, Development, Work' programme, which sought to ease the Labour Code (Chancellery of the Prime Minister, 2002) and make it easier to both hire and fire workers. In Poland, whilst successive governments, on the left and right, did move to make the Labour Code more flexible and to control government spending, this was associated, in the 2004 Hausner Plan,[4] with attempts to better target key social benefits (Millard, 2006) and to develop more effective labour market institutions (EIROnline, 2004). More recently, elections in both Poland and Slovakia have encouraged a tempering of welfare reductions and labour market flexibilization as new governments have focused on a partial rejection of the singularly neo-liberal state (Millard, 2006; Smith & Rochovská, 2007).[5]

In Kraków and Bratislava, however, the key labour market issue has not been unemployment. As we noted in Chapter One, in Bratislava and Kraków unemployment rates were 2% and 7% respectively in 2007, significantly lower than the national rates of 8% and 11% respectively. Rather, the key issue has been the quality and security of employment, connected to the emergence of in-work poverty. The 'working poor' is a relatively new phenomenon in the post-socialist world, and a largely urban one, reflecting the segmentation of urban labour markets (Mitra, 2008; CBOS, 2008a).[6] In both cities, there has been a notable process of labour market restructuring since the early 1990s (Figure 4.1), involving a decline in employment in manufacturing and construction and a considerable growth in tertiary sectors. Particular growth was witnessed in retail and wholesale, financial intermediation and real estate, which, as we noted above, are characterized by markedly different wage levels (see Table 4.1).

This polarization of pay has been connected, in Kraków and Bratislava as across the region as a whole, to a polarization of the experience of work. Post-socialist worlds of work are characterized by phenomena – both positive and negative – which were rarely experienced in the era of state socialism, such as unemployment (particularly persistent unemployment and/or worklessness), in-work poverty, transnational work, and self-employment. Other phenomena such as vocational training and retraining and informal and illegal work have taken on new forms in new contexts. Together, as we explore in more detail below, these transformations have challenged and remade subjectivities of work and class, destabilizing older identities formed on the basis of stable employment in state enterprises and introducing new, often transitory, identities based on much less secure work. In these ways, labour market transformations not only influence the flow of income into households but also reposition household members' relationships to the economy, the household and the city more generally. In short, they transform households' economic standing and their economic opportunities.

Experiencing Labour Market Change

In this context, households reflected, in interview, on the impacts that changes in the sphere of work were having on the process of social reproduction (see also Stenning, 2005a). In both districts, though more extremely in Nowa Huta given the dominance of the steelworks within the community (Chapter One), work had played a defining role in social and economic development and in the lives of households. Not only did work provide a route to social mobility and to security, but enterprises across ECE took on a range of activities well beyond their core production focus, including education and training, childcare, housing, recreation and leisure, health facilities, retail and consumption, and heating and energy (B. Domański, 1992,

Bratislava

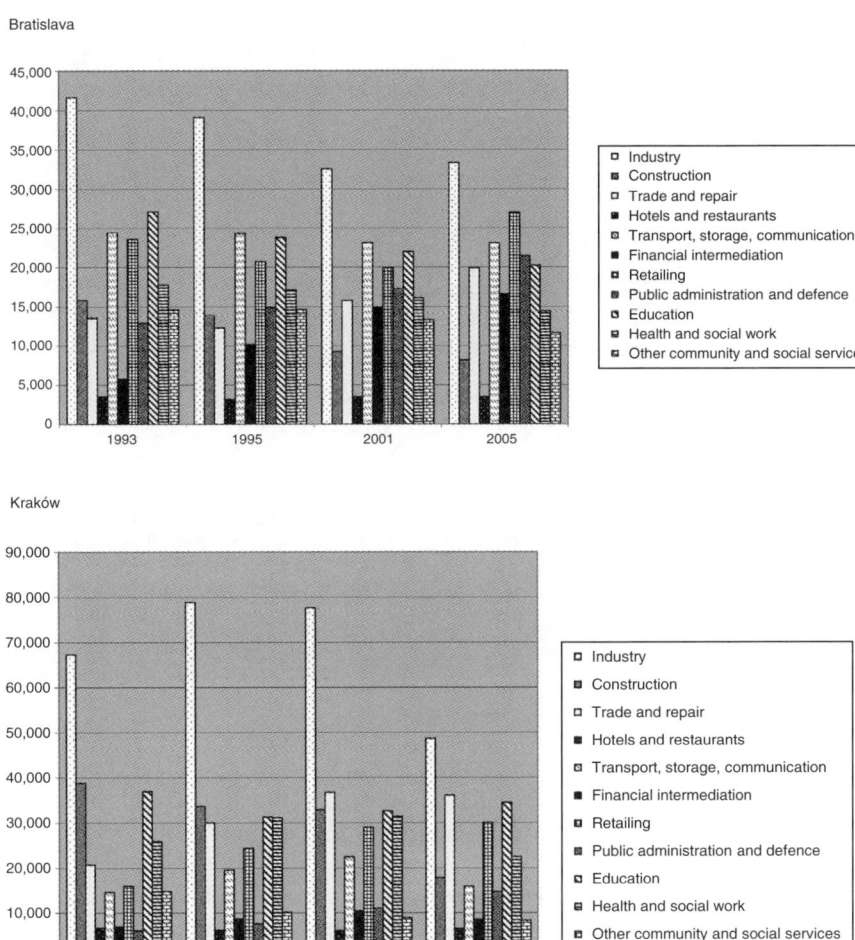

Figure 4.1 Sectoral employment change, Bratislava and Kraków
Source: Slovak Statistical Office; Polish Statistical Office

1997; Stenning, 2010). The value of this 'social wage' was not insignificant: in state socialist Czechoslovakia it was estimated to account for an additional 17–20% of the average money wage (Clark & Soulsby, 1998: 36).

For Petržalka residents, reflecting the diversified geography of their employment, employers and enterprises across Bratislava were key to the provision of an extensive social wage. As we explore in Chapter Five, the provision of

Plate 4.1   A steelworker at Arcelor Mittal, Nowa Huta

housing by employers was particularly important, but household members also had access to a wide range of amenities and an extensive social wage, from subsidized transport and meals, to vacation facilities and medical provision. In Nowa Huta, the steelworks supported a range of social and cultural facilities in the town, financed a health service, established premises for vocational training, a metallurgical training school, cultural centres, a sports club and stadium, a theatre, two cinemas, subsidized holidays and assisted in the maintenance and construction of much of the town's stock of housing (see Chapter Five; see also Hardy & Rainnie, 1996; Soja, 1986, 1990; Stenning, 2000). Many of these benefits extended to other Kraków employers, as Mrs Kielak, who worked for the state distillery, Polmos, explained:

> At Polmos when I worked there, I had it very good because I had a nursery on site, so I could take [my daughter] and leave her, and collect her later. And I had lunches; there was a canteen. And I could take loans; that was a huge comfort.

In these ways, work was at the core of household social reproduction, and in ways far beyond simply providing an income.

The perceived benefits of work were not, however, limited to the social wage. A number of interviewees in both communities recalled the sociability of work, alongside the more obvious material benefits. Others, particularly those with household members who worked for large state enterprises, shared a strong sense of security, both material and ontological. Mr Mokrzycki, Mrs Sedlak and Mrs Myszka – all living in Nowa Huta and now in their fifties – recalled how there was no need for additional work or secondary jobs, since the income from two stable jobs easily enabled a reasonable standard of living. Such views were echoed throughout many interviews in both Nowa Huta and Petržalka and framed perspectives on the current situation, as neo-liberalizing labour markets eroded income and employment security. The loss of income security is, for example, captured by Mrs Dawidowicz, one of our Nowa Huta interviewees, whose household was struggling to make a living on the basis of her, her husband's and her daughter's insecure and occasional work:

> It's changed a lot. What can I say? Well, we never earned extraordinarily well [in the past]: my husband earned more, me a little below the national average. But you knew what your wages were each month and you could plan and live, and now it's barely possible to live, only to survive, right?

The wider shift to greater insecurity of employment is described by Mrs Sieradzka, an unemployed Nowa Huta woman in her forties, who had trained and retrained three times in her working life:

> There was much more security and stability for workers … And it was easier, you could count on concrete abilities. Then, if you worked, it was possible to advance and to have a sense of security. Now you don't have that. So about a year and a half ago I worked as a graphic designer, the firm collapsed and the employer didn't pay any wages. It was a huge amount … And before there was this stability, that simply if you had a job, you had stable earnings. Before I had this continuity, if I changed work, then I found another job. It was easy to find work. Now it's so much more difficult. You have to have acquaintances, there's no other way.

Even for those fortunate to have been able to carve out new careers and employment opportunities in the restructuring labour markets of both Bratislava and Kraków, there was often a clear ambivalence about the new forms of work. For example, Mr and Mrs Kiedrowski, a couple in their thirties who both worked as economists for a major international corporation, explored the difficulties of these new forms of work: 'It's high stress work, flexibility etc. etc. It's constantly cranking up. A big difference over the last 15 years.' Mr Kiedrowski went on to note that:

> From the point of view of security, work was ideal in socialism, because throwing a worker out of work was a pretty difficult thing, but even if you were thrown out of work, then you'd very quickly find another job. Now it's the other way around, because throwing someone out of work can be just a question of one telephone call; you're removed, deprived of work. However, if

you do have work, then the bonuses that follow, that is the improvement in the quality of life and financial benefits, are disproportionately better than they were. And that's not to mention increased spending power, or the potential spending power of that money, which is a completely different thing. For sure now, I'm talking for myself now, work gives you much more; in any case it gives me much more satisfaction and independence.

The marked shifts in these households' experience of their local labour markets, and the increasing difficulties associated with ensuring a living wage, begin to point not only to the ways in which households are challenged to negotiate varied labour markets to secure an income sufficient to ensure social reproduction, but also to the dramatic polarization of employment experience. Whilst for some, such as the Kiedrowskis, new forms of work provided opportunity, for the majority of our interview households, the experience of post-socialist work was increasingly problematic. Emerging secondary labour markets were characterized by pay levels so low that they raised critical questions about the ability of such jobs to provide a living wage and the restructuring of work threatened the stability of housing, social networks and consumption too.

Negotiating Segmented Labour Markets and the Emergence of In-Work Poverty

Despite the existence of low levels of unemployment in Kraków and Bratislava, exclusion from the labour market remained an important issue for many households in Nowa Huta and Petržalka. In 2005, unemployment levels among surveyed households averaged 11% of the total sampled population in Petržalka and 9% in Nowa Huta, higher than the cities' unemployment rates as a whole.[7] The incidence of unemployment was significantly higher among those living in surveyed households with equivalized incomes below 60% of the regional median (i.e. those 'at risk' of poverty), and much lower in the highest income group (Table 4.2). Unemployment was thus very closely related to poverty. Not only were benefit levels generally very low, but also in most instances benefits were only paid for the first six months of unemployment. In Petržalka, 31 of the 150 surveyed households had at least one unemployed household member, yet just four households reported income from unemployment benefit and in Nowa Huta, 35 of the 200 surveyed households had at least one unemployed household member yet just six households reported income from unemployment benefit.

While being out of work was clearly related to poverty, it was also the case that around one-third of members of households 'at risk' of poverty were *in employment* in both Petržalka and Nowa Huta, suggesting the existence of

Table 4.2 Employment structure of households in Nowa Huta and Petržalka relative to 'at risk' of poverty levels (% of households)

	Below 60% of median income	*61–100% of median income*	*101–140% of median income*	*Over 140% of median income*
Nowa Huta				
Employed	28	44	48	56
Self-employed	0	8	3	9
Carer	0	2	2	0
Not working for health reasons	12	6	8	4
Maternity/paternity leave	2	1	1	2
Studying	4	3	12	4
Unemployed	39	13	3	2
Retired but working	0	1	0	4
Retired	10	20	21	16
Studying and working	0	1	0	3
Other	6	2	3	1
Total (*n*)	51	116	102	185
Petržalka				
Employed	32	45	59	72
Self-employed	3	6	5	6
Carer	0	0	0	0
Not working for health reasons	3	1	0	0
Maternity/paternity leave	6	6	1	4
Studying	13	10	8	4
Unemployed	31	8	5	1
Retired but working	3	2	5	4
Retired	6	17	15	3
Studying and working	0	2	0	5
Other	4	4	1	1
Total (*n*)	71	174	80	115

Source: Household survey. Figures relate to proportion of household members in each income group

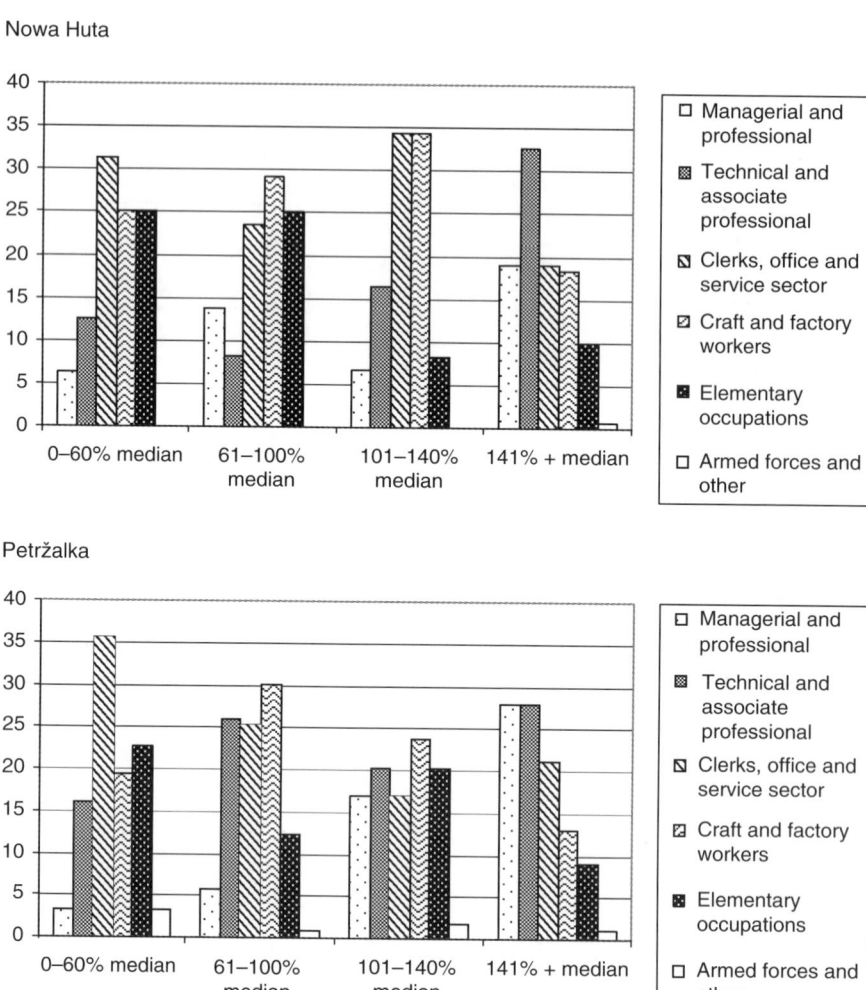

Figure 4.2   Occupational profile of household members relative to poverty risk levels, Petržalka and Nowa Huta (proportion of household members in each income category)
Source: Household survey

significant levels of in-work poverty (Table 4.2). Those 'at risk' of poverty tended to occupy jobs characterized by low pay in lower skill, lower status service sector and elementary occupations (such as cleaning and security). Over half of adults living in surveyed households in both districts with the lowest incomes, and therefore at risk of poverty, worked in basic service sector jobs and elementary occupations (Figure 4.2). At the other extreme, over half of adults living in surveyed households in the highest income group

Table 4.3   Average equivalized monthly income for households with different employment structures in Nowa Huta and Petržalka (euros)

	Nowa Huta	Petržalka
Managerial and professional	471	480
Technical and associate professional	374	380
Clerks, office and service sector	270	368
Craft and factory workers	276	363
Elementary occupations	230	359

NB: Data for 'other' households are not included because of the low count
Source: Household survey

Table 4.4   Gender and occupational structure in Nowa Huta and Petržalka

	Nowa Huta		Petržalka	
	Total (%)	Women (%)	Total (%)	Women (%)
Managerial and professional	14	16	15	17
Technical and associate professional	22	27	25	29
Clerks, office and service sector	24	32	23	33
Craft and factory workers	25	12	22	8
Elementary occupations	14	13	14	11
Armed forces and other	0	0	1	1
Total	291	145	317	166

Source: Household survey

worked in managerial, professional and technical jobs. In both Petržalka and Nowa Huta, average monthly equivalized household income was lowest among those surveyed households with members employed in elementary occupations, clerks, office and service sector jobs, and craft and factory worker occupations (Table 4.3).

Labour market segmentation and the emergence of in-work poverty were also associated with the feminization of certain sectors of the labour market (H. Domański, 2002). Although the proportion of women in higher status jobs (managerial and professional, and technical and associate professional occupations) was slightly above average in Nowa Huta and Petržalka, there was a marked concentration of women in office and service sector occupations (such as retailing and hotels/restaurants) (Table 4.4). While some of these jobs may have been held by so-called 'secondary earners' (Rashid et al., 2005), many women were in fact prime earners, as a result of male unemployment or male absence. For example, of the 41% of employed women in Petržalka who worked in basic service and elementary occupations, approximately one-third (36%) were living without a male partner in the same household. It was also clear that young people experienced significant labour market segmentation and were noticeably concentrated in service and elementary occupations, which are characterized by low pay levels and insecurity: in Nowa Huta, 69% of 18- to 24-year-olds who were working were employed in these sectors.

Highlighting the analytical value of gender and generation, unemployed household members tended to be either older men and women, whose skills no longer matched the demands of the labour market, or younger people who had struggled to make the transition from education to employment. In Nowa Huta, for example, Mrs Kwiatek explained that her husband, a trained electrician in his mid-forties, had been unable to find work because of the increasing conditions attached to employment: 'an electrician always finds work but they're always putting conditions: if it's not age, then a driving licence, if not a driving licence then a computer'. These changing contexts enforced for some a process of continuous training and retraining. Many of the older workers interviewed in the course of our research had been employed in sectors of the economy which had been at the heart of state socialism but which had been downsized in post-socialism. This not only applied to the thousands of steelworkers made redundant during the process of restructuring in Nowa Huta, but also workers in both Nowa Huta and Petržalka who were employed in other manufacturing enterprises and in the administrative sector. For some, redundancy was alleviated, or masked, by access to early retirement or disability pensions (see Chapter Seven), but for others, often those in their forties and fifties, redundancy was followed, sometimes repeatedly, by efforts to retrain and reskill in an attempt to fit better in the new economy. Mrs Sieradzka, for example, an unemployed woman in her mid-forties living in Nowa Huta, had trained in her youth as an electronic engineer but, as socialism collapsed and the industrial sector declined, she retrained as a tailor, a job in which she worked for 10 years. When tailoring also dried up, she took employment with a printer and eventually retrained in informatics. While her latest reskilling has not led to more stable employment, it had enabled Mrs Sieradzka to offer her IT skills to friends and family in return for other favours (see Chapter Seven). This kind of repeated retraining evokes notions of the neo-liberal, entrepreneurial self, 'a subject who is capable of constant self-invention' (Walkerdine, 2003: 241; see also Rose, 1999; Larner, 2000) in the rapidly changing and demanding labour markets of neo-liberal capitalism (Hörschelmann, 2008). Yet, as Mrs Sieradzka herself noted, despite the invocation to reskill and up-skill, it was increasingly difficult to translate skills into work, to 'count on concrete abilities', as the requirements of the new economy were often less tangible than those of older forms of work.

Mr Kowalik, also from Nowa Huta and in his mid-twenties, was typical of the younger unemployed worker who had failed to make the transition from education to employment. Educated during the transition, Mr Kowalik had had to negotiate a rapidly changing school system and had completed his education without identifiable occupational skills. This lack of focused training had created problems in the search for work, as Mr Kowalik explained: 'I've been registered with the labour office for two years ... When they make an offer, because I'm without an occupation ... then I go to the place of work and it turns out someone else has already started.' Two daughters in the Sinicki household, also in Nowa Huta, found themselves similarly excluded from stable employment after completing their education. Each had had a series of casual jobs in bars and restaurants and in promotional work (such as leafleting), but neither had found a decent job that might enable them to achieve some kind of independence from their parents.

For many, young and old, the experience of long-term unemployment was common; for those with particular barriers to employment, such as single mothers and those with disabilities, unemployment occasionally stretched for five or more years. For the majority, unemployment benefits had long since ceased; older workers waited desperately for when they could start receiving their pensions and younger workers were forced to rely on their families, one-off emergency benefits (see Chapter Seven), or informal work. For others, movement into and out of work, between unemployment and insecure employment, was the key characteristic of their working life. For example, Mrs Modzelewska, a single mother in her thirties, living in Nowa Huta and out of work at the time of interview, explained:

> For now I don't work, for some time, because it's hard to find work. And before, yes, it worked well for me ... then I worked as a sales assistant in a small bar, for more than a year, then I had my child and for maybe five years I was out of work. I worked in [a second-hand clothes shop], but that was really brief. And I cleaned in a shop here in Huta. That was more that more than five years ago ... it was very casual work.

Mrs Zajacová, a 50-year-old female respondent living in Petržalka with her partner, her adult son and her former husband, represented another typical experience of more unstable work patterns:

> I changed [my job] a lot. I lost my job in Pozemné Stavby [a construction company] in 1991, when the enterprise was closed. I got a redundancy payment and I was then registered at the labour office. Then I was employed in a kindergarten. I worked there for four years, but it was a very poor salary, so I decided to go to [work for a] private entrepreneur. ... He went bankrupt after half a year, [and] he didn't pay me. He still owes me SKK10,000 [€250][8] and also a redundancy payment. Then I was unemployed for half a year after

which I went to [work at] Minigril. It was also a private enterprise and they also went broke ... so I had to leave and I was at the labour office again for around two months. I met the director who works in the kindergarten. She told me they have a vacant position ... and she asked me if I wanted to come back. So I am there ...

Yet, the pay levels at the kindergarten remained very low and Mrs Zajacová was forced to supplement her income by working in a second job at a local hypermarket as a cashier. Such employment trajectories mean that household members negotiating the low-wage service economy in both cities rarely experienced a stable career path. They invariably moved from one low-paid, insecure job to another, to periods without work, and back again, combining multiple jobs during periods of employment in order to earn enough to ensure basic social reproduction.

For some, this temporality was mediated by labour market institutions, such as temporary work agencies, which were often used in conjunction with personal networks to access casual and irregular work. There were, however, a number of disadvantages to such institutions, resulting from their lax regulation. Evidence in Petržalka suggested that those registering with such agencies paid an initial fee, which was frequently too high for the very poor, whilst interviews in Nowa Huta indicated other risks. For example, Mrs Sasnowicz, a woman in her late forties living with her husband and daughter, had worked in a printing firm through a temporary agency on a series of 355 one-day contracts for a year and a half (four days on, one day off). When the work dried up and she tried to register as unemployed, she found that she lacked one day's work to be eligible for unemployment benefit. Yet, notwithstanding these significant difficulties, such agencies often provided the easiest way for those with the lowest qualifications and without work to find short-term work.

Labour market precarity was also reflected in concerns over the risk of losing a job if a worker became ill, or was otherwise forced to take time off work. Mrs Futyma, for example, a widow living in severe poverty in Nowa Huta, had only an informal employment agreement and was extremely reluctant to take time off for illness, holidays, or family responsibilities, reflecting wider experiences of labour market insecurity in other contexts (Burchell et al., 2002). Within the context of increasing employment insecurity, many households felt under increasing pressure to work longer hours and to work harder whilst at work in order to demonstrate their commitment to their employer, and there was growing evidence of a 'culture of presenteeism' (in which workers worked even if they were unfit to do so, simply to ensure that they were not marked with a record of absence). The greater time constraints (Tarkowska, 1996) engendered by developing labour market insecurity had important implications for other spheres of social reproduction, not least the ability of household members to find the time to work on allotments, to care for elderly relatives and to engage in secondary work.

Even for those in work, pay and conditions were rarely stable. Recent years have seen the withdrawal by employers of elements of the 'social wage'. Reported levels of in-work benefits were higher in Nowa Huta than Petržalka, reflecting the continuing role of the steelworks as a major employer. A significant number of households had access to free or subsidized food at work, to subsidized holidays and, occasionally, subsidized transport and medicines. However, many interviewees, particularly in Petržalka, noted the erosion of the social wage. While workplaces continued to provide access to health care, it was frequently remarked that such services tended to be provided at a lower standard than in the past and that employers were 'looking for savings everywhere', as Mr Niemczyk in Nowa Huta suggested. Nevertheless, in Nowa Huta, 44% of surveyed households also had access to very cheap or even interest-free loans through their employers, contrasting with just 9% in Petržalka (see Stenning et al., 2010). In Nowa Huta, access to loans through the workplace was a very important means of managing household budgets. Ms Senecka, a single woman working for a housing association on an above-average income, was typical of such households:

> I use a mutual assistance fund [Kasa Zapomogowo-Pozyczkowa, KZP] and Workers' Repair Fund [Pracowniczy Fundusz Remontowy] ... it's certainly [a big help to the budget] because it's an interest-free loan, or a very low rate. And it's good even just to take it into your account and deposit it and then buy something, or do some small repairs ... very useful; those funds are very useful ...

In contrast, Mrs Kwiatek, living in a very low-income household and struggling financially, lost access to such funds as her workplace was contracted out (from a hospital to a private provider). Whilst she had previously had access to such loans, she no longer does and 'it makes a big difference'.

Articulations Beyond the Formal Labour Market

The precariousness of the formal labour market forced poorer households to engage with a range of other work practices in their attempts to achieve social reproduction. While income from primary employment was the most important source on average for all households involved in the research (see also S. Clarke, 2002), it was considerably less important in households at risk of poverty (Table 4.5). To supplement income from formal employment, poorer households drew not only on other forms of informal and illegal labour, but also on their other assets – housing, land, citizenship rights and social networks (Smith & Stenning, 2006; Stenning et al., 2010;

Table 4.5   Average proportion of income derived from various sources

Income group relative to local median	Main job	Other jobs	Pensions	Child benefit	Unemployment benefit	Other social benefits	Other sources
Nowa Huta							
≤60% median	25	0	15	11	15	3	31
61–100% median	49	7	22	1	4	1	17
101–140% median	53	4	30	1	0	0	13
≥141% median	72	6	19	0	0	1	3
Total	59	5	22	1	2	1	11
Petržalka							
≤60% median	55	5	20	3	2	3	9
61–100% median	58	4	28	2	0	1	5
101–140% median	70	1	21	1	0	4	3
≥141% median	92	3	4	0	0	0	1
Total	70	3	18	1	0	4	3

Note: In Nowa Huta, 'other sources' is primarily comprised of incapacity benefit.
Source: Household survey

see also Chapters Five and Six). In these ways, engagements with formal labour markets have become intimately domesticated across a wide range of sites and practices.

Informal and illegal employment

One of the main ways in which household members attempted to secure a livelihood in the context of low-paid work was through combining several jobs – a kind of 'portfolio employment' – either in the formal economy, or through informal employment. Engaging in additional and informal employment was rarely a choice, but was widely seen as a necessity to secure a living wage. Ms Senecka, for example, a single woman in her forties living in Nowa Huta, formally worked as a caretaker in a neighbouring housing block. In addition, she earned a supplementary income from doing odd jobs (shopping, cleaning, caring) for an elderly couple who lived in the block where she worked, occasionally worked extra shifts to cover for her colleague, and, as a trained seamstress, took in small sewing jobs from friends and acquaintances in the neighbourhood – many of whom she knew from her caretaking work – and 'charged' anything from a cup of coffee to a few złoty (Pawlik, 1992). Like many individuals engaging in secondary work, and in an echo of socialist practice (Kalleberg & Stark, 1993; Smith & Stenning, 2006), such additional income-earning opportunities were founded on the basis of the skills, knowledge and contacts acquired through primary paid work. This is also exemplified by Mrs Cukrikova, who lived in a 'working poor' household in Petržalka with a male partner employed as a carpenter, and argued that: 'In fact this moonlighting of my husband is very important. He gets paid SKK100 [€2.50], sometimes SKK200 [€5], which we save so that we will have at least something to buy things with for Christmas. Otherwise, I don't know what we would do.'

Many individuals and household members, especially in poorer households, were actively engaged in work in the informal economy that involved 'illegal' practices, often as an alternative to being registered as unemployed. The low level of state benefits, coupled with a desire to avoid state surveillance, acted as a disincentive to register, especially in Slovakia where the state had been doing its utmost to monitor labour market participation and benefit payments. Mr Pustelak, a man in his twenties living in Nowa Huta, provides a good example of the shift from formal to informal employment. He had a series of legal jobs, mostly working as a security guard, but struggled to support his family. His wife explained that her 'husband worked but not much and he didn't earn enough to support the family'. Consequently, he left legal employment and, he continued: 'Now I work on the black. I earn a lot more money than if I was on unemployment, but [being registered as out of work] at least I have child benefit.'[9]

For others not eligible to receive social assistance benefits, informal work provided a small but important additional income supplement. For example, the Bombová household in Petržalka, comprising a retired woman in her late sixties and her middle-aged son, supplemented the pension income they received with income from the son's periodic informal work cleaning windows and flats. This accounted for about one-third of their monthly income of SKK17,000 [€425]. For others, the margins of informal employment were a means to manage flows of benefit and employment income. A typical example of this is the Lastovičková household in Petržalka, comprising a woman in her thirties, her young son, her parents and her single brother. Mrs Lastovičková was formally unemployed and received some state benefits for herself and her child, yet she worked informally in a kitchen for 3–4 hours a day. However, she had no contract for this work; rather her retired mother had the contract of employment enabling Mrs Lastovičková to continue to claim benefits and her employer to avoid tax and insurance payments. For some, especially younger workers who had struggled to make the transition to employment, poor quality, casual work was the only option, as the experience of the Sinicki household in Nowa Huta illustrates:

> they [the family's daughters] don't have work. They simply aren't able to find it. Occasionally they work with me [in a hotel] 'on the black'. One of them worked for a bit and the other worked last year for a while in the hotel … for 2 złoty (€0.5). One daughter worked once, and I had to pay for the journey to work. I paid for a taxi because otherwise it wouldn't have been safe. She also worked on the black, in some pub. And it really didn't make any sense, for 2 złoty an hour, you know: it's simply ridiculous.

While illegality and informality in the labour market provided a way of accessing some form of income, such employment experiences also created other significant constraints. For example, Mr Brestovič, a Petržalka resident, worked as a barman in the centre of Bratislava and received irregular salary payments from his employer. Officially, Mr Brestovič was paid the minimum wage and received the rest 'cash-in-hand'. This enabled his employer to pay lower taxes, but meant that Mr Brestovič was often uncertain of his income and never had sufficient 'official' income to access a mortgage from a bank. As a result, the Brestovičovás had to rely on their family, mostly working in similar low-paid jobs, in order to try to balance their household budget. In this way, external labour market pressures to reduce the costs of employment by resort to forced informality were literally domesticated, brought into the household. Mrs Kowalik, a young woman with an unemployed husband living in Nowa Huta, had found herself in a similar position, with no employment contract or certifiable income. She had attempted to formalize her employment contract, but had, in the process, seen a reduction in her take-home pay:

> Yes, for now I have a contract, but I worked for this woman for almost a year without a contract. I asked for a contract because of my child. … She said to me, you're a young woman, you have time to earn for your pension … so I asked again for a contract, and now I have a contract for a year, but I don't know what will happen … I used to earn more, but when I got a contract … she had to cut my wages because she had to pay for [social] insurance…

In a number of cases, then, informality had been imposed by employers, sometimes 'subcontracting' employment and transferring workers to positions of self-employment. While reported self-employment in the household survey was relatively low (7% of the economically active age population in Petržalka and 9% in Nowa Huta),[10] the experience of self-employment varied according to the position in the labour market. While some encountered insecurity, long hours and the loss of in-work benefits, others saw advantages in the opportunities for additional work and greater autonomy. In one Petržalka household, Mr Senzo, a former employee at the local rubber enterprise, Matador, was told by the management of the privatized former state-owned enterprise that he either had to become self-employed or he would be made redundant. He chose self-employment and as a consequence now had to find work on his own (some – but only some – of which was contracted to Matador) with the consequence that he worked very long hours (sometimes up to 80 per week) and experienced periods without work. As a result, the household's income was insecure and remained reliant on Mrs Senzová's wages from her relatively low-paid secretarial job, belying the argument that low-income female workers are secondary earners. In a contrasting example from Nowa Huta, Mr Wolak, a qualified accountant, was required to work freelance so that his former employer could avoid paying his social insurance and pension contribution. Yet, despite some months of real insecurity, at the time of interview in 2006, he had more recently seen his income increase as he was able to work both for his former employer and for other firms, and informally for friends and acquaintances.

Households and labour migration

For some households the flexibility and temporality of employment was linked to opportunities for labour migration to Western Europe. More and more attention has been drawn to the significance of remittance income in the region, not only in the poorest European countries, such as Albania (King & Vullnetari, 2004) and Moldova, but also in those states with long histories of international migration such as Poland and Slovakia, where patterns of mobility and remittance have been revived in recent years with accession to the European Union (Mitra, 2008). Even before EU accession, it had been estimated (in 2003) that official remittances to the transition economies equalled more than US$10.8 billion (Schrooten, 2005: 5). Since EU accession, remittances and migrant savings have played an even greater role in household budgets, especially those of poorer families (Kupiszewski, 2005). Indeed, much of the wider remittance literature argues that migration is a household financial decision to add transnational earning and saving to the portfolio of financial resources available (see, for example, Poirine, 1997).

Since this research was carried out as labour migration to the old EU member states (particularly to the UK, Ireland and Sweden) was rapidly growing, we identified a number of households – especially in Nowa Huta (reflecting prevailing patterns of labour migration in the two countries)[11] – where, during the course of our research, members had migrated within Europe for short periods. For some, labour migration had been a feature of socialist work too, providing means for major purchases (such as apartments and cars), although given the longer and deeper history of international migration from Poland, the significance of remittances tended to be greater among Nowa Huta households. In Nowa Huta, seasonal and occasional work overseas prior to 1989 was a common activity, as workers employed their manual skills on building sites and in factories in Western Europe and North America or were seconded by their employers to work in 'friendly' states. The Byjoch household in Nowa Huta exemplified this clearly, demonstrating the dependence of this kind of strategy on family networks:

> my husband's oldest sister went to Sweden and my husband, for a month each year [from 1984 to 1999], during his vacation, went to Sweden and earned money there … I remember it was US$300 for purchasing the flat at that time … if he hadn't been able to earn some extra money, we wouldn't have bought this flat so soon.

After 1989, the opportunities – legal and illegal – to earn and save overseas grew exponentially and many households used this route to ease daily budget pressures and to finance more significant purchases. A number of different experiences of remittances were evident. First, there were those where one household member worked abroad for an extended period and saved their earnings such that the household as a whole could rely on these for some time afterwards, either for everyday expenses or for major purchases. For instance, Ms Senecka, in Nowa Huta, covered her sister-in-law's maternity leave from her job in Brussels for seven months and Mrs Dawidowicz, also from Nowa Huta, had worked for a number of years as a care assistant in Switzerland, relying heavily on the income earned there in the two years since her return. Second, others relied on regular remittances from family members living overseas for their everyday – or emergency – finances. Two examples from Petržalka exemplify this 'altruistic' pattern of remittance. Mrs Badunická, a pensioner, relied on monthly remittances from her 43-year-old daughter who had been working in Austria as a medical technician since 1991. The increasing costs of medicine and Mrs Badunická's failing health meant that she was reliant on this remittance income to purchase the medication she required. In a similar way, Ms Blatová, a woman in her mid-thirties, had been working as a poorly paid shop assistant and living with her parents, adult siblings and their children in somewhat overcrowded circumstances. Following a theft that resulted in the family having to resort to a very high interest loan and an increasing realization that it would be impossible to enhance their financial situation in Bratislava, Ms Blatová decided to seek work in Austria through her personal networks. She explained: 'I promised my mum that I will regularly send her money ... if the work in Austria can be arranged and I manage to earn some money.' Third, there was increasing evidence that younger people were using periods of work overseas to achieve financial independence, enabling them to avoid reliance on either their parents or on credit institutions. A number of the households involved in this research, notably in Nowa Huta, where levels of out-migration appeared higher, had children or grandchildren working overseas with a view to investing their savings in property or in creating a small business (see Eade et al., 2006). In all these ways, for many households, especially in Nowa Huta, short-term labour migration was a regular option within the breadth of income strategies considered. Of course, such opportunities were structured by household characteristics (age, skill, independence etc.) and thus were not equally available. Labour migration, though an option, was not unproblematic.

Combining multiple jobs within households

These examples demonstrate that many households combined multiple jobs – legal and illegal, full-time and part-time, local and international – in the attempt to secure social reproduction. The experience of multiple job holding was a very real one, as households tried to balance work and domestic responsibilities to increase the number of hours worked, and thus the income received. The creation of 'portfolios' of employment, both simultaneously and consecutively, was a key mechanism for maintaining household income.

For some households, increasing the number of household members was used to increase the size and number of jobs (and income) in a single (extended) household unit. For example, the case of the Brestovičová household in Petržalka, introduced above and comprising three generations of seven people living in a three-room apartment, clearly demonstrated the struggles involved in daily social reproduction. All three adult women in the household were unemployed at the time of interview, although each pursued occasional informal work. The two adult men (the father and husband of the main respondent) both worked in low-pay service sector jobs in Bratislava. Their combined household income was based on the wages of the two men, occasional irregular and informal work of the women, and regular short-term borrowing from a network of family members living in the neighbourhood (Stenning et al., 2010). This enabled the household to survive month by month, but provided no opportunity to save and little prospect for the couple with a young child to get their own apartment.

In other examples, a number of poorer households pointed to the fact that their younger members – schoolchildren and full-time students – took on part-time and casual work in order to supplement household incomes. For the Dawidowicz household in Nowa Huta, for example, the occasional work of the 22-year-old daughter was essential for easing difficult moments in the family budget, and for allowing the daughter to treat herself to a social life. What had begun as very occasional leafleting work in a local shopping centre had been complemented at the time of interview by additional cleaning work, in the same shopping centre, two to three times a week. A similar experience was evident in the Kielak household, also in Nowa Huta: Mrs Kielak, an unemployed single mother who was registered disabled, struggled to manage the household budget and relied occasionally on income from her 18-year-old daughter's casual work. This income not only supplemented the household budget but reduced the financial pressures that a teenager's developing consumption habits had on more essential expenditures, as Mrs Kielak explained:

> My daughter somehow also comes up with something. She has this acquaintance, and she goes and simply earns herself some money, some pennies, for cosmetics or something … once or twice a week, arranged by these friends, all on the black.

In Petržalka, too, low parental incomes were supplemented by children taking on casual work – for example, the regular, but low (SKK15,500 [€408]), income from Mrs Slamková's work as a kindergarten teacher was supplemented by the income from her student daughter's work in a variety of short-term and informal jobs, to which she committed up to 30 hours a week. In other instances, it was extra work taken on by household members living on disability or old-age pensions that eased the flow of income and expenditure in poorer households. Mr Wrzosek, Mr Mokrzycki and Mr Wiatroszczak, all older men living on incapacity benefit after careers in industrial employment in Nowa Huta, took on occasional odd jobs on the recommendation of friends and family, despite not being able to work formally or full-time. This additional informal work was incredibly important for these household budgets, as Mr Wiatroszczak notes: 'If it wasn't possible to do extra work, then it would be really difficult'. Multiple job holding in large households thus played a critical role in trying to ensure social reproduction, with the benefits often disseminated through kinship networks.

Work and social networks

The importance of kin and friendship networks extended through a number of spheres of household economic activity, and we return to the role that such networks play in the following chapters. In the sphere of employment, the most direct connection was the use of social networks to access work. The failure of job centres to offer reasonable work meant that most found work through acquaintances and recommendations, although this was not always easy, as Mrs Sieradzka, unemployed for 18 months, illustrated:

> Mmm, I use every possibility, and the most effective is through acquaintances. But I don't have the possibility to rely on finding work through acquaintances. Everyone is themselves without work, or looking after their own. ... Every newspaper, the job centre, labour exchanges, the internet ...

For the self-employed, too, contacts provided by friends and neighbours were crucial for continuity of income, and, in the sphere of informal work, such contacts were often the only means to secure work. For example, in the case of the Bombová household in Petržalka introduced above, the son's opportunities for informal cleaning and maintenance work were identified almost entirely through his mother's social networks.

For others, family and kinship networks provided a source of childcare and enabled access to the labour market among those of working age, which would not normally have been possible. The most common version of this relationship involved grandparents caring for their grandchildren while their adult children, usually daughters, took paid work (see Chapter Seven). In Nowa Huta, Mrs Futyma, after some 12 years on the margins of the labour market, worked as an office cleaner. She limited her working hours, however, in order to take care of her granddaughter whilst her daughter worked full-time. In other instances, shifting labour market opportunities resulted in a reversal of working responsibilities and the remaking of non-commodified labour in the home. While Mrs Kwiatek in Nowa Huta continued to go to work, her husband – the unemployed electrician discussed above – stayed at home to take care of their daughter and to maintain the home.

In other cases, social networks formed at work proved particularly useful for other spheres of life. In Nowa Huta, Mrs Sedlak, employed in local government, used networks established through workplaces to access scarce services:

> I went to work and I said that [her daughter] had to go [to hospital] because something was wrong with her eye, and selflessly my colleague called and said, listen, but E____, that's her son-in-law, he works somewhere and he has

this acquaintance who's a doctor ... And later I got a [business] card, and I went to that woman, and she already knew on whose recommendation, and so it was...

Whilst connecting back to the role of such work-based networks under state socialism, the use of work networks in the current era may also have served to reinforce exclusion. Poorer households were disadvantaged not only by limited funds for bribes and gifts, but also by the fact that they had less access to the kinds of contacts (whether through professional spheres or with the 'right person') that might be useful. Consequently, they were less likely to use such contacts to access services. As one of our Nowa Huta interviewees, Mrs Kowalik, living on a very low income and employed in marginal jobs, suggested: 'No, we don't do things in that way, because we do not have the sort of acquaintances who have access [to services].' In contrast, in both districts the use of professional contacts to access services and employment opportunities among the most affluent households was very common, demonstrating how such households could use job-based networks to further consolidate their labour market position and access to services.

Work and benefits

For some, the small flows of income within extended families and social networks rested on the presence of one or more secure, if small, incomes from the state, most often in the form of a pension.[12] Despite the liberalization and relative decline in the value of pensions in several countries (Muller, 2002; Smith & Rochovská, 2007), they continue to be an important source of money income (Table 4.5). For many households, these sources provided a small but stable income base and articulated in complex ways with various forms of employment. In some cases, for example, pension or other benefit income provided a basis for the running of very small businesses or the taking on of part-time insecure work (Cellarius, 2004), as we saw above in the case of men living on incapacity benefit. In labour markets where restructuring has led, through early retirement programmes, to significant numbers of young retirees, this kind of combined pension/employment strategy was quite common. In Poland, for example, early-retired pensioners can earn between 70% and 130% of the average monthly salary with a concomitant reduction in pension payments.[13] In Nowa Huta, one of our respondents, Mrs Idziak, attempted to sustain a living through a couple of informal activities – she gave massages and copied paintings to order – but until recently struggled financially. However, she had qualified for a disability pension and explained that her financial situation had 'improved a bit because I have this permanent allowance and it's secure, because I used to be without money and it lasted up to three months'. Household members therefore combined employment with benefit income and, in some cases, used their citizenship status as pensioners to negotiate contract and benefit situations. However, neo-liberal pressures to restrict state expenditures and cut back on benefit payments raise questions about the continuing potential for this kind of combination.

Material assets: Land, home and other income-generating activity

A household's home space and other material assets, such as garages and cellars, also enabled additional employment and earning (see also Chapters Five and Six). Not only did available space in the home allow households to increase in size and incorporate more income-earners (as discussed above), but it also enabled a range of 'entrepreneurial' activities, ranging from starting small businesses to ad hoc work. In addition to the examples of home-based casual work mentioned above, a young Nowa Huta couple, Mr and Mrs Wojnowicz, ran a successful publishing business from a spare room and had started up a manicure business from the home of Mrs Wojnowicz's mother. In Petržalka, Mrs Brestovičová, a woman in her late forties, ran a small, informal second-hand clothing shop from her cellar. In all, our survey revealed that 15% of 'other jobs' (that is, any additional jobs beyond the 'main job') were located in the home in Petržalka, and 12% in Nowa Huta, demonstrating the importance of domestic space in household economic practices (see also Burawoy et al., 2000).

In addition to employment in home-based enterprise, a significant number of households also engaged in work on the land, either on their own or family plots, or in labour offered reciprocally to friends and neighbours (Smith, 2002a; Smith & Rochovská, 2007). We focus much more fully on the role of land and food provisioning in Chapter Six, but here we explore some of the ways in which land and labour were connected in the struggle for social reproduction. The labour expended and shared in the production of food was rarely commodified, even when employed on other people's land, but more often than not involved some kind of exchange, either through the receipt of vegetables, meat, and fruit or through the provision of other forms of non-commodified labour (such as painting and decorating, repairs or childcare). The Slamková household in Petržalka, for example, met up to 70% of their food consumption needs from a family plot some 60 km from Bratislava in exchange for reciprocal labour provided in looking after the house and tending the land. This kind of reciprocal labour was often enacted by the very household members who were the least productive in the formal economy (pensioners, teenagers, unemployed workers), and involved skills developed previously in the workplace. In one Nowa Huta household, for example, the husband who was a retired steelworker, regularly did welding work on his friends' and neighbours' allotments. In this way, the attempt to sustain livelihoods through work involving commodified wage labour was also articulated with a range of reciprocal practices of unpaid and 'self-employed' labour on the land (Cellarius, 2004; Smith, 2002a).

Conclusions

This chapter has drawn attention to the neo-liberalization of work and labour markets in post-socialist Bratislava and Kraków. Labour markets are increasingly fragmented, and segmented, and work is increasingly experienced as precarious and contingent. There has been a sharp contraction in employment and the emergence of persistent unemployment, even in relatively buoyant urban labour markets, and the jobs that have been created in the wake of this decline have often demanded new skills (and/or repeated reskilling) but offered little of the security and few of the additional benefits associated with work in state socialism. Many of the new jobs have been marked by low pay, low status and high levels of insecurity. As a result, both cities have witnessed the emergence of in-work poverty as the income from such work is not sufficient to lift a household out of poverty. The emergence of such poor quality work has taken place alongside the erosion of social welfare and a completely inadequate unemployment benefit system, leading many households into increasingly precarious financial positions.

Unable to secure an adequate income from primary employment or to rely on in-work benefits, the working poor, in particular, have been impelled to engage in a diversity of working practices. Thus, households' working practices rested not only on regular jobs in the formal labour market but also on complex strategies shared amongst household members. These included additional, secondary jobs; attempts to multiply household incomes by encouraging young, retired and incapacitated household members to take on work as and when they could; a preparedness to engage in informal and sometimes illegal employment practices; and a readiness to retrain or to pick up new skills in order to make the most of new opportunities. The variety of practices in which households engaged has drawn them into a range of diverse class processes. The fact that most working household members combined numerous forms of labour meant that many also experienced a shift in their working identity, from wage-labouring employee, to contingent labourer, to self-employed, for example. These shifting identities also had to be balanced with a range of family and social roles enacted through domestic and reciprocal labour.

These working practices articulated with other spheres of households' everyday economies and with their social networks, material assets and benefits, in particular. Thus, for example, the search for work, both formal and informal, often relied on friends and family to make recommendations or identify opportunities; periods of overseas working enabled households to save for major purchases, such as housing; and the presence of relatively stable benefit incomes created some continuity with which to manage unstable and temporary work. In other ways, the pressures and precarities of neo-liberal work impacted on households' ability to engage in other practices, such as education, caring, leisure, and the production of food. For some, life on the margins of formal labour markets led to 'compound exclusion' (Speak & Graham, 2000) as access to housing markets and financial products, for example, were limited by labour market exclusion and as households' ability to maintain social networks was eroded by poverty and, sometimes, shame. For both those struggling to find and keep hold of insecure work, but also those under increasing pressure to work more and work harder, the time spent at work, or in search of work, detracted from other spheres of life (Stenning, 2005a), leaving little time to invest in social and kinship relationships, or work the family plot. In all of these ways, households' working practices were shaped by, and also shaped, the multitude of other economic practices in which households engaged.

The need to manage the articulations between work and other household practices draws attention to the importance, and transformation, of the geographies of work. Although this is a point of differentiation between Nowa Huta and Petržalka, as we discuss in more detail below, during state socialism the interconnections between work and life were eased by the proximity of home and workplace and by the infrastructures that supported transitions between the two. In the post-socialist period, the fragmentation of work has created a fragmented geography: households' varied working practices took place in much more diverse locations, not only locally, but also nationally and internationally, and the task of juggling this diversity has become all the more difficult.

Households' working practices were not only articulated with each other and with other household practices, but also with wider structures and infrastructures, which in turn intersect with subjectivities such as class, gender and generation. Spheres such as education, childcare, public transport and the benefits system articulated with the labour market to disadvantage certain workers, such as women, manual workers and young people in particular. These structural constraints were often reinforced by more discursive features – the moral rationalities we discussed in Chapter Three – which suggested, for example, that women should prioritize childcare over work, or that older manual workers should adapt to the new working conditions, or that young people could be paid less. Some of these moral rationalities have deep historical roots; others have developed alongside the neo-liberal governmentalities we discussed in Chapter Two.

These articulations point to some of the legacies of state socialism. Work, as we have seen, was particularly central to social reproduction during state socialism and the influence of work extended well beyond the workplace. This has both material and discursive echoes today in, for example, access to low-cost loans in Nowa Huta and in particular understandings of the gender division of labour. But the diversity of work was also, in part, inherited from state socialism – and from earlier histories – as diverse working practices have been translated from households' rural pasts or from the strategies developed to negotiate the shortages of late socialism. These histories indicate, in turn, points of comparison and contrast between Nowa Huta and Petržalka. In Nowa Huta, the steelworks and associated institutions were at the heart of a geographically concentrated labour market and marked out the enduring legacies of state socialist forms of paternalism. It has only been relatively recently that Nowa Huta has become more of a 'dormitory' settlement for the wider Kraków labour market. In contrast, Petržalka's households had long engaged in commuting within the wider city and had never been able to rely on a single, embedded, local employer. In the context of post-socialism, this has meant that some households in Nowa Huta had, to some extent, been protected from the extremes of neo-liberalizing labour markets, whilst some in Petržalka had perhaps been less isolated from the rapid transformation of work.

In both districts, however, neo-liberalizing labour markets have been domesticated in two ways. On the one hand, the transformations, insecurities and diversifications of the labour market have been brought into the homes of Petržalka and Nowa Huta workers. Households' preparedness – willingly or unwillingly – to take on complex working practices to secure an adequate income in many ways enabled the proliferation of new forms of work which failed to pay a living wage. Instead of being borne by the employer, the costs of employment uncertainty were brought into the home and absorbed, more or less successfully, into households' economic practices. The precariousness and plurality of work have had very real impacts on the material shape of households, introducing pressures not only on household budgets, on time resources and on the balance of work, pleasure and other responsibilities, but also on relationships, within and beyond the home. On the other hand, these practices are also evidence of the ways in which households have sought to make neo-liberalizing labour markets tolerable. Some of these appeared as active contestations of the neo-liberal but most were more mundane attempts to ease the experience of labour market transformation and to respond to it.

In both senses, this process of domestication highlights the ways in which the lives of households in Petržalka and Nowa Huta have been radically altered by these labour market transformations. In the context of post-socialism, many households have struggled to pull together a set of working practices that might offer an adequate income and have had to develop proactive strategies in the search for work. Together with the emergence of in-work poverty, such forms of engagement with work raise real questions about the ability of households to ensure social reproduction in the context of post-socialist neo-liberalization.

Chapter Five

Housing: Markets, Assets and Social Reproduction

Introduction: Housing and Its Geographies

Housing invokes a wide range of meanings and values: it offers shelter and security; it has profound and emotional connections to 'home'; and, increasingly, it is seen as an economic asset, ripe for development and investment (Blunt, 2005; Blunt & Varley, 2004; Christie et al., 2008; S. Smith, 2008). These multiple meanings imply an 'interweaving of economy and emotion' (Christie et al., 2008: 2299) and illustrate clearly the complexity of value in economy (Lee, 2006), such that any exploration of the place of housing in everyday economies and social reproduction demands a multifaceted analysis of housing markets and their geographies, household relationships, the interconnections of socio-economic circumstance and inheritance, and the changing structures of housing ownership and finance. The particular significance of housing in the context of post-socialism is highlighted not only by the very rapid and wholesale transformation of housing markets since 1989 – from a situation of overwhelmingly state-owned provision, these economies now record some of the highest rates of owner occupation in the world (Lux, 2003) – but also by the almost mythologized value of the home under socialism. Despite the predominance of state ownership and the often poor quality of much living space, the home was seen as 'the last defense against the rapacious socialist state' (Burawoy, 1999: 307; see also Boym, 1994), a space where families and friends could hold on to their eroded autonomy and plan their everyday lives together.

Since the collapse of state socialism, the transformation of housing and of housing markets has been dramatic, with markedly uneven social and geographical consequences. Much has been made of the differentiated consequences of privatization (Pichler-Milanovich, 1994, 2001; Falt'an & Dodder, 1995; Clapham, 1995; Marcuse, 1996; Kovács, 1999; Grime, 1999; Cirman, 2006), the appropriateness of different housing finance schemes (Stephens, 2005), and the changes wrought in the urban fabric, including socio-spatial differentiation and emergent gentrification (Sýkora, 1999; Ira, 2003; Matlovič, 2004; Dawidson, 2005). Much less attention has been given, however, to understanding how individuals and households reconfigure their housing and negotiate housing markets, at a time when ownership structures are being radically reformed, housing markets are developing and diversifying, costs are escalating dramatically, and access is increasingly constrained by issues of affordability. The neo-liberalization of housing markets is swiftly domesticated, as transformations in this sphere change the meanings, values and practices of home, that most domestic of spaces. How households make sense of and engage with these transformations is the focus of this chapter.

Across the region since 1989 most housing has been privatized and the social housing sector has become residualized; real estate markets have been established and formalized, and real estate professions have developed; there has been a boom both in house prices and housing construction (following a stagnation in the early 1990s); and there has been increasing housing turnover and mobility. All of these processes reshape housing practices – the ways in which households understand, occupy and employ their housing – and have profound implications for housing market and wider social inclusion and exclusion. This chapter focuses on these housing practices and their contribution to household social reproduction in Nowa Huta and Petržalka. It analyses the ways in which households capitalize on and develop their housing assets; how they negotiate the marketization of housing and deal with housing market exclusion; and how they manage the increasing costs of housing (utilities, maintenance etc.). The chapter also pays attention, following the framework established earlier, to the articulations between housing and other spheres of everyday economic life through an exploration of the use of housing for informal economic activities and the proximity of households' housing to land, to shops, workplaces and family and friends. Understanding these practices demands that attention is given to the ways in which earlier forms of housing allocation and tenure sedimented an uneven social geography which continues to explain, in part, differential housing experiences today. Importantly, the differentiated housing practices and outcomes we explore are not only a consequence of the uneven positioning of households in neo-liberalizing property markets, but also a legacy of housing practices under state socialism.

The Transformation of Housing in Poland and Slovakia

Hegedüs and Tosics (1992; see also Hegedüs et al., 1996; Clapham, 1995) identified an 'East European housing model' under state socialism, which was characterized by certain key features but varied from country to country. Common features included: state, enterprise or municipal ownership and allocation of most housing; a universal right to housing; fixed low rents, unrelated to costs and typically around 5% of income; increasingly long waits for housing allocation; and a growing predominance of poor quality, panel-built high-density apartment blocks (Blunt & Muzioł-Węcławowicz, 1998; Markham, 2003; Pichler-Milanovich, 2001; Zapletalova et al., 2003). This system resulted in the almost total absence of housing markets under state socialism, a striking conformity of provision, low levels of segregation (D. Smith, 1996), very low levels of housing turnover, and significantly deferred maintenance. Yet, for all this, there was much more variability than is often assumed. ECE housing stocks included not only the post-war high-rise blocks so common in Nowa Huta and Petržalka, but also pre-war tenements and single-family homes. Different periods of post-war construction varied considerably in terms of quality, build and facilities and the size, location and accessibility of neighbourhoods varied noticeably. Access to housing was often mediated by employment status, formally and informally. There was also a persistent tradition of self-build (Sik, 1995) and, in the late socialist period in particular, alternative forms of ownership, including cooperative and private forms, grew in significance (Bodnár & Böröcz, 1998; Bodnár, 2001; Pichler-Milanovich, 2001). Moreover, in some contexts, allocated leases were inheritable, exchangeable and able to be sub-let, such that quasi-markets developed in later years (Bodnár & Böröcz, 1998). As a result of these variations and nascent markets, the inheritance of housing in the post-socialist period has been very uneven.

Despite attracting considerable subsidy (Hegedüs et al., 1996), housing was also a sector marked by severe shortage in late socialism, such that by 1989, housing in many ECE countries, including Poland and Slovakia, was a sector in crisis. This crisis had both quantitative and qualitative aspects. Firstly, most of the post-socialist countries inherited very significant housing deficits. It is estimated, for example, that there was a deficit of around 2 million dwellings in Poland in the late 1980s, a figure which increased to 3.5 million if overcrowded households are also included (Ciechocińska, 1990; see also Uchman & Adamski, 2003). This shortage had resulted in waits of 20 to 25 years in Poland and real difficulties for young couples in establishing independent households (Ciechocińska, 1990). Comparative data for Slovakia are not available, but a UNECE report (1999) found that there were clear indications of overcrowding in Slovakia suggesting housing shortages, with 1.14 persons per room in 1994, compared to 1.02 in Poland. Secondly, the fiscal situation in late socialism, coupled with the low rents charged and the reliance on hasty construction methods, had created a huge backlog of housing maintenance, such that a large proportion of the housing stock was in urgent need of repair and/or renovation (Ciechocińska, 1990; UNECE, 1999). This meant that many households, on the eve of transition, were living in sub-standard, overcrowded accommodation, which proved to be a problematic inheritance as provision was privatized.

The transformation of housing in ECE has been characterized by a number of common features and by some national specificities. The common features of this transformation centred on the enthusiastic promotion of markets, owner occupation, deregulation, and the marketization and residualization of social housing. It is easy to see here the influence of other neoliberal housing reforms, particularly the privatization of council housing in the UK (Pichler-Milanovich, 2001). Pichler-Milanovich, for example, identifies the imposition of a World Bank Privatization Housing Model on the post-socialist states which resulted in a privatization carried out under the influence of 'neoliberal ideology, privatization rhetoric and budget constraints' (Pichler-Milanovich, 2001: 150). Thus, the overriding feature of housing transformation was a 'general tendency ... to reduce government budget expenditure and to shift responsibilities for housing policy to local and/or individual level' (Pichler-Milanovich, 2001: 155).

In practice, the core of ECE housing transformation was a heavily subsidized privatization which saw sitting tenants eligible to 50% to 80% discounts on the market price of their property (Zapletalova et al., 2003; Markham, 2003; Uchman & Adamski, 2003). This has resulted in very high levels of owner occupation (74% in Poland (Uchman & Adamski, 2003) and 77% in Slovakia (Zapletalova et al., 2003))[1] and a housing market in which social housing is minimized (Priemus & Mandič, 2000). Yet, despite the 'give-away terms' (Yemtsov, 2007: 1; see also Markham, 2003) of post-socialist housing privatizations, they created some marked inequalities and exclusion, growing housing burdens, and some tough management issues, each of which has raised important questions about how households have been able to negotiate access to decent, affordable housing.

As Yemtsov has suggested (2007: 1), 'housing privatization affected the distribution of personal wealth and inequality', often exacerbating already emerging inequalities as wealthier households captured more valuable housing assets on equally subsidized terms. The privatization benefits for already-privileged groups 'dwarf[ed] what the poor have received as a result of marketization of poorly constructed buildings on city outskirts' (Yemtsov, 2007: 7; see also, Pichler-Milanovich, 2001). By subsidizing privatization to sitting tenants, 'housing privatization programmes created winners and losers depending on where people happened to be living at the beginning of transition' (Yemtsov, 2007: 10). As a result, 'losers' in the privatization process often found themselves the owners of poor quality accommodation in high-rise blocks on unattractive estates, which was not only worth less and more expensive to maintain and heat (Buzar, 2007), but was also much more difficult to sell or exchange. Even if they were lucky enough to take ownership of good housing assets, low-income households still tended to find themselves in weaker positions in the new housing market; they often had difficulties investing in property to maintain its market value (Schmigotski, 2004; Uchman & Adamski, 2003), found energy expensive (Buzar, 2007), and had 'subprime' access to housing loans (Stenning et al., 2010). For some, housing purchase led to an increase in the costs of shelter and created significant difficulties in meeting maintenance costs.

Such problems are exacerbated by the management structures established after privatization. Responsibility for the management and maintenance of blocks largely shifted to individual tenants. Tenants were then forced or encouraged to establish residents' associations or to contract an administrator to manage the collective upkeep of the building, its common areas and facilities, and to share the costs of this maintenance (Zapletalova et al., 2003). Such practices rarely recognize the variation among residents. Households will have varying sources of capital and credit on which to draw; blocks may include a variety of tenure types since not all apartments will have been privatized (Ball, 2007); and the demand for maintenance and upgrading will vary according to desire and income. In all these ways, these management structures have the potential to create conflict between neighbours.

The vehement promotion of owner occupation as the normalized housing form has led, in an echo of the British experience, to the residualization and stigmatization of social housing. Those who do not or cannot purchase their property are deemed to have failed and the figure of the owner-occupier sits alongside the entrepreneurial self in the development of neo-liberal subjectivities.[2] In both quantitative and qualitative terms, the social housing sector has been diminished since 1989 (Ball, 2007; Pichler-Milanovich, 2001), creating major problems of access to social housing. In Poland, for example, the wait for social apartments can be over five years in large cities (Uchman & Adamski, 2003) where the loss of stock through privatization has been exacerbated by the low level of new-build social housing (Schmigotzki, 2004). As a result, households with delayed or no access to social housing resort to overcrowding, squatting or to paying high rents in the private rental market. Municipalities are obliged to provide social housing, with low rents, for households in particularly dire situations but this social housing stock tends to be of poor physical quality, poorly located and intended only for temporary residence (Uchman & Adamski, 2003; Pichler-Milanovich, 2001). The provision of housing benefits has also been devolved to local government, which has resulted both in considerable variability and increasingly stringent conditions of eligibility (Lux, 2000). Limited access to both social housing and housing benefits – arising from the neo-liberalization of social welfare – leads Ball (2007: 95) to conclude that 'widespread poverty exists with large numbers of households concentrated in un-privatized apartment blocks who, in the absence of housing allowances, can afford to pay little or nothing for their housing'.

The weak development of the private rental sector (Hüfner, 2009) and the limited availability of affordable private housing in Poland and Slovakia mean that housing choices for new households, created by family formation or breakdown, are very limited. This is a particular issue for young people, as a demographic surge creates a wave of household formation at a time when access to the housing market, through rental or purchase, is difficult (Ball, 2007). As a result, and as we discuss below, 'growing numbers of young people [are] living in "involuntary cohabitation" with parents' (Lux, 2000: 190) or, when parents are unable or unwilling to shelter adult children, are forced into an informal rental sector, characterized by high rents, insecurity and low standards.

Difficulties with access to the housing market are exacerbated by a poorly developed mortgage finance sector. The heavily subsidized nature of housing privatization meant that many households were initially able to buy their apartments outright, limiting the need for mortgage finance in the early years of transformation. It is only in recent years that mortgage markets have developed in Poland and Slovakia, and evidence suggests that recent growth has been rapid (Stenning et al., 2010; Anderson, 2007; Schmigotzki, 2004). In Slovakia, mortgage rates for younger households with incomes less than 1.3 times the national mean were subsidized by about half (Zapletalova et al., 2003), evidence of the normative promotion of owner occupation. By 2005, however, in the light of the neo-liberal policies of the Dzurinda government, state subsidization of mortgage markets had ceased, only to be re-introduced in late 2006, following the election of the centre-left Fico government (Anderson, 2007). In Poland, mortgage interest payments have also been subsidized for some low-income families, but at a scale deemed to be almost negligible (OECD, 2008b). At the same time, the weak development and high entry costs of mortgage finance means that 'many transactions still occur without recourse to mortgage lending' (Ball, 2007: 95), as 'home buyers have to produce large cash down-payments … drawn from their savings, assets and equity contributions from relatives and friends' (Pichler-Milanovich, 2001: 166). For those households without down payments, the possibility of stepping onto the housing ladder is all but non-existent (Ball, 2007). One means to circumvent these difficulties is through complex exchange and part-exchange deals, arranged informally by buyers and sellers with the aim of avoiding major cash outlays. As Ball suggests (2007: 20), 'further down' the housing market transactions become

Plate 5.1   New private housing development in Petržalka

'more informal and opaque', pointing to the domestication of neo-liberal market relations by informal practices.

Recently, ECE cities have been marked by a housing and house price boom (Ball, 2007), a trend particularly evident in large, attractive cities such as Bratislava and Kraków. In Kraków, house prices increased by 55% in 2006 (compared with 33% in Warsaw) and in Bratislava prices increased by 33% in 2007. These increases were caused not only by domestic pressure but also by speculative international investors following EU enlargement, especially from the UK and Ireland where property investment cultures have encouraged the purchase of foreign property (see Cook, 2010, on Prague).[3] These growth rates are driven most by market developments in the 'more fashionable districts' (Ball, 2007: 17) where international developers have identified significant potential. House price growth has been much lower in places like Petržalka and Nowa Huta. In 2007, the price of 1 m^2 of residential property in the heart of the old town of Kraków was almost three times that of Nowa Huta (*Małopolskie Nieruchomości*, 26 June 2007, page 6). Even domestic house buyers have tended to reject peripheral housing estates, if they can, reinforcing the growing differentiation between such estates and city centre locations (Bodnár, 2001; Sýkora, 1999). There have, nevertheless, been both new housing developments (Plate 5.1) and price increases in Petržalka and Nowa Huta, with significant implications for affordability and access. It is within these contexts that we now turn to assess the housing practices of households in Nowa Huta and Petržalka.

Housing in Nowa Huta and Petržalka

Nowa Huta and Petržalka comprise significant parts of the housing market and infrastructure of both Kraków and Bratislava, housing approximately 30% of each city's total population. Indeed a significant part of the rationale for our focus on these two districts, as discussed in Chapter One, lies in their built form and their position as major residential districts on the edge of booming cities. Both districts were largely constructed during the post-war period and reflect the housing structures of state socialism. The overwhelming image of both districts is of high-rise, panel-built housing from the 1960s and 1970s (see Plates 1.1–1.8) but, in marked contrast to their image as homogenous estates, both Nowa Huta and Petržalka are characterized by considerable variety of housing type. The variation in built form was coupled, during state socialism, with a socially mixed population. Unlike peripheral housing estates in Western Europe, these large-scale developments in ECE were home to households from a very wide range of social and economic circumstances (D. Smith, 1996; van Kempen et al., 2005).

Some notable features of the housing history of the two districts are worth highlighting because they have a strong influence on the contemporary development of housing markets. Reflecting its place at the forefront of Polish post-war urbanism, and the particular significance attached to the steelworks at its heart, Nowa Huta benefited from considerable housing investment. New housing technologies were developed in Nowa Huta and a factory for the production of pre-fabricated housing panels for Nowa Huta was built at Łęg, just to the south of the district. This has meant that much of the district's housing stock from the late 1950s to the early 1990s was based – like that in Petržalka – on fairly sub-standard building techniques, leading to relatively high levels of dilapidation, energy inefficiencies (causing issues with heating and higher energy costs), and increasing maintenance costs. Large-scale investment in housing in both Nowa Huta and Petržalka meant that waiting lists were shorter than in many other parts of Kraków and Bratislava, and in other cities. Many families moved to Nowa Huta – and took jobs in the steelworks or associated plants – explicitly to access housing more quickly. This meant that the steelworks played a very significant role in the allocation of housing in Nowa Huta and employment in the steelworks was one of the best routes to acquiring property. As Table 5.1 demonstrates, 28% of surveyed Nowa Huta households originally

Table 5.1   Means of acquisition of current apartment, by income category (% of households)

	≤60% median	61–100% median	101–140% median	≥141% median	All households
Petržalka					
Inherited	0	2	0	2	1
Received from workplace	32	19	46	22	27
Bought from cooperative	9	20	11	9	13
Bought privately	5	9	11	24	13
Allocated by municipality	23	20	21	20	21
Rented	0	2	0	11	4
Exchanged	5	20	11	4	11
Other	27	7	0	7	9
Nowa Huta					
Inherited	10	11	4	12	10
Received from workplace	10	33	31	27	28
Bought from cooperative	15	25	29	32	28
Bought privately	0	0	8	12	8
Allocated by municipality	30	19	10	2	10
Rented	10	6	6	10	8
Exchanged	10	6	6	5	6
Other	15	0	6	1	4

Other: includes replacement accommodation as compensation (e.g. for a compulsory purchase elsewhere), restitution, squatting etc.
Source: Household survey

acquired their home directly through their workplace, with a further 28% acquiring it through a cooperative, the majority of which were workplace-based.[4] In Petržalka, there are quite strong internal differences in how housing was first accessed, based on age of construction and style, but despite a much more diversified employment base in Bratislava, workplace allocation mechanisms were also important, especially through some of the largest employers (including state agencies). The allocation of housing thus created a set of reciprocal relations between homes and workplaces as the two housing districts were developed.

Table 5.2   Tenure status of surveyed households (% of households)

	Nowa Huta	Petržalka
Own apartment	74	89
Apartment rented from municipality	14	5
Private rented apartment	8	3
Apartment belongs to another family	3	1
Other	2	3
Total	100	100

Source: Household survey

By 2005, housing in both districts had been thoroughly commodified and transformed through privatization, with three-quarters of surveyed households owning their own apartment in Nowa Huta and almost 90% in Petržalka (Table 5.2). Yet, in comparison with other similar housing districts in central Europe, the cost of buying an apartment relative to average national wages was very high in Petržalka (Table 5.3). These figures are supported by a survey of advertised sale prices for apartments in early 2007. As Table 5.4 shows, average prices in Petržalka were between 70 and 111 times the average Bratislava wages and were even more unaffordable in Nowa Huta, at between 91 and 182 times average Kraków wages. In both Nowa Huta and Petržalka, however, prices were significantly lower than the city average. Indeed, the low desirability of housing in Nowa Huta is illustrated by advertisements seeking housing which regularly include the phrase '*Nowa Huta wykluczona*' ('Nowa Huta excluded'). Two of Kraków's three 'intervention blocks' are located in Nowa Huta (Bukowski et al., 2006) and 'problem' tenants are regularly re-housed by social services in other Nowa Huta blocks, many of which are seen to be difficult to let or sell (Stenning, 2005b). Low prices and cheaper rents do however mean that both Nowa Huta and Petržalka are increasingly attracting younger couples and student households who struggle to pay for housing in more desirable districts. This inflow of younger people has very positive impacts on what are otherwise seen as aging districts.

Internal differentiation

Turning to the housing situation of our researched households, Tables 5.5 and 5.6 summarize the age, location, built form and internal differentiation of the neighbourhoods. As noted in Chapter One, in Petržalka, the Gessayova neighbourhood comprises one long main 12-storey block of apartments with multiple staircases and about 60 households resident in each staircase.

Table 5.3   Average apartment prices in selected central European cities, 2004

	1-room apartment[a]		*2-room apartment*[a]		*3-room apartment*[a]	
	Sale price in local currencies[b]	*Relative to average annual national wages*[c]	*Sale price in local currencies*[b]	*Relative to average annual national wages*[c]	*Sale price in local currencies*[b]	*Relative to average annual national wages*[c]
Petržalka	1,150,000	72.7	1,550,000	97.9	1,900,000	120.1
Prague 8	1,160,000	64.3	1,399,000	77.6	1,565,000	86.8
Vienna (Josefstadt)	140,000	43.8	163,000	50.8	187,000	58.4
Warsaw	129,000	53.6	163,000	67.8	236,000	98.1
Budapest (18th district)	8,900,000	61.1	12,700,000	87.2	15,500,000	106.4

Notes:
(a) Definition of apartment sizes:
1-room apartment: Petržalka (40 m²); Prague 8 (40 m²); Vienna (70 m²); Warsaw (28 m²); Budapest (37 m²)
2-room apartment: Petržalka (58 m²); Prague 8 (52 m²); Vienna (56 m²); Warsaw (38 m²); Budapest (52 m²)
3-room apartment: Petržalka (75 m²); Prague 8 (75 m²); Vienna (75 m²); Warsaw (63 m²); Budapest (76 m²)
(b) Local currencies are: Petržalka (Slovak koruna); Prague 8 (Czech koruna); Vienna (euros): Warsaw (złoty); Budapest (forints)
(c) Clearly there are issues relating to using average *national* wage levels, given that wages tend to be higher in Bratislava than in Slovakia as a whole, for example, but this limitation also applies in the other capital cities
Source: www.reality.sk/Articles.aspx?DocID=obr30426 (accessed 12.09.06)

Gessayova has the lowest social status of the three neighbourhoods. The Haanova neighbourhood mainly consists of four-storey blocks and has the highest social status. The Lúky-Sever neighbourhood has social characteristics similar to the average for Petržalka as a whole, although it is internally much less homogenous than the other neighbourhoods, as we discuss in greater detail below. In Nowa Huta, the key difference is between the smaller, brick-built blocks of 'old' Nowa Huta, built in the late 1940s and early 1950s, and the larger blocks dating from the 1960s onwards. In Willowe and Górali, housing blocks are built around courtyards and tend to consist of small apartments, many one- or two-roomed, some with three or four rooms. Górali is also home to one of Kraków's so-called intervention blocks, where the local authority houses families in financial or other difficulties. In both Przy Arce and Dywizjonu 303, most housing stock consists of

Table 5.4   Average apartment sale prices in Petržalka and Nowa Huta (January 2007)

	Average price (SKK or PLN)	Average price (€)	Average price per square metre (€)	Average price relative to average annual wages
Petržalka (*n* = 78)				
30–40 m²	1,751,760	50,050	1,339	70.4
50 m²	2,407,898	68,797	1,267	96.9
65–75 m²	2,763,560	78,959	1,140	111.2
All	2,307,739	65,935	1,249	92.8
Nowa Huta (*n* = 75)				
30–40 m²	212,716	54,842	1,543	91.4
50 m²	305,475	78,757	1,465	131.3
65–75 m²	424,577	109,464	1,292	182.4
All	314,256	81,021	1,433	135.0

Sources: Authors' survey of advertised sale prices; average wage data for Bratislava www.statis tics.sk/webdata/ks/ksbrat/mesacmzda.htm (accessed 25.06.07); for Kraków, wage data for 2006 derived from the Polish Central Statistical Office

Table 5.5   Surveyed neighbourhoods in Petržalka

	Gessayova	*Haanova*	*Lúky-Sever*
Period of construction	1971–80	1971–80	1981–90
Type of construction	A 12-storey block, with multiple staircases	Many 4-storey blocks, set around grassed areas	Combination of 6-, 8- and 12-storey blocks
Location	Close to the city centre	Close to the city centre	Quite distant from the city centre

prefabricated blocks in varying states of repair, with some blocks in Przy Arce housing around 250 households. Dywizjonu 303 has lower social status, with high levels of rent arrears and a fairly poor social reputation. Oświecenia comprises newer housing, much of which was built by cooperatives[5] in the 1980s and 1990s. Apartments here are bigger than other parts of Nowa Huta and the neighbourhood is seen as much more desirable, on

Table 5.6   Surveyed neighbourhoods in Nowa Huta

	Willowe/Górali	*Przy Arce*	*Dywizjonu 303*	*Oświecenia*
Period of construction	1947–56	1966–70	1970–75	1975–
Type of construction	Brick-built, mostly 2- or 3-storey, smaller apartments	Large panel-built blocks, 8–12 storey, with multiple staircases	Large panel-built blocks, 8–12 storey, with multiple staircases	Large, multi-storey blocks; some single-family homes
Location	'Old' Nowa Huta, closer to steelworks	Good communications; close to major markets	Closer to Kraków and close to major markets/ hypermarkets	Closer to Kraków; further from steelworks. Good communications and close to major hypermarkets

account not only of apartment size, but also the location (closer to Kraków, with views of the old city and mountains to the south).

All our surveyed households lived in apartments in multi-storey blocks (though some single-family homes do exist in both Petržalka and Nowa Huta) and the majority of surveyed households in both areas are now owner-occupiers. The pattern is, however, more mixed in Nowa Huta than in Petržalka (Table 5.2). There are some marked differences between neighbourhoods, especially in Nowa Huta, where the level of owner occupation is significantly lower in Przy Arce and especially low in Willowe and Gorali. In Petržalka, the only neighbourhood with surveyed households living in municipal apartments is Lúky-Sever. In both Petržalka and Nowa Huta, poorer tenants are more likely to rent from the municipality and wealthier tenants from private landlords. In both districts, housing turnover has been fairly limited. Our questionnaire survey showed that in Petržalka there has been relatively little internal housing mobility, though this has increased through the 1990s and 2000s. In Nowa Huta, reflecting the longer history of residential settlement and thus the varying household profile, movement in to the current apartment tends to be later than movement into Nowa Huta. This suggests that some households moved from older parts of Nowa Huta to the newer neighbourhoods as they were built in the 1980s and 1990s. Very significant numbers of households in both districts, however, moved into their current apartment on the day the block was occupied and have remained there for

Table 5.7   Total living space (m²)

	Minimum	Maximum	Mean
Nowa Huta	15	87	47.2
Petržalka	20	100	70.5

Source: Household survey

20 years or more, providing the basis, as we show in more detail in Chapter Seven, for the development of extensive intra-block social networks.

In both districts, despite the key role of major enterprises, there was considerable variety in the means of acquiring the current home (Table 5.1). In Nowa Huta, this variety reflects the different histories of the neighbourhoods and the households' residential histories: for example, more than half (54%) of households in Osiedle Oświecenia, a more recently built neighbourhood where the steelworks and other key employers allocated apartments, received their apartment from their workplace. Since so much housing in Nowa Huta was allocated by the steelworks, the municipality played a smaller role than in Petržalka. A higher percentage of apartments in Nowa Huta were inherited from parents or grandparents. This reflects the longer history of settlement and has been an important feature of housing acquisition in the district: many young households in Nowa Huta take the first step on the housing ladder by inheriting their grandparents' apartment, as the older generations move in with their children for care, move back to their home villages on retirement, or die. Yet, even inheriting the rights to an apartment does not guarantee housing security. In Nowa Huta, Mrs Kielak went through a complicated legal procedure to take on the lease for her grandmother's flat before she turned 18; some 25 years later, however, Mrs Kielak found herself with such large housing debts that she had been served with eviction orders and was awaiting removal at the time of interview.

Living space in Nowa Huta and Petržalka varied quite markedly. Although both districts have apartments of varying dimensions, the mean apartment size of respondents was considerably smaller in Nowa Huta than Petržalka (47.2 m² in Nowa Huta; 70.5 m² in Petržalka) (see Table 5.7).[6] The differences in living space reflected very clearly the age of the housing stock and the density norms of different construction periods. Table 5.8 demonstrates further that poorer households had less living space per person. Poorer households tended to live in smaller apartments, but they were also more likely to share their space with more household members (see also Chapter Seven). Stanisława Urbaniak, past vice-president of Kraków city council responsible for social affairs, suggested that some 500 families were living in overcrowded conditions in Nowa Huta

Table 5.8   Living space per person in Petržalka and Nowa Huta (m²)

	Mean	*Median*	*Minimum*	*Maximum*
Petržalka				
≤60% median	21.5	18.3	9.0	61
61–100% median	23.2	18.8	8.8	77
101–140% median	28.4	23.7	13.3	69
≥141% median	29.4	24.0	10.0	80
All households	25.7	22.2	8.8	80
Nowa Huta				
≤60% median	12.5	11.0	4.2	28
61–100% median	14.5	12.8	3.6	56
101–140% median	18.6	16.7	7.4	50
≥141% median	21.5	19.0	7.0	72
All households	18.6	17.0	3.6	72

Source: Household survey

and raised concerns about the social and psychological problems such overcrowding engenders (interview, 8 November 2005).

For many households, their apartment was their most valuable material asset. Some households also possessed some land, sometimes with a small cabin or cottage (see Chapter Six), but for everyday shelter and security, their apartment in Nowa Huta or Petržalka was key. For this reason, the ways in which households managed, deployed and developed their domestic space, their home, was central to both their ontological and financial security (Hiscock et al., 2001; S. Smith, 2008). The security that a home offered created opportunities for the household to extend its benefits by selling and exchanging to maximize available space, by making space for others (within or beyond the family), by developing property through investment and renovation, by employing domestic space for business purposes, or by extending their housing portfolio (through borrowing and building). Many of these practices were aimed at enabling younger generations to take their first step in the ever-tightening housing market. The limits placed on the ability of a household to capitalize on its property assets by the quality of the home and its location and size, and by the financial capacities of households, were very real. Together these practices draw attention to the ways in which households have sought to domesticate developing housing markets through their attempts to understand the nascent markets, the ensuing differentiation of housing, and their own changing place within these new markets. The following section explores these practices before we turn our attention to those struggling to negotiate housing crises and housing market exclusion and those for whom the ownership of housing is becoming an increasing burden.

Capitalizing on Housing Assets

One of the main strategies employed by households to adapt their housing assets to their changing needs was to sell or exchange their apartments. Such practices took multiple forms, often reflecting the life cycle situations of different family members and commonly involving the assets of more than one household. Sometimes this was a straight non-commodified exchange within a family, as Mr and Mrs Zych in Nowa Huta explain:

> We've lived here since 1992. My daughter lived here once, and we swapped. We had a big three-bedroom apartment in Na Skarpie, but because for two people that didn't make any sense and they are a developing family, right? So we moved, we simply swapped.

Yet even in such cases of straightforward exchange, further life changes could engender additional switches. Mrs Cała, also in Nowa Huta, exchanged her larger flat, on the death of her husband, for the one-room apartment of her son and daughter-in-law, as they started a family. Yet, when the son's marriage broke down after three years, they swapped back. Mrs Cała continued to hope that her son and daughter-in-law would rebuild their relationship and that the two households would once again swap their apartments. Other exchanges involved wider transactions that enabled households to ease their financial situation and improve their housing conditions. Mrs Sedlak and her elderly parents each lived in apartments in the same Nowa Huta neighbourhood. On the death of her father, Mrs Sedlak and her mother exchanged their two apartments for a single, larger apartment, not only increasing space for Mrs Sedlak and her children but also enabling her to offer her mother 24-hour care. The use of flat exchanges was much less prevalent among households in Petržalka, with only one case of non-market exchange mentioned in our interviews. This more limited development of an economy of non-monetized flat exchange reflected both the fuller development of the private market for housing in Petržalka and the more limited local familial connections (see Chapter Seven). Where exchange did occur, it enabled households to avoid formal housing markets and often relied on word-of-mouth flows within a household's social networks to find and arrange a suitable swap. Such practices, then, point to households' desires, needs and/or abilities to avoid formal, market-based transactions and to reduce the monetary cost of housing mobility.

Instead of simply exchanging property, a noticeable alternative strategy saw households sell their family homes elsewhere in the city and relocate to cheaper property in Nowa Huta and Petržalka. This practice enabled the redistribution of equity within family networks as house price differentials often meant that households could release enough equity to purchase two apartments, one for the parents and one for the adult children. For example, the Portiš family of two non-working pensioners sold their house with a garden in a 'better' part of Bratislava (Karlova Ves) to reduce their own housing costs and to enable their adult children to gain access to the otherwise prohibitive housing market in the city. This transaction involved using the equity released to purchase a new flat in Petržalka, to provide a down payment for their children to purchase their own flat, and to purchase an allotment in another part of Bratislava. For others, the sale of property elsewhere in the city and relocation to Petržalka was a means of realizing some liquidity to cover increasing costs in other parts of the household budget. For example, Mrs. Badunická, a single pensioner, sold her large five-room flat in the Ružinov district of Bratislava in order to help her daughter buy an apartment and to help fund the purchase of her own increasingly costly medication. Because of the higher costs of property in Ružinov, compared with Petržalka, Mrs Badunická was able to sell one apartment and buy two.

However, the financial costs and benefits of such sales and exchanges were not the only consideration; such moves disrupted important social networks, critical to the easing of everyday life (see Chapter Seven). Mrs Badunická had lived in Ružinov for many years and the move to Petržalka had led to her becoming isolated from her old social and support networks in Ružinov, as she explained:

> I regret it a lot [moving to Petržalka]. Not because the flat isn't good, or the neighbourhood, but my friends are there [in Ružinov] and I miss them. I have to go there when I want to see them.

In contrast, for Mrs Sedlak the attraction of exchanging her and her mother's apartment in Nowa Huta for a single larger one was that the exchange enabled her to stay 'right here in the neighbouring courtyard, so it's the same shops, the same, so to speak, shop assistants, neighbours, and everything was the same'. For some, the potential loss of social networks meant that the possibility of moving, and thus realizing their illiquid assets, was all but non-existent. This gives lie to the conception, common amongst policy makers in both cities, that many poor households are in fact 'housing rich' and in a position to work their way out of poverty through housing mobility. The inability of households to access the equity held in property ownership was complicated still further by the fact that homes were often occupied by multiple generations and occasionally by more than one household (see below) such that any potential relocation was an extremely complicated, if not impossible, act.

For some, moving home demanded a combination of exchange and additional payments, highlighting the ambiguity of transactions that enabled households to improve their housing conditions without making excessive demands for capital. Although this kind of transaction tended simply to involve an agreed additional transfer, in the case of the Gwizdek family in Nowa Huta, their move from a small, poorly equipped studio flat (with no kitchen, a shared shower in the corridor, no hot water and no gas) to a fully equipped one-room flat involved them exchanging homes with a family friend and taking on half of his housing debts.

Persistently low levels of housing turnover (Mandič, 2001) meant that for many households, the focus of their housing investments and negotiations was the renovation, repair and maintenance of their current home (Plate 5.2). The years since 1989 have seen a boom in the DIY market in ECE,[7] with major international companies establishing DIY hypermarkets and warehouses in most towns and cities and specialist domestic firms (for roof tiles, double-glazing, security, and plumbing, for example) developing a ubiquitous presence in the region. Households' investments in their property reflected the desire to increase its value as an asset as well as to improve liveability. Many of our researched households had spent considerable time and effort updating and renovating their homes since they had bought them (often after a long period of disrepair and disinvestment), installing double-glazing or new bathrooms, or buying new fitted furniture. For some in Nowa Huta, these improvements had been funded by low-cost or interest-free workplace loans (from mutual assistance funds (Kasa Zapomogowo-Pozyczkowa, KZP) or the Workers' Repair Fund (Pracowniczy Fundusz Remontowy); see Stenning et al., 2010), which tended not to be available to households in Petržalka. For others, renovations had been funded by commercial loans, which in some cases had become a significant burden, leaving families heavily indebted and, ironically, creating a financial situation that threatened housing security. This was most often the case for those households who were renting (or squatting) sub-standard housing which required considerable work to make it liveable. For example, in Nowa Huta, Mrs Czarnocka, a single mother in her thirties, had spent PLN7,000 (€1,750) replacing the floors, redecorating the walls and furnishing her illegally occupied squat. Through such involvement in both emerging DIY markets and with new housing finance

Plate 5.2   Balcony renovations in Nowa Huta

products, households are increasingly engaged in the growing property industry, reflecting the neo-liberal commitment to owner occupation and its responsibilities.

Many households in both Nowa Huta and Petržalka said they *would* spend extra income (if they had it) on their homes, suggesting that many were not actually in a position to do so. Although the strains of delayed repair and refurbishment could be acute, budgetary pressures created even more problems when, following privatization, residents' associations sought to make financially demanding collective repairs. As we suggested above, the diversification of residents' socio-economic status and financial health during the period of transformation has created growing inequalities in both the willingness and the ability of households to pay for the upkeep of communal spaces (such as lifts and staircases) and for major refurbishments (such as the insulation of blocks and new roofing). These common investments rest on, but also potentially strain, the strength of neighbourly relations and shared understandings of the housing block's value.

It is clear, then, that the use of housing assets in these ways – the realization of equity to reposition an extended family network in the wider housing market and investment for potential future gain – is structured around the social position of households and articulated with the uneven legacies of state socialist housing. As noted above, despite the narratives of uniformity, housing in Poland and Slovakia varied considerably in terms of quality, size and location, and these variations articulated with often opaque allocation mechanisms to produce micro-geographies of social differentiation within housing districts such as Petržalka, as Mr Šiška explained:

> There's a difference in the quality of apartments between those which were cooperative and those which were state-owned. State apartments during socialism were free after joining a waiting list, but it was necessary to pay for cooperative flats [often available only to state employees or key factory workers]. They didn't cost a lot but poorer people couldn't afford them. This block [a 12-storey one] was completely made up of cooperative flats. Eight-storey blocks were mainly state-owned and were given to people who weren't from Bratislava – people who moved here as factory workers from East Slovakia – or former residents of 'old Petržalka' [the original village next to which the new housing was built]. These four-storey blocks were also state-owned and for the Roma and others being assimilated into society.

The result has been increasing differentiation in social status as different allocation mechanisms have translated into clear distinctions in desirability. This is an emerging process. There are still considerable levels of social mixing in the districts as a whole, but the contrasts between individual blocks are growing. One respondent in Petržalka, Mrs Červíková, herself a divorcee, described in very graphic terms the situation in her former state-owned apartment block as follows: 'the well-to-do people moved away and left only "bastards", divorcees and widows behind'. These varying ownership structures articulate with other factors, such as location, build quality and block size, to result in increasingly significant variations in value, as some neighbourhoods and housing styles are identified as desirable and others to be avoided. For those who found themselves in apartments increasingly identified as unattractive, the potential for sale, exchange or investment was considerably lessened and the allocation mechanisms of state socialism were seen to have material and long-lasting impacts. For financial reasons, as well as the more social ones outlined above, some privatized homes – especially those of poor households unable to invest in their property – were an unrealizable asset. In this way, the distinctions of the market were lived and negotiated every day, strengthened all the more by the evident polarization of housing experience.

Thus, whilst some were burdened with unmarketable assets, others saw the benefits accrued from a strong employment and housing position in the socialist period extended still further. The housing status of these households was strengthened by their ability to acquire additional housing assets, either with savings amassed from secondary and seasonal work or with loans negotiated with the security of existing property. In both these ways, some households in Nowa Huta and Petržalka had been able to support younger generations' first steps onto the housing ladder. The Byjoch family in Nowa Huta, for example, not only managed to buy their apartment early in the process of privatization on the basis of money earned by Mr Byjoch in Sweden, but were also later in a position to buy a piece of land and to use this as collateral for loans to build a house for their son as he reached adulthood.

The impact of living space on wider household strategies to achieve social reproduction was also important. There were, for example, households using their surplus space for small businesses, extra informal work (see Chapter Four) and for renting to tenants. In Nowa Huta, Ms Senecka, a single woman who lived in an apartment which absorbed about 75% of her expenditure, had, whilst waiting to arrange an exchange, let a room to a student on a short-term basis, thereby offsetting some of her housing costs. The letting of rooms within family apartments highlights the connection between some households' housing wealth and the difficulty with which younger people, in particular, could acquire independent housing, either through purchase or rental. The relatively undeveloped formal rental market in central European cities feeds a hidden rental sector within the owner-occupied sector.

Negotiating Housing Crises and Housing Market Exclusion

The housing shortages at the end of the state socialist period and the haphazard and skewed development of neo-liberalized housing markets in post-socialism have created serious problems with access to housing in contemporary Poland and Slovakia. Rapid price inflation in the property market, a slowly developing and stringent mortgage market, and very limited low-cost new-build housing articulate with growing levels of labour market exclusion and social stress (including ill-health and family breakdown) to threaten exclusion from housing markets and housing crises for many households. Levels of recorded overcrowding have grown since 1989, despite already worrying levels on the eve of transition. Olech (2008) cites estimates of anything from 4 million to 12 million Poles living in overcrowded conditions (10% to 30% of the population) and notes an increasing shortage of housing through the post-socialist decades. At the same time, homelessness has emerged as a phenomenon, despite being almost unknown during state socialism. Activists and social workers estimate that there are currently around 60,000 homeless people in Poland (Wygnańska,

2006) and 1,200 in Kraków (Bieńkowska, 2008). Comparable figures in Bratislava stand at approximately 1,000 (Stanková, 2009). In part, the increase in homelessness reflects a growing number of evictions during the 1990s (Południkiewicz, 2005) – usually for non-payment of rent – but also as a result of family breakdown and personal crises. Importantly, though most evictions are related to the municipal and social housing sector, non-governmental organizations working amongst the homeless have seen mortgage default increase as a cause of homelessness (Olech, 2008). Homeless shelters have been opened in both Nowa Huta and Petržalka (the majority run by NGOs and charities, often church-related), predominantly housing men who have left, or been forced from, their homes as a result of family breakdown, alcohol abuse, violence, redundancy, and personal crises.

One phenomenon that has emerged in Nowa Huta is households illegally occupying vacant municipal apartments. Three households living in the Górali neighbourhood had effectively squatted their current homes, and all faced eviction because of this. Each of these three households had found themselves in a dire housing situation, with all other options closed off to them. The Kwiateks and the Kowaliks were both young families living on less than 60% of the median income and in precarious labour market positions. Like many young families, neither had achieved the kind of financial position that might have allowed them to establish their own home, either rented or owned. Yet where both families differed from others in our research was that they could not live with their parents; nor could they have called upon them for any substantial financial support. Mr and Mrs Kowalik did live with Mr Kowalik's mother for six years after getting married, but the birth of their son in 2003 altered the situation. At this point, it was simply not possible for all three to be accommodated in Mr Kowalik's mother's small apartment. With no other local family, no means to rent or buy their own home, and long waits for both municipal and 'emergency' social housing, they felt they had no option but to illegally occupy their current apartment, having found out about the vacancy from friends. For Mrs Kwiatek, the impossibility of living with family was founded not on their absence but on the breakdown of relations with her mother-in-law, with whom Mrs Kwiatek, her husband and their daughter had previously lived. Mrs Czarnocka's housing difficulties had also in part emerged from the absence of a family safety net. She had moved to Nowa Huta for work from a small town 20 miles from Kraków and for three years had rented a home privately. However, as the costs of renting increased more than her income, and as she reduced her working hours to care for her daughter, Mrs Czarnocka found it increasingly difficult to balance the books. Without the option to move in with family – who remained in her home town outside Kraków – and unable to find better paid work to coordinate with her childcare responsibilities, Mrs Czarnocka decided to move into an apartment in

Osiedle Górali without permission. She was angry that she had been excluded from discounted privatizations – since she had not then had a home to purchase – and resentful that her rent payments were so high when others had bought so cheaply.

For all three families in this position, the illegal occupation of municipal property had increased their housing insecurity. Not only had all three been evicted and were awaiting removal and relocation by the city council, but all had also been fined significant amounts for their illegal occupation. They were thus all in a position of paying rent (once their illegal occupation had been noted by the city council), and additional fines, for very small apartments in sub-standard conditions; all three apartments comprised just one room without adequate facilities and in a poor state of repair. Each had spent their own money on improving the apartments (with Mrs Czarnocka, as we have seen, taking on considerable debts to do so). As a result, none had been in a position to save towards renting or buying their own home. Each had also lived for some years with the insecurity of squatting, always waiting for the city council to find out and act and, in some cases, experiencing considerable harassment from neighbours who objected to their illegal occupation. Such insecure housing therefore had real impacts on other forms of security and well-being. The extreme precariousness of their housing situation reflected a potent combination of a failing social housing system, labour market exclusion, and weak, difficult or absent familial networks, all of which have been caused or exacerbated by processes of neo-liberalization.

The combination of family relationships, financial stability and a novel and rapidly transforming system of tenure, to a lesser degree, played a role in the housing position of many of the other households in our research. The difficulties experienced in moving onto the housing ladder – even through renting – suggest that the ability of family and friends to accommodate or financially support young families was absolutely critical. For those who had not been in a position to purchase their home as property was privatized, the cost of owner occupation was often prohibitive. Even for some households who had lived in their apartments for 20 or 30 years and would have been, in theory, able to buy them with a large discount, the idea of home ownership was a distant one as low incomes and more pressing needs eroded the potential to buy.

Similar constraints played into the attempts of younger families to buy their own homes. Despite being a relatively wealthy young couple in good employment, Mr and Mrs Juszczak struggled to be able to move into their own home. Not only did they opt for Nowa Huta, instead of their preferred location closer to the city centre, in order to find the cheapest apartment, but they actively pulled together all possible financial resources to make the purchase. Both sets of parents made a contribution, they drew on savings accrued when Mr Juszczak worked in Frankfurt, and they took out credit to meet the remaining expense. Others in both districts, in similar financial positions, struggled to purchase and watched house prices rise much faster than their incomes or savings, raising questions about whether they would ever be in a position to buy.

For those unable to buy – or even to rent privately – sharing with family was a common solution. Although survey evidence suggested that the vast majority of homes in both Nowa Huta and Petržalka were occupied by only one household (94% in Nowa Huta; 95% in Petržalka), follow-up interviews suggested that home-sharing strategies were much more extensive, although often hidden by close family relationships. In a number of cases, for example, single mothers continued to live with their parents and siblings, and adult children, both sons and daughters, returned home when their relationships broke down. Adult siblings sometimes shared the apartments inherited from their parents, such that two intertwined households lived in one home. And many adult children, having completed their education and moved into employment, lived with their parents long after they might have hoped for independent living. While many of these arrangements – as well as reducing housing costs – had considerable additional benefits (most commonly, care and support for younger and older family members, see Chapter Seven), they also created tensions and strains. Not only were younger generations restrained, but their parents also often had to accept their children moving in and out as their economic and social circumstances changed. In this way, the dislocations of post-socialism are brought home.

An extreme example of sharing space involved the Blatová household in Petržalka. The flat of the parents (both in their sixties, Mrs. Blatová was retired) represented a very important asset to the extended family, housing a total of 13 people in three rooms. This included three daughters in their thirties, a son in his twenties, two of the daughters' partners, and their five children. The insecurity and change in this kind of living arrangement is evidenced by the fact that, at the time of our survey, the household consisted of eight people but shortly afterwards another daughter, her husband and three children found that they were no longer able to afford separate rented accommodation in Petržalka and so moved back with their parents. Only by sharing with their parents were the adult Blatová children able to save any money, with the hope of eventually securing a mortgage to purchase their own flat, which, at the time of interview, still seemed like a distant dream.

The difficulties for lower income households of accessing the increasingly costly housing market were compounded by the tenuous labour market positions of many households. The growth of precarious employment and an expanding low-wage service sector has meant that poorer households found it increasingly difficult to access products, such as mortgages, in the developing financial industry (Stenning et al., 2010). Take, for example, the

Brestovičová household of six persons living in Petržalka in a former state-owned apartment which had been purchased by the parents who were in their fifties. The household comprised Mr and Mrs Brestovičová, their two daughters, a son-in-law and three-year-old grand-daughter. The men in the household were the only ones in regular employment, albeit in low-paid, casualized bar and restaurant work. The three adult women worked occasionally or informally to supplement the household budget. Living conditions were overcrowded, with the younger, unmarried daughter sleeping in the living room. The married daughter and her husband would have readily moved to their own apartment but their positions in the labour market have meant that getting access to a mortgage was all but impossible. As we noted in Chapter Four, the partial payment of her husband's salary as unregistered 'cash-in-hand' meant that the official salary he received on his pay slip – the official minimum wage – was inadequate to secure a mortgage from a bank. As our respondent explained:

> I think that my parents would definitely live better if we weren't here. But what can we do? It is like this: we have to try to get a mortgage for a flat, but you can't get one. It is impossible. Maybe if my husband earned, I don't know, SKK20,000 (€500), maybe we could get one, but when he has on paper only SKK6,800 (€170), it's impossible …

In Nowa Huta, the Sinicki family were living in similar circumstances. Only Mrs Sinicka was in work, and her three adult daughters had struggled to find secure jobs in which they would earn enough to establish financial – and residential – independence. With a fourth, younger child still living at home and a grandchild on the way, the Sinickis were desperate for a larger apartment but had not even been in a position to buy their current flat on privatization.

Sharing was still more uncomfortable when difficulties in accessing housing meant that divorced couples were forced to live together after marital breakdown, creating the potential for increasing levels of conflict. In Petržalka, Ms Červíková had been forced, following her divorce, to continue to live with her son in the same apartment as her former husband. While sharing the same living space, Ms Červíková and her son effectively operated as a separate household budget unit, although they paid a nominal 'rent' to her former husband who had legal title to the apartment. Ms Červíková worked as a kitchen helper, had two other jobs to try to make ends meet, and received about SKK11,000 (€275) each month in income. Of this, she paid her former husband SKK2,000 (€50) in 'rent' to cover utility costs, considerably less than she would be paying for rent for an independent apartment.

The disarticulation of family lives and housing resulting from difficulties in the housing market was a recurring theme in our research. Not only did the costs of housing force family members to share when they would rather not, but in some cases they also demanded that households were divided. In Nowa Huta, Mr Chmielecki lived apart from his wife and children, though he was not separated. The small size of their family home was exacerbated by the fact that Mr Chmielecki, his wife and their two children were all musicians with nowhere to practise but their home. That Mr and Mrs Chmielecki both needed to work, and the two children study, made living in a three-roomed apartment as a family all but impossible. In other instances, too, the availability of space (or its lack) at parents' homes sometimes meant that young couples had to live apart in the early years of their marriages. Mrs Futyma, a widow in her fifties, for example, usually shared her small Nowa Huta apartment – in fact just one room with a kitchen corner – with her younger daughter and two small grandchildren, whilst her son-in-law lived with his mother. Only because Mrs Futyma's niece had gone to the US for a few months were her daughter and son-in-law able to live together, temporarily, as a family.

Mr Chmielecki's housing solution points to another strategy to acquire property in adverse circumstances: that of converting non-residential space to make a home. It is estimated that 11,500 Poles live in space not designed for residential use, such as attics, laundry rooms, garages and cellars (Olech, 2008: 10). Mr Chmielecki and a second Nowa Huta household, the Wolaks, were good examples of this. Mr Chmielecki was allocated, by the city council, an attic space in some disrepair as a music workshop, for practising and for giving private lessons, with no expectation that he would live there – he was still registered for residential purposes in the flat in which his wife and children lived. On moving into the attic, Mr Chmielecki noticed that there were two separate spaces with two distinct access points. Mr Chmielecki converted both spaces to residential use, kept one for himself, and sub-let the second to another family. In this way, Mr Chmielecki subverted the city council's property allocation system and worked it to his advantage, yet he still owned neither space. The Wolaks, by contrast, bought a utility room, having rented an apartment elsewhere, and converted it into a residential space for themselves and their two daughters. After five years in that converted apartment, they sold it and moved into a 'regular', three-roomed apartment in the same neighbourhood. In this way, they successfully moved onto and up the housing ladder, something that would not have been possible without their first unconventional purchase.

In the context of such a housing crisis and significant housing market exclusion, it might be expected that the social housing sector would play a considerable role. As we have noted (Table 5.2), 14% of our Nowa Huta households and 5% of our researched households in Petržalka rented from the municipality, and a number of households also received some housing benefit. Yet, the relatively low levels of such housing support, in a context of often severe relative poverty, points to the inadequacy of neo-liberal housing policy. As with issues of access to benefits more generally (see Chapter Seven), many households recounted tales of real difficulty in claiming housing benefits. In Poland and Slovakia, all housing benefits are temporary, meaning that households have to repeatedly reapply, submitting new documents to confirm their household budgetary situation each time. Those in receipt of benefits – or resident in municipal apartments – were subject to heightened surveillance and, as Mrs Giewon noted, must be exemplary tenants. One of Kraków city council's vice-presidents explained in interview how the city recently added to the criteria of eligibility for municipal housing a requirement that households had had no interventions from the police or municipal guard (*straż miejski*) in the last three years. Given that much of the need for social housing came from households which had experienced family breakdown, this was a demanding criterion. Tough eligibility criteria frequently restricted access, as households fell foul of occupancy rates or income categories. In two contrasting cases, Ms Myszka and her mother failed to qualify for housing benefit because her father, though estranged, was still registered in their home and, thus, his income was recorded as part of the household's budget, even though it was not, whilst Mrs Kwiatek had to wait longer to acquire a municipal apartment because her husband was *not* registered as living in her apartment, and thus his presence was not used in calculations of housing priority.

In an echo of British policy, the social housing sector in Poland and Slovakia is being progressively eroded. Sales from this sector exceed new construction and cash-strapped local authorities are reducing the availability of both social housing and housing benefit, at a time when housing market exclusion is growing. That local authorities exacerbate housing insecurities by imposing large fines on those who fall into rent arrears or 'opt' for illegal occupation of municipal property serves only to underline how unfit for purpose the social housing sector is in Poland and Slovakia. As in the UK context (S. Smith, 2008), this sector has been increasingly residualized – and stigmatized – with those living in social housing increasingly identified as dependent and problematic, lacking the enterprise, agency and self-respect to own their own homes and falling short of neo-liberal ideals. Owner occupation has quickly become normalized in central Europe, yet for those excluded from the sector, home ownership is an unattainable fantasy.

Housing Costs, Energy Liberalization and Poverty

The weakness of housing support structures meant that housing costs were a real burden, consuming a large part of some households' budgets. As Table 5.9 demonstrates, housing expenditures (rent or mortgage payments and utilities) accounted for, on average, 32% of total household

Table 5.9   Average proportion of household expenditure on housing by income groups

	≤60% of median income	61–100% of median income	101–140% of median income	≥141% of median income	Total
Petržalka					
Rent or mortgage repayments	8	4	5	6	5
Utilities	29	31	30	19	27
Total housing costs	37	35	35	25	32
Nowa Huta					
Rent or mortgage repayments	19	20	20	13	17
Utilities	15	18	17	13	15
Total housing costs	34	38	37	26	32

Source: Household survey

expenditures in both Petržalka and Nowa Huta, although the cost of utilities was a significantly higher proportion of expenditure in Petržalka than in Nowa Huta. The differences reflected both variations in housing tenure and in the price of utilities. On the one hand, while most households in Petržalka owned their own apartments and many purchased them outright at the point of privatization in the early 1990s, in Nowa Huta more households – especially poorer households – remained in the rental sector or burdened by mortgages. On the other hand, higher utility expenditures reflected the fuller liberalization of energy prices in Slovakia (Fankhausen & Tepic, 2007), although for many Nowa Huta households, the costs of utilities were hidden within their rent payments or service charges. In both cases, utility prices had risen dramatically in the post-socialist period and in many households the costs of electricity, heating and water exceeded the threshold of afford-ability (Lovei et al., 2000; Fankhausen & Tepic, 2007; Buzar, 2007).[8] There is, of course, considerable variation by income group, with these costs being a noticeably lower proportion of expenditure amongst higher income house-holds. Our interview research, moreover, revealed a number of cases where housing costs accounted for more than half of household expenditures, often in cases where rent arrears had led to fines being imposed on top of rent payments. In such cases, the magnitude – and immutability – of hous-ing costs had a crippling effect on all other aspects of the household budget, pushing households into palpable poverty.

A somewhat extreme example of the prohibitive costs of housing and the implications it had for adult children continuing to live with their parents is provided by the Veselá household in Petržalka. The household comprised two disabled pensioners, who received small disability pensions, and two adult children, one of whom was unemployed while the other worked as a low-paid security guard. The household lived below the risk of poverty level and nearly half (46%) of its monthly expenditure was spent on housing costs. This meant that meeting their housing costs was a monthly priority, as Mrs Veselá explained: 'Even if I didn't have enough money for food, the first thing I would do each month is to run to the post office to pay for the flat. I've lived in Bratislava for 32 years and each month this is my regular habit ...'. The pressing need to ensure that housing costs were met meant that there was no additional money to support the children in finding apartments of their own:

> I feel quite hopeless when I see people who can buy neighbouring flats for SKK2 million (€50,000) and they change everything from the ceiling to the floor for another half a million. You know what, I just can't believe this, I feel so hopeless because I don't know when I have three children and I wanted to educate them and give them some financial support, I can't imagine how my child would be able to buy a flat for SKK2 million ... they just can't afford it. Windows cost 100,000 (€2,500) and they just throw everything out and change everything. I always look from my window and my heart is bleeding when I see more changes going on in the neighbourhood. I don't know how people get the money for this ... it's not from honest work. Maybe they borrow the money for this ... I don't know ...

Consequently, her children had to stay at home:

> And what about my son – he's 24 – what if he wanted to get married? Where would he live? On the street? ... He tries to save as much money as possible in case he wants to get a mortgage for a flat. If he leaves ... I can't imagine where he could afford to go. He has to find a rich woman with a flat or house. If all three of my children stay at home, they can't go anywhere else.

For some, these excessive housing costs were incurred because the uneven inheritance of state socialist housing allocation had left them with apartments which were too big for their needs. Ms Senecka, a single woman in her late forties living in Nowa Huta, offers a good example of this. She had acquired her current apartment as a result of working in a neighbouring block as a caretaker but had come to realize that she could not maintain it, since it absorbed about three-quarters of her total expenditure. However, her room for manoeuvre was limited since her job meant that she had to live in one particular neighbourhood and the importance of her social networks meant that she was reluctant to move far anyway. Having until recently sub-let a room to a student, Ms Senecka was, at the time of interview, working with an intermediary to find a suitable exchange in a neighbouring block which would enable her to move to a one-roomed apartment, better suited to her needs and her budget. This example highlights the ways in which housing mobility – and the ability to address excessive housing costs – is limited by considerations of work, social networks and other spatialized connections. That so many of our households had lived in their current homes for so long – sometimes for up to 50 years – meant that many were reluctant to move, concerned about the adjustments which would have to be made to their social networks and their everyday geographies.

The cost of additional housing space was linked to the costs of energy in particular, with some households – mostly small, adult-only households – finding themselves heating and lighting empty rooms and tripping into energy poverty.[9] The dramatic increase in the costs of heating, hot water and electricity as a result of utilities privatization and price liberalization has had a profound impact on household budgets. In this context, households were having to engage in more and more inventive ways to reduce their housing costs, not only living in temperatures below 'comfort' level but also occasionally, acquiring electricity 'on the side'.[10]

Conclusions

This chapter has explored and analysed the ways in which households in Nowa Huta and Petržalka have negotiated the very rapid development of a marketized and commodified housing sector, the emerging cultures of housing investment, and some of the highest levels of owner occupation in Europe. These transformations have radically altered the housing outcomes of individuals and families in both Nowa Huta and Petržalka. The development of neo-liberalized housing markets has taken place alongside the marked residualization of social housing and the weak development of benefit systems, which are almost wholly inadequate for their purpose. Rising house prices during the post-accession boom reinforced issues of housing affordability, created real problems for low-income households and for newly formed households and led to some problematic housing outcomes, including rising homelessness, squatting and precarious housing situations. For many households, these transformations have been exacerbated by the liberalization of utility prices and the consequent emergence of energy poverty.

These processes of neo-liberalization resulted in a variety of housing practices oriented to mediating and negotiating – or domesticating – these transformations. These included exchanging or selling and 'downsizing' to realize housing assets; sharing homes between households in order to guarantee shelter for those unable to achieve or maintain housing independence; adapting or improving existing properties to better suit households' housing needs; and pooling all available financial resources to enable household members' first steps onto the housing ladder. These all point to the diversity of practices employed and clearly highlight the blurring of market and non-market housing practices. Some households, especially those with the time, money, skills and inherited housing advantages, benefited from these transformations and were, through the development of housing markets, able to extend their housing assets through purchase, development and construction. For many, though, the negotiation of housing market transformation has carried significant costs, not only the material costs of repair and maintenance but also concerns about privacy, independence and the possible loss of valuable social networks.

Housing transformations are articulated strongly with the spheres of care and work, and also with wider social networks, with access to finance, and with family absence or breakdown. The relationship between housing and family has pointed to disarticulations too, as housing provision conflicted with changing housing needs in the light of family transitions. All of these articulations point to spatialized connections between housing and the other spheres of everyday life that we explore in *Domesticating Neo-Liberalism*. These spatial interdependencies challenge the idea that households can easily sell their sometimes valuable housing assets to ease their budgets. Housing is more than simply a material asset: it is a home and the centre of interlocking geographies of everyday economic practice. But it is a material asset, and often one in which households could base other economic practices.

The uneven development of housing practices reflected some incredibly important historical articulations. The nature of housing allocation during state socialism and of privatization in the post-1989 period resulted in very uneven housing inheritances as the development of housing markets differentiated housing value and encouraged buyers and sellers to distinguish aesthetically and socially (Bourdieu, 1984) between properties. However, the legacies of state socialism were not only a result of housing allocation policies but also of the shortages, overcrowding and delayed maintenance which characterized the late socialist period. These uneven inheritances were played out within Nowa Huta and Petržalka, as micro-geographical differences have been exacerbated and as national and urban patterns of housing development have differentiated the two districts. Nowa Huta has a more striking legacy of social housing, one that has been enhanced still further in recent years as particularly impoverished, evicted and 'problem' tenants are regularly re-housed in the district. In Petržalka, housing privatization has been taken further, such that almost no social housing remains. Its location within Slovakia's capital has seen house price increases which have excluded significant parts of the population, even though it is also the site of some of the least expensive housing in the city.

The kinds of housing practices outlined here demonstrate the ways in which neo-liberal housing market transformations have been domesticated, quite literally, within households' homes. Some of these practices, such as squatting and illegal supplies of electricity, could be seen to be examples of explicit contestation, yet even these were perhaps better seen as extreme responses to austerity. In all these practices, though, we can identify the persistence of values that extend beyond the market, and the desire or, at least, the willingness to try to maintain these through relationships and practices which make poor housing outcomes just about tolerable. But in this tolerance, we see households once again taking the strain for excessive marketization. Without doubt, households in Nowa Huta and Petržalka have experienced very dramatic housing transformations in the post-socialist period. For many households, these changes have been for the worse, but their articulations with family, care and social networks and the significant investments made, even by the poorest households, in their properties maintain the value, broadly defined, of apartments, blocks and neighbourhoods. In this context, predictions of the 'ghettoization' of socialist era housing districts (Szelényi, 1996) fail to capture the dynamics, differentiations and micro-geographies of everyday life in post-socialist cities.

Chapter Six

Land and Food: Production, Consumption and Leisure

Introduction: The Meanings of Land and Food

As much recent work in the context of post-socialism has shown (*inter alia* Chelcea, 2002; Smith, 2002a; Burrell, 2003; Smith & Jehlička, 2007; Torsello, 2003), echoing wider analyses (Miller et al., 1998; Crewe, 2000), food and land not only make a critical contribution to households' attempts at social reproduction, but are also entwined with important social and symbolic values connected to family relationships, urban–rural connections, and national identity. These important connections reflect a number of characteristic features of the countries of the post-socialist world. These are countries with very recent rural pasts; their urban industrial populations – like those who live in Nowa Huta and Petržalka – are often only the first or second generation to live in cities and many can still identify grandparents or cousins, for example, who have lived off the land all their lives. For this reason, attachment to the land is a common trope in many families, and is one that is reinforced by struggles for land during the twentieth century.[1] In a still more recent historical past, each of the countries of ECE, Poland and Slovakia included, witnessed periods of complex food politics in late socialism, when food shortages and food price hikes were key features of everyday life and provoked more or less political responses (Chase, 1983; Kenney, 1999). The absence of key food products in the formal spaces of provision and consumption fed an expansion of domestic production and of the social – and economic – capital of those households with productive rural connections.

These inherited landscapes of food provisioning and attachments to land have, in the post-socialist era, rapidly come into contact with new spheres, circuits and imaginaries. Both food and land have been rapidly commodified, as international markets in both have been developed as part of the process of economic transformation, and the relationship between domestic agriculture (including the small-scale, subsistence and urban production of food) and food consumption has been transformed. On the one hand, the retail market has been radically remade with both domestic and foreign firms developing and redeveloping retail sites, including markets, chains of neighbourhood shops, supermarkets and hypermarkets. On the other, the development of land markets has enabled and encouraged shifting land use, especially in urban hinterlands, as pressures for development, not only of housing and infrastructures (in particular, roads) but also, paradoxically, new shopping malls, has seen land previously given over to food production subsumed into more thoroughly urban uses.

This chapter explores households' attempts to understand and negotiate these interrelated transformations. It begins by exploring the domestic production of food and pays attention to the history of such practices, the meaning – economic and social – of land ownership and food production, and the limits and threats to the domestic production of food. This discussion of the threats to domestic production includes an analysis of the commodification of land and the growing development pressures on urban allotments in Petržalka and Nowa Huta. For many without access to land, the connection to home-grown food relies on access to circuits of food which flow through familial and social networks, what Smollet (1989) called 'the economy of jars'. The following section of this chapter, then, examines the ways in which households exchange and gift home-produced and home-processed food within their social and kinship networks. This highlights both the social and economic importance of such exchanges and their cultural value, reflecting the inheritance of skills and interests, such as gardening and cooking. For the majority of our households, however, the purchase of food in markets and shops is the main means for acquiring food. Thus, the final section explores households' food shopping practices, exploring not only where they shop and why, but also tracing the connections between food shopping and other household economic practices (including food production and processing, but also work, caring and budgeting).

Land and the Domestic Production of Food

The close articulation between urban households and rural and peri-urban land has been a major and continuing issue in studies of the economic practices and social reproduction of urban households in Central Europe. The relatively recent, and in some cases continuing, reverberation of peasant economies across the region – reflecting relatively late industrialization and rural–urban migration patterns in the post-war period – mean that many urbanized households retain close connections to rural and peri-urban areas

(Clarke et al., 2000; S. Clarke, 2002; Smith, 2002a, 2007). In 1921 in the former Czechoslovakia, for example, 61% of the Slovak population were employed in agriculture, compared to only 32% in the Czech Lands, and three-quarters of the Slovak population lived in rural areas in 1930 (N. Swain, 1994: 8–9). Furthermore, the process of post-war urbanization and the construction of urban housing districts such as Nowa Huta and Petržalka were accompanied by the expansion of vibrant allotment societies and urban gardening provision, often on the basis of earlier development (Bellows, 2004). Indeed, throughout the state socialist era, continuing access to land, either in the form of historic family plots or urban allotments, provided important means with which households sought to achieve social reproduction. The continuing use of allotments and other gardens both rested on the cultivation skills and practices inherited from rural pasts and ensured the survival of these skills into the current period (Smith, 2002a) (Plates 6.1, 6.2 and 6.3).

These plots and these practices have been seen as a private space which offered some autonomy and some maintenance of tradition that articulated with the regulated and modern spaces of the state (such as the workplace and the housing block) (Smith, 2002a). At the same time, private plots

Plate 6.1 Vegetable plot on an allotment in Nowa Huta

Plate 6.2   Workers' allotment garden, Nowa Huta

Plate 6.3   Allotment garden and small cottage, Petržalka

served a number of explicit purposes for the state. For example, Bellows (2004: 257) notes that 'allotments served the state to distance and isolate individuals from each other because workers went directly to their gardens from work and did not spend time socializing'. Allotments supported state-led economic policies during the socialist period by enabling these states to attract agrarian labour to new industries in towns and cities and to ease the transformation of peasants into workers (Siemieńska, 1967). In the short-age years of late socialism, they also mitigated these states' inability to provide food for their populations by offering alternative sources of produce not only to allotment owners but also to wider populations through expanded rights of sale and through the 'charitable' acts of allotment associations (Bellows, 2004).

On the eve of transition, vast numbers of the population in both Poland and Slovakia, and across ECE more generally, had access to land for production and for leisure. In Poland in 1985, some 2.7 million families – a quarter of the population – were engaged in allotment gardening (Kleer, 1987). This continuing importance points to a need to consider the changing role of allotments through the transformations since 1989, a question that has attracted much debate in recent years. For many analysts of household survival strategies in post-socialist societies, land is seen as critical to household sustenance in the context of the austerity and inequality brought about by neo-liberal transformations because it provides vital additional food. For example, Seeth et al.'s study of three Russian regions 'addresses the question of how households *respond* to the economic stress of the transition economy' (1998: 1611; our emphasis) and seeks to understand how households 'cope with poverty by increasing subsistence food production'.

However, others have argued that food production is a practice more ambiguous than one of solely survival in times of austerity, and that it should be understood at the intersection of class and wider socio-economic change (S. Clarke, 2002; Smith, 2002a). Simon Clarke (2002) has argued that it is not the poorest households who engage in domestic food production. Rather, what Clarke calls the 'dacha economy' in Russia is seen as a relatively inefficient form of food production, which is both time consuming and undertaken largely by middle-income groups who can afford to do so. It is not therefore a survival strategy developed in response to employment loss and declining income. Similarly, Meurs (2002) has suggested, in the context of Bulgaria, that there has been no absolute growth of self-provisioning in the context of post-socialism, but rather a truncation of formal wage earning opportunities that gives domestic food production greater relative weight in household budgets. Food provisioning is not reducible to wider processes of commodification and class transformation, but is articulated with them in ways which highlight how 'peasant' legacies and the cultural economies of land and farming, and of the garden, have today become articulated with wider political economies of neo-liberalism (Smith, 2002a).

These themes echo through our analyses of domestic self-provisioning in Nowa Huta and Petržalka, where access to land was unevenly distributed and reflected a range of different household practices, some social and some economic. Around three-quarters of Nowa Huta households and 70% of Petržalka households across all income categories had no access to any kind of land (defined as an allotment, a plot of land, a kitchen garden or a piece of land connected to a recreational cottage) (Table 6.1). They either relied upon market provisioning of food and/or on the receipt of food from plots of land used by relatives or friends (see below). However, around a quarter of households – a similar level to Polish national figures – did have access to land and, for many, the food produced on that land contributed in important ways to the diversity of their economic practices and their negotiation of neo-liberal change. Those with the lowest incomes, relative to the regional median, were least likely to have access to land. In both districts, it was households in the highest income group who also had the highest level of access to land. In Nowa Huta, in particular, the preponderance of higher income groups using land is partly explained by the historical distribution of allotments through the workplace (Bellows, 2004), meaning that for some households in good, stable employment in former state-owned enterprises, ownership of an allotment was an additional benefit. The main reason, however, for such an uneven distribution of allotment ownership is that not only were there very few *significant* financial advantages derived from using land, but also, moreover, the costs of allotment cultivation could be prohibitive.

Beyond questions of income, those using allotments were distributed across a range of social groups. Unlike some previous research which has pointed to the unevenly gendered nature of work on domestic land (Meurs, 2002; Smith, 2002a, 2002c), our research suggested that both men and women took primary responsibility for work on allotments and plots (Table 6.2), often with numerous family members, of both genders, engaging in activity on the land. However, the generational profile of allotment users was markedly different from that of the surveyed population as a whole (Table 6.3). Older generations, especially those who had retired and those in middle-age, were much more likely to be engaged in work on the land than younger generations. This echoes patterns more widely, in Poland at least, where almost half of all allotment holders are retired (Polski Związek Działkowców, 2008) and is suggestive of a wider concern that the necessary skills and knowledge required to maintain an allotment are not being handed down through generations.

However, it is important to note that, even if one family member was primarily responsible for work on the plot, many others were drawn in, at

Table 6.1 Access to land by income categories

Income category	Households with access to land			Households without access to land		
	No.	% of income category	% of households with land	No.	% of income category	% of households without land
Nowa Huta						
≤60% median income	2	10	4	18	90	12
61–100% median income	10	28	20	26	72	17
101–140% median income	10	20	20	39	80	26
≥141% median income	27	28	55	68	72	45
Total	49		100	151		100
Petržalka						
≤60% median income	5	23	11	17	77	16
61–100% median income	8	15	18	46	85	44
101–140% median income	12	43	27	16	57	15
≥141% median income	19	42	43	26	58	25
Total	44		100	105		100

Source: Household survey

Table 6.2 Gender of the main household members with responsibility for working on land

	Men (%)	*Women (%)*
Nowa Huta	52	48
Petržalka	50	50

Source: Household survey

Table 6.3 Generational structure of household members working on household plots (compared to surveyed populations)

	Nowa Huta		*Petržalka*	
Period of birth	*% of those working on land*	*% of total household members*	*% of those working on land*	*% of total household members*
Before 1940	12	7	6	4
1941–54	55	19	50	24
1955–69	27	21	38	19
1970–89	6	35	6	41
After 1989	0	18	0	12

Source: Household survey

particular times during the season and on a casual basis. Households with land also had to have access to the available labour to work on the plot and this proved increasingly difficult for some households as the domestic production of food was but one part of a their diverse economic practices. Most household members were simultaneously engaged in employment and in other social and economic roles (caring, studying, etc.) and, as we detail in Chapters Four and Seven, neo-liberal transformations in these spheres have resulted in them consuming more and more of households' time. Given the relatively small size of most plots, most of the labour employed on land was that of immediate household members, although on some plots neighbours, friends or other relatives were also involved. In most cases, work on land was undertaken in free time and involved very little by way of payment, in cash or in kind. Only three households with land in Petržalka, and six in Nowa Huta, provided payment in kind to others who worked on the plot, and just three households in Nowa Huta paid people who worked on their plots in cash. As we noted in Chapter Four, work on allotments was often performed by those household members who were the least productive in the formal economy and involved skills acquired in the workplace. In this way, 'a household's surplus labour (embodied in the products of the land) is used to sustain a network of familial and friendship relations which embed families and individuals in local communities' (Smith, 2002a: 243).

However, financial pressures had been starting to impact on usage in important ways. Amongst those households without access to land in Nowa Huta and Petržalka, 33% and 43% respectively reported that they were unable to afford to keep a plot of land. Among the poorest households involved in the research, the inability to afford the use of land as a factor in not having access to it increased to 44% of households in Nowa Huta and 72% in Petržalka. For some of those with access to land, costs were a primary explanation for their withdrawal from direct ownership or production. Such costs, however, related not only to the investments in seeds and other inputs, but also to the financial and temporal expense of travel, as Ms Senecka, a single woman in her late forties living in Nowa Huta above the median income, explained:

> We do grow things, but not carrots or parsnips, simply because you need to spend almost three hours on the return journey. If we're having a heatwave then you have go there practically every day to water. So it just doesn't pay. [You can get there] by one bus, but it goes all round the houses … it goes through all the neighbourhoods it possibly could. And it simply takes up lots of time – and then when you get there you have to walk a bit. So it just doesn't pay to grow carrots there.

The pressures of time were exacerbated by the need, real and perceived, to spend more time at work to maintain security of employment (see Chapter Four) and by the rationalization and increasing cost of public transport, which meant that travelling to allotments became more difficult and more time consuming. For some, however, related developments offered a partial solution. Until both parents lost their jobs (through unemployment and early retirement), the Dawidowicz family in Nowa Huta had travelled to their allotment in 10 minutes in their family car. Since giving up their car, they had eased the journey to their allotment somewhat by taking a hypermarket's free bus half the way. Yet, they still had to walk a further 3 kilometres, making each journey last about one and a half hours. The cost of bus tickets, added to other rising costs, had caused a number of the households in our study to all but withdraw from growing fruit and vegetables on their plots. Cost, however, was not the only deterrent. Mr and Mrs Chilkiewicz, a Nowa Huta couple in their late fifties, had recently been forced by vandalism to give up the allotment which had been used by the family for 30 years to grow carrots, parsnips, celery, radishes, peaches, apples, pears, cherries and plums (see also Round, 2006b).

Reinforcing this question of production costs, many of the poorer house-holds noted that they would happily take on an allotment, if their financial position were stronger. In many of these cases of wished-for allotment own-ership, the key motivation was the cultivation of fruit and vegetables to sup-port the family diet and reduce retail expenditures, highlighting the ways in which self-provisioning is seen to underpin other forms of consumption (Smith, 2002a). This desire to grow food was, however, inflected with a strongly felt commitment to *self*-provisioning, as Mrs Szwacz, an elderly widow living in Nowa Huta below the median income, explains:

> I would grow vegetables, if [the land] was big enough, I would grow potatoes, and yes, vegetables, and some flowers. I like flowers. With pleasure I would have an allotment, but who would give me one? Yes, if someone gave me an allotment, with pleasure I'd plant myself some potatoes, vegetables; my own carrots, parsnips I'd have on an allotment.

Mrs Szwacz's sentiments were echoed by others, especially those living in small, cramped apartments, who stressed the more-than-economic motiva-tion for an allotment, highlighting their desire for some of their own space, to reduce their shopping bills, and to secure good food in their families' diets. Of course, these aspirations do not reflect the realities of allotment ownership, but do point to a continued valuation of land cultivation.

The costs and concerns of producing food on allotments – and the con-centration of ownership amongst wealthier households – connect to the more-than-economic motivation that our poorer households flag. Of the surveyed households with access to land, many were in fact using a plot or allotment primarily for leisure purposes (Table 6.4), for growing flowers,[2] for barbecues, for space beyond the city. For example, the Panák household in Petržalka, consisting of a man in well-paid work and his employed wife, had a plot approximately 40 kilometres from Bratislava. They travelled there by car each weekend, but they only grew a little food. The allotment mainly provided a place to relax and to spend free time: 'you cannot calculate the fact that the journey there and back is so expensive ... it is not only about growing food, but also to relax and to spend time on our hobbies'. As Mr Panák explained:

> I can buy very cheap vegetables. And if I have to water the plants, and to go by car only to do this, the whole thing would be very expensive. I only have a bit of wine ... but we provide very good company there, now and then we have a barbecue party outside and such like.

Another Petržalka family with two working adults and one small child, who had a household income below the regional median, had a plot of land

Table 6.4   Primary purpose of having access to land

	Petržalka		Nowa Huta	
	No. of households	%	No. of households	%
Basic source of food	0	0	1	2
Additional food	18	44	16	37
Source of income for rainy day	2	5	1	2
Hobby	16	39	15	35
Other	5	12	10	23
Total	41	100	43	100

Note: The different reported column totals from those in Table 6.1 reflect different response rates to this question in the household survey
Source: Household survey

50 kilometres from Bratislava. They grew lots of food, vegetables and fruit, and made preserves. But this was a secondary activity for them, because the main reason for using the land was to allow them to be out of the city and to meet with their extended family. Of those households in both Nowa Huta and Petržalka whose allotments were closer to home, a number regularly visited during the week and for long weekends, often staying in the small chalets, or *altanki* (in Poland) and *chaty* (in Slovakia), that they had built there. For many families, the allotment was thus an important social site, not only for gathering extended family but also for meeting wider circles of friends. Indeed, for some households, having access to a plot of land provided the basis for the development of new social networks. For example, the Portiš household from Petržalka had a plot of land in another part of the city, which they bought when they moved to Petržalka having sold a larger house in another part of Bratislava in order to assist their adult children to purchase their own apartments (Chapter Five). Mr Portiš, who is retired, told us:

> we have [a garden] where we have a cottage, an excellent cellar, our own sitting area with electricity. In the cottage, we have a small bedroom and kitchen. We have fruit trees and grow vegetables. We spend our free time there and meet with friends there to socialize, where we've also made lots of new friends.

In other cases, the time spent on allotments made up for the loss of holidays in the post-socialist era, as the decline of enterprise subsidies for vacations and increasing work pressure eroded the longer breaks previously taken (Stenning, 2005a). For some of these more recreational users, allotment ownership was a more a recent practice, taken up since 1989 in an attempt to find some time and space for relaxation in an increasingly pressured world of work. For others, spending time on the allotment was an important activity in the light of redundancy: a number of older men amongst our interviewees, in particular, had increased the time they spent on their allotments, tending their plants and socializing with their neighbours, after they had lost their jobs through unemployment or incapacity. Thus, as Round (2006b) also suggests, allotments were critical in the development and maintenance of social networks, within the context of increasingly atomized and neo-liberal work relations. Of course, the distinction between allotments as sites of cultivation and sites of socializing is not unambiguous, and these practices often reinforced each other. As Mrs Byjoch from Nowa Huta explained, developing relationships with allotment neighbours aided the process of cultivation through the sharing of seeds and seedlings, and of knowledge:

Yes [...] for example he [her allotment neighbour] brings me green beans, because I do not have green beans. Apart from that he is there from early spring till late autumn. He is there non-stop, so he can grow anything. For example, he gave us raspberry seedlings, and I have raspberries now. We cannot grow parsley, neither him nor I; it doesn't ever want to grow. So we are going to try another one, a local one.

Of those households with access to land, nearly half in Petržalka and over a third in Nowa Huta used their land as an additional source of food. Amongst our research households, allotments produced all manner of fruit and vegetables,[3] as well as, in some cases, also being the site of chicken and rabbit rearing.[4] While virtually no households used land to provide basic food, the additional role that food produced on plots of land played was important for many, enabling households to reduce the proportion of cash expended on food items. For some households, the produce grown on their allotments accounted for approximately one-third of their fruit and vegetable consumption (Tables 6.5 and 6.6). For those households in serious financial difficulties, access to land played a particularly important role in mitigating their difficulties in affording food in the market economy. For example, the Holmanovás in Petržalka were a poor household, comprising a woman who had taken early retirement to care for her elderly mother and her daughter, who engaged in very careful shopping practices (see below) and for whom the use of an allotment in another part of the city was absolutely critical. Although travelling to the allotment was complicated, they used the plot to grow fruit and vegetables in order to reserve their money for commodified transactions in local shops and supermarkets. They processed most of the food they grew and stored any surpluses for the future. As Mrs Holmanová explained: 'I appreciate everything, each carrot,

Table 6.5 Average proportion of household expenditure on food, leisure and savings (% of total household expenditure)

	Nowa Huta		Petržalka	
	Households with access to land	Households without access to land	Households with access to land	Households without access to land
Food	29	33	32	35
Leisure	3	3	4	3
Savings	2	3	8	3

Source: Household survey

Table 6.6 Average household provisioning of vegetables and fruit (% of average total household consumption on each item)

	All households with access to land	Households with access to land, for which production provides basic or additional food	Households without access to land
Nowa Huta			
% vegetables bought	79	60	93
% vegetables produced	15	33	0
% vegetables received	7	7	7
% fruit bought	77	65	94
% fruit produced	17	31	0
% fruit received	6	4	6
Petržalka			
% vegetables bought	76	65	89
% vegetables produced	21	32	0
% vegetables received	2	4	11
% fruit bought	75	62	91
% fruit produced	23	36	0
% fruit received	2	2	10

Source: Household survey

all the parsley … we have fruit, apricots, peaches, plums, cherries … the surplus is always for processing … I couldn't afford it otherwise.'

The ability to use land, and to enter into the wider economy of reciprocity through the products of land, was fundamentally connected to the wider resources and assets to which households had access. The income from formal employment allowed households to subsidize relatively inefficient forms of food production and the availability of other assets, such as a car to travel to a distant plot or enough space at home for the storage of the jars of pickles and preserves, also shaped households' ability to work the land. But households did not enter into such activity as simply rational, profit-seeking, sufficing economic subjects; they drew upon a range of economic practices that had cultural as well as economic meaning. The products of land did, of course, provide economic resources to households, which could then be offset against expenditures in the market, but this was not the only set of rationales within which food cultivation was embedded.

Land and Land Development

These domestic limits to allotment activity were not the only ones that threatened food production in Nowa Huta and Petržalka. In recent years, the development of land markets and the pressure to release land for urban development have seen allotment gardens, often located in key development sites on the edges of towns and cities, become the focus of potential land conflicts. In both Bratislava and Kraków, the desire to establish the respective city regions at the forefront of national and regional economic development processes and to create residential and commercial spaces for thriving cities meant that there are particular pressures to release land for development. In Petržalka, the city planning authorities have designated six of the seven main allotment sites for development, ranging from offices to shopping centres (Územný plán hlavného mesta Slovenskej republiky Bratislavy, 2007).[5] In Nowa Huta, one of the largest allotment sites is threatened by the mooted construction of a new arterial route skimming the northern edge of the Kraków conurbation. This is just one example of similar pressures across Poland,[6] where contentious political debates have been taking place over the proposed wholesale reclassification of urban agricultural land as available for investment (*Warsaw Business Journal*, 2008). The legislation, proposed by a centre-right Civic Platform MP and supported by business groups in an attempt to 'enliven' urban economies (tvn24.pl, 2008), was opposed by the allotment owners' union (Polski Związek Działkowców, PZD) and vetoed by Poland's president, Lech Kaczyński. This followed related debates about the forms of ownership which dominate Poland's allotments. As it stands, those who occupy allotments are only lease-holders and have very limited rights of sale; they can pass the use rights to family members but formal ownership of every plot resides with the local branch of the PZD. This restricts the potential sale of land for speculation or investment, and proposed moves to create full ownership rights are being strongly resisted by the PZD (Dziennik Polski, 2007). In Petržalka only private land rather than allotments can be sold but there remain complex and somewhat opaque property rights surrounding most of the urban allotments in Bratislava.[7] These debates over ownership articulate with concerns that the ageing of the population engaged in using household plots may increase expectations of the sale of land for development as it is no longer seen to be important for household food production.

In other parts of East Central Europe, urban and peri-urban allotments have witnessed development pressures as poorer households informally convert their garden sheds or huts to residential use (Timár, 1998).[8] In neither Poland nor Slovakia is there much evidence of allotment sites being informally taken over by residential development in this way, but our research presented some evidence that older generations are living on their allotments in warmer weather, both through choice and to relieve pressure in the family home (see Chapter Five). For a small number of households, the ownership of land was linked not to food production and recreation, but to housing development, either as an investment for the future or as a means of developing alternative housing strategies for different generations. For example, the Wolaks, a young Nowa Huta family living well above the median income, had bought some development land outside of Kraków, later adding to this with a neighbouring plot which was purchased from a mortgage raised on an apartment. This process of land and property acquisition was especially found among higher income households who had the financial resources to use land in this way, and who had other relevant resources, such as a car, which enabled regular and timely access. In this sense, land development represented a strong process of asset reproduction among wealthier households. For others, however, the sale of land, provided important resources for poorer households, particularly during periods when they may be struggling – for a variety of reasons – to sustain the use of the area of land they own or have access to. For example, in Petržalka, one of our respondents, a divorced woman, sold her allotment located in Rača (another part of the city) because her adult daughters were neither interested nor able to help her look after the plot any more. Although it had been an important asset, the allotment had become useless without the social and other material assets needed to work it. Through the sale, she converted an unusable asset into capital that eased her household budget.

Social Networks and the Circulation of Food

As we have already suggested, the flows of products from allotments and other plots rarely stayed within the household. Those owning land were often embedded in intricate networks of exchange, whilst those without direct access to land often sought to source fresh and processed fruit and vegetables from their land-owning family and friends. However, integration into such an economy of favours resonated beyond just the poorest households. The ability to provide labour at the weekends on rural plots, the receipt of vegetables, meat, and fruit in exchange for the provision of labour, and the wider involvement in an 'economy of jars', all act to link the urban, peri-urban and the rural economy of domestic food production.

For those households that produced and procured food, the overwhelming majority of produce *was* kept within the household itself. This was especially true of poorer households with between 80% and 100% of vegetable and fruit production used by the household. Many non-producing households were, however, in receipt of food produced by friends and family. For some, these were local connections within Nowa Huta or Petržalka; for others, they revolved around long-distance and long-standing connections with the countryside, often with home villages where siblings, aunts and uncles, or cousins continued to cultivate food on family plots. As we noted in Chapter Four, the Slamkovás from Petržalka, comprising a divorced woman who worked as a low-paid nursery school teacher and her student daughter, received about 70% of their consumption of vegetables, fruit and animal products from a family plot in Galanta, some 60 kilometres from Bratislava, in return for work on the plot and other assistance to their rural family. Because the Slamkovás very often found themselves in financial difficulties, the food they received represented a very important part of their overall consumption:

> they give us everything, mainly in summer, fruit, vegetables; we have everything from them, so it is good … sometimes also poultry, hens, rabbits … we don't buy expensive food, only cheap Tesco products and fruit and vegetables we have from relatives …

Whilst the Slamková household in Petržalka accessed a significant part of its diet from their family's plot, for others such food was simply a supplement to their diet, albeit an important one. Neither the Stanis nor Pustelak households in Nowa Huta, both living below the median income, bought any potatoes on the open market, instead relying on supplies from friends or family. The Juszczaks, a young couple keen on providing good food for their small daughter, received vegetables, potatoes and preserves from Mr Juszczak's grandfather's plot (cultivated and processed by Mr Juszczak's mother) and apples from a friend who owned an orchard in eastern Poland. Mrs Idziak, a single Nowa Huta pensioner, not only processed the peppers, tomatoes and plums that she received from a friend's garden for herself, but also then distributed them to her children and her neighbours. In poorer households, the close articulation of the urban and the rural economy of domestic food production, and the products that flowed from it, enabled a level of consumption – in quantitative and qualitative terms – that would otherwise have been impossible to achieve. The Šenzová household in Petržalka, for example, struggled to make ends meet from their insecure and poorly paid work, yet their apartment was full of jars of products from Mr Šenzová's mother's family plot. Despite the fact that they provided very little by way of direct input to the production of food on the plot, they estimated that these products provided about 20% of their consumption of fruit and vegetables.

These circuits of food relate not only to food produced on household land, but also to products gathered or bought and then processed. Approximately 50 of our interviewed households in each district (about one-third of Petržalka households and one in four Nowa Huta households) were involved in gathering mushrooms, picking berries, fishing or some other form of food procurement. These were less likely to be the poorest households, suggesting that wealthier households not only had the resources to facilitate this (cars, money for fishing licences, access to land) but also the time to dedicate to such activities (which was often associated with holidays and time away from the city). As Chapters Four and Seven also demonstrate, the poorest households were often preoccupied by multiple jobs or the search for work, by negotiations with social services, and by caring responsibilities, or were fearful that time spent away from work would compromise their job security. Yet, many of those households who did not procure or gather food for processing did buy fruit for juicing and jamming, and cucumbers and mushrooms for pickling, such that the processing of food combined both commodified and non-commodified circuits. The Pustelak household in Nowa Huta, for example, who had no access to an allotment, were engaged in a deep and complex economy of pickling and reciprocity. While they used a good deal of products bought commercially in this process, they also relied on products supplied from friends' allotments: 'through friendship we help each other, simply'. The processing of food also sustained a wider, partially commodified network of family and close friends. As Mrs Šenzová, a respondent in Petržalka, explained:

> Yes, we buy [fruit for pickling]. We do some research locally and find the cheapest, and my husband's mother gives us a lot of food and because she is on her own she doesn't need so much herself ... Our neighbours and friends are used to us, as kind of wholesalers of pickled cucumbers for example which they offer to us for a symbolic price.

In some households, as we explore further in Chapter Seven, the exchange of processed food bled into wider shared practices of cooking and eating.

Mothers and daughters shared home-made food, particularly traditional dishes (such as *pierogi* and *gołąbki*[9] in Nowa Huta and *bryndzové halušky*[10] in Petržalka). Such practices reflected not only relations of care, but also concern about the transmission of traditional recipes. At times, these practices spilt over into socially mediated connections of shared cooking and eating within and beyond the family, as Mrs Pustelak explains:

> Yeah, it used to be that we actually ate our dinner at their [husband's parents] place. Later, in turn, I cooked. I also cooked for two homes, and it stays like that until now, we simply go to and fro … we go to and fro with food; sometimes it looks funny, my husband with some pot, me with a cake tin, non stop. It's very important, and in the block as well.

The concern about the transmission of these culinary practices echoes that related to gardening know-how. Interviewees noted how they had less and less time to commit to pickling and preserving and that, moreover, the purchase of such goods was easier, and sometimes cheaper, in supermarkets and hypermarkets. For others, however, the limits to pickling and preserving were enforced by their small homes. Mrs Kwiatek, for example, a trained cook living on a very low income in a marginal housing block in Nowa Huta, expressed a desire to prepare and store more food but explained: 'I find that it's not worth it, because we don't have anywhere to store it. This [her apartment] is just $18\,m^2$ and we don't have anywhere to keep it.'

The Transformation of Retail Landscapes and Food Consumption Practices

As these examples of processing and pickling suggest, there are numerous articulations between the commodified and non-commodified sectors. Most households, even those which grew a significant proportion of their fruit and vegetables, relied primarily on purchased food to meet their dietary needs (Table 6.6). These patterns point to the ways in which households' engagements with the retail sphere were mediated by, and articulated with, other economic practices; the purchase and production of food were not distinct spheres.

As a result, the particular transformations of food retailing[11] deserve attention. Changing culinary and consumption practices reflect the restructuring of this sector as much as changing patterns of self-provisioning and, as we have already suggested, the development of retail is one of the forces encroaching on allotment land. During state socialism, the retail sector was noticeably underdeveloped as the focus of investment and planning was centred on the more productive manufacturing sector (Michalak, 2001).

Retail provision was sparse and unvaried, and shopping was commonly characterized as an unrewarding and difficult practice, all the more so as the scarcities and rationing of the late socialist period led to empty shelves and still more restricted choice. Although there is evidence that state socialist shops were domesticated and that, for some, shopping was quite an animated, social experience (Búriková, 2004; Stenning, 2005b), it is clear that by the 1980s the purchase of food and other consumer goods was marked by delay and frustration. These difficulties provoked some innovative responses. Not only did domestic production become more important, as we have discussed above, but individuals, families and communities cultivated networks of alternative supply, developed queue committees to manage the ubiquitous lines in shops, and became increasingly adept at repair and recycling (Hraba, 1985; Chase, 1983; Burrell, 2003; Chelcea, 2002). In part because of its underdevelopment during state socialism, after 1989, the restructuring of retail was one of the earliest and most rapid processes of corporate transformation, as individual stores and small chains were privatized, cooperative ventures were created and spontaneous retail spaces, such as kiosks, stalls and bazaars, emerged on the streets of towns and villages (Michalak, 2001). This early restructuring has had a lasting impact on the retail landscapes of post-socialist cities, but further change has been driven by the incursion of major international (mostly West European) retailers into regional markets (Wrigley, 2000).

The entry of major international retailers into Central European markets dates to the mid-1990s (Michalak, 2001) when German and British firms, in particular, began to buy up existing retail chains and to establish new stores on greenfield sites. The most marked growth in large format stores (hypermarkets and supermarkets) came, however, during the late 1990s and early 2000s. In Poland, from 1997 to 2005, the number of hypermarkets grew from 22 to 264, whilst in Slovakia, between 2000 and 2006, the number grew from 2 to 83 (Machnicka, 2005; GfK Slovakia and INCOMA, 2006). This expansion involved many of the leading European retailers, such as Tesco, Carrefour and Kaufland (Plate 6.4). Notwithstanding this general picture, there are some important contrasts between the Polish and Slovak experiences. Despite the fact that hypermarkets entered the market earlier in Poland and that, in 2005, there were more than three times as many hypermarkets in Poland as in Slovakia, the spread of hypermarkets in Poland is much sparser. In Poland there were just 6 hypermarkets per million inhabitants, compared with 12 per million in Slovakia (GfK Slovakia and INCOMA, 2006; Machnicka, 2005). Most hypermarkets are located close to the main consumer markets, in larger towns and cities, where they tend to have an increasingly dominant position in the market. In Poland, recent years have seen something of a backlash, nationally and locally, against hypermarkets as concerns have been raised about their impact on employment, on local shops

Plate 6.4   Carrefour Hypermarket in Nowa Huta

and independent traders, and on lifestyles (Gardawski, 2002; Cienski & Buckley, 2005; McLaughlin, 2005; Hardy et al., 2008; Tchorek, 2008). In Slovakia by contrast, hypermarket development has continued apace. In both countries, alongside the growth of hypermarkets, there has also been a significant expansion of no-frills supermarkets or discounters. Over half of all 'modern' outlets in Poland are discounters (Machnicka, 2005: 2), such as Biedronka (a previously domestic chain bought by the Portuguese firm Jeronimo Martins in 1998), Netto and Lidl. These discounters locate in the small towns and on peripheral housing estates often avoided by larger hypermarkets in Poland, and are often more easily accessible on foot, frequently being located within neighbourhoods and amongst tower blocks.

In Poland, foreign multinationals' share of retail turnover is relatively low (just 8% in 1998 (Michalak, 2001: 497)) and 'large format' stores (hypermarkets, supermarkets and discounters), regardless of ownership, accounted for just a quarter of the grocery market in 2005 (Szaleniec, 2008). In Slovakia, by contrast, the market share of the 'large format' retail sector was over 50% in 2003 while almost half of the ownership share of the top 50 retail firms was non-Slovak, suggesting a higher degree of internationalization in Slovakia (FAO, 2005). The relatively small size of the Slovak market and increasing internationalization of ownership has meant that levels of competition are high, leading both Carrefour and Ahold to sell their Slovak stores in 2008. In Poland, small, domestic retail outlets continue to dominate the retail landscape, despite the physical presence of hypermarkets. Without doubt the role of hypermarkets and large supermarkets is growing but in Poland, in 2004, less than half of all households shopped in large supermarkets (CBOS, 2008b: 3). Small, local shops (with three tills at the most) were the favoured source of purchased food, whilst significant numbers also shopped at markets and street stalls. The local shop sector has itself been transformed in recent years with a small number of domestic chains (such as Żabka, ABC, Lewiatan, and Groszek in Poland)[12] consolidating ownership or management, sometimes through franchises. Indeed, the persistent importance of this segment of the retail sector has led some foreign supermarkets to enter this market by 'going compact' (Machnicka, 2005: 3) and either launching their own neighbourhood or convenience chains or seeking to acquire smaller chains.

In these patterns, it is already clear that major European retailers have developed responsive strategies to the particular retail routines of Poles and Slovaks. In this sense, then, these foreign retailers have been domesticated.[13] However, Poles and Slovaks have had to negotiate these changing retail landscapes, too, and these processes have been mediated by very uneven patterns of access and usage. Within Nowa Huta and Petržalka, class, location, age and preference all played a part in shaping households' shopping practices, but shopping was a sphere in which some of the distinctions between the experiences of Petržalka and Nowa Huta were clearest, reflecting both national differences and the particular retail and consumption histories of the districts themselves. However, as a result of significant, spatially concentrated markets, under-provision during state socialism, and available land, both districts are marked by a significant presence of foreign retailers. In Petržalka, Tesco, Carrefour, Kaufland, Terno, Albert, and Lidl all had a presence, while in Nowa Huta, Carrefour, Geant, Lidl, Biedronka and a number of smaller chains had local outlets.

In general, hypermarkets were seen more positively in Petržalka than in Nowa Huta. Until the 1990s it was widely recognized that Petržalka had a very underdeveloped service economy, particularly relating to retail outlets (Mládek, 1994). More recent research has suggested that people from Petržalka usually see the new consumption possibilities offered by the expansion of hypermarkets very positively, despite some of their environmental consequences, the consequent loss of open land and the impacts of noise on local residents (Ira, 2003). In our research, too, many Petržalka households, especially those on lower incomes, saw the expansion of hypermarkets as positive. Yet, while poorer households in Petržalka shopped in hypermarkets to access lower prices, others noted that the absence of other local stores meant there was little real choice. In Nowa Huta, by contrast, few households expressed a preference for hypermarket shopping; most continued to shop in small local stores, often shopping daily to meet needs for fresh food, with only occasional visits to hypermarkets for bulk items. The few households that did choose to shop regularly in hypermarkets were wealthier, time-poor households who could use their cars to do large, weekly shops. The majority rarely saw hypermarket prices as cheaper, and were also dissuaded from shopping in larger, foreign-owned stores by concerns about the quality of food products, by their size and anonymity, by fears that they would spend too much in a store with such choice, and, occasionally, by concerns about the employment practices of foreign retailers (reflecting widespread public debate over this issue; Hardy et al., 2008). Independent traders in Nowa Huta have themselves been active in contesting and mediating the impact of foreign retailers in the district, through the establishment of the Małopolskie Stowarzyszenie Kupców i Przedsiębiorców (MSKiP, Małopolska Association of Traders and Entrepreneurs). This association was initially established in 1999 to represent Nowa Huta's independent traders in the context of the perceived threat of hypermarkets, but has developed its range of activities to include the dissemination of information, lobbying and training. More recently, MSKiP launched a loyalty scheme, Złoty Punkt (Golden Point), in which shoppers accrue and redeem points by shopping in participating local, independent stores. It is unclear how successful the scheme is – although the Złoty Punkt logo is visible throughout Nowa Huta and the scheme has been extended to other localities – but the active response is important to note nonetheless.

For Nowa Huta households, the proximity and convenience of a dense network of local stores and local markets enabled them to avoid hypermarkets to a much greater degree than in Petržalka. Nowa Huta is home to two large markets (Tomex (Plate 6.5) and the market at Plac Bieńczycki (see Figure 1.2)) and a number of smaller, neighbourhood marketplaces. These are easily accessible from most of the district, either on foot or by public transport, and present a very wide range of product choice. All of the markets incorporate not only traditional stalls but also kiosks and small shops, and in addition are home to occasional informal sellers (such as the flower-grower discussed above, but also those selling cigarettes or second-hand goods). Some of the vendors are farmers, selling their produce direct to consumers, but other outlets are more standard retail concessions. In season, all the Nowa Huta markets attract informal sellers of fruit and vegetables, from makeshift stalls or from the boots of cars and vans. Over 7,000 people work at Tomex (*Rzeczspospolita*, 11 June 1999), as many as now work at the steelworks, and alongside the stalls and kiosks, there is a branch of PKO Bank and a currency exchange.[14] By contrast, despite the existence of a small market in Petržalka, the biggest open-air market in Bratislava is some way from Petržalka

Plate 6.5   Tomex, a market in Nowa Huta

and access depends on having a car. Although it does offer access to flowers, fruit and vegetables from south Slovakia and to other less readily available products, those who did use it tended to visit once a month or less.

The use of local outlets did not simply reflect rational concerns of time and money, but also social attachments to particular retailers in Nowa Huta (Stenning, 2005b). A number of our Nowa Huta households explained, in detail, how they regularly shopped at the same stores or market stalls, where they knew the owners or assistants, and trusted them to sell good quality produce at a fair price. Others noted, further, that they liked shopping locally as it meant that they bumped into their neighbours, maintaining social networks as they shopped. These variations reflected a number of the different features of the two districts' retail and consumption histories, not least the fact that during state socialism, the economic and political importance of Nowa Huta's steelworkers meant that the district as a whole benefited from a denser and better-supplied retail network than many other parts of Kraków. Krakowians from other parts of the city would often come to Nowa Huta's shops during the 1980s 'because there they always sold better meat' (Sadecki, 1994: 3). The continuing presence of local shops also reflects the persistently small geography of many households' everyday lives in Nowa Huta, with much everyday activity focused on the block and neighbourhood. This is reinforced by recent market research, which noted that when asked as to the most important factors when choosing a place to shop, almost one-half of Poles (47%) acknowledged that the proximity of the store to home was one of their top considerations. In addition, a survey carried out by Pentor Institute indicated that two-thirds of Polish consumers shopped for food every day in stores they could reach on foot within five minutes of their residence, and a total of 85% of respondents shopped in stores which they could walk to within ten minutes (Machnicka, 2005: 3).

By way of contrast, the relatively underdeveloped retail economy of Petržalka under state socialism (Mládek, 1994) and its development as a dormitory settlement have meant that residents often established relationships with retail outlets beyond the district, often in locations which fitted with their travel to work patterns elsewhere in Bratislava. Reinforcing the geographical disconnect between home and work, shopping patterns did little to foster community in Petržalka, in contrast to the experience in Nowa Huta.

A further influence on the particularity of Nowa Huta retail practices, in contrast to those in Petržalka, was the continuing possibility, and desire, to buy direct from farmers. This was a practice developed during the shortage years of late socialism on the basis of the longstanding urban–rural connections which we have already highlighted, but one that persisted in the presence of farmers and small producers in Nowa Huta's markets. Mr Mokrzycki, from a large, three-generational Roma household with a long residence history in Nowa Huta, was, for example, pleased that he could continue his father's habit of buying from small farmers. Although his father had had personal contacts with farmers and sourced good quality products directly, Mr Mokrzycki instead sought out small farmers at his local market on Plac Mogilski, ensuring good quality fresh fruit and vegetables at reasonable prices, which he and his wife then pickled and preserved.

That Petržalka residents were happier to shop in hypermarkets does not mean that they did not have concerns about such food consumption practices. In particular, many complained that the cheap food purchased in hypermarkets was often close to or past its sell-by date. As Mrs Červíková, from one of the poorest households in our survey, explained:

> in Tesco, there are discounts, milk just before it expires, but I go and buy it for half price. Three times I bought bread, which cost normally 16 koruna (€0.4), and I bought it for 8. I noticed that next day it was mouldy … all mouldy …

Indeed, complaints about the quality of food sold in supermarkets and hypermarkets was, as we have already suggested, one of the reasons why some households continued to grow their own food, despite the high costs of such a practice. This balancing of the price benefits of hypermarkets against their perceived quality reflects the ways in which both Nowa Huta and Petržalka households negotiated their options in retail. Many households engaged in active and complex practices, echoing those undertaken during the shortage years of late socialism, to make the most of the opportunities offered by hypermarkets and other retailers and to balance household budgets. Perhaps the most common of these practices was intense research into the cheapest source of various food products, reflecting the competitive pricing of food amongst hypermarkets. In both Petržalka and Nowa Huta, promotional leaflets are delivered regularly and frequently to letterboxes, and posted on retail websites,[15] advertising latest prices and special deals. Within households, these leaflets were often read carefully and formed the basis of strategies that took shoppers to the store where particular products were cheapest. The search for special discounted prices on food was often the responsibility of one household member in lower income households. For example, in the Holmanová household introduced above, the responsibility for this practice of detailed price monitoring lay with the Mrs Holmanová's daughter: 'We have a habit that my daughter always reads these leaflets, she monitors all the prices … and we only buy things that have a special price … our shopping is very well thought out.' Knowledge about deals and bargains was spread through networks of family, friends and neighbours, and the search for promotions often meant that households traipsed around multiple stores to save often very small amounts of money,[16] rejecting the 'all under one roof' strategy promoted by hypermarkets. Shopping habits were sometimes changed from week to week in response to the various promotions identified, and other households regularly bought their meat, vegetables, dairy products and bread from different shops or stalls, reflecting their very detailed knowledge of prices. As Mrs Szwacz in Nowa Huta, explains:

> I search for where it's cheapest … I go to Carrefour – there I buy bread, cheap bread. I can buy a roll there for 18 grosze[17] (€0.05), but here in the shop under my nose, even a roll costs 50 grosze (€0.13), and I'm not in a position to buy a roll for 50 grosze.

In Slovakia, these considered shopping practices were supported by numerous websites, such as www.konzum.sk, which offer 'information and advice in shopping, advertising bargains and sales in several chains of super and hypermarkets' (Búriková, 2004: 1) and create forums for discussion. Such careful shopping practices were not just the preserve of poorer households, with many wealthier households also exhibiting price sensitivities and 'smart shopping' habits (GfK Slovakia and INCOMA, 2006). As Mrs

Šenzová, from a household where both adult members were working and with two children at university, explained: 'When we go shopping we do a small survey, to see where the cheapest products are.' Since, as we have seen, the Šenzovás also consumed food produced by family and friends, it is clear that for many, even those who are not struggling with poverty, these careful yet commodified shopping practices articulated with a wider 'economy of jars'.

Managing Retail Exclusion

The complex shopping routines of our researched households echo the experiences of 'disadvantaged consumers' in Western Europe and North America (see, for example, Bromley & Thomas, 1993; Piacentini et al., 2001; Williams & Hubbard, 2001). In exploring the shopping practices of poorer households, Piacentini et al. (2001) categorize shoppers, suggesting that 'economic shoppers', who primarily seek value for money, are particularly well represented among poorer households. While our research certainly supports the economic rationality of many Petržalka and Nowa Huta shoppers, the particular agency of their shopping practices was notable. For this reason, they might be better characterized as 'smart shoppers', 'who take pride in their ability to take maximum advantage of the retailer's offerings, such as sales and discounts, in order to get the best value for money' (Piacentini et al., 2001: 145). This ability is 'considered to be an important skill' (Piacentini et al., 2001: 154) and draws attention to the very active and considered ways in which households domesticate the changing retail landscapes of their localities. Williams and Hubbard (2001: 269) note that 'for the disadvantaged consumer, consumer choice is often no choice at all', suggesting that the agency of poorer shoppers is all but eroded. In contrast, our research suggests that poorer Nowa Huta and Petržalka households worked hard to make the most of the many options available. Unlike peripheral districts in UK cities, for example, hypermarkets had not avoided Nowa Huta and Petržalka. The lengths the Nowa Huta and Petržalka households went to shop 'smartly' reflected the large proportion of household budgets spent on food, especially among poorer households. Just over 40% of average monthly household income was spent on food and drink by the poorest households, compared to just 28% among the wealthiest households (Table 6.7).

Of course, for poorer households, the options were not unlimited, and various facets of their disadvantage restricted their retail choices. Consumer disadvantage connects not only with poverty, but also with health, ageing, gender and household size (Williams & Hubbard, 2001). One of the clearest ways in which these disadvantages played out was through car ownership,

Table 6.7 Average proportion of household expenditure on various items by income groups relative to median income

	≤60% of median income	61–100% of median income	101–140% of median income	≥141% of median income	All house-holds
Nowa Huta					
Food and drink	43	33	34	28	32
Clothes and footwear	4	4	6	6	5
Rent or mortgage repayments	19	21	18	13	17
Utilities	16	18	16	13	15
Childcare, education and training	1	2	2	3	2
Medicines and medical services	6	6	6	4	5
Transport	2	5	4	8	6
Other basic needs	2	3	3	3	3
Leisure activities	1	2	3	5	3
Repayments for loans	6	6	4	7	6
Savings	0	0	2	6	3
Other	0	1	2	4	2
Petržalka					
Food and drink	42	37	34	28	34
Clothes and footwear	4	7	8	9	7
Rent or mortgage repayments	8	4	5	6	5
Utilities	29	31	30	19	27
Childcare, education and training	2	1	0	1	1
Medicines and medical services	3	4	4	2	3
Transport	5	6	7	6	6
Other basic needs	3	3	3	4	4
Leisure activities	1	2	7	7	3
Repayments for loans	3	4	4	4	4
Savings	1	2	2	12	5
Other	0	0	1	2	1

Source: Household survey

the absence of which limited access to the full range of retail options. Only half of our researched households in Petržalka and Nowa Huta owned a car, leaving half reliant on public transport, foot, or lifts from friends and family. In this context, the connection – or disconnection – between public transport and shopping facilities was critical, and a number of households drew attention to the negative impact of declining or changing provision on their shopping practices. In Petržalka, this had been exacerbated by the re-routeing and withdrawal of key bus routes, a result of budget cuts within the city, and a process which had been strongly contested within the district. Although all of Nowa Huta's and Petržalka's hypermarkets were accessible on foot and by public transport, households without cars were much more likely to rely on local shops, preferring restricted choices and higher prices to difficult journeys and the additional price of tickets. In Nowa Huta, Mrs Myszka, a working woman living below the median income with her adult daughter and young granddaughter, explained how she knew that the cheapest food was available at the big outdoor markets, but could only access those by bus. Juggling the cost of public transport and time pressures (Mrs Myszka spent three hours a day commuting to and from work), she opted instead to do all her shopping at the local Biedronka, to which she could walk. Managing the costs of public transport, and available time, often meant that households did their shopping en route to or from work, children's schools, or other activities. In this way, the geographies of shopping were articulated with those of other economic and social practices. The complexity and geographical diversity of household shopping routines means that they can be very time consuming, and, as we discuss in more detail in Chapter Seven, this was a sphere of household activity which fell predominantly to female household members. Not only did women tend to take primary responsibility for researching prices and promotions, but they also carried out the bulk of family shopping, coordinating this with work and other responsibilities. The burdens of shopping perhaps reinforced some women's concern to shop locally, not only for convenience, but also in order that shopping was a sociable practice too. Paradoxically, perhaps, one group of apparently disadvantaged shoppers sometimes found themselves with wider options. These were pensioners, who had both time and free travel on public transport, which together enabled them to travel widely to access cheaper prices. For a number of Nowa Huta pensioners, free public transport was the key to household budgeting.

For those in particular poverty and without the social and kinship exchange of food, which might enable them to avoid commodified exchange, charitable sources were important. The European food aid programme (PEAD, Programme Européen d'Aide aux plus Demunis), for example, redistributes EU food reserves (including flour, pasta, cheese, milk, rice, buckwheat and sugar) through both individual donations and meals served in soup kitchens, shelters, schools and nurseries, and is administered in Poland by the Federation of Polish Food Banks, the Catholic charity Caritas, the Polish Social Welfare Committee (PKPS) and the Polish Red Cross (Federation of Polish Food Banks, 2008). In 2007, PEAD food was distributed to almost 3.8 million Poles (*Warsaw Voice*, 2008) and was a recurring source of nutrition for many of the poorest families in Nowa Huta.[18] By contrast, the role of EU food aid in Slovakia appeared to be almost insignificant. It was not mentioned in any household interview in Petržalka and a monitoring study undertaken by the European Commission in 2008 indicated that Slovakia did not contribute to PEAD at all (EC, 2008).

Conclusions

In the years since 1989, the spheres of food and land in Poland and Slovakia have been rapidly transformed by processes of neo-liberalization. The most visible of these transformations has been the emergence of multinational retailers and the proliferation of other new providers on the cities' retail landscapes, resulting in an apparent expansion of choice but also in the rapid commercialization of food provisioning and the erosion of older forms of retail provision. Yet this neo-liberalization of retail landscapes has occurred alongside the persistence of self-provisioning, not only through food production but also through practices of food preparation and exchange. These too, however, were under pressure from the forces of neo-liberalization, as land development threatened to encroach on the peri-urban land at the heart of households' self-provisioning strategies and as the growing precarity of labour markets reduced time available for food production and preparation. Paradoxically, however, for some, new or renewed engagement with the land could be seen as a direct result of neo-liberalizing labour markets, as some sought out the space of allotments for relaxation, in lieu of longer holidays, and others resorted to practices of cultivation in the face of redundancy and exclusion from the labour market.

In this context, this chapter has drawn attention to the diverse practices of production, exchange and consumption employed by households to domesticate the neo-liberalization of land and food and to meet their daily dietary needs. Different sources and different shops were used for different purposes and articulated with each other at different times of the year, and households often engaged in complex and calculated consumption practices which intertwined retail with self-provisioning, exchange and the occasional use of charitable sources. In these ways, households combined both commodified and non-commodified provision in their attempts to ensure their social reproduction. Many of these practices were also articulated with leisure and labour, and, in some cases, with housing practices, as family land was employed or developed as an alternative or potential site of shelter. These articulations already point to the interplay of different economic and social practices, but other connections were important too, including infrastructures, such as public transport, or material assets, such as car ownership, which enabled or constrained households' access to land and/or to a choice of shops.

These in turn highlight some of the legacies of state socialism, and more distant pasts, as contemporary transformations echoed the historical meanings and contestations of land and food, built on state socialist development and allocation of allotments. The kinds of practices discussed here are suggestive of both those developed in the context of the scarcities and rationing of the late state socialist period and those maintained from households' recent rural pasts. All of these articulations draw attention to the geographies of food provisioning, which rested on, as we have suggested, the local geographies of transport and everyday life but also on longer distance rural connections, invoked by the location of households' land, or that of their friends or family, and by the persistent presence of farmers at urban markets.

In many ways, the cultures and practices of self-provisioning were very similar in Nowa Huta and Petržalka, with households in both districts involved in the production and circulation of home-produced and home-processed food. However, the wider practices of food consumption were quite different, perhaps the most contrasting sphere in all those explored in *Domesticating Neo-Liberalism*. Households in Petržalka were much more likely to access lower cost food items from the hypermarkets that had been established in the area, while in Nowa Huta reliance on independent and Polish-owned food retailers was of continuing importance. These different experiences of recent retail transformations reflected markedly different retail histories – Nowa Huta's economic and political importance meant that it had been relatively privileged during the late socialist years of shortage and had, as a result, maintained a network of more independent, local shops – but they also suggested different social and cultural values, such that households in Nowa Huta placed considerable emphasis on the social practices of local shopping.

However, in both districts the financial pressures that many households experienced meant that for most the primary aim was to reduce food expenditures through a range of consumption and purchasing practices. Whilst in part this meant that households succumbed to the growing dominance of multinational retailers, it was also clear that many actively and knowingly sought the cheapest or best sources of food for their family. The new spaces of retail demanded new skills – as households, for example, used hypermarkets' leaflets and promotions to their benefit and chose, apparently, not to submit to hypermarkets' suggestions that all shopping should be done under one roof – but these were practised in concert with older skills, such as gardening and cooking, and with networks of exchange, which countered the complete commodification of food cultures. These new and persistent practices reflected, also, a continuing attachment to food quality and to value, and this in itself fed into more explicit contestations of multinational retailers, as households shunned their sometimes poor quality food, protested their employment practices and played them off against each other in the search for bargains.

Yet, just as households have been learning to domesticate multinational retail, so too the retailers have responded to the shopping practices of post-socialist consumers by extending their networks of domestic suppliers and by developing smaller, more local and discounter stores. Moreover, the complex ways in which households have responded to the changing retail landscape enabled the ongoing neo-liberalization of urban life in other ways. Their practices of self-provisioning and exchange facilitated partial reproduction outside the formal sphere and thus, in turn, enabled social reproduction on the basis of insecure work which paid less than a living wage. The receipt and production of domestic food items also, paradoxically, created opportunities for a fuller engagement with the market economy as the provisioning of essentials beyond the market increased potential spending on commodified purchases and in other spheres, such as leisure and tourism.

In all of these ways, households' food provisioning practices were intimately articulated with neo-liberalism and were characterized by ambiguous boundaries between domestic, reciprocal and non-market forms of food provisioning and the neo-liberalization of the food retailing market in the two districts. Most households combined diverse provisioning practices in complex ways, but households' particular combinations varied according to the resources, incomes and time households were able to draw upon and to the differentiated retail options available.

Chapter Seven

Care: Family, Social Networks and the State

Introduction: Care and Its Geographies

Care and the geographies of care have attracted increasing amounts of academic attention in recent years (Phillips, 2007; Fisher & Tronto, 1990; Sevenhjuisen, 2000; Staeheli & Brown, 2003; McKie et al., 2004), exploring and highlighting the myriad practices which come together in a series of interlocking spaces to express and enact 'affection, love, duty, well-being, responsibility and reciprocity' (Phillips, 2007: 1). This chapter explores the place of care and caring practices within and between households in Nowa Huta and Petržalka. It focuses on the ways in which households bring together multiple spheres of care in their attempts to ensure their social reproduction, and to domesticate neoliberalism, by mediating the impacts of neo-liberal transformations, by enabling households to learn the policies and strategies of neo-liberal governance, and by creating spaces for the contestation of and resistance to neo-liberalism. This chapter also explores the ways in which neo-liberal transformations have remade the landscapes of care, through reductions in the provision of and access to public, state-funded care and through the growth of private care. The increasing privatization of care rests not only on commodified provision by growing numbers of commercial providers, but also on increases in fees, supplements and bribes paid within public provision (Stenning & Hardy, 2005). It has also resulted in the individualization of care within households and extended families, a process which paradoxically takes place alongside the mooted erosion of social networks and communities, under pressure from neo-liberalization in the labour market and in the sphere of consumption.

In her introduction to 'care', Phillips (2007) neatly identifies some of its quandaries: care is ubiquitous, yet such a part of everyday life that it is often taken for granted and all but unnoticed. We understand care to mean the practices which support households – emotionally, financially, practically – in their everyday lives, both routinely and casually and in more extreme, emergency situations. Such practices are those which households 'use to deal with daily life, seize opportunities, and reduce uncertainties ... They underpin the informal arrangements crucial for a household's survival, expansion and reproduction' (Wellman & Wortley, 1990: 559). These might include emotional support, advice and companionship; lending, giving or exchanging household items or cooking ingredients; support in negotiating bureaucracies; repair work; help with housework, home maintenance or gardening; assistance with childcare, care of the elderly and in times of illness; loans and gifts of money; assistance with shopping; enabling access to goods, services and work; giving lifts and helping with moves; watching over empty homes (including taking in post and watering plants), other property or pets; and maintaining contact and celebrating or marking birthdays, holidays and important events (see, among others, Wellman & Wortley, 1990; Crow et al., 2002; Gilbert, 1998; di Leonardo, 1987; Stack, 1974; Perren et al., 2004). In all these acts, care employs both physical and emotional labour and draws on 'time, material resources, knowledge and skill, social relationships and feelings' (Phillips, 2007: 311; see also Fraad, 2000). Care is rarely simply a rational act, but also implies a relationship which reflects values of community, empathy and, sometimes, obligation (Stack, 1974). As one of our Polish interviewees suggested: 'A good gesture on the part of one person inspires another person.' Much care reflects reciprocity – both within families and social networks and in the context of state provision – such that 'investments' in care are reciprocated through care received, even if 'payback' is deferred (see also Smith, 2002a). Care may be of particular importance at times of pressure or crisis, such that care is a critical element of so-called 'survival strategies' in impoverished and deprived communities (Young & Willmott, [1957]2007; Stack, 1974; Gilbert, 1998).

In much work on care, the family is seen as the natural, primary and most important site of care. But the care provided within the nuclear family is articulated with and complemented by that provided by the extended family, by friendship networks, by communities, and by organizations including the state, charities, churches, other non-governmental organizations and, increasingly, by commercial providers. It is also practised in a range of 'interlocking locations' (McKie et al., 2004: 4), the routes through which are negotiated according to household schedules, lifecourses and work lives. The overlapping kin, neighbour and workmate networks (Bridge, 2002) of many – particularly working class – communities are mooted to offer a particularly important source of care, especially in the context of low residential turnover (a common feature, until recently, of socialist-era housing districts such as Nowa Huta and Petržalka; see Chapter Five). But this 'spatial rootedness' may act as both a resource and a constraint on 'survival strategies' (Gilbert, 1998) because the insularity and the poverty of such networks may limit the quality and range of care provided. Caring can also take place, however, 'at a distance' (Silk, 1998), such that the 'everyday activities of care work ... are not simply a local matter. They are effects of the stretching of social, political and economic relations over space, constructed and negotiated at interlocking scales of bodies, homes, cities, regions, nations and the global' (Dyck, 2005: 235). Notwithstanding these multiple geographies, most care – in whatever form, in whatever location – is performed by women (Phillips, 2007; Young & Willmott, [1957]2007; Stack, 1974; di Leonardo, 1987; Gilbert, 1998) and it is often assumed that women are the natural providers of care. Of course, there is a gender division of caring labour, such that men do have a role in the tasks highlighted above. And, moreover, transformations in the labour market, in moral rationalities, and in policy and politics, are enabling and/or forcing men to take on new caring roles.

Transforming Landscapes of Care: Neo-Liberalizing Care?

Given the presence and connections of care across a number of spheres, landscapes of care are regularly transformed by shifts and reforms in fiscal policy, labour markets, gender and family cultures and governance, among others. In recent years, reforms in these spheres have driven – in ECE and beyond – a neo-liberalization of care. This has introduced (or extended) the role of the market in care, sought to reduce state expenditures in the field of welfare, devolved responsibility for care to individuals, connected the right to welfare to the duty to work, and downgraded claims for equality and justice. These transformations contrast markedly with the system of social security under state socialism, which was characterized as 'universal, comprehensive and centralized' (Read & Thelen, 2007: 7; see also Ferge, 1997), founded on a paternalist connection between employment and care provision (B. Domański, 1997; Offe, 1996), and coupled with the persistent importance of kinship, patronage and other networks (Ledeneva, 1998; Wedel, 1986). The particular ways in which these processes of neo-liberalization are being played out in this context are explored in the following sections, but it is worth noting that neo-liberal pressures on caring practices in the post-socialist world have been particularly acute. As we noted in Chapter Two, the implementation of neo-liberal reforms in Poland and Slovakia has been inconsistent. Yet, within the sphere of welfare, the trend has undoubtedly been towards a reduction and rationalization of provision, although this does not necessarily equate to state withdrawal (Read & Thelen, 2007). Increasing poverty and unemployment, declining tax and insurance incomes, and external pressures for fiscal austerity have combined to encourage a reduction in state spending on welfare and a concomitant reduction in the coverage, levels and duration of social benefits. In Poland, for example, the 2004 Hausner Plan aimed to reduce social expenditures by PLN30 billion (€7.25 billion) between 2004 and 2007 (Ministry of the Economy, Labour and Social Policy, 2004; see also Chapter Two). In Slovakia, similar expend-iture cuts were encouraged after the 1998 election, following the implemen-tation of the flat tax regime.[1] In both countries, means-testing has been introduced for many benefits; income replacement rates have been reduced and tied to price rather than wage indices; and eligibility for benefits has been tightened and, often, tied to so-called 'activation' measures. After a brief increase in the early 1990s, the period since 1992 or 1993 has seen both the proportion of GDP spent on social benefits (especially family ben-efits such as childcare allowances, family allowances, and social benefits for households living in poverty) and the number of beneficiaries decline markedly (Fultz & Steinhilber, 2003; Balcerzak-Paradowska et al., 2003). Even those benefits introduced in the post-socialist period to respond to the costs of transition – such as unemployment benefit – have been eroded by successive reforms. In many of these reforms, Poland and Slovakia stand out: both countries' benefits systems can be characterized as the toughest in terms of eligibility, coverage, replacement rates and duration (Cerami, 2008). For example, to qualify for unemployment benefit in Slovakia, a claimant must have been employed for three of the previous four years, and in Poland for 365 days over the previous 18 months (Cerami, 2008: 9).[2] With respect to social benefits aimed at bringing household incomes up to a social minimum – generally available for an unlimited period – the dura-tion of assistance is limited to 24 months in Slovakia and all access is deter-mined by the discretion of social services in Poland (Cerami, 2008: 12; see also Chapter Two).

Within these contexts, care has been subjected not only to agendas of neo-liberalization but also to conservative agendas which 'valorize hierar-chical and historical relations of gender, race, class, or sexuality' (Staeheli & Brown, 2003: 772). This particular mix of neo-liberalism and conserva-tism can clearly be identified in Poland where neo-liberal transformations have been combined with a Catholicism which encourages welfare res-ponsibilities to be privatized within the family (Glass & Fodor, 2007).[3] Yet, even in Poland, where the Catholic Church wields considerable political influence, fiscal support for pro-family social policies has been tempered by budgetary pressures (Saxonberg & Szelewa, 2007). In Slovakia, the role of the church is important, though perhaps less influen-tial than inPoland, and similar conservative values regarding gender and sexuality have combined with neo-liberal values, especially with respect to perceptions of women's traditional role in the home. The family has been at the centre of conservative discourses in Slovakia, despite (or perhaps because of) the increasing significance of divorce and childbirth outside marriage.

These welfare reforms have 'radically reshaped the relationships between individuals, families, citizens, communities and states' (Staeheli & Brown, 2003: 771), leading to 'reconfigurations of public and private spaces, institutions, moralities and subjectivities' (Read & Thelen, 2007: 9). They demand that we explore the ways in which households negotiate these changing landscapes of care in their attempts to secure their social reproduction, drawing analytical attention to the dynamics that shape the nature and quality of care in communities. In this chapter, we begin by exploring domestic and familial caring practices, asking who performs what forms of carework within households and considering what shapes these patterns of care. We then extend the analysis beyond the household to map the flows of care between other family members, paying attention to the presence and absence of family support in household lives. In these ways, we ask how the family enables individuals and households to manage the pressures of neo-liberalization. In the next section, we shift our attention to the wider social networks of households, centring their relationships with friends, neighbours and acquaintances, asking what affects the shape and nature of households' social networks, what forms of care flow within these social networks and what happens when households are isolated from supportive social networks. Finally, we focus on the more institutional forms of care with which households engage. We explore the changing role of state welfare systems in household lives, asking how households understand and negotiate the neo-liberalized welfare systems and how their familial and social networks, work practices and material assets articulate with state support. We explore how 'citizenship assets' (Burawoy et al., 2000), the claims that households can make on the state for support, are employed within the household and through wider social networks. In the context of the reconfiguration of state provision, we also explore the role of non-governmental and community organizations in the provision of care, and ask similar questions about the ways in which households negotiate this provision to secure social reproduction.

Domestic Work and Family Support

For the overwhelming majority of the households involved in this research, and for many Poles and Slovaks more generally (Synak, 1990; Ornacka & Szczepaniak-Wiecha, 2005), the family remains a – if not *the* – key social unit, with relatively high levels of family contact and quite close patterns of residency.[4] Around 60% of households in both Nowa Huta and Petržalka

Table 7.1 Household composition in Petržalka and Nowa Huta

	Petržalka		Nowa Huta	
	No. of households	%	No. of households	%
Total households	150		200	
1 single adult	16	11	27	14
1 single adult + children	3	2	5	3
2 adults	34	22	44	22
2 adults + children	14	9	36	18
3 and more adults	47	31	59	30
3 and more adults + children	36	24	29	15
Of 1+ households:				
One generation	18	14	35	20
Two generations	83[a]	61	113[b]	65
Three generations	31	23	24	14
Including extended families (i.e. with siblings, nieces, nephews, in-laws etc.)	14		4	
Four generations	1	1	0	0
Others/Unknown	1	1	1	1
Without children under 18	97	65	130	65
1 child under 18	36	24	43	22
2 children under 18	12	8	24	12
3 children under 18	4	3	2	1
4 children under 18	1	2	1	1

Notes:
[a] includes three households with two adult generations (i.e. elderly parents)
[b] includes one household with split generations (i.e. grandparents and grandchildren), two with two adult generations and one extended family
Source: Household survey

were composed of two generations (i.e. parents and children), though just 9% of households in Petržalka and 18% in Nowa Huta comprised the apparently traditional model of two adults and children under 18 (Table 7.1). In addition to households including adult children, 23% of Petržalka households and 14% of Nowa Huta households comprised three generations. In Nowa Huta, the most common pattern was for an adult couple to live with one or more of their parents and with their children (i.e. a simple, three-generational household) but in Petržalka, almost half of the three-generational households included more complex combinations of cohabitation, such that siblings, in-laws, and cousins, nieces and nephews all lived with shared grandparents.

In part, the presence of multi-generational households is explained by strategies to negotiate increasing vulnerability in the housing market (see Chapter Five), but further explanation lies in the wider family geographies of households. Whilst Nowa Huta households were less likely to include different relatives, they were considerably more likely to have them living in very close proximity. In Petržalka, close relatives were more likely to be living in other parts of Bratislava, reflecting the particular populating of Petržalka in the 1970s and 1980s through (in large part) migration *within* Bratislava, in addition to households moving from other regions of Slovakia. Across both districts, over half of surveyed households' close relatives (parents, grandparents, siblings, children, grandchildren, uncles and aunts, and cousins) lived within 25 kilometres of Bratislava and Kraków, and of these significant proportions lived within Petržalka and Nowa Huta, or elsewhere in the two cities. The variations in the patterns presented here reflect two key factors. Firstly, histories of migration to, and settlement in, Nowa Huta and Petržalka, such that the earlier establishment of Nowa Huta and the 'chain' migration which its construction encouraged (Stenning, 2005b) led to the presence of wider family networks within the district; and, secondly, the nature of housing allocation under socialism and the development of housing markets more recently, through which households could, more or less successfully, seek apartments close to family and friends (see Chapter Five).

These figures, coupled with the data on household composition, suggest that many households had significant local family networks on which to rely for support. This echoes earlier analysis of the role of family networks which, in the Polish context, argued that the 'family continues to function as the fundamental self-help group of the society' (Synak, 1990: 42). As Pickup and White (2003) have argued, large, functioning families can be very useful, as they expand networks and opportunities, for example by bringing in a larger number of incomes (Chapter Four) or by enabling the household balancing of domestic responsibilities. However, large families can also be problematic, especially if the ratio of working to non-working members is disadvantageous. Whilst the centrality of family is a theme that echoes through our research, there is also considerable evidence of change in family structures (Ornacka & Szczepaniak-Wiecha, 2005). There were, for example, numerous 'non-traditional' households in both Petržalka and Nowa Huta, including single-person households and single-parent families (both types of household which could find themselves particularly disadvantaged in the negotiation of neo-liberalization) and occasional examples of households comprising unrelated groups, including small but growing numbers of student households.

Domestic work

The division of domestic labour in the household played a decisive role in the wider economic practices of household members – it often shaped labour market participation, for example (see Chapter Four) – and was subject to significant transformation in the context of external pressures. For these reasons, an exploration of domestic work within an account of neo-liberalization is critically important. At the same time, domestic work, for many women in particular, constituted one of the most time-consuming of all everyday activities and, as such, demands attention for that reason alone. Patterns of domestic work in Petržalka and Nowa Huta reflected very clearly the generally recognized persistence of gender divisions of domestic responsibility and labour (Ornacka & Szczepaniak-Wiecha, 2005; Voicu et al., 2008). In a 1995 Polish survey, 87% of men and 84% of women agreed with the statement: 'It is considerably better for the family when the husband earns money and the wife takes care of the home and children' (Ornacka & Szczepaniak-Wiecha, 2005: 211). Such gendered attitudes were supported by our data (Table 7.2), which see women taking primary responsibility for almost all routine household tasks. The imbalance between the work taken on by men and women in the home was very marked in those areas traditionally seen as 'women's work' (such as childcare, cooking, cleaning, washing, ironing) but was also surprisingly significant in areas such as financial and administrative matters and helping with homework, two spheres which are less commonly gendered. While it was most frequently the female head of the household who was responsible for these domestic tasks, in the majority of cases where another household member took on such work, that household member was also female (a daughter, mother, mother-in-law, daughter-in-law). This is clearly illustrated in the case of the Blatová household in Petržalka, a large extended household with 13 members, as one daughter explained:

> It varies. It depends who has time. When I have time, I clean the flat, or my sister does it ... we wash clothes every day ... and mum cooks. We cannot cook separately for each family, we wouldn't have enough cookers and fridges ... mum does it centrally to cook everything for everybody.

In both districts, men did play a predominant role in some tasks: renovating and decorating, equipment repairs, and looking after household vehicles. However, none of these were tasks which demanded time and energy every day, not all households performed these tasks at all and, as we discuss below, these were the areas in which households were also most likely to employ external professional help. In short, those areas in which men did make a contribution to domestic work were far less time-consuming than

Table 7.2   Domestic work: gender of primary responsible household member[‡]

	Nowa Huta		Petržalka	
	Male (%)	Female (%)	Male (%)	Female (%)
Looking after children	15	85	5	95
Looking after elderly or disabled people who require care	27	73	18	82
Everyday food preparation	16	84	10	90
Washing up	19	81	24	76
Cleaning the home	20	80	23	77
Washing	15	85	11	89
Renovating and/or decorating the home	75	25	76	24
Repairing home equipment	92	9	86	14
Shopping for food and groceries	26	74	44	66
Food processing (pickling, juicing, jamming, freezing)	12	88	18	82
Responsibility for financial and administrative matters	37	63	37	63
Looking after a car or other vehicles	78	22	84	16
Helping children with homework from school	24	76	29	71

[‡] Not all households perform all tasks
Source: Household survey

those for which women were responsible, further underpinning the significance of gendered divisions of labour in domestic work.

The explanations for such a persistent gender division of domestic labour are manifold. Perhaps the most influential is an enduring set of moral rationalities (Duncan & Edward, 1997; see Chapter Three) that deems domestic work to be feminized. A number of our interviews invoked gendered assumptions in their explanations of divisions of domestic labour, often explaining their foundations in local and familial cultures. Mr Kiedrowski, a married father in his forties from Nowa Huta, for example, explained that domestic tasks in his home were divided according to 'innate abilities', although he did insist that many household tasks were shared so that both he and his wife could find time in the day for relaxation. In Petržalka, Mrs Zajacová, a separated woman in her fifties, explained her burdensome load through reference to men's 'innate' inability to look after themselves and their families:

> It was always my responsibility, to arrange food, because I know what is needed and what's not. Men never in their life know about these things. It's very exceptional when a man knows something about these things. When you don't tell him that it is necessary to buy toilet paper, he won't do it, because it is not important for him. And when he is hungry and has no bread, he is unhappy, but he doesn't know what he should do, if he should buy bread or not; if you should eat or not …

Of course, in identifying men's inabilities as natural, Mrs Zajacová was herself contributing to the persistent inequalities in domestic work. However, men's withdrawal from housework reflected not only their apparent inability to take on such work but also their unwillingness. Mr Šiška, a 50-year-old father of two, living with his wife in a 'middle-class' household in Petržalka, illustrated this in a most extreme way, as he explained why he did not share responsibility for household tasks with his wife: 'My wife shops, because I don't like it, I only like sport'. In terms of explaining these 'innate' roles, our interviewees recognized the importance of socialization, both within the family and beyond. Mrs Sasnowicz, a married mother in her late forties from Nowa Huta, suggested 'it's genetic, from our parents, I suppose', whilst Mrs Sedlak, a single mother with two children, drew attention both to the example of her parents and the particular breadwinner model dominant in post-war Nowa Huta. She explained that 'my parents had that kind of typical marital model; that is, my father worked in the steelworks and my mother brought up the children', illustrating the 'contract' between male employment in the labour market and the female work of social reproduction. The transmission of gender roles through the generations is clear here, and recurred in other interviews. Indeed, the Šanovnas in Petržalka celebrated the fact that their older son had found a wife who, despite also working full-time, would look after their son:

> He only comes home in the evening at ten. At least he has such a good girl; she cooks and cleans the flat, because he wouldn't have time for it. But she also works all day till the evening in an estate agency; she works till the evening.

The persistent responsibility that some women felt for the men in their lives resulted in some very peculiar, though occasional, scenarios in which women continued to support ex-partners even after the breakdown of relationships. Mr Šmoliar in Petržalka, for example, a single-parent with an income below 60% of the regional median who lived with his 20-year-old son, continued to be cared for by his ex-wife. Despite the fact that his ex-wife worked nights, she visited him and her son twice a week to cook and clean, since Mr Šmoliar had no one else to call on for help but his 'football friends'.

These ingrained cultures, however, are not the only explanation for the continuing imbalances in domestic labour. They are also in part explained by real inequalities in the capabilities – physical, temporal or otherwise – of household members to perform such tasks and by the apparently increasing struggle many households engaged in to balance their multiple commitments. In a number of households, ill-health, incapacity and old age limited the tasks which household members could take on, and often resulted in such members being forced to withdraw from roles they had previously fulfilled. For example, in the Mokryzcki household, a large Roma family in Nowa Huta – comprising a couple, their three children and the wife's mother – a stroke had recently incapacitated Mr Mokryzcki such that he was no longer able to assist in any household tasks. While there were some examples of men taking on additional roles to compensate for their wives' and mothers' incapacity, the gendering of paid work, especially in Nowa Huta through employment in steel production, meant that men were more likely to have suffered from industrial injury or ill-health (Watson, 1998). The presence of relatively high levels of incapacity not only reduced the number of household members able to contribute to housework but also increased the demand for caring labour. The erosion, rationalization and marketization of health care have meant that care for ill, disabled or elderly family members is increasingly 'familialized' (Saxonberg & Sirovátka, 2006), or domesticated, as it is brought into the family home. Again, in this caring labour we see a complex interplay of gendered moral rationalities and neo-liberalization (through the increasing cost of professional care). As Mrs Holmanová, in her late fifties and living in Petržalka on less than the median income, explained, both poverty and a desire to ensure a high level of care meant that she took the difficult decision to leave work to look after her mother who was suffering with dementia:

> I would never earn enough to pay for care for her. When you take care of her for 14 years, you have this care in your blood, in your eyes, in each touch … so how could I leave her, such an old lady, where? It was a hard decision …

Alongside ill-health and old age, the most significant limitation on a more even gender division of domestic labour involved patterns of paid work among household members. A common feature of post-socialist labour markets has been that women tended to be made redundant more often and more quickly, that they struggled harder to find new work and that they are likely to be employed, when they did find work, at a lower wage on average (see Chapter Four for more on this; see also, Hardy & Stenning, 2002).

An additional influence was the pressure for those in employment to work longer hours, either for fear of losing their job or from a necessity to work overtime to secure a living wage, such that working household members were less able to contribute to the tasks of daily social reproduction. For all these reasons, women were more likely to take on the majority of everyday housework, either because they found themselves in the home more or because the loss of their income was easier to bear if someone in the household had to forgo paid work to take on major caring roles, for children, the elderly or incapacitated. The latter scenario was reinforced by the rationalization of carer and income support benefits, which might have provided a decent replacement income for carers. Although women appeared most likely to replace paid work with work in the home, labour market transformations have also resulted in some men taking on traditionally feminized roles within the household as they were forced out of the labour market. Not only did this result in men increasing their contribution to housework simply because they were at home more, but also, in a few examples, in a 'swap' of gender roles, as women went out to work and men became 'househusbands', as the case of the Kwiatek family, introduced in Chapter Four, highlighted.

The difficulties with which households balanced paid work and the work of social reproduction points to the heavy burdens of caring work, even to ensure that basic domestic tasks were adequately performed. Many of the women involved in the research spent hours each day cooking, cleaning and shopping; for some, this was a second shift (Hochschild, with Machung, 2003) fitting around paid work, for others it became a full-time job. The demands of housework appeared, once again, to reflect both perceived moral obligations and the pressures of negotiating ongoing transformations. Processed food, supermarkets and other labour-saving 'inventions' had not yet fully transformed the domestic lives of households, within which many, women in particular, clung to traditional notions of good housekeeping. They also maintained very high standards of cleanliness and home cooking, but the need to spend time 'sorting things out' and stretching minimal budgets as far as possible had increased. Together these patterns imposed a heavy burden of household labour. In this context, some men had taken on some housework. This increasing contribution is often explained by the need to 'help out' women who were also engaged in paid work. Women were still seen as primarily responsible for housework but 'given a hand' by 'compassionate' men when they were struggling to fulfil all household tasks. In such scenarios, children, young or adult, though often daughters first of all, also took on housework, either 'helping out' their mothers from time to time or, occasionally, becoming the primary 'homemaker'.

Despite the growing demands of paid work and housework, very few households engaged non-household members in routine domestic tasks.

Table 7.3 Percentage of households engaging non-household members in routine tasks

| | Nowa Huta | | Petržalka | | |
	Relative/ friend	Professional employed person	Relative/ friend	Professional employed person	Others
Renovating/ decorating	13	23	11	9	11
Repairing home equipment	9	35	11	11	11

Source: Household survey

In the handful of cases where this did happen, assistance was most likely to be provided by relatives or friends living within close proximity (see below). The only areas in which people from outside the household did assist to any significant extent involved renovating and decorating and equipment repairs (Table 7.3). In these spheres, relatives and friends (and very occasionally neighbours) did play a key role, but some more affluent households employed paid labour to complete renovation, decoration and repair work. As we have already suggested, some households, especially those negotiating precarious work and ill-health or old age, did struggle to complete routine household tasks. If these households did not have access to the sorts of kinship and wider social networks which we explore below, then they may have been forced to pay for caring labour, despite their poverty. The example of Mrs Czarnocka, a single Nowa Huta mother living around the median regional income, is illustrative. Until recently she had paid a neighbour to look after her young daughter whilst she went out to work, bringing in the household's only income. Yet exemplifying the fragile moral and monetary balance of this situation, Mrs Czarnocka had more recently decided to leave work in order to bring up her daughter herself. This case also points to the connections between household livelihoods which are played out in the sphere of care. In the way that Mrs Czarnocka's need for childcare provided an income for her neighbour, the Juszczaks, a relatively well-off young Nowa Huta couple, considered employing their neighbour to look after their small daughter, in part because they knew it would help her out financially. This kind of informal yet paid inter-household care could also be an explicit part of the income strategies of poorer households: one of the unemployed daughters of the Sinicki family in Nowa Huta had done paid but casual childcare work for acquaintances in the absence of more substantive employment.

Table 7.4   Frequency of family help (% of households)

	Petržalka		Nowa Huta	
	How often extended family provide help to interviewed household	How often interviewed household provide help to extended family	How often extended family provide help to interviewed household	How often interviewed household provide help to extended family
Every day	14	13	13	13
Once a week	15	21	10	16
At least once a month	9	11	12	14
Less than once a month	11	8	10	8
Rarely	21	21	20	19
Never	31	26	36	31

Source: Household survey

For most households, however, the employment of outsiders in household labour was seen as the last option. Only when household members could not themselves complete the task in question did they turn to others. Moreover, in the overwhelming majority of such instances, the first port of call for help were the kinship and wider social networks, which we explore below, since in these networks questions of trust, reciprocity and standards of care were already answered.

The extended family

Extended families also played important roles in sustaining the social reproduction of households and care systems. In total, about two-thirds of all surveyed households in Petržalka and Nowa Huta provided and received help from their extended families; many on a regular basis. However, for around one-fifth of all households in both Petržalka and Nowa Huta this help was only rarely given or received (Table 7.4). Most of this assistance was part of a mutual economy of favours, with help flowing in both directions over extended periods of time. It might be expected that the geographical proximity of family would have had an impact on the scale and frequency of flows of family assistance, but this did not appear to be the

Table 7.5 Help given and received from family, friends, neighbours, colleagues and organizations (% of households)

	Money		Food or other things		Labour or time[a]		Money; Food or other things		Money; Labour or time[a]		Food or other things; Labour or time[a]		Money: Food or other things; Labour or time[a]	
	To	From	To	From	To	From	To	From	To	From	To	From	To	From
Nowa Huta														
Parents	2	12	1	7	33	5	2	15	6	6	4	7	10	18
Children	2	5	1	0	4	12	3	2	4	2	4	3	13	0
Grandparents	0	6	2	1	12	2	0	4	0	1	3	1	1	1
Grandchildren	1	1	3	0	1	1	2	0	3	0	4	0	9	0
Other relatives	17	19	14	8	30	35	6	8	10	6	8	12	11	9
Friends	12	22	9	8	43	45	4	5	16	7	3	0	8	10
Colleagues	12	14	5	10	40	47	3	4	15	8	2	0	5	2
Neighbours	14	24	5	5	49	43	12	9	6	3	4	0	8	13
Allotment neighbours	1	0	2	3	5	2	0	1	0	0	0	1	0	0
Church/NGOs	65	30	21	35	9	0	0	10	0	5	0	0	0	0
Others	13	40	75	20	13	0	0	20	0	0	0	0	0	0
Petržalka														
Parents	5	4	2	3	14	3	1	5	4	1	4	4	8	11
Children	5	5	5	1	2	4	1	1	1	2	4	4	7	3
Grandparents	0	1	0	2	5	1	1	2	1	0	3	1	2	2
Grandchildren	1	1	1	0	2	0	1	0	0	0	1	1	3	0
Other relatives	3	4	2	5	17	7	1	4	1	3	8	5	3	6
Friends	11	7	5	6	17	12	3	2	4	1	7	8	6	3
Colleagues	3	1	3	4	14	11	0	0	3	1	2	5	3	1
Neighbours	1	2	11	9	14	5	0	1	0	0	3	5	3	0
Allotment neighbours	1	0	1	1	3	3	0	0	0	0	2	2	0	0
Church/NGOs	13	0	5	0	0	1	4	0	1	0	1	0	1	0
Others	3	2	3	0	0	0	1	0	0	0	0	1	0	0

Note:
[a] Time = assistance involving the time of others
Source: Household survey

case. Significant proportions of those who never gave or received family help also had family living locally. Households also received support from (and gave support to) more distant family, not only those living elsewhere in Poland and Slovakia, but also those who had migrated internationally. Contacts and advice supported migrating family members, while remittances played a critical role in the budgets of some households (see Chapter Four and Stenning et al., 2010).

For those households who frequently gave and received help within their extended family networks, the kinds of help provided were varied (Table 7.5). There were some distinct generational patterns, such that households were more likely to give their parents and grandparents their time and labour and receive money, food and other things from them. Likewise, they were more likely to receive labour or time from their children than give it to them. For many households, these exchanges were casual and taken for granted, but nonetheless important. In general, there appeared to be a gendering of family support, with female household members generally playing a larger role in familial exchanges. This reflected a widespread recognition that it was primarily women who maintain and develop kinship networks (di Leonardo, 1987; Smith & Stenning, 2006). Within this, the mother–daughter relationship is one which has been regularly identified in work on kinship relations as powerful and important (Young & Willmott, [1957]2007) and which did seem to play a particularly strong role in Nowa Huta and Petržalka. A considerable amount of the assistance provided flowed along the daughter–mother–grandmother axis, with a significant number of the women in our interviewed households reporting that they saw their mothers very regularly. Mrs Sieradzka, a divorced, unemployed mother of two in Nowa Huta, for example, saw her mother every day, spending much of the day at her mother's home and sharing most of her everyday tasks with her. For others, an exchange of home-cooked food between mothers and daughters appeared to take on both a symbolic and material value. The material importance of gifts of home-cooked food to poor households was clear, but it was also an act of caring that was not especially costly and enabled mothers to continue to 'mother' their daughters.

Despite the critical importance of the mother–daughter relationship, male relatives played particular roles in family networks, reflecting the gender divisions of domestic labour outlined above. Older male relatives (fathers and uncles) helped out with those domestic tasks identified as 'male', such as repairs, renovation and decoration, and these and other male relatives (brothers, cousins, in-laws) also offered professional advice, contacts and assistance with bureaucracies, often reflecting work-based skills and contacts. For Ms Myszka, for example, a young single mother living with her young daughter and her mother in Nowa Huta, her father's assistance in domestic repair and renovation work was critical. Still more important, however, was his support in her negotiation of social services, as she explained: 'I take Dad with me, because my dad is that bit wiser and has more experience than me'. Ms Myszka believed that older people were more respected by social services, and her father's presence and his skills were valuable assets as she struggled to acquire the benefits to which she was entitled.

Above and beyond this gendering of family support, three key 'modalities' of care were evident within extended family networks. Firstly, for many, the role of grandparents in the lives of their children and grandchildren was critical. Secondly, often in situations where parents were unable or unwilling to offer high levels of support, siblings played a major role. Thirdly, some households found themselves connected to large, close, multi-generational family networks which, in Nowa Huta in particular, reflected long-standing connections to the district.

Grandparents

The central role of grandparents in household social reproduction is rooted in both cultural and structural legacies. The traditional family model which predominates in Poland and Slovakia values the nurturing of relationships between generations. Yet these relationships have also been supported, over the years, by family policies that have sought to devolve responsibility for childcare and wider welfare to the family. In Poland, for example, state provision of nurseries and kindergartens stood at a much lower level than other European states, both East and West (Saxonberg & Sirovátka, 2006) and changes to pension policies in 1975 were targeted to encourage grandmothers to take early retirement so that they might take on caring roles for their grandchildren. In this way, their daughters (in-law) were freed to return to work (Heinen & Wator, 2006) and the state was able to relinquish responsibility for childcare.

Neo-liberal transformations in the post-socialist period have reinforced these trends, leading to the identification of 'refamilialization' as a key trend in post-socialist social policy (Glass & Fodor, 2007; Saxonberg & Sirovátka, 2006). Across the region, state budget cuts and the transfer of responsibility for childcare facilities from enterprises and central government to local authorities have led to a dramatic reduction in the public provision of nursery places and to an increase in the average cost of childcare (Balcerzak-Paradowska et al., 2003). Early retirement has also been used extensively to avoid unemployment, especially in localities dependent on heavy industries (Balcerzak-Paradowska et al., 2003), thus creating a cohort of healthy retirees to take on caring roles. The loss, or reduction, of childcare and other family benefits, coupled with changes in the labour market, has also lessened women's ability to reconcile motherhood with paid work. These changes have led Glass and Fodor (2007: 337) to conclude that 'working women must drop out of the labour force to care for their children or depend on non-working or retired relatives', a trend they describe as 'private maternalism'.

In this context, many of our households relied on their parents to meet childcare needs. For some, this was a casual and occasional, though critical, role, taken on when one parent was ill or work pressures temporarily extended the working day. For others, this was a much more regular arrangement which was central to the balancing of work and care. For example, Mr and Mrs Wojnowicz, a young couple with a small son, chose to live in Nowa Huta in order to be close to their parents, who had agreed to take on a large share of childcare. In Petržalka, Mr and Mrs Brago, a retired couple in their early sixties, looked after their nearby grandchildren at least twice a week. For the Kiedrowskis from Nowa Huta, the role of both grandmothers was especially critical, as both parents had demanding jobs and their young daughter had a severe disability and high care needs. As Mr Kiedrowski explained: 'Fortunately we have … these wonderful grannies, who both take her two or three times a week to the sanatorium, and it's very important.' So critical to their household lives were their mothers that the Kiedrowskis never considered moving. In these cases, we can see that the provision of childcare by grandparents (predominantly grandmothers) was absolutely critical for some young families to balance parenthood with paid work and engagement in the labour market in the absence of adequate state provision. But what was also important was that carework provided grandparents with a continuing sense of value in retirement, redundancy or unemployment. Mrs Futyma, for example, had been unemployed for ten years and at the time of interview was employed in an extremely precarious manner as an office cleaner. She lived in poverty in a marginal housing block and was all but dependent on her daughter for survival; she explained: 'I mean, simply, my family helps me to live, maybe that sounds a little not so nice, but, simply, I earn nothing … without it, how is it possible to survive?' In this context, the reciprocity engendered by Mrs Futyma caring for her grand-daughter offered her an important fillip. As Zajicek et al. (2007: 65) have suggested, this kind of caring labour offers older family members 'some degree of autonomy or status in what might otherwise be a dependent family relationship'. These kinds of relationships might not always be reciprocal, however, and there is a danger, as we noted in Chapter Three, that gendered and generational inequalities within the family may tend to exploitation (see also Synak, 1990).

Over and above providing childcare, parents/grandparents were also critical in other ways to the social reproduction of households. The early acquisition of pension income and the relative stability of their past working lives (as compared with their children and grandchildren) often meant that grandparents were in a position to support their younger families in material ways too, to greater or lesser extents. Despite fears of poverty amongst pensioners, cash flows from older to younger family members are a widely recognized phenomenon (Zajicek et al., 2007; Siemeńska, 2002 in Glass & Fodor, 2007). Mr and Mrs Zych, a Nowa Huta couple in their late seventies, for example, purchased apartments for their children and helped to establish a dental surgery for one son with money saved during time that Mr Zych worked abroad. Mrs Zych continued to work for about ten years after her retirement 'in order to help the children' and 'would like to have a pension two times bigger, just to help the children – I don't need anything'. Mr and Mrs Brago, from Petržalka, also sought to help their children, preferring to invest their money in their family than 'sit on it'. In numerous more minor ways, grandparents contributed to household livelihoods and offered a defence against the winds of neo-liberal transformations. Mothers brought round home-cooked food; grandchildren popped in to grandparents for meals and treats; grandparents with cars used them to ferry grandchildren around; and grandparents gave grandchildren occasional gifts of clothes, books and pocket money, critical in households where budgets were tight. Such flows of help also operated in reverse: many households took on some of the household tasks which elderly parents and grandparents were no longer able themselves to complete (Table 7.5). As the Kowaliks, a young couple from Nowa Huta living in severe poverty, explained: 'If help is needed, then we must, of course, it's our duty. Our parents brought us up and we have responsibilities to them too' (see also Synak, 1990; Read, 2007).

Siblings

A second key relationship, which complemented the parental/grandparental role, was that between siblings. While many households had regular, casual contact with their siblings, for a few households, this relationship was critical, often in the absence of parents who were able or willing to play a supporting role. In some cases the reluctance of parents to support their children resulted from family breakdown. In others, poverty, ill-health and old age restricted parents' ability to offer help, financial or otherwise. Mrs Kielak, for example, a single mother in her forties living in Nowa Huta, used to receive financial and other help from her parents, but at the time of interview her parents were both dependent on disability pensions and rarely able to help. As a result, it was more likely that her sister helped out:

> My sister, either she buys something for me, or gives me or the children some money ...When she has more money, then I go to her. Practically every month, because I don't have money. So I'll pop in to hers. And if for example she has

an ill child or something, then she says, 'B_____, this month, I can't help you, I can't give you, or even the children, anything, because I don't have anything'. But you can say that she helps me every month; sometimes it's more, sometimes less, because it's different amounts but often she tries to help.

Another Nowa Huta mother, Mrs Dawidowicz, recounted a similar story. Since her mother retired, she had more frequently turned to her sister for help, money and food. In this case, however, Mrs Dawidowicz reciprocated by looking after her nephew before he started pre-school.

For some, the help offered by siblings was more substantial, in response to particular financial needs. For Ms Senecka, a single woman in her late forties from Nowa Huta, the everyday assistance of her brothers in repairs and maintenance was important (she lived in a large flat and her brothers worked in the building trade). But most important was the fact that one brother repaid a PLN40,000 (€10,000) debt for her, a debt incurred by an estranged friend which Ms Senecka had guaranteed. In Petržalka, Mr Šmoliar, out of work and living on a disability pension, formally arranged a SKK28,600 (€715) loan from his sister, who found herself in a better financial situation, to pay for his flat. These examples point to inequalities in the post-socialist experiences of varying family members. Those who found themselves in more stable family situations and with two incomes were often called upon to support their siblings, and other family members, who had not fared so well.

Dense family networks

The final example of family support involved those households who had very dense, close networks of relatives living in and around Nowa Huta and Petržalka with whom they shared high levels of care and support. Although many Nowa Huta and Petržalka households had a lot of proximate relatives, only a few had especially rich and helpful networks which provided support in *all* circumstances. In all cases, these were families who had long been resident in Nowa Huta and Petržalka, had strong rural roots, and often had multi-stranded and long-standing connections with their neighbourhood. In particular, the Roma families interviewed in Nowa Huta testified to dense and supportive family networks based on large extended families living in adjacent blocks and neighbourhoods. Importantly, interviewees noted how they could draw on these networks at any time, without forewarning, despite the poverty of the wider family. As Mrs Gwizdek, a Roma woman living in Nowa Huta, explained:

I mean, these are such difficult times, that one helps another, right? I mean, how am I to explain this ... This is family, it's not really close family, it's slightly more distant family, so when, for example, I have some clothes which are too small, then I go and take these clothes … and it's not just me, because everyone helps out here, this family is a poor family.

In Nowa Huta, the most illustrative example of extended family networks was the Sinicki family, who with their extended family were re-housed in Nowa Huta from their family home in Łęg, a rural district just to the south of Nowa Huta where a power station was constructed in the late 1960s. Mrs Sinicka's parents, siblings, cousins, aunts and uncles also acquired apartments in Nowa Huta, mostly in adjacent neighbourhoods. One sister, one aunt and some cousins lived in the same block as Mrs Sinicka in Przy Arce. Mrs Sinicka bemoaned the fact they they no longer had as much time to see each other as before, but noted that they did not have to arrange to meet: 'We just pop in on each other'. They helped each other out as much as they could, circulating through their family network not just their own financial and material resources, but also those gathered from wider social networks, as Mrs Sinicka explained:

So of course after all if I receive something from a colleague at work, then I take those clothes for the children, I pass them on to my brother for the youngest children … Yes, yes, in general, I get things from my sister, and from her daughter. Because she's my sister, and in general also from granny and great-granny … Great-granny, yes, yes. And I get things from my grandsons, so that they're shared. Once, for example, I received a whole outfit for my daughter, and that whole outfit I must pass on to my goddaughter, with boots, that's how it is. Everything is looked after, respected, so that it can be used once again.

In addition to this exchange of clothes, one brother had an allotment, from which he distributed fruit and vegetables throughout the family (see Chapter Six), and another brother had a car which he used to give lifts to various family members. Mrs Sinicka and her family helped one brother set himself up in a new home after the birth of his daughter, assisting him both financially, when they had money to spare, and in fitting out his new apartment. At other times, when Mrs Sinicka and her husband were without work and struggling financially, her brother helped her out. In all these cases, Mrs Sinicka explained that there was no need to ask for help; family members simply knew when others needed some support. Mrs Sinicka implied that there is both an expectation of and a duty to help, implicit in the family relationship (Wierzbicka, 1997; Wedel, 1986). Similar dense flows of support were evident in Petržalka, where the Brestovičová family had very close contacts with their relatives. They met regularly, every weekend, for tea at 5 o'clock on Sunday, and if necessary even more often. The whole extended family was in a very similar financial situation but they lent and borrowed money within the family, often involving small amounts from 100 to 200 korunas (€2.50 to €5), which they returned as soon as they got some money from irregular informal work.

Family support and its limits

Poverty, ill-health and old age were often the context in which family support networks were mobilized, but they also proved to be a limit on such support. As Mrs Kowalik from Nowa Huta suggested: 'Of course everyone's in a difficult situation, of course we try to help each other out in any way, but it's not great.' For some the costs of care – in terms of time and money – meant that it was often difficult to reconcile the desire to support family members with constraints and competing demands, as Mrs Mad'arová from Petržalka explained:

> He [my father] cannot help me because he's 83. My sister takes care of him, because she has a car so she can travel and help him. For me, the journey is expensive, it's 800 crowns [€20], and also I have nobody to take care of my dogs, because my daughter is working and she is never at home, so it would be financially too difficult.

For others, it was the absence of family – through distance or conflict – that reduced the benefits of family support networks. Although the Juszczaks in Nowa Huta had access to Mrs Juszczak's mother's bank account – a real help for a young family – they had no everyday support from their parents or wider family who were either too far away or too busy with their own family needs. The trust placed in family support, and the consequent distrust of potential carers beyond the family, meant that the Juszczaks had no help with their daughter, the absence of which placed real limits on their wider lives, both socially and economically. In many instances of absent family, households turned to their wider social networks for support, but in these wider networks, issues of trust and reciprocity were more complex, as we explore in more detail below.

For those lucky enough to have important family connections, family support was a key way to ensure survival. The various forms of support – emotional, financial, material, technical and so on – which flowed within family networks literally made life possible, enabling households to manage working patterns and tight budgets, and sometimes to take the next step in family life cycles (starting a family, buying a flat; see Chapter Five). In the context of neo-liberalization, they enabled households to negotiate increasingly precarious and pressurized labour markets (see Chapter Four) and to reduce expenditures through the sharing and circulation of second hand goods and home-grown or home-cooked food (see Chapter Six). They also strengthened households' capacity to navigate the institutions they encountered. In these ways, family networks mediated the processes of neo-liberalization and made them more tolerable, but they also pointed to other narratives and rationalities which valued more than economic motivations. Yet, such networks of support were also very demanding, in terms not only of expectation and trust, but also of resources. The provision of care within families was dependent on the ability – in material, technical and other terms – of family members to contribute to, as well as draw from, the flows of support. Thus the wealth, in the broadest terms, of family networks depended on the assets of family members, and the distribution of these assets was uneven. As the examples of grandparents and siblings demon-strated, the provision of care within families rested on flows from asset-rich to asset-poor family members. For as long as some reciprocity was main-tained – for example, if financially poor grandmothers could give their time to time-poor parents – then networks could be maintained. However, the growing impoverishment of some households and the polarization of wealth in post-socialism threatened to erode this long-standing reciprocity and to wear away the bonds of family.

Neighbours and Networks

Family networks were also complemented by support offered by friends, acquaintances and neighbours. Recognition of the critical importance of these sorts of relationships during state socialism (Wedel, 1986; Ledeneva, 1998; Sik, 1995), and their persistence into the present day, has encouraged reflection on the nature of friendship across ECE. Linguistically, 'all Central and East European cultures have words that distinguish between different degrees of friendship' (Rybak & McAndrew, 2006: 151), most often distin-guishing between friends, colleagues and acquaintances (in Polish, *przy-jaciele, koledzy* and *znajomi*; in Slovak, *priatelia, kolegy* and *znami*) whose role and importance varies significantly (Wierzbicka, 1997; Wedel, 1986). All of these groups, even those described as acquaintances, play a critical role in the circuit of mutual help and trust. Colleagues and acquaintances can gen-erally be trusted with requests for help and, in turn, are 'permitted' to ask for help themselves while friendship invokes much greater expectations, as Wedel (1986: 104) suggests:

> A lot of Poles would go very far both in their expectations of real help and in terms of offering such help to their friends. Having a circle of *przyjaciele* increases the feeling of safety, both in psychological as well as in very 'practi-cal' aspects of life.

As has been noted in the post-socialist Russian context, real friendship is 'an intimate relation with serious obligations' (Nafus, 2006: 620), 'perhaps in itself a kind of emotional survival strategy' (Pickup & White, 2003: 428). The strength of friendship means that, for some, family-like relationships are developed with close friends, leading to the identification of fictive kin. A number of households in Nowa Huta and Petržalka identified friends with whom their ties were so strong and long-standing – often built through a combination of both neighbourhood and workplace relationships – that they saw them as all but family, evoking the same expectation of help offered and received.

Table 7.5 demonstrates, however, that households in Nowa Huta were, on the whole, more active in support networks with friends, colleagues and neighbours than those in Petržalka. The most common form of mutual support was the sharing of labour or time. In Nowa Huta, around half of all households exchanged this kind of support within their networks, compared to less than 20% in Petržalka. With respect to the exchange of money and food and other things, the role of friends in Nowa Huta was also generally higher than in Petržalka. Social networks established beyond the family were often critical, however, in both districts, for both practical and social needs. For some, rich, tight friendship groups provided considerable network resources to households. In most instances, these friendship groups were developed on the basis of long-standing and interlocking relationships from school, study, work and the neighbourhood, and were most likely to occur in households which had lengthy family connections with Nowa Huta or Petržalka. Both Mr and Mrs Niemczyk, a middle-aged couple with two adult children, had been born and brought up in Nowa Huta and still had family living in neighbouring parts of the district. But it was with their group of a dozen or so friends (their *grono przyjaciól*, or circle of friends) that they had forged support networks within which they not only lent and borrowed money, food and advice, but which also enabled them to access scarce services, such as good doctors, through acquaintances or *po znajomości* (Wierzbicka, 1997). Having known these friends for more than 20 years, they knew well who to approach for what kinds of help and found the help and advice offered to be very effective. While the Niemczyks were reasonably well-off (with an equivalized household income above 140% of the median) and were as likely to go skiing with their friends as to need their help, the poorer Sieradzki family relied on their *grono przyjaciól* in more critical ways. In particular, Mrs Sieradzka counted on (she used this phrase repeatedly in interview) her five closest friends, who lived in adjacent neighbourhoods, for a range of support. She explained:

> So, yes, it's like that, that if someone needs something ... it has a friendly form, so they phone and I ask 'what's up?', I pop round for coffee ... Another time I want to borrow something, so it's simply, it's a friendly exchange, so that one can count on another.

Each member of the circle helped the others according to their skills, such that Mrs Sieradzka, an information technician, helped her friends with their computer problems, and she received other favours in return. In the context of economic insecurity, Mrs Sieradzka noted the importance of close friends, as 'acquaintances' were less and less likely to help out:

> Well, obviously, on account of these finances, but not only because there's also this principle that if it's not that close a friendship, just some sort of more distant 'colleague [koleżenski]' friendship, then rather simply there comes a time when you have to distance yourself, because maybe I'll ask to find me work. So simple, they're afraid and they turn away if someone has a problem. I think that it's a sort of self-defence, so that it [the problem] doesn't touch me. But this relates mostly to those more distant acquaintances. Close acquaintances simply aren't afraid of this. And those further, contacts, colleagues, occasionally they're afraid ...

The importance of dense friendship networks, especially for young couples with children who might not be able to call on family for support, led two of our Nowa Huta households – the Kiedrowskis and the Wolaks – to plan, with their friends, to live in the same neighbourhood. Both of these households were 'born and bred' in Nowa Huta and had social lives rooted in the district and negotiated with their friends, as they all set up households independent of their parents, to live in close proximity, such that they might be able to socialize together and support each other.

The final example of a critical friendship group in Nowa Huta was of a group of three of our interviewees, Mrs Kielak, Mrs Modzelewska and Mrs Czarnocka, who all lived in one block in Osiedle Górali. Mrs Czarnocka was occupying her flat illegally and had been given notice of eviction, while Mrs Modzelewska and Mrs Kielak had both been served with eviction for non-payment of rent (see Chapter Five). All three women were single mothers and unemployed, having experienced insecure and patchy work histories, and thus lived on a combination of family benefits, discretionary benefits and occasionally alimony (discussed in more detail below).

The three women had known each other for some time, meeting through their co-residence and through their children of roughly the same age. They met daily, sometimes with other neighbours too, for coffee at the very least, but more usually to exchange various forms of help – emotional, practical and material – exchanges which took them beyond the block and into Nowa Huta. As Mrs Kielak explained:

> With my friend [koleżanka – Mrs Modzelewska] I go shopping, or to social services, for example, where we sort things out together.[5] We go to the church to the priest, because more than once the priest has helped us out,

for example, in the form of food, and we also go together. To holy mass, also together. We go practically everywhere together. And sometimes we pop somewhere together for a beer.

While it was clear that Mrs Kielak and Mrs Modzelewska had a considerable amount of affection for each other, it is the practical support they lent each other which appeared to be critical. This related not only to their negotiations of formal bureaucracies – in particular, social services – but also to sharing information and ideas about where to access other forms of support. Each told the other of help available from charities and parish churches, for example. Given their difficult financial position and their complex negotiations over benefits, alimony, housing and work, Mrs Kielak, Mrs Modzelewska and Mrs Czarnocka spent much of their day 'sorting things out'. The support and company which each offered the others in these negotiations was critical, both practically and psychologically. Together with the small amounts of money, the flour and the soap powder, which amongst other things these women exchanged, their relationship covered all bases, providing them with very high levels of support in very difficult circumstances and when more formal channels of support were unhelpful and difficult. The presence of three women in the network also helped to iron out difficulties; if Mrs Modzelewska and Mrs Kielak could not help each other, then they turned to Mrs Czarnocka. Each also fulfilled a different role in support: Mrs Modzelewska was more likely to borrow money from Mrs Czarnocka but food and ingredients from Mrs Kielak. The particular strength of these networks in this block, in a context most often caricatured as anti-social and fragmented, is acknowledged by local research (Bukowski et al., 2006), which draws attention to the relatively high levels of trust, in neighbours and in institutions, and explains the strong neighbourly relations through the proximity of key social institutions and the presence of some educated, young and working residents. Nevertheless, the concern that the insularity and poverty of networks weakens the opportunities presented through them is very real here (Gilbert, 1998).

While we have noted the greater extent and usage of friendship networks in Nowa Huta compared to Petržalka, it is also the case that for many of the poorest households in Petržalka friendship was a fundamental basis for the establishment of local networks of support. For example, Mrs Červíková, a 52-year-old Petržalka respondent living with her former partner and adult son, had an income from invalidity benefit worth SKK3,450 (€86) a month, of which she had to spend nearly one-third on medicine. In order to supplement this income she worked with her friend and neighbour, Mrs Veselá, to collect paper for recycling from rubbish containers around Petržalka. Operating in a commodified informal economy in which they go on to sell the paper they gather to a local recycling company, they received the princely sum of SKK1 (€0.03) for each kilo of paper. Over two days Mrs Červíková expected to earn SKK350 (€9) to supplement her benefit income (Smith & Rochovská, 2007).

Everyday neighbouring

These relationships were rooted in the fact that these households were neighbours, living very connected lives together, often in poverty. But they also often reflected the intertwining of their children's lives, their shared negotiations with local institutions, their common experiences and, in Nowa Huta, their church-going. These shared experiences and overlapping spaces of everyday life meant that, for some, neighbours became an important part of a household's social networks and central to their negotiation of complex forms of poverty and exclusion. Neighbourly relations became, at times, indistinguishable from friendship (Wedel, 1986). In both Nowa Huta and Petržalka, the particular forms of urban life and, until recently, the slow pace of residential change (see Chapter Five) reinforced the interlocking geographies of everyday life, which enabled and sustained such strong neighbourly relations. While much of this 'everyday neighbouring' reflected deep-seated urban social interactions, such relationships took on new meanings and values in the context of the tumultuous transformations of neo-liberalization and associated social exclusions. In many instances, relationships which began as nodding to acquaintances in the lift, stairwell or in public spaces (Plate 7.1) developed into more multi-stranded relationships as children enrolled in school together, mothers and grandmothers shopped in the same neighbourhood shops, families regularly attended the nearest parish church, and dogs were walked along the same paths. Particularities which supported the development of these relationships included the fact that many households moved into the same block around the same day immediately after construction and that workplaces often allocated apartments in newly built blocks such that a household's new neighbours were likely in many cases to also be their workmates (Stenning, 2005b; see also Chapter Five). Mrs Idziak, a divorcee in her fifties in Nowa Huta, initially met three of her neighbours through her children's activities in the 1980s and came to recognize them in the neighbourhood as they all walked their dogs. Over the years, Mrs Idziak gradually increased the contact she had with her neighbours, such that they exchanged food and food ingredients, money, and used clothes,[6] and socialized together. Indeed, the friendship that developed between Mrs Idziak and her neighbours animated their staircase more generally as these women organized a New Year's Eve party for the whole corridor in 2005. Similar sets of relations were also reported among households in Petržalka. For example, the Šanovná family not only organized

Plate 7.1   Pensioners talk in Nowa Huta

New Year's Eve parties with their neighbours but also weddings and other major events. For the Šanovnás, the longevity of their residence, the slow turnover in the block, and the transfer of apartments between generations supported the maintenance of these neighbourly relationships.

While such very close and animated relationships were not the rule, most households did have important functioning relationships with some of their neighbours. As Table 7.6 demonstrates, the majority of households in Nowa Huta had some level of everyday contact with their neighbours. The same was also true of the Petržalka neighbourhoods of Haanova and Lúky-Sever, but not of Gessayova. These neighbourhood differences reflected a number of factors that influenced neighbourly contact. In Nowa Huta, the highest level of daily contact was in the neighbourhoods of Willowe and Górali, which are characterized by the highest levels of poverty and marginalization, by smaller blocks built around shared courtyards, by longer residential histories and, often, by older residents and others (the unemployed, single mothers) who are likely to spend more time in the neighbourhood than at work. In Petržalka, the lower levels of neighbourly contact in Gessayova resulted from the combined impact of the preponderance of poorer households and the physicality of the district, with its large 12-storey long blocks creating a physical environment in which social interactions were often more limited and atomized. In Haanova,

Table 7.6 Households with some level of contact with neighbours, by neighbourhood (% of total respondents)

Neighbourhood		Some level of contact every day	Contact once a week	Contact once a month
Nowa Huta	Willowe/Górali	90	78	62
	Przy Arce	60	56	38
	Dywizjonu 303	64	84	88
	Oświecenia	60	70	56
Petržalka	Gessayova	24	56	20
	Haanova	86	90	82
	Lúky-Sever	66	80	90

Source: Household survey

social interactions were more intense, reflecting the presence of higher income groups, who not only had more time and resources to invest in their social networks, but were also supported by a built environment dominated by four-storey blocks positioned around sociable grassed courtyards. Thus, whereas in Nowa Huta the social limitations of poverty were somewhat relieved by a built form that supported social interaction, in Petržalka the social burdens of poverty were exacerbated by an atomizing built form. In addition to issues of built form and poverty, the presence of children also mediated and enabled contact between neighbours, not only because contact between children led to contact between parents, but also because, given existing gender divisions of labour, mothers with young children were likely to be in and around the neighbourhood during the day. More recently, both life-cycle and wider demographic changes within neighbourhoods in Petržalka and Nowa Huta reduced the presence of children and thus their role as mediators. In other ways, the passing of time and the coincidence of life cycles was seen to have a positive impact on neighbourly relationships, as Mrs Paštéková in Petržalka explained: 'We are here with our neighbours all our lives – 26 years is quite a long time – so we were here like one big family; we have children in the same age, so its good... we all know each other ...'. The simple fact of living in a neighbourhood for a long time shaped the frequency and character of contact with neighbours and the number of recognizable faces on the benches and paths of the neighbourhood.

The most common forms of assistance exchanged with neighbours were mutual visits and what Perren et al. (2004) call 'watch-and-ward' functions, involving looking after each other's flats, plants and pets (Table 7.7). Also common, however, were the exchange and gifting of food (see Chapter

Table 7.7   Forms of neighbourly support (% of households)

	Nowa Huta	*Petržalka*
They look after our flat when we are away	42	40
We look after their flat when they are away	42	42
We borrow food or goods from them	28	24
They borrow food or goods from us	33	23
We give food or goods to them	16	21
They give food or goods to us	24	20
We borrow money from them	22	11
They borrow money from us	25	11
We look after their children	12	9
They look after our children	14	11
We visit them	50	53
They visit us	49	53
We help them with repairs	34	21
They help us with repairs	25	18
We help them on the allotment	3	–
They help us on the allotment	3	1

Source: Household survey

Six), the exchange of time and labour (repairs, childcare) and the lending and borrowing of money. The vast majority of this assistance was mutual, with households both helping and being helped. In interview, the routine and taken-for-granted nature of neighbourly contact became clearer. The value of very mundane exchanges, of painkillers, an onion or a lightbulb, for example, was downplayed as households explained how their relationships with their neighbours were minimal. Yet, as the Pustelak household in Nowa Huta acknowledged, such petty support is in fact 'a big help, very big'. For the Pustelaks – a young couple with three children – the help they received from an elderly neighbour meant that juggling cooking and childcare or managing minor illnesses, for example, became easier. These small gifts and loans meant that the business of everyday life was eased and they could focus attention on managing the more complex negotiations of work, care and other responsibilities. In the context of this everyday, routine support, two particular modalities are important to highlight. Firstly, in Nowa Huta a number of households had taken on informal and occasional caring roles in relation to elderly neighbours, often when those neighbours had absent family. Thus, for example, households visited and kept an eye on elderly neighbours, did shopping for them, collected medicines, did occasional housework or repairs, and walked their dogs when they were ill.

On occasion, this care was reciprocated by the elderly neighbour keeping on eye on the household's children from time to time, or by gifts of home-cooked food.[7] Secondly, a particularly important role was played, in both the giving and receiving of neighbourly assistance, by those household members and neighbours who had particular technical skills. The Lastovičková family in Petržalka, for example, often exchanged the grand-father's plumbing skills for the carpentry skills of their neighbour, whilst their adult son offered his electrical expertise to neighbours and the grand-mother her sewing skills. All this help was offered in the expectation that, at some point, it would be reciprocated. In these ways, skills, often devel-oped at work and sometimes now redundant in the formal workplace, were circulated within housing blocks and wider social networks. Although some women provided IT support, sewing and cooking in this way, this was a sphere dominated by men engaged in fixing locks, repairing TV antennae, and repairing electrical appliances.[8] In the exchange of expertise, house-holds avoided commodified repair services and, thus, both costly repairs and an unremitting engagement with market forms of exchange. These repair cultures and mutual economies of non-commodified exchange ena-bled some households to focus their limited incomes on those goods and services increasingly only available through market exchanges (and often experiencing price increases), but they could also be seen as a less than perfect alternative to consumption.

Networks of Care

In Nowa Huta and Petržalka, a very large proportion of all caring work was carried out within the kinds of kinship and friendship networks discussed already. Such networks made up for the absence of more formal provision (see below) and enabled households to manage tight budgets, busy sched-ules and the demands of care. The exchange of skills, as well as more tangi-ble resources, such as money and food, and the more intangible expression of care, demonstrates the ways in which the help that circulates within social networks reflects the broadly conceived 'assets' of households and those of their friends, family and neighbours. Households fed into the flows of cir-culating support what they could and sought support in spheres they lacked. Thus households with cars found themselves offering friends and family lifts; those with IT skills, help with computers; those with free time, child-care and errands; and so on. In many cases, what this meant is that the gender divisions of labour evident within both the household and within the formal labour market tended to extend the forms of care provided within wider social networks. Women were predominantly engaged in personal care, in shopping, cooking and emotional support; men contributed technical skills, bureaucratic know-how and heavy labour. The feminized burdens of care begin to point to some of the tensions present in these flows.

Such tensions were exacerbated by the apparent erosion of networks, and of reciprocity within them, by the processes of neo-liberalization, which are feeding growing poverty and polarization, increasing work pressures and/or, paradoxically, job loss, and housing turnover. Contact and community became eroded, and networks of support were placed under considerable pressure, as many of our interviewees testified. That families were increasingly remaining behind closed doors was a notion that recurred throughout our interviews in both Nowa Huta and Petržalka and was increasingly expressed physically through the adoption of security systems and stronger front doors (see also Stenning, 2005b). As Mrs Sasnowicz, from Nowa Huta, explained, voicing the concerns of many, 'Now everyone closes their doors, they want a bit of peace. Everyone is at work a long time. They have to go to work all day ... Before, doors really weren't closed and now it's not like that.'

Yet, notwithstanding these real concerns, the density of support offered by family, friends and neighbours in Nowa Huta and Petržalka was considerable, and surprisingly resilient. The acts of generosity performed by households in very difficult social and economic situations, and the willingness of many to share whatever resources – time, money, food, second-hand clothes etc. – they did have suggests the persistent importance of these non-market exchanges. But such transactions also worked to constitute neo-liberalism in the wider economy by allowing savings to be directed to other expenditures and by absorbing – or domesticating – the loss of state support and welfare through the networks of family and friends.

The State and Other Institutional Forms of Care and Support

Notwithstanding the erosion of social security provision discussed in Chapter Two, and the powerful role of informal support and transfers in the everyday economies of households discussed here, state benefits continued to play an important role in sustaining incomes and in redistributing income within extended household networks, particularly amongst poorer households. As Table 7.8 shows, a significant proportion of household income in both Petržalka and Nowa Huta was derived from state benefits. This was particularly marked in Nowa Huta, where the restructuring and 'downsizing' of the steelworks had led to high levels of disability pension claimants (included in Table 7.8 as 'other sources') and relatively high levels of unemployment benefit claimants. In both districts, pensions were an important contributor to household income, reflecting the age profile of the districts, the tendency to use early retirement as a means of 'reducing' unemployment

Table 7.8 Average proportion of income derived from various sources

Income group relative to local median	Main job	Other jobs	Pensions	Child benefit	Unemployment benefit	Other social benefits	Other sources
Petržalka							
≤60% median	55	5	20	3	2	3	9
61–100% median	58	4	28	2	0	1	5
101–140% median	70	1	21	1	0	4	3
≥141% median	92	3	4	0	0	0	1
Total	70	3	18	1	0.4	4	3
Nowa Huta							
≤60% median	25	0	15	11	15	3	31
61–100% median	49	7	22	1	4	1	17
101–140% median	53	4	30	1	0	0	13
≥140% median	72	6	19	0	0	1	3
Total	59	5	22	1	2	1	11

Source: Household survey

(Balcerzak-Paradowska et al., 2003),[9] and the *relatively* generous pension benefits granted by earlier pensions systems. This was particularly the case among poorer households in Petržalka below median income levels. However, the shift of unemployment and other social benefits to a means-tested basis (although see the discussion below about child benefit) meant that these other benefits contributed much less to overall household income than in Nowa Huta (notably for the poorest households).

Those households which received a significant amount of their income from pensions, in both Nowa Huta and Petržalka, were not especially likely to find themselves in the poorest income category. They were much more likely to be clustered around the median income level, suggesting that one or more pension income lifts a household out of relative poverty (see also S. Clarke, 2002). In both districts, there were pensioner households in the wealthiest income category, though in Petržalka these were more likely to be where pensions accounted for less than half of the total household income, suggesting the presence of other working household members and/ or more diverse income generation strategies (see Chapter Four). In contrast, the relatively few households with significant proportions of their income from unemployment benefit tended to be clustered below the median income level. With respect to other social benefits (including child benefits), the greater the proportion of household income from benefits, the more likely the household was to be in the poorer income categories. This reflects a marked shift in recent years in Poland towards the means-testing of benefits, including family benefits. In Poland, apart from a one-off payment on the birth of a child (the so-called *becikowe*, introduced by the PiS government in 2006), there is now no universal access to maternity, child-rearing or family benefits (Balcerzak-Paradowska et al., 2003). Not only has this reduced access to benefits but it also increased, as we discuss in more detail below, the difficulties of accessing such benefits and the stigma attached to them. Paradoxically, in Slovakia, despite the wide-scale neo-liberalization of social policy during the 1990s and early 2000s, family benefits were never moved to a means-testing system. One-off payments on birth have been retained and the parents of every school-age child, regardless of household income, are eligible to receive child benefit.

These regular benefits were supplemented in some households by one-off assistance from local authorities, although the relative significance of the specific type of assistance varied considerably between Nowa Huta and Petržalka (Tables 7.9 and 7.10). On the whole, levels of support were low, with just a handful of households receiving such assistance. In general this support was granted more frequently in Nowa Huta, reflecting the greater preservation of social security in Poland. In Nowa Huta, assistance provided in association with children's education stood at a much higher level, with 15% to 25% of all households receiving some remission of fees

Table 7.9 Households receiving state or local authority assistance in previous 12 months (% of households)

	Nowa Huta	*Petržalka*
Tax remissions or credits	2	7
Financial family support	10	5
Financial support for pensioners	3	1
Financial support for medicines or glasses	7	2
Emergency social assistance	2	3
Assistance at Christmas or Easter	5	1
Material support (e.g. food, regular free meals, clothing)	3	0
Took part in cultural programmes (e.g. special dinners or social events)	2	3
Other	8	4

Source: Household survey

Table 7.10 Households receiving school assistance in previous 12 months (% of households)

	Nowa Huta	*Petržalka*
Scholarship for children	6	2
Remission of some fees	26	1
Free school meals	16	1
One-off assistance at the beginning of the school year	19	0
Access to after-school clubs or summer camps	12	3
One-off allowance or payment	1	0
Other	2	1

Source: Household survey

(for additional school services), free school meals and assistance at the beginning of the school (for the purchase of books and school clothes). For some of the poorest households in Nowa Huta, the provision of hot meals for children was extremely important. As Mrs Modzelewska, living without any income while her ex-partner was pursued for alimony (see below), explained: 'Lunches, for example, really help, because if for example there is a time when I don't get any alimony, then at least the children have a hot meal.' There was a complex relationship between receipt of some of these forms of assistance and income, with some benefits more likely to be received by wealthier households. There are a number of potential explanations for this. Firstly, some benefits remained universal (e.g. financial support for medicines for pensioners) and were thus likely to be received by households in all income groups. Secondly, in some instances, benefit income was enough to lift a family above the poverty level (as discussed above). And thirdly – and most problematically – the poorest households may not have been accessing the benefits they were entitled to, an issue we explore in more detail below.

The accounts of households living on benefits flesh out the social security landscape further. In most instances, households with benefit incomes put together a portfolio of benefits, from the state and local authorities (often coupled with non-state assistance, see below), and spent much of their time applying and reapplying for this income. Whilst some benefits were only available for fixed periods (such as unemployment benefit), others were granted for short periods, with a requirement to reapply every 3, 6 or 12 months. This created enormous demands on households to maintain 'a mass of papers of different evidence', as Mrs Dawidowicz noted, and to regularly visit social services offices to process their claims. It also meant that the flow of income into 'benefit-dependent' households was uneven, with periods of non-payment severely disrupting the household budget and creating some very precarious situations.

The case of the Kowalik household, a young couple with a small baby, illustrates this point well. Mr Kowalik was out of work, without any right to unemployment benefit, and Mrs Kowalik was employed in a low-paid and precarious job. They were also caring for a young son. At the time of interview, they were in receipt of temporary benefit from municipal social services (MOPS) at a level of PLN250 (€60) a month for six months, plus housing benefit which varied between PLN100 and PLN200 (€25–50) every month or two, and one-off benefits of PLN100–150 (€25–35) for medicines, food and electricity payments. As Mrs Kowalik explains:

> Yes, it demands a lot of time and a lot of paper. You could say that bureaucracy drives bureaucracy … You have to spend a lot of time … sometimes I have to provide them with proof how much I earn, although social services already know that, how much I have gross every month, but each time for example I have to take them proof from my employer about my wages. Sometimes for that proof I have to wait a week or two, because my employer doesn't have a permanent office where I can go … My husband for example has to provide evidence that he's looking for work at the job centre where he's registered. And that takes up a bit of time too, he has to go from firm to firm, getting these stamps that say he's looking for work, that that firm really has refused him work. This also takes a lot of time. It really is a little time consuming.

For some households, the costs of trying to access social assistance were not only temporal but also financial. The time and money Mrs Sieradzka in Nowa Huta spent collecting, photocopying and delivering the necessary paperwork to social services outweighed any possible benefits received. The burden of negotiating social services was also almost exclusively absorbed by women. While this picture is skewed by the number of single mothers claiming benefits in Nowa Huta, even in those households where husbands were present, women took on the majority of this activity. In this context, the support that women gave each other in their navigation of social services and the benefits system was critical. These informal channels were often the most important means for households to find out what benefits were available and what they might be eligible for. Only in a very few instances were women alerted to possible benefits by authorities, such as social services or schools. The key exception to this formal flow of information and advice was for those groups for whom specialist help was offered. In Nowa Huta, this was the case for two groups: those with almost permanent contact with social services[10] and Roma families.[11] With respect to the former, the continuity of contact was reflected for some in important relationships with key social workers, though it is important to note that others had had ongoing contact with social services over a number of years, but had not been supported in such a productive and personal manner. This reinforces the view, cited above (Cerami, 2008), that social worker discretion plays a considerable role in the provision of state care in Poland.

Households' personal experience with social services, and with particular social workers, raises questions about equality of access to eligible benefits. Social workers told a number of our households that, regardless of their legal eligibility, other families had greater needs which would be met first. Other household members found themselves judged by social workers for their personal circumstances or disadvantaged by inflexible eligibility rules. Some, for example, found themselves ineligible because of the informal and insecure nature of their employment contracts, which meant that, sometimes unknowingly, they had failed to pay insurance contributions (see Chapter Four). Still others were reluctant to trust social services with personal information, not only because of a generalized lack of trust in state authorities but also because the poorest households were often forced to access illegal employment and to resort to other illegal practices. All of these difficulties, together with the withdrawal of universal benefits and the attack on so-called 'cultures of dependency' (Stenning, 2005a), encouraged the stigmatization of benefits in Nowa Huta and Petržalka. A number of households in both districts described the shame and indignity they felt in accessing benefits, expressing clearly in their accounts of the tortuous process of claiming the difficult emotions evoked. A perhaps contrary, but related, sentiment frequently expressed saw some household members seeing themselves as unworthy of support, despite often being in extremely precarious financial positions. As Mrs Futyma, a widow in her fifties in real poverty and dependent on precarious part-time employment, explained:

> No, I've never used social services, and I don't now ... you know, I'm now on my own ... and I think, let those who really are in a worse situation, who have children, use it [social services].

Together with the increasingly stringent criteria employed in the assessment of benefit rights and the ongoing reduction in the level and duration of most benefits, questions of trust, stigma and worth, obstacles to claiming, poor information and technical problems with eligibility all reduced the access that needy households had to benefits and other forms of state assistance.

One area where access to benefits was particularly difficult, but also particularly important, was the sphere of alimony benefits, paid by the state to single parents (predominantly mothers) when absent parents (fathers) failed to pay the alimony payments set by the courts. For a significant number of single-parent households in Nowa Huta, these alimony benefits were the primary source of stable income, often supplemented by other occasional benefits. These single-parent households were amongst the poorest in our sample because single mothers often struggled to combine child care with employment (as discussed above; see also Krakowskie Centrum Praw Kobiet, 2005; Hryciuk, 2005).[12] Indeed, recent benefit regulation changes in Poland meant that single mothers would almost certainly lose these benefits if they were in work, since their income would rise above the social minimum threshold for payment of benefits. In both our interviews and in broader accounts of the alimony system, there are repeated tales of ineffectual bailiffs, both unable and unwilling to pursue fathers for their debts (Krakowskie Centrum Praw Kobiet, 2005).[13] As a case in point, Mrs Modzelewska had been without income for three months, since her ex-partner had ceased paying alimony. Whilst the bailiff confirmed that she had no concealed income and began to press her former partner for payment, Mrs Modzelewska was living off loans and the goodwill of her friends and family.

We have already drawn attention, in Chapter Four, to the ways in which benefit – especially pension – income offered a relatively stable basis on which to develop riskier, entrepreneurial income strategies, but it is also important to note the wider household and network benefits of such income and to reiterate, in particular, how pension income was redistributed within families, from grandparents to their children and grandchildren (Zajicek et al., 2007; Tarkowska, 2000). We noted above that grandparents offered a range of material, emotional and practical support to their families, but this was often complemented by financial assistance. For example, a Petržalka household comprising a divorced middle-aged woman, Mrs. Uhlíková, living on invalidity benefit with her school-age daughter, received a regular financial contribution from her pensioner parents living elsewhere in Bratislava since she lost her job due to health problems: 'I pay SKK3,000 [€75] for my flat and my parents pay the rest [SKK4,500; €113]. But they won't [continue to do that anymore] when my daughter finishes school … They have helped me for many years in this way. …'

Other institutions

As we have shown, state benefits often failed to meet the needs of poorer households, forcing them to seek additional support elsewhere. In the post-socialist period, there has been a marked growth in charitable, particularly religious, organizations providing assistance to struggling households and offering new care services, such as hospices and substance abuse pro-grammes (Read & Thelen, 2007; Caldwell, 2004a; Sokolowski, 2001). As in the USA and the UK, these institutions have moved to fill gaps left by the neo-liberal state and become a kind of 'shadow state' (Wolch, 1989; see also May et al., 2005). In some instances, the activities of these charities were intertwined with international programmes, supported by organizations such as the EU and reflecting the connections between anti-poverty pro-grammes and international structures and agendas. Perhaps the clearest example of this is the European food aid programme (PEAD) discussed in Chapter Six, but international aid and know-how was also channelled to other charitable activities. All of the organizations involved in the distribu-tion of PEAD food were also involved in other forms of charitable support. In Poland, Caritas offers regular monthly and more occasional emergency assistance, in the form of food, clothes and money for medicines, to the poor and elderly. The Polish and Slovak Red Cross both run soup kitchens, homeless hostels and pensioners' clubs, and donate clothes, soap powder, schoolbooks, furniture and domestic equipment to poor families. The Polish Social Welfare Committee (Polski Komitet Pomocy Społecznej, PKPS) pro-vides 'material and organizational support and the restoration of hope and a feeling of security to people who find themselves in difficult life situations, in particular to the poor, the homeless, the lonely and the neglected'[14] and offers a range of material and financial help. It also organized clubs for pen-sioners, youth clubs, summer camps and Christmas and Easter festivities. In addition to these national and international actors, smaller charities, often associated with parish churches and other local organizations, are also involved in providing material and moral support to struggling families.[15]

In Nowa Huta, reflecting the persistent centrality of the steelworks and its associated institutions, a key welfare role was also played by trade unions

Plate 7.2   Towarzystwo Solidarnej Pomocy (Mutual Assistance Association), Nowa Huta

(Stenning, 2003), echoing wider experiences of community unionism (Wills, 2001). Each of the steelworks' trade unions – there are half a dozen – expended considerable energy and funds on the welfare of its members in the community, offering financial assistance to both current and former employees for the purchase of medicines, holidays and housing renovations, for example. Subsidiary organizations fulfilled complementary welfare roles. The Towarzystwo Solidarnej Pomocy (TSP, or Mutual Assistance Association; Plate 7.2), for example, distributes donated medicines to the community through a free chemist, subsidizes school meals, provides Christmas and Easter dinners and other hot meals for those in need in the winter, donates Christmas presents, clothing and food packages and pays the utility bills of those in desperate need. And the Centre for Old Age and Disability Pensioners, funded by the steelworks through its Social Fund but managed jointly by the three largest unions, distributes funds to pensioners in need and acts as a collection and redistribution point for in-kind benefits and as an advocate and social centre for pensioners.

While the broad provision of support for poor families was a positive phenomenon, two issues were troubling. Firstly, the multiplicity and complexity of sources of help made the search for support complicated and time consuming and the importance of shared information meant that exclusion from knowledgeable networks reinforced daily struggles for some, even though some of the help received through these channels did circulate beyond individual households. Secondly, most charitable donations came with conditions attached – recipients were rarely free to consume as they wished – and these conditions were coupled with the occasional moral judgements of charity workers, as Mrs Kowalik explained about her dealings with Caritas:

> It's simply, really, this humiliation of everyone. They ask what your situation is, how you spend your money, what's in your kitchen ... no, I simply don't have the nerves for it ...

Conclusions

This chapter has drawn attention to the interlocking spaces and practices of care and the ways in which family, wider social networks and the state all play a role in supporting households in the troubled times of neo-liberalism. Above and beyond the wider strains created by neo-liberalization – most noticeably the sheer increase in the burdens of 'getting by' – these processes of change have had a direct impact on landscapes of care in a number of ways. Most importantly, perhaps, this is seen in the neo-liberalization of welfare and the concomitant reduction and rationalization of state-led care, in the context of national pressures to domesticate budgetary prudence. These transformations have had impacts across the welfare sector but are most evident in the growing limits on eligibility and the reduction of available benefits. Post-socialist welfare has been marked, in most cases, by an end to universal benefits, an associated extension of means testing, the growing prevalence of agendas for 'activation' (in an echo of Western 'welfare to work' programmes) and a widespread stigmatization of benefit income. As the latter suggests, these reforms have developed alongside the devolution and individualization of responsibility for care, in an echo of wider neo-liberal governmentalities which reverberate also through religious and conservative agendas in both Poland and Slovakia. Within these discourses, we see a downplaying of the structural sources of poverty and a denial, often within impoverished households themselves, of evident need and deprivation. The changing governmentalities, and moral economies, of care are exacerbated by the promotion of third, or private, sector providers with particular conditionalities.

These neo-liberalizations have occurred at a time when households' kinship and social networks have been under strain from job loss, poverty and the polarization of opportunity, all experiences which have threatened the reciprocity at the heart of networks of care. Neo-liberalizing labour markets, increased housing turnover driven by developing housing markets and rising poverty all, in the experience of households in Nowa Huta and Petržalka, encouraged declining levels of sociability. The neo-liberalization of work echoed in other ways through landscapes of care too, as redundancy, male unemployment and the relative growth of 'female' jobs led to shifting domestic divisions of labour.

Nevertheless, in spite of these powerful transformations, our research testified to the presence of extraordinary networks of care, many of which were themselves testament to an incredibly strong impulse to community within Nowa Huta and Petržalka. These social spaces made some of the most difficult consequences of neo-liberalism tolerable, and were evidence of a resistance to the overwhelming impulses to individualism promoted by neo-liberal rhetoric. Households drew on and contributed to a range of social and kinship networks, engaging in different circuits and exchanges for different caring practices (such as elder care, DIY, financial support, advice) and used these social networks to ease their negotiation of state and charitable spheres too. The critical role played by kinship and social networks in households' landscapes of care pointed to real concerns for those households who found themselves isolated from family and friendship networks, as a result of family breakdown or other social crises.

As we have suggested, the state remained central to welfare provision in both Nowa Huta and Petržalka, notwithstanding the evident processes of retrenchment and rationalization. This reflected, in part, the dominant role of the state in state socialist welfare regimes, despite the fact that the structures of paternalism, which offered 'cradle to grave' support before 1989, have been significantly eroded. In some ways, though, such as inadequate public childcare provision and the expectation that grandmothers play a key role in childcare, we can see the clear echoes of state socialist policy decisions. These legacies were articulated with a host of long-standing and culturally significant practices (such as the re-use and circulation of commodities within networks and the persistent use of wider family and kinship networks to sustain social reproduction) and with moral rationalities and subjectivities, especially of gender and generation. Not only did these shape who does what within social and kinship caring practices, but they were also key to understanding the practices of state welfare, such as the provision of childcare, the alimony system, and support for elderly or disabled household members.

Households' caring practices and their historical roots point to a whole array of articulations, not only within and between caring practices and the networks which supported them, but also with other spheres of everyday life. In addition to the knock-on impacts of neo-liberalizing labour markets, it was possible to identify myriad other interconnections between care and work. The enduring provision, in Nowa Huta in particular, of a social wage by key employers, the translation into caring practices of skills derived at work, and the circulation within households and their wider networks of income earnt at work were all ways in which work articulates forcefully with care. Similar articulations can be identified with housing, since social networks often rested on low levels of housing turnover (see Chapter Five), and with consumption practices as social networks and kinship relations mediated the engagement with commodified spheres through exchange, repair and recycling, as we discussed in this chapter and in Chapter Six. These articulations point to interlocking geographies of everyday life in which overlapping networks of kin, neighbour and family relationships and interconnected geographies of household practices either enabled and strengthened caring relationships, or reinforced the exclusion of those on the margins.

These everyday geographies differed, however, between Nowa Huta and Petržalka. The two districts have quite distinctly different patterns of family and wider social networks, which reflect to a large extent the districts' geographies, both of settlement and of the development of their built form. Households in Nowa Huta had denser and more resistant sets of social networks, even within and around extremely marginalized households. These household networks were supported by a particularly 'thick' institutional geography, with soup kitchens, parishes, charities, trade unions and other local organizations contributing to the district's landscapes of care. There are differences within Nowa Huta and Petržalka, too, given the apparent importance of the built form and social make-up of blocks. In some neighbourhoods, proximate family offered greater opportunities (and demands) while residence within a particularly 'hostile' housing block may have reduced the potential for caring relationships. However, extreme poverty did not seem to be a barrier to robust and productive social networks, though the poverty and insularity of these may have limited the range of households' economic practices. Through these local differences, however, were refracted differentiated national neo-liberalizations. In contrast to other spheres, Slovakia does not seem to have neo-liberalized welfare more than Poland, where the strong commitment to solidarity (see Chapter Two) barely seems to have tempered the rationalization of welfare provision. Indeed, both countries' welfare forms stand out within regional comparisons as particularly neo-liberal.

The caring practices of households were time-consuming, especially for women, involving not only the actual practices of care, but also the work of maintaining social networks and negotiating bureaucracies. Moreover, these burdens have increased markedly in recent years as the struggle to achieve social reproduction seems to have become more and more difficult. Through these diverse caring practices, households – and women in particular – have sought to domesticate post-socialist transformations, to smooth some of the most difficult experiences of neo-liberalization, to fill the gaps created by the downsizing of welfare, and in these ways to try to make neo-liberalism more tolerable. Yet, in doing so, households have picked up the slack of other providers and have taken responsibility for ensuring social reproduction, not only easing the lives of younger, older and disabled household members, but also enabling low-paid workers to juggle diverse working practices and to bring home some sort of income (see Chapter Four). They have also, through articulation of their social and kinship networks and negotiation of state and charitable providers, found ways to fill the gaps between the incomes flowing into households and their everyday needs for food and shelter. In all these ways, households' caring practices have paradoxically both made neo-liberalism possible and highlighted the spaces of kinship and community which have not, yet, succumbed to the rhetoric of neo-liberal individualism. The strains on these domesticated landscapes of care, however, create real concerns over the extent to which further neo-liberalization is sustainable and raise real questions over issues of achieving social justice in post-socialist societies.

Chapter Eight

Conclusions

Domesticating Neo-Liberalism

Across East Central Europe, the processes of neo-liberalization have dramatically reshaped the nature and experience of everyday life and, for many, intensified struggles for social reproduction. In the preceding chapters we have documented some of the diversity of economic practices, in the spheres of work, housing, land, food and care, with which households in Petržalka and Nowa Huta have sought to domesticate these uneven neo-liberal transformations. We have argued that the domestication of neo-liberalism can be analysed in three overlapping ways.

First, households have employed diverse economic practices in an attempt to make the processes of post-socialist neo-liberalization tolerable, if only at times a little more tolerable, and to enable the process of social reproduction. Through their work, housing, consumption and caring practices, households have attempted to create the means to survive, if not in most cases to thrive. They have negotiated markets, familiarized themselves with new practices and new institutions, invested time, and sometimes money, in maintaining their kinship and friendship networks, and sought ways to make a living. In these ways, as Creed suggests, households domesticate neo-liberalism '[b]y simply doing what they could to improve their difficult circumstances, without any grand design of resistance' (Creed, 1998: 3). For some households, however, social reproduction is only just achieved, and is achieved precariously, such that the efforts to create a set of economic practices which do sustain household economic life are immense and stressful, and shocks to the complex practices constructed hit hard.

Second, the efforts households have made to find ways of making a living, despite the adverse and rapidly changing social and economic environments of 'transition', have enabled neo-liberalism to work (see also Shevchenko, 2009). In their preparedness to take on badly paid and insecure work, to absorb the inequalities of transition in their social networks, to seek out alternative, non-market sources of consumption, and to pool housing resources to guarantee shelter, households in Nowa Huta and Petržalka have borne the burdens of neo-liberalism, and in this way domesticated it. They have absorbed the costs of neo-liberalization, externalized by the disarticulation between markets, welfare and the costs of living. The costs of and responsibilities for well-being are shifted from the public to the private realm and this shift, John Clarke (2007: 976) argues, 'enables the dynamic of the new economy'. In short, if the households had not developed complex sets of economic practices to make a living, then it is difficult to see how they would have been able to secure their social reproduction. Without households' own efforts, institutions of both state and market would have to readjust their own pay, conditions, prices and practices in order to ensure that workers could return to work tomorrow and that capitalism could be sustained.

Finally, households' negotiation of markets and bureaucracies thus point to the differentiated processes of neo-liberalization in Poland and Slovakia, and in Nowa Huta and Petržalka. As we discuss in more detail below, neo-liberal markets, institutions and policies have developed differently in the cases explored here. This 'domestic' variation reflects not only the differential commitments of policy makers, firms and other agents of neo-liberalism, but also the variegated landscapes of post-socialism and contrasting household practices. All of these highlight the importance of a view of neo-liberalism as always historically and geographically contingent (Tickell & Peck, 2003) and the limits of 'big' picture neo-liberalism.

In each of these ways, it is clear that households' domestication of neo-liberalism is both regressive and progressive, such that the process of domestication entails an ambivalence of both hegemony and empowerment. In contrast to other accounts of domestication (see Chapter Three), we argue that domestication cannot be seen as *either* a process of disciplining, imposition and forced adaptation *or* a process of negotiation, subversion and resistance. Instead we have demonstrated that household engagements with the neo-liberal reflect both acts of domestication and experiences of being domesticated. As we suggested in Chapter Three, despite claims that everyday practices are subaltern acts of resistance, many are in fact aimed – explicitly or implicitly – at maintaining the status quo, in this case enabling neo-liberalism.

Some practices are also exploitative. Not only are some of the working practices we have outlined evidence of class-based exploitation of wage labour, but some of the caring practices, in particular, also suggest the domestic exploitation of women, of older generations, and sometimes of younger generations too. These latter practices remake and reinforce domestic and gender divisions of labour in their attempts to achieve social reproduction. In contrast, some practices can be seen as explicit attempts to circumvent 'the strategies of instituted power' (de Certeau, 1984: 23) through illegal and/or informal acts. Such explicit circumventions include, among others, accessing electricity illegally, squatting vacant properties, applying for credit on behalf of other family members, and claiming benefits while working. Yet, in the ways in which these were practised within households in Petržalka and Nowa Huta, it is difficult to claim that they should be characterized as calculated acts of resistance. Rather, they appear to be acts of desperation in circumstances where legal options are exhausted. These acts, then, like the majority of practices identified are part of a portfolio of mundane, yet creative, practices enacted in the attempt to secure household social reproduction.

These 'apparently insignificant' and mundane activities of everyday life (Simonsen, 2007: 168) are economic and social practices which households employ across a range of different spheres of work, care, housing and consumption. They draw on household members' resources – including their skills and embodiments, social networks, property and other material assets – and articulate with the wider geographies of moral rationalities, cultural practices, built forms, infrastructures and political economies in ways which both enable and constrain a household's everyday life and their success in securing social reproduction. In these ways, the practices of domestication can be theorized in a number of ways. Firstly, the articulation of different aspects of a household's economic practices and of those practices with 'external' institutions, conditions and rationalities points to the structuring of everyday practices by the contours of inequality. The result is that household economic practices develop unevenly, often reinforcing advantage or exclusion. Secondly, these practices are often routine and mundane, such that they can be taken for granted and either ignored or characterized as accidental or reactive. Thirdly, they reflect a continuous process of negotiation between the 'internal' and the 'external', between the household and its wider geographies. Fourthly, they are built on both new, emergent economies and on cultures, assets, institutions and practices inherited from the era of state socialism, and earlier historical periods, and these legacies are played out at a number of scales, from the individual and household, to the community and nation-state, highlighting the importance of a comparative analysis of domestication.

In *Domesticating Neo-Liberalism* we have drawn attention to the ways in which households' abilities to secure their social reproduction rested on uneven access to a range of resources, skills and assets, and to how, in many cases, the absence of assets which could be employed, exchanged or invested in the expansion of household social reproduction appeared to be cumulative, resulting in a reinforcing of poverty and exclusion. For example, we noted how those without secure work also often lacked access to work-based social networks, to the residual 'social wage' or to a stable income that might have enabled access to loans or mortgages. Or how the absence of a private car restricted not only the choice of food retailers but also reduced a household's ability to cultivate fruit and vegetables on their own land. Or how poor-quality residential accommodation restricted not only a household's current living conditions but also their ability to move up the housing ladder as its low value reflected a disadvantageous market position and limited access to loans for possible renovation. In these ways and more, we have indicated how many poor households in Nowa Huta and Petržalka experienced compound exclusion as their disadvantaged position in one market or hierarchy delimited their engagement with others.

We return to the issue of increasing inequality below, but here we wish to stress three key aspects of households' economic practices that appear to be particularly central markers of inequality. Firstly, while throughout *Domesticating Neo-Liberalism* we have stressed the necessity of exploring and understanding the diversity of economic practices which come together (or not) to secure a household's social reproduction, we have also shown that access to quality, stable employment is at the heart of 'successful' portfolios of practices. Quite simply, households with members working in 'good' jobs (i.e. relatively secure, relatively well – and regularly – paid work) were significantly less likely to be at risk of poverty than those without. Those in the increasing number of marginal jobs or in unemployment were very likely to be living in poverty and struggling to achieve sustainable social reproduction. Secondly, for those living in or at risk of poverty, access to information – about benefits, job opportunities, cheap sources of food, clothes etc. – was critical in making a bearable living; and such information flowed through strong social networks. Among those living in or on the margins of poverty, those without strong family and friendship networks appeared to be especially disadvantaged. Thirdly, the complexity of household economic practices meant that shocks to the household – from illness, death, job loss, family break-up, for example – could quite easily endanger social reproduction and tip households into poverty and social exclusion. In those households with a history of familial crisis, the number of working household members was often reduced (through illness, absence or the necessity of other carework); caring responsibilities were increased or increasingly concentrated; time was increasingly pressured, reducing the potential for more creative and time-consuming practices; and social networks were stressed by a declining reciprocity. In all these ways, social reproduction had become increasingly fragile. All of this points – despite our arguments for an appreciation of the diversity of economic practices in the constitution of neo-liberalism – to the fundamental centrality of daily social reproduction (Lee, 2006).

The complexity of household economic practices also highlights the importance of recognizing the effort, skill and creativity embodied within such practices. There is some debate (see, for example, Kideckel, 2008) over the extent to which post-socialist practices reflect proactive planning, control and agency or, on the contrary, are better characterized as short-term and reactive. As we noted in Chapter Three, much of the 'practice turn' has sought to counter the binary of autonomy and determinism, suggesting that practices are the result of a more or less successful process of learning and negotiation of wider structures and institutions. For Simonsen (2001: 44), this is an 'everyday skilful coping or engagement' founded on often tacit skills and knowledge. Within our research, there is without doubt evidence of some proactive strategies to increase household income, including retraining, emigration and enterprise, in particular. But in many more mundane ways too, households in Petržalka and Nowa Huta demonstrated careful, thoughtful and planned practices of consumption, work, housing and exchange, amongst others. These included, for example, shopping practices which incorporated prior research, multiple sites and knowledge shared within networks, or housing practices which improved property value through investment and renovation or which maximized the housing situation of extended families through exchange, or caring practices which recognized the complementary competences of family, friends and neighbours and exchanged favours accordingly. Whilst these may not be dramatic acts of autonomy, they do reflect agency and planning. Other apparently mundane practices demonstrate households' processes of adaptation and learning. For example, some households had learnt quickly how to shop in the large hypermarkets, seeking out promotions, buying in bulk, or purchasing recently out-of-date products at much lower cost; some had mapped out the sources of charitable help available as a burgeoning third sector expands to fill the gap of a shrinking state welfare system; some had adapted existing skills to new demands in the labour market; and others had studied the new landscapes of loan and mortgage finance in an attempt to understand their chances of borrowing. Information about the sites and sources of economic life was critical in the construction of sustainable economic practices, and many of the households had not only demonstrated their ability to acquire new knowledge and skills, but had also shared these within their kin and social networks. Of course, while skills, knowledge and learning are important, they are just one of the assets which shape household economies and are rarely sufficient to counter the material and structural inequalities which restrict household economic life. They often, moreover, demand time, and this too was distributed unevenly among households and their members, according to matrices of class, gender, generation and health.

All of these articulations and inequalities in practices point to the relationships between households' 'internal' lives and a variety of 'external' structures, practices and institutions. As we argued in Chapter Three, a focus on everyday practices need not necessarily privilege the micro or local scale. The lens of domestication highlights clearly and explicitly the juxtaposition between the apparently local and the apparently global. Not only are households' domestic negotiations with neo-liberalism evidence of the global in the very local – that is, in the food that households eat, in the employment strategies they consider, in the mortgage finance they seek, or in the charity they receive, for example – but they are also evidence of the remaking of global neo-liberalisms in their everyday lives. In the economic practices of households, it is difficult to identify what is local, what is national, and what is global, such that the processes of domestication can be seen as a collapsing of scales, and a weaving together of spaces. On the one hand what this perspective draws attention to is the nested geographies of neo-liberalism. Neo-liberalism is not just an economic project which sits 'out there' in the circuits of international policy and business, but a set of practices, rationalities and commitments which flow through homes, communities, workplaces and institutions. On the other hand, our perspective also highlights the complex geographies of household economic practices (Smith & Stenning, 2006), which draw in myriad spaces at multiple scales. The practices explored in *Domesticating Neo-Liberalism* are enacted in and echo through the home, the street, work, shops, allotments, the branches of transnational banks, other neighbourhoods, cities and countries, schools and universities, national ministries, churches, and elsewhere. These nested geographies point to the role of what Jarvis (2005: 135) calls the 'infrastructure of daily life' in enabling or constraining households' everyday geographies. Issues of public transport, the built environment, the proximity of home, work and school, among many others, influence the ease with which households managed their complex, multi-sited economic practices. These infrastructural geographies articulated, moreover, with influences on personal mobilities, such as age and health, to enable or constrain social reproduction and, in many cases, to reinforce inequalities.

For many households, notwithstanding the many wider links and flows, everyday life *is* decidedly local. Family and friends often lived locally; local shops were preferred to those further afield; work was a bus or tram ride away; and schools or nurseries were in households' own or adjacent neighbourhoods. The role played by largely proximate and carefully maintained social networks was often critical and reinforced an attachment to the block, neighbourhood or district for many. As a result, for some – especially those managing particularly precarious livelihoods – there were real concerns about any disruptions to the spatialized connections that enabled their economic practices. This relates particularly to the development of housing markets and the suggestion that housing mobility was a rational response to poverty.

While some of the practices explored here were emergent, many of the processes of domestication have long histories, stretching back not only to the era of state socialism, but also before then, and to the path dependencies of 'transition' itself. As we suggested in Chapter Three, post-socialism is built on the ruins of socialism, as new practices and institutions are grafted on to and reworked from inherited practices (Stark & Bruszt, 1998; Pickles, 2004b). That the practices explored here are *post-socialist* does make a difference, as the legacies of state socialism were seen in, for example, the cultures of repair and self-provisioning, in the practices of reciprocal exchange of access and favours, in the particular childcare role of grandmothers, in the wariness towards bureaucracies, in the stigma of poverty and unemployment, in the differential inheritance of state socialist housing, and in the contrasting retail geographies of Nowa Huta and Petržalka. It is, however, also possible to identify longer-standing traditions, which have been filtered through the state socialist years or revived anew after decades of abeyance. Households' attachment to the land and to cultivation was perhaps the clearest example of this, but the influence of long-standing commitments can also be illustrated, in Poland in particular, by the importance of the Catholic Church and its profound impact on gendered moral rationalities.

Twenty years after the end of state socialism in ECE, it is increasingly clear that the choices made – by households and other institutions, private or public – during the early years of 'transition' can also be seen to have an impact. For example, the headlong rush to housing privatization in the early 1990s resulted in particular patterns of inclusion and exclusion in the housing market and the lax planning ordinances of commercial development immediately after 1989 created a dense network of supermarkets and hypermarkets in both Petržalka and Nowa Huta. These histories, which echo through various timescales, were grounded in different ways and at different geographical scales in the everyday practices of households. Some shaped uneven household inheritances or, for example, embodied gender roles; others highlighted inherited skills which extended the breadth of conceivable economic practices; and others still formed the contexts of policy, markets and institutions – at local, national and international scales – within which households in Nowa Huta and Petržalka acted.

Diverse Economies of Post-Socialism

All of these takes on everyday economic practices in Nowa Huta and Petržalka highlight their complexity and diversity. Although documenting and explaining this diversity is important in itself, in order to better represent the economic lives of the households in our research – and by extension in post-socialist Poland and Slovakia – it is also important because such a recognition of diversity enables, or even demands, a rethinking of economy and of neo-liberalism. As we noted in Chapter Three, a number of writers have sought to draw attention to the ways in which a particular idea of the economy is performed and practised by key actors, such as states, international lending agencies and banks. In the context of post-socialism, the dominant metaphor of economic change was the 'transition', an apparently linear, singular and predictable path of reform and restructuring which would create a neo-liberal economy (see Chapters Two and Three). This account of transition has been widely critiqued on the grounds that the processes of economic transformation have rarely been straightforward or linear, but there have been fewer critical accounts of the post-socialist economy emerging out of 20 years of transition.

Domesticating Neo-Liberalism has focused on the economies of 'actually existing post-socialism' (Stenning & Hörschelmann, 2008) in an attempt to understand the kinds of economic practices that have resulted from 'transition'. This analysis reaffirms the view that capitalism is just one part – albeit a very important part – of a diverse economy of post-socialism (Smith & Stenning, 2006) and is articulated in the everyday economies of households in Petržalka and Nowa Huta with a range of non-market and alternative market practices (Community Economies Collective, 2001; Chakrabarty, 2000).

Non-market practices can be seen in, among others, the domestic production of food, in the networks of gift and barter within which households exchange food, clothes and other goods, in the lending of money between households, in the acts of care enacted between family members and within social networks, in the remaining structures of state support and redistribution, and in the reciprocal labour offered on allotments and in repair and renovation. Alternative markets can be identified in the informal labour markets within which many household members were employed, in the street market supply of consumer goods, and in the recourse to other systems of financial lending (see also Stenning et al., 2010). Many of the everyday economic practices of households in Nowa Huta and Petržalka, however, were characterized by hybrid constructions of both commodified and non-commodified exchange. For example, much of the property 'market' that exists in the two districts combined both a cash transaction and an agreed non-commodified swap; and many households consumed a combination of purchased food, food that had been domestically produced, and food that had been purchased, processed and exchanged. Moreover, in addition to the articulation of different modalities *within* particular practices, every household drew together different forms of economic activity – market, non-market and quasi-market – in its attempts to achieve social reproduction and to domesticate neo-liberalism. No household relied solely – for work, food, housing, care or any other economy – on market practices. This conclusion leads us to ask, with Gibson-Graham (1996: 244), 'what it might mean to call the countries of eastern Europe "capitalist"'.

Neo-Liberal Subjectivities and their Others

As we noted in Chapter Two, part of the project of neo-liberalism rests on the cultivation of neo-liberal subjectivities which seek to promote an individualizing ethics of autonomous self-improvement and to erode communal and social relationships (K. Mitchell, 2006; McCarthy, 2006; J. Clarke, 2007; Weiner, 2007). In the process of neo-liberalization, then, there is an expectation of new practices that reflect this new ethics (Popke, 2006) and in Petržalka and Nowa Huta it is possible to identify ways in which individuals and families did enact these new subjectivities. Most evidently, these were seen in individuals' attempts to retrain for restructured labour markets, to emigrate in search of better prospects, and to invest in property through a commitment to owner occupation. These are many of the practices described above as proactive and it is interesting to note that is these practices which Kideckel (2008) and others see as evidence of control and agency. By contrast, viewing these apparently proactive practices from the perspective of neo-liberal subjectivities, it is possible to see them as evidence of compliance with the dominant narratives of neo-liberalism.

However, a closer analysis of these practices – and the others in which households engaged – reveals that in most instances they were inflected with a set of rationalities that extended beyond the narrowly neo-liberal. There was considerable evidence of other-than-neo-liberal subjectivities. Contrary, however, to many accounts of informal and diverse economies, these subjectivities only rarely reflected attempts to explicitly and intentionally contest neo-liberalization. Instead, what we repeatedly identified in the diverse practices of households in Nowa Huta and Petržalka was a commitment to relationships, to community and to solidarity, to an 'economy of generosity' (Community Economies Collective, 2001: 17) which countered the individualizing subjectivities of neo-liberalism.

These commitments were seen, for example, in the generous networks of care established and maintained by Nowa Huta and Petržalka households, in the loans of money, even amongst impoverished households, in the sharing of information about retail bargains or charitable sources, in the continuing shelter offered to adult family members, and in the gifts of food and clothes. Households in Petržalka and Nowa Huta shared their resources, skills, knowledge, time and energy with their family, friends and neighbours in ways that belie the individualizing ethics of neo-liberalism. It is possible to speculate that these alternative subjectivities are rooted in the intertwined cultures of rurality, family and (especially in Poland) church, and perhaps nourished by socialist narratives of collectivity, but they have persisted and developed in the more urban settings of Nowa Huta and Petržalka, even in the context of economic upheaval and, for some, impoverishment. While there was some evidence that such an economy of generosity was being eroded – as families withdrew from wider social circles or as resources were concentrated on the needs of immediate family and close friends – there was also evidence that households struggled to maintain these commitments despite their adverse circumstances.

The value of these more-than-neo-liberal subjectivities is not insignificant. They reveal a set of spaces that not only mediate neo-liberalism but also offer a respite from it and a reminder that neo-liberalism is not the only rationality. In the tenacity with which households held on to these economies of generosity, the relationships of care and community have the potential to transform wider political economies and to challenge emerging notions of neo-liberal citizenship (Popke, 2006). In part, the wider impact can be seen, in Poland at least, in the party political commitment to solidarity explored in Chapter Two. But their value can also be identified within Nowa Huta and Petržalka where the energies of key actors were directed at building active communities of hope and potential which seek to create better forms of work and to recognize and validate the diversity of economic practices important to those in the community (Stenning, 2010; Hardy et al., 2008). This can be seen, for example, in the community organizations and projects devised by the Partnership of Nowa Huta Initiatives,[1] in the Centrum komunitného rozvoja (Centre for Community Development) in Petržalka, and in the support for pensioners' clubs in both districts.

In both communities, however, there was also evidence of a level of resignation (Buchowski, 2003), which reflected an apparent acceptance of poverty and the struggles for social reproduction and a disbelief in any alternatives to neo-liberalism. This was particularly evident in households' relationships to welfare (Chapter Seven), such that poor households denied or downplayed their impoverishment and their need for benefits and often claimed that they could survive regardless. As one of our Petržalka interviewees, who was living close to the poverty line despite both he and his wife being in formal employment, explained: 'We can't complain about everything, about how we live, but it could be a little easier…'. In another case, a single mother, working as a nursery teacher on a low income, illustrated the 'normalization' of poverty in post-socialist cities: 'It is possible to survive, if you get used to spending less, and to live normally. I don't mean that we are paupers. There are people in worse situations. And I am used to our situation, so I don't mind that we live like this. It seems to be normal for me.'

These sentiments have also been reflected in election results in Petržalka[2] where support for the neo-liberal coalition in 2002 and 2006, in the light of the injuries of post-socialism, suggest a generational postponement of the possibility of a more stable or affluent future (Smith & Rochovská, 1997) and a reluctance to return to the anti-European, anti-democratic, nationalist populist politics of the HZDS. The threat of populism confirms the concerns that the social and spatial cleavages of post-socialist Poland and Slovakia might result in the emergence of illiberal, reactionary and nationalist alternatives (Bohle & Greskovits, 2007), a threat more fully realized in Poland with the recent (though inconsistent) electoral success of the right-wing League of Polish Families (and its support network in Radio Maryja) and, more importantly, the rightward shift of Prawo i Sprawiedliwość (Chapter Two; see also Day, 2005; Dempsey, 2007).

The Violence of Neo-Liberalism: Class, Gender, Generation and Ethnicity

These phenomena suggest that the presence and value of other spaces of economy and community development cannot fully detract from the violence of neo-liberalism (cf. Žižek, 2008). The privatization of housing, the restructuring of the labour market, the marketization of consumption and the erosion of welfare have led to social dislocations and exclusions, to a polarization of income and opportunity, and to increasingly unequal power relations. As we have already suggested, many of the costs of neo-liberalization are borne by households and the 'the onslaught of postsocialist forces' (Kideckel, 2008: 209) has provoked emotional and material violence through poverty, fear, alienation and stress, among others (Kideckel, 2008; Svašek, 2008). Many households have had to try to secure their social reproduction in the context of job loss and labour market restructuring, increasingly insecure incomes, ill-health and family breakdown, and personal crises, which in many cases have been brought about or exacerbated by neo-liberalization.

These costs have been unevenly felt, and the inequalities have been increasingly marked. Inequalities have been compounded not only by uneven inheritances from state socialism, but also by the articulation of different spheres – work, finance, housing, land and transport, for example – such that exclusion from one sphere often resulted in exclusion from others. The processes of neo-liberalization have reconfigured class inequalities, not least as capitalist class processes subsume the myths of equality and the bureaucratic inequalities of state socialism (Weiner, 2007). The working class, often though not always venerated during state socialism, has become increasingly impoverished as working-class jobs disappear or are devalued and their struggle to 'survive' is made more difficult by their exclusion from key markets and opportunities (Stenning, 2005c). As Kideckel (2008), echoing Burawoy et al. (2000), has suggested, the working class are increasingly forced to rely on reactive, defensive strategies, many derived from earlier practices, while wealthier households can engage in newer, more entrepreneurial strategies. This results in a bifurcation of post-socialist experience as the benefits accrue to those who already have the potential for more expansive strategies. Of course, the inequalities of post-socialism are not wholly new. As we have suggested, inherited resources, embodiments and skills are extremely influential as households and individuals use their existing resources as leverage to develop further. This can be seen most starkly in the inherited advantages of households' property assets, as discussed in Chapter Five. The polarization of inequality reflects the limits on social mobility in post-socialism; as Weiner (2007: 124) suggests: 'there is no climbing up; holding on proves enough of a challenge'. While there is a danger that this perspective exaggerates the narratives of 'oppression, loss and victimization' (Weiner, 2007: 125; see also Stenning, 2010) and downplays the agency and resilience of impoverished households, it is certainly the case that the options of poorer households are more limited.

However, the reconfiguration of class identities does not allow for the easy identification of a singular post-socialist working class. The diversity of spaces and practices in which household members were engaged draws them into a range of diverse class processes. Their employment beyond the home may construct them as a waged worker, for example, but not their reciprocal labour in friends' and neighbours' homes as a volunteer freely offering their time; their engagement in secondary or informal labour markets for occasional work as a contingent labourer; and their cooking and cleaning at home as a carer (Gibson & Graham, 1992; Gibson-Graham, 2006). In these ways, the diverse geographies of social reproduction are interwoven with diverse class processes, with political implications, which we explore below.

It is not just identities and inequalities of class that have been remade in the context of post-socialist neo-liberalization. Gender and generation, too, have been transformed and the intersections between class, gender and generation have played a key role in shaping the practices of social reproduction and the domestication of neo-liberalism. We have highlighted the ways in which the continuity and change in the spheres of material structures, moral rationalities and cultural formations have resulted in a reshaping of gender relations and of gender divisions of labour, within and beyond the home. Firstly, it is important to note the extraordinarily heavy burdens that have been placed on women. As the costs of neo-liberalization have been domesticated, in households in Nowa Huta and Petržalka women have taken on many of the new and expanded tasks of social reproduction. They remained predominantly responsible for maintaining and developing kinship and social networks; they had to commit 'laborious hours' (Weiner, 2007: 126) to shopping; they were primarily responsible for negotiating social services and accessing welfare benefits; and they were increasingly likely to be the sole or main earner in a household. These burdens were exacerbated still further in households marked by ill-health or family breakdown; many women were caring for disabled husbands or fathers and all of the examples of single-parent families were headed by single mothers, most often in receipt of no help at all from absent fathers. Of course, these phenomena point clearly to the transformation of masculinities too, not least the 'redundant masculinities' which are also evident in post-industrial communities in Western Europe (McDowell, 2003; van Hoven and Hörschelmann, 2005). Some men have, of course, thrived in the context of neo-liberalization. Indeed, many of those who engaged in the proactive, entrepreneurial strategies explored above – starting their own businesses, developing property, migrating – were men. Others have taken on new roles as domestic divisions of labour have been remade, and the number of young men pushing prams on the streets of the two communities is testament to this.

The remaking of gender roles in younger families points to the articulation of gender and generation, and to the importance of generation in analyses of social reproduction in Nowa Huta and Petržalka. Generation can be seen as another axis of inequality as, for example, both younger and older workers appeared to be disadvantaged by the neo-liberalization of the labour market, as younger households struggled particularly to get a foot onto the housing ladder after having often missed out on post-socialist privatizations in the early 1990s, and as older households, socialized during state socialism, found the negotiation of new market practices especially difficult. In short, generation shaped the range of everyday economic practices available to households in Nowa Huta and Petržalka. However, in addition to generational inequalities, the processes of neo-liberalization and their domestication have also remade intergenerational relationships (Vanderbeck, 2007; Hopkins & Pain, 2007) as new interdependencies and conflicts emerge. There are dangers that the increased pressure on the intergenerational exchange of time, money and care will exhaust familial bonds, as, for example, care for the elderly creates additional burdens for overworked women, as cohabitation erodes familial goodwill, and as the pension income and carework of grandparents is exploited by struggling young families.

Of course, in wider accounts of neo-liberalization and inequality, ethnicity is a key concern. In this research, however, it is only really in the positioning of the regions' Roma communities, vividly illustrated by the Slovak events narrated in Chapter One, that the impact of ethnicity on everyday economic practices can be clearly seen. The particularities of Roma households have been drawn out in earlier chapters, which have highlighted both the exclusion of Roma families from housing, labour and retail markets and the dense and supportive extended family networks of our Roma interviewees. That the issue of Roma marginalization was integrated into EU accession negotiations and has been taken up by national and regional authorities across ECE points to its severity, and it is clear that, as a community, the Roma have become increasingly impoverished during post-socialism (Stewart, 2002).

Comparative Neo-Liberalisms

The increasing inequalities of class, gender and generation are not the only evidence, however, of the uneven development of neo-liberalization in Poland and Slovakia. This research and the analyses derived from it have also focused on the uneven geographies of neo-liberalization, drawing attention to the contrasts and comparisons that can be drawn at scales from the housing block and neighbourhood, to the urban and the national. These comparisons, we argue, arise from contrasting political economies, moral rationalities, built forms and infrastructures, among others, which, at interlocking scales, construct the 'rules of the game', the contexts within which the processes of domestication take place.

The contrasts between Petržalka and Nowa Huta can be seen in, for example, the more persistent social wage in Nowa Huta, the wider labour markets of Petržalka, the more extensive geographies of migration amongst Nowa Huta households, the differing experiences of retail transformation in the two districts, the contrasting inheritances of housing – both in terms of built form and ownership structure, and the distinctive histories of settlement and family formation. These, in turn, derive from contrasts at both the national and the urban scales. At the national scale, it is perhaps the experiences of post-socialism which produced the sharpest contrasts. As we discussed in Chapter Two, notwithstanding strong commonalities, there have also been key differences in the development of neo-liberal policy in Poland and Slovakia. Most importantly, we have suggested that Slovakia has experienced a more thoroughgoing marketization in recent years across a range of spheres, and certainly since 1998. The Dzurinda government, for example, promoted an extreme commitment to a 'work first' agenda, which sought to replace welfare with work of any quality, and a flat tax regime which discursively devalued and financially deprived the public sector. In this environment, consumption was significantly commodified and monopolized as domestic retail was, like many other sectors, partly displaced by foreign-owned supermarkets and hypermarkets. By contrast, in Poland, neo-liberal transformations in labour markets and welfare have been consistently tempered by a continuing policy commitment to solidarity (small 's') and protectionism, and the incursion of multinational capital has been mitigated by a persistent attachment to local, domestic markets. In Poland, too, the costs of neo-liberalization have also been mediated by a range of institutions, such as credit unions, a very active charitable sector, trade unions and community organizations, which have offered various forms of support to the poorest households.

Explaining the particular resilience of other logics in Poland is not simple, but it is possible to speculate that the central role of the Catholic Church and the continuing influence of Solidarity (big 'S') and its legacies are important. These two institutions are, of course, intertwined, and the Catholic Church was at the heart of Solidarity's success in the 1980s. The two institutions also foster – or reflect – social attachments to families, communities, workplaces and other collectivities, and the evidence derived from households' everyday economic practices in Nowa Huta does suggest that these are important aspects of the processes of domestication there. In Slovakia, by contrast, the 'old' forms of resistance, which were less institutionalized in the former Czechoslovakia other than through explicit political movements (such as Charta 77 and the environmental movement), have either mutated into institutionalized political formations (for example, HZDS was in part an offshoot of the Public Against Violence anti-communist movement in 1989 but later engaged in the development of populist nationalism) or (in the case the green movement) have waned in overall significance. What, in turn, accounts for these differences in contemporary Polish and Slovak politics is more difficult to explain. The theorization of national cultural difference lies beyond this book, but it is important to point to the possible influence of a set of more intangible socio-cultural formations (what we might call Polishness and Slovakness) in shaping the differences between Nowa Huta and Petržalka. In shopping practices, cultures of cultivation and familial responsibilities, for example, we can perhaps see the contrasting influence of 'national' values and identities.

These national contrasts articulate with contrasts at the scale of the city and district. At the urban scale, it is perhaps the legacies of socialism – and the districts' geographies – which mark out the key differences. Notwithstanding their foundation as archetypal large-scale housing districts during the rapid urbanization of ECE during the post-war period, Nowa Huta and Petržalka have quite distinct histories, geographies and political economies, as we explored in Chapter One. The legacy of Nowa Huta's construction from the late 1940s in concert with the development of the then Lenin Steelworks can be seen in a number of ways. The steelworks' legacy of the centrality of work and a single dominant workplace, strong social institutions (such as trade unions and community centres) and a privileged position in the political economy of state socialism (manifested not only in industrial investment but also cultural, retail and educational developments, among others) have shaped a very particular post-socialist landscape. In addition, the interlocking networks of family, friends and colleagues have deep roots in Nowa Huta's neighbourhoods and the built form of these

234 DOMESTICATING NEO-LIBERALISM

neighbourhoods, especially those constructed in the 1950s with small blocks and inward-looking courtyards, has reinforced the density and strength of Nowa Huta's social networks. Nowa Huta's particular geographies were reinforced still further by its cultural and functional isolation from Kraków, a reflection of the wider city's strongly felt antipathy towards Nowa Huta. By contrast, Petržalka is characterized by a higher level of integration with the city of Bratislava, evident in its labour market, retail and residential geographies, which are all articulated fully with the wider city, and the orientation of its households out across the city. State socialist Petržalka possessed no single dominant workplace (although there were several important local employers such as Matador), and was instead constructed largely as a dormitory town, whose residents were expected to maintain their connections to work, friends and family beyond its administrative borders, as well as within. It received no special treatment during state socialism but its residents did benefit from their integration into the capital of the Slovak Federal Republic before 1993. In addition to these tangible contrasts, the districts are differentiated by more intangible, local cultures, practices and moral rationalities derived, as Schatzki (1998: 247–8) suggests, from the 'realm of the setting', that is, 'particular rules, paradigms, ideas and so on' which result from the shared routines of everyday life (Beynon & Hudson, 1993). These local contrasts articulate with the national contrasts outlined above and shape, positively and negatively, the development of everyday economic practices, making a difference to the array of possible practices and their success.

The logic of differentiation and contrast extends beyond the national and urban scales to draw attention to comparisons within Nowa Huta and Petržalka, between neighbourhoods and blocks. As we discussed in Chapter Three, the 'very space of the neighborhood' (de Certeau et al., 1998: 7) both shapes and is shaped by everyday economic practices. The axes of differentiation highlighted above – labour markets, social networks, demographics, the built environment, infrastructural and institutional geographies, and so on – are also played out at the scale of the neighbourhood, and our analyses of household economies in Petržalka and Nowa Huta highlight some important contrasts at the micro scale. For example, issues of residential built form and location differentiate not only the benefits of housing privatizations but also the shape of neighbourhood networks; micro-geographies of public transport and retail clearly shape the work and consumption practices of households; the demographic make-up of neighbourhoods – in particular, the age profile and life stage of residents – appear to influence the strength and success of networks of care. These micro-geographical differences link back to contrasting individual and household positions, of class, gender, generation and ethnicity, and the socio-economic make-up of neighbourhoods and blocks.

Conclusions

The discussions here have highlighted the uneven experiences of neo-liberalization in Nowa Huta and Petržalka, drawing attention in particular to the inequalities reinforced or generated by this project of political, economic and social change. It has been suggested that, in domesticating neo-liberalism, households have borne the often heavy costs of neo-liberalization and that many have paid a high price, emotionally and materially. Yet, there have been relatively few active, public challenges to neo-liberalism in Poland or Slovakia, notwithstanding those evidenced in Chapter One (see also Hardy et al., 2008).

There have been a number of explanations for this absence of explicit political contestation. Firstly, attention has been drawn to the power of neo-liberal agendas, and their agents. In general and in the particular context of post-socialism and EU accession, the strength, ubiquity and seduction of market motifs have subsumed the ideological space for alternatives to neo-liberal capitalism (Kennedy, 2002; Weiner, 2007; for a critique, see Gibson-Graham, 1996), creating an environment in which contesting the dominance of the market and imagining other economies becomes inconceivable. As we have suggested, even those at the sharp end of neo-liberalization in ECE appear to have taken on narratives of self-governance and personal responsibility (Weiner, 2007; Hörschelmann, 2008). Secondly, however, commentators have argued that the absence of active contestation in post-socialism results not simply from a process of co-option, but also from the heightened poverty and insecurity of life in neo-liberal times. Kaldor (1996), for example, has explored the impact of what she calls 'the strains of transition' on the ability or willingness of individuals or communities in ECE to participate in protest politics (see also Stenning, 1999); this is a theme developed by Kideckel (2008) and others who argue that for the poorest and most marginalized, the fight for survival and daily social reproduction overrides any potential for political action or for working-class challenges to neo-liberalism.

Others, however, have suggested that, instead of focusing solely or primarily on dramatic acts of political protest, more attention should be paid, echoing Creed (1998), to the mundane challenges to neo-liberalism (see Chapters Two and Three) and to the potential spaces of transformation opened by the diverse economic practices of households and communities. This is the vein in which we have analysed the domestication of neo-liberalism in Slovakia and Poland, arguing not only that households have domesticated neo-liberalism through the performance of their everyday economies but that in the enactment of diversity they have created spaces for transformation which 'do not necessarily involve social upheaval and hegemonic transition' (Gibson & Graham, 1992: 116).

Throughout *Domesticating Neo-Liberalism* we have emphasized how the small, mundane acts and practices attempt to make a difference to the social reproduction of households but also feed into wider political economies. This suggests that some of the everyday concerns and practices of households might be developed into political commitments and policy ideas which could contribute to the enhancement of social justice in the context of post-socialist neo-liberalism. In the sphere of work, the establishment of a living wage in the two cities would help to ensure that the negative impacts of labour market restructuring and the emergence of in-work poverty are countered. In the context of housing, insecure employment, household shocks (such as illness and family break-up) and lack of creditworthiness have meant that many find themselves excluded from the housing market and reliant on extended families. Providing low-interest loans and access to credit and sustaining a social housing sector are thus critical to enable housing security. This connects to the potential to develop community financial institutions to mitigate the uneven access to financial resources that many households in Nowa Huta and Petržalka experience. Although Poland has a well-developed system of credit unions and some households still have access to workplace funds, the development and extension of these kinds of institutions would offer poor households access to better forms of credit. Questions of financial security also rest on access to the kinds of state benefits (including pensions) which might provide stable incomes and enable households to invest their time and energy into retraining, seeking work or supporting their families. An extension of state benefit levels and coverage would do much to increase household financial security, especially for the poorest households, and would dramatically reduce the risk of poverty. But, since difficulties with benefits also emerge from an unwillingness to engage with state institutions, a weariness with the process of application, and even an ignorance of benefit entitlements, any extension of benefits could also be accompanied by improving information about benefits and the application process.

What these possibilities suggest is that active resistance is not the only way to remake neo-liberalism (see Smith et al., 2008a). Our analytical focus on domestication highlights the 'contradictory, contingent and *constructed* nature of neoliberal present' (Peck, 2008: 4), drawing attention to the ways in which neo-liberalism is tempered in the political process – by implementation, by intervention, by coalition – and by everyday engagements on the ground. These domestications indicate 'the gaps between ambition and achievement' (J. Clarke, 2004: 30) and the ambiguities of the neo-liberal project itself. Whilst the neo-liberal project can be seen as a very powerful set of forces which has transformed the political economies of Poland and Slovakia and the everyday lives of households in Nowa Huta and Petržalka since 1989, the process of neo-liberalization is always partial and unfinished. In this sense, neo-liberalism is never fixed and determinant but can be mediated and tempered.

This contention is borne out in the identifiable turns away from neo-liberalism in Poland and Slovakia in the early and mid-2000s respectively (see also Larner et al., 2007), and, increasingly in the discourses and events of the current global economic crisis, provoked by the failures of a particular logic of neo-liberal financialization. Indeed, the impacts of the current global crisis on Poland and Slovakia, and the rest of ECE, continue to unfold (Smith and Swain, 2010). On the one hand, the crisis is seen to threaten millions of post-socialist citizens with a return to poverty and vulnerability since, as even the World Bank concedes, the rapid liberalization of these states has left them particularly vulnerable to financial crisis (World Bank, 2009). The recognition of these particular threats has led to calls for investment in social policy, in a strengthened safety net and, indeed, in many of the everyday practices highlighted in *Domesticating Neo-Liberalism*, rebuilding much of that which has been destroyed by two decades of neo-liberalization. In this sense, the ongoing crisis can be seen as a reworking of the particular forms of neo-liberal transitions discussed here.

On the other hand, however, the policy agendas of ECE's neo-liberal states have been held up as a model for managing the crisis. The *Washington Post* (2009; see also Ratajczyk, 2009) used a recent editorial to critically compare US President Barack Obama's high-spend crisis plan with 'the Reaganite bearing of post-communist Poland', expressing admiration for the way that Poland's Prime Minister Donald Tusk had 'slashed marginal tax rates, cut government spending and temporarily suspended some government regulations'. In contrast then to the fears of rising social costs, an alternative perspective sees the current crisis as an opportunity to strengthen and extend the neo-liberalization of ECE economies.

These debates about neo-liberal transformations and their costs reaffirm the importance of a grounded analysis of actually existing neo-liberalization in Poland and Slovakia. Notwithstanding the current global crisis, neo-liberalism continues to reverberate across the economies of ECE and within the everyday economies of households in Nowa Huta and Petržalka. Any serious commitment to social justice for households and communities across the region therefore demands a recognition of the complexity and violence of neo-liberalism in people's everyday lives.

Appendix I

Summary Information on Interviewed Households

Household (HH) name	Neighbourhood	Income category[a]	HH size	HH make-up (including age at time of interview)	Employment status
Nowa Huta					
Chmielecki[b]	Os. Willowe	Over 140%	1	Married man (52); wife and two teenage children living in Kraków	Works as musician and music teacher
Guzik	Os. Willowe	60–100%	3	Widowed mother (53), son (22) and daughter (19)	Mother works as computer technician; student son does occasional odd jobs
Gwizdek	Os. Willowe	Below 60%	4	Husband (26), wife (24), daughter (5) and wife's father (52)	Husband and wife unemployed with no real work history; wife's father on incapacity benefit
Mokrzycki	Os. Willowe	60–100%	6	Husband (51), wife (44), two sons (17, 8) daughter (14) and wife's mother (78)	Husband worked in steelworks, on incapacity benefit since 2002; wife worked in printers and as caretaker but unemployed and seeking incapacity benefit
Stanis	Os. Willowe	60–100%	1	Separated man (48); wife and daughter living beyond Kraków	On temporary incapacity benefit following accident; otherwise works as trainer

Household (HH) name	Neighbourhood	Income category[a]	HH size	HH make-up (including age at time of interview)	Employment status
Wojnowicz	Os. Willowe	Over 140%	3	Husband (31) and wife (26) and infant son (1)	Husband runs successful magazine from spare room; wife is manicurist
Wrzosek	Os. Willowe	100–140%	3	Husband (73) and wife (69) with adult son (48)	Husband and wife now retired after years on incapacity benefit, husband worked at steelworks; son works as plumber
Czarnocka	Os. Górali	100–140%	2	Single mother (35) with daughter (9)	Unemployed after leaving work to care for daughter
Futyma	Os. Górali	Below 60%	1	Widowed woman (55); adult daughter and granddaughter usually also resident	Worked in canteen for 12 years, unemployed 1995–2003 and in insecure, casual cleaning job since 2003
Giewon	Os. Górali	Below 60%	3	Mother (42), son (20) and daughter (9)	Unemployed for 10 years, with no right to benefits
Kielak	Os. Górali	Below 60%	4	Divorced mother (44), two sons (12, 14) and one daughter (18)	Trained as hairdresser but currently registered as disabled and incapable of work (but without benefits); daughter does some part-time work

Name	Area	Income	No.	Household	Notes
Kowalik	Os. Górali	Below 60%	3	Husband (26) and wife (28) with infant son (2)	Husband unemployed and never had more than casual job; wife works as caretaker with irregular hours and, until recently, no contract or insurance, after 2 years of unemployment
Kwiatek	Os. Górali	Below 60%	2	Mother (29) and daughter (6), with husband occasionally resident	Wife works shifts in catering at local hospital; husband trained as electrician but unemployed for 8 years
Modzelewska	Os. Górali	Below 60%	3	Single mother (36) with two sons (12, 13)	Fragmented work history and currently unemployed
Pustelak	Os. Górali	60–100%	5	Husband (28) and wife (26), two daughters (6, 6 months) and son (6 months)	Husband worked in security but now in canteen; wife employed in a series of jobs in retail
Sedlak	Os. Gorali	Over 140%	3	Divorced mother (55), son (25) and daughter (13)	Mother works for city council in investment and construction; son studies
Szwacz	Os. Górali	60–100%	1	Widowed woman (73)	Retired after years on incapacity benefit; previously worked at steelworks

Household (HH) name	Neighbourhood	Income category[a]	HH size	HH make-up (including age at time of interview)	Employment status
Byjoch	Os. Przy Arce	Over 140%	4	Husband (57) and wife (55) with two sons (27, 32)	Wife took early retirement from trading company; husband worked as welder at steelworks and had periods of work in Sweden, company now privatized; older son works for private firm; younger son had worked in UK without much success and now employed in factory
Cała	Os. Przy Arce	100–140%	1	Widowed woman (60)	Retired for 5 years, previously employed in office work at wholesalers
Idziak	Os. Przy Arce	60–100%	2	Woman (52) and adult daughter (26) (left home between questionnaire and interview)	On incapacity benefit after 10 years of running small enterprises; does occasional casual work to supplement benefit income; previously employed as social worker
Sieradzki	Os. Przy Arce	Below 60%	3	Divorced mother (44) with daughter (19) and son (14)	Unemployed for 18 months; trained in IT, tailoring and printing

Name	Location			Household	Notes
Sinicki	Os. Przy Arce	Below 60%	6	Husband (52) and wife (49), three daughters (22, 20, 17) and one son (16); grandchild on way	Wife works long hours in hotel; husband on incapacity benefit after work in electricity plant; adult daughters unemployed though occasional casual work
Zych	Os. Przy Arce	Over 140%	2	Husband (78) and wife (73)	Husband retired from steelworks; wife retired, but continued occasional work as medical technician
Chilkiewicz	Os. Dywizjonu 303	60–100%	2	Husband (55) and wife (58)	Husband on incapacity benefit for 20 years after work in renovations and exports; wife worked as chambermaid, recently retired
Juszczak	Os. Dywizjonu 303	Over 140%	3	Husband (37) and wife (30) and infant daughter (2)	Husband works in German project design firm in chemical industry; wife on maternity leave
Sacharuk	Os. Dywizjonu 303	Over 140%	2	Husband (75) and wife (71)	Both retired but continued to run small accountancy business
Sasnowicz	Os. Dywizjonu 303	100–140%	3	Husband (48), and wife (48) and daughter (15)	Wife works on factory floor after over 1 year on temporary contracts; husband works shifts as a driver

Household (HH) name	Neighbourhood	Income category[a]	HH size	HH make-up (including age at time of interview)	Employment status
Wolak	Os. Dywizjonu 303	Over 140%	4	Husband (36) and wife (35) and two daughters (4, 6)	Husband self-employed in financial services; wife works as receptionist for language school
Dawidowicz	Os. Oświecenia	Below 60%	4	Husband (56) and wife (51), daughter (22) and son (16)	Husband took early retirement from steelworks subsidiary; wife made redundant from same firm, now unemployed, worked in Switzerland for 2 years; daughter does some part-time cleaning and leafleting work
Kiedrowski	Os. Oświecenia	Over 140%	3	Husband (41) and wife (37) and disabled daughter (6)	Both work for multinational corporation as economists
Myszka	Os. Oświecenia	100–140%	3	Divorced mother (51), daughter (22) and granddaughter (6 months)	Mother works as bookbinder; daughter caring for her daughter, previously worked in hypermarket
Niemczyk	Os. Oświecenia	Over 140%	4	Husband (51), wife (48), daughter (24) and son (21)	Husband and wife both work in steelworks, wife for repair firm
Senecka	Os. Oświecenia	Over 140%	1	Single woman (48)	Works as caretaker in neighbouring block

Household (HH) name	Neighbourhood	Income category[a]	HH size	HH make-up (including age at time of interview)	Employment status
Petržalka					
Brago	Haanova	Over 140%	2	Husband (58), wife (56)	Husband took early retirement and works part-time; wife heads an insurance office in Bratislava
Blatová	Haanova	60–100%	8/13	Husband (60), wife (56), son (40), daughter (36), daughter (34), son (22), grandson (13), granddaughter (12); plus at time of follow-up interview, husband of one daughter and third daughter, who returned to flat with husband and two other children	Husband works in a local factory as a machine operator; wife is retired; son is a cabinet maker; oldest daughter is a shop assistant; middle daughter is on maternity leave but works informally; youngest son works as a kitchen helper
Cukriková	Haanova	60–100%	4	Wife (43), husband (47), two sons (19, 8)	Wife works as shop assistant; husband as cabinet maker
Gubová	Haanova	100–140%	4	Wife (57), husband (53), two sons (32, 25)	Wife is on medical leave; husband is a security guard; both sons unemployed
Holmanová	Haanova	60–100%	3	Divorced women (58), grandmother (84), adult daughter (30)	Divorced woman took early retirement to care for ill mother; adult daughter works in a care home for children

Household (HH) name	Neighbourhood	Income category[a]	HH size	HH make-up (including age at time of interview)	Employment status
Klasický	Haanova	Over 140%	1	Adult male (36)	Works as a technician in an international firm
Lastovičková	Haanova	60–100%	5	Wife (55), husband (57), daughter (33), son (34), grandson (3)	Wife works as a nurse; husband as a plumber; daughter is unemployed and son is a technician
Paštéková	Haanova	Over 140%	1	Divorced woman (47)	Employed as an administrator in a pharmaceutical firm
Slaninová	Haanova	Over 140%	3	Wife (36), husband (35), daughter (8)	Both adults work as a teacher and printer respectively
Uhlíková	Haanova	60–100%	2	Mother (42), daughter (22)	Mother is on incapacity benefit and daughter is unemployed but works occasionally
Badunická	Gessayova	100–140%	1	Retired woman (65)	Retired and receives regular remittance income from adult daughter abroad
Bombová	Gessayova	60–100%	2	Mother (68), son (41)	Mother retired; unemployed son does occasional informal work
Hazlen	Gessayova	Below 60%	5	Husband (46), wife (41), daughter (16), two sons (14, 10)	Husband unemployed at time of interview but works as a musician without permanent employment; wife works as a bursar/economist

Name	Location	Income	No.	Household	Description
Johánek	Gessayova	Over 140%	2	Father (53), son (25)	Father works as a school caretaker and son as a receptionist
Maďarová	Gessayova	Over 140%	2	Divorced woman (54), daughter (23)	Woman works as an economist/bursar; daughter is a student but works also as a financial adviser
Panák	Gessayova	Over 140%	3	Husband (49), wife (47), daughter (23)	Husband is a state employee; wife works in the health care sector; daughter is a student
Panterová	Gessayova	Below 60%	3	Wife (44), husband (43), daughter (1)	Wife is on maternity leave from job as a cashier; husband works as a watchman
Portiš	Gessayova	60–100%	2	Husband (76), wife (73)	Both are retired and living on pension income
Slamková	Gessayova	60–100%	2	Woman (48), daughter (20)	Woman works as a kindergarten teacher; daughter is a student who works occasionally to supplement household income
Šenzová	Gessayova	Below 60%	4	Wife (45), husband (51), two daughters (22, 19)	Wife works as a secretary; husband runs his own business; both daughters are students
Bleková	Luky-sever	60–100%	4	Wife (43), husband (46), two daughters (21, 18)	Wife works as an administrator; husband works as a chef

Household (HH) name	Neighbourhood	Income category[a]	HH size	HH make-up (including age at time of interview)	Employment status
Brestovičová	Luky-sever	Below 60%	6	Wife (47), husband (48), daughter (26), son-in-law (26), second daughter (22), granddaughter (3)	Wife is unemployed but works occasionally informally; husband is a waiter as is the son-in-law; the daughter with the child is on maternity leave and the other daughter is a hairdresser
Červiková	Luky-sever	100–140%	3	Divorced woman (51), living with ex-husband (59) and son (22)	Woman works as a kitchen helper and has two other informal jobs; former husband is retired; son is unemployed
Kováčová	Luky-sever	60–100%	7	Wife (48), husband (48), daughter (29), son-in-law (36), granddaughter (2), grandson (8), daughter (18)	Husband and son-in-law work as factory workers; wife is unemployed; older daughter is on maternity leave.
Rámová	Luky-sever	Over 140%	4	Wife (55), husband (53), son (26), daughter (24)	Wife has taken early retirement; husband works on an assembly line; son is a manager; daughter an office clerk

Name	Location	Income	No.	Household	Description
Šanovná	Luky-sever	60–100%	3	Wife (50), husband (57), son (15)	Wife works as an administrator and husband as an electrician
Šiška	Luky-sever	Over 140%	4	Husband (49), wife (45), daughter (23), son (21)	Husband and son work as technicians in local companies; wife and daughter are both employed as office workers and daughter also gives informal English lessons
Šmoliar	Luky-sever	Below 60%	2	Father (54), son (20)	Father is on a disability pension; son is unemployed
Veselá	Luky-sever	Below 60%	4	Wife (52), husband (51), daughter (25), son (23)	Husband and wife are both on incapacity benefit; daughter is unemployed; son works as a security guard
Zajacová	Luky-sever	Below 60%	5	Woman (50), estranged husband (44), woman's partner (32), son (20), daughter (22)	Woman works as a machine operator; daughter as a shop assistant; others are all unemployed but have occasional informal work

Note:

(a) Equivalized household income in relation to regional median income

(b) All names have been altered to provide anonymity

Appendix II

Semi-Structured Interviews with Key Informants

Position of person interviewed	Organization	Focus of discussion
Slovakia		
Director	Mestský výbor záhrad-károv (Urban Association of Allotments)	Allotments in Petržalka
Department Head and staff responsible for social affairs	Department of Social Affairs and Health, Town Council, Petržalka	Social situation in Petržalka, responsibility of the department for poor
Associate Professor, Department of Human Geography and Demogeography	Comenius University, Faculty of Natural Sciences	Role of allotments in Petržalka, development of Petržalka
Staff members	Department of Social Affairs and Health, Town Council, Petržalka	Programmes of social assistance
Director	Hayek Foundation	Pension reform
Senior researcher	Centre for the Study of Work and Family, Ministry of Labour, Social Affairs and the Family.	Social situation and policy changes
Staff member	UNIFEM (United Nations Institute for Women) Bratislava	Reform of social assistance laws
Director	Club of Large Families and Slovak Anti-Poverty Network	Establishment and role of the APN

Position of person interviewed	*Organization*	*Focus of discussion*
Director, with responsibility for allotments	City Council	Allotments, strategy of the City Council
Department Head	Department for Local Development and Transport	Urban plans and development of allotments in Petržalka
Staff member	Institute of Housing	Strategies for questionnaire surveys in Petržalka
Staff member	Úrad práce, sociálnych vecí a rodiny (Office for Work, Social Affairs and Families)	Data concerning social support programmes
Staff member	Krízové centrum Brána do života (Crisis Centre: Life Protection)	Mission and activities of the centre and its role in Petržalka
Gardeners	Allotment area in Pri Chorvatskom ramene district of Petržalka	Work on allotments, the situation in Petržalka, relations with allotment neighbours
Former Director	Slovak Red Cross	Role of Red Cross in assistance for the poor and for the homeless, assistance programmes for pensioners and financing of activities
Department Head	Housing Department, Town Council, Petržalka	State and cooperative flats
Director	Social Assistance Department, City Council, Bratislava	Social assistance and responsibility of the City Council
Staff member	UPSVAR (Institute for Labour, Social Affairs and Families)	Social assistance programmes
Staff member	Pensioners' club, Haanova	Activities for pensioners, discussion with pensioners
Staff member	Slovak Red Cross	Role of the Red Cross in social care
Staff members	Department of Social Inclusion, Ministry of Labour and Social Affairs	Living wage, social assistance, social policy
Social assistants	Dom tretieho veku (Home of the third age)	Role of the organization in the local area, activities for pensioners, situation and possibilities for poor pensioners

Position of person interviewed	Organization	Focus of discussion
Staff member	Department of Schools, Culture and Sport, Town Council, Petržalka	Leisure activities and development in Petržalka
Nuns	BETLEHEM sv. Matky Terezy (Nunnery of Mother Teresa, Petržalka)	Voluntary work with homeless, interview with nuns and other volunteers, interviews with homeless people
Deputy Director	Leisure centre, Gessayova, Petržalka	Details concerning the role of the leisure centre, interviews with visitors
Priest	Saleziáni Dona Bosca (Social Centre of Don Bosca)	Development of the centre, activities for children and adults, situation of the poor
Staff member	Centrum mentálneho zdravia Matka (Centre for women's mental health)	Role of the centre in the local community, situation regarding the mental health of the population
Staff member	Children's Club SLNIEČKO	Activities for children and parents, situation for teenagers, discussion with children
Director	Pensioners' club Osuského, Gessayova	Role of the club in activities for pensioners, interviews with pensioners about their social situation
Director	Centre for Community Development in Petržalka	Community activities in Petržalka, social situation in different neighbour-hoods
Staff member	Zariadenie opatrovateľskej služby (Organizaton of repair services)	Activities of the organiza-tion, building of a new centre, changes in demographic situation in Petržalka
Directors	Culture centres Lúky, Háje, Dvory	Facilities and opportuni-ties for observation

Position of person interviewed	Organization	Focus of discussion
Poland		
Teacher	Primary School, Os. Kazimierzowskie, Nowa Huta	Social help in schools, identification of areas of social exclusion
Manager	Emaus Community Kraków (homeless organization)	Emaus community, rules of operating, everyday life in community
Head of Centre	U Siemachy Association (Sociotherapy Day Centres), Os. Willowe	Work of the sociotherapy day centre for young people, everyday activity, cooperation with local institutions, families and individuals
Head of Social Programs Department	MOPS (Municipal Centre for Social Services)	Social situation in Kraków and Nowa Huta, activity of MOPS, excluded groups
Manager	Night Shelter	Organization of night shelter, homelessness in Poland, major problems of homeless
President of PCK Kraków branch	PCK (Polish Red Cross)	Activities of PCK, cooperation with local government and NGOs in social service provision
Vice-President, City of Kraków	Kraków City Council	Condition of social service in Kraków, major social issues in the city, local social policy
Head	Instytut Zdrowia Publicznego CM UJ (Institute of Public Health, Jagiellonian University of Kraków)	Polish studies of poverty and social exclusion, change of situation in social policy during transformation, previous research projects
Manager	Warsztaty Terapii Zajęciowej (Occupational Therapy Workshop)	Programs supporting socially excluded population in Nowa Huta, organization of WTZ
Priest responsible for aid for poor	Parish Bieńczyce, Nowa Huta	Poverty in Nowa Huta, social structure of the parish, major problems of the poor in Bieńczyce

Position of person interviewed	Organization	Focus of discussion
Nun	Parish Bieńczyce, Nowa Huta	Poverty among children in Bieńczyce, Parish Centre for Children Help
Councillor, Committee Chair	Social Aid Committee, Kraków City Council	Social aspect of trans-formation in Kraków (Nowa Huta), social policy of city council, social differentiation in Nowa Huta
President of PKPS Krakow branch	Polski Komitet Pomocy Społecznej (Polish Committee for Social Aid)	Social policy in Poland, activities of PKPS, conditions of retired workers, financial sources for tasks connected to social aid
Gardeners	Allotment Association Wandy	Work in allotments and everyday practices of allotments owners, social contacts in allotments association, importance of allotments
President	Roma Association in Kraków	Condition of Roma minority in Nowa Huta, major difficulties of local Roma communities, aid programs, activity of Roma Association
Head of Department	Division of Social Problems and Planning, Department of Sociology, Warsaw University	Review of Polish research concerning social exclusion, most vulnerable groups in Polish society (under communism and during transition), methodological problems with studying poverty and social exclu-sion issues
Staff member	GUS (Polish Statistical Office), Warsaw	Measures and indicators of poverty and social exclusion, national and international programs for measuring social exclusion

Position of person interviewed	Organization	Focus of discussion
Head of the Social Policy Department	Ministry of Labour and Social Affairs, Warsaw	Social policy and social justice in Poland, major problems of govern- ment programme imple- mentation, international cooperation in solving social problems, national programs against social exclusion and poverty
Nun	Mogiła Parish, Nowa Huta	Activities of Mogiła Parish in supporting poor and fighting social exclusion and poverty, support of the church to most vulnerable groups
Social Worker from Nowa Huta	MOPS (Municipal Centre for Social Services) Kraków (Os. Teatralne)	Access to data about social exclusion for Nowa Huta from MOPS
Director	OKN (Cultural Centre) and Partnership of Initiatives for Nowa Huta (PIN)	Ongoing EQUAL project, history of Nowa Huta (especially central districts), selection of estates, situation of old Nowa Huta districts
Priest	Head of Grębałów Parish	Social exclusion in Grębałów and in Nowa Huta
President & Vice- President	Housing Cooperative Czyżyny	Selection of estates, questionnaire research, Dywizjonu 303 district
President	Housing Cooperative Victoria	Questionnaire research, Dywizjonu 303 district, data about Cooperative Victoria
Manager	Centrum Informacji Gospodarczej Nowa Huta (Centre for Economic Information: Nowa Huta)	Additional contacts
President of District Council	Bieńczyce (XVI) District Council	History of Nowa Huta, selection of the estates, history and problems of Os. Przy Arce

Position of person interviewed	Organization	Focus of discussion
President of District Council	XVIII (Nowa Huta) District Council	History of Nowa Huta (especially central districts), selection of estates, situation of old Nowa Huta districts
Vice-President	Czyżyny housing cooperative	Problems, housing market, access to households in Os. Dywizjonu 303
Manager	Communal Buildings Management (ZBK), Os. Urocze, Nowa Huta	Communal buildings management
Head of Social Aid Commission	Czyżyny District Council	Social aid in Czyżyny
Vice-President	Adrem Housing Cooperative	Condition of housing and financial conditions of Nowa Huta inhabitants
Staff members	Administrators of Willowe and Wandy estates (Adrem)	Condition of Willowe and Wandy estates
Department Head	Social Aid Department, Kraków City Council	Differentiation of Nowa Huta estates, data on housing allowances
Administrator	Górali and Krakowiaków Estates (Adrem)	Condition of Krakowiaków and Górali estates
Administrator	Adrem (Przy Arce) and Promos (Przy Arce) Housing Cooperatives, Nowa Huta	Situation and problems of Przy Arce district
Former Councillor of XVIII (Nowa Huta) district	Head of Mistrzejowice allotments association, Górali estate activist	History of Nowa Huta and Górali estate, financial condition of Górali estate inhabitants, allotments in Nowa Huta
Administrator, Former Councillor of Bieńczyce District	Housing Cooperative Jutrzenka	Condition and problems of inhabitants in Jutrzenka housing cooperative (Przy Arce), data about Przy Arce
Head of Social Aid Commission	Mistrzejowice District Council	History of Nowa Huta and Mistrzejowice district, problems of Mistrzejowice districts
Vice president	Housing Cooperative Oświecenia	Condition of Oświecenia estate

Position of person interviewed	Organization	Focus of discussion
Manager	Department of Communal Buildings Management, Kraków City Council	Data about apartments in Os. Przy Arce, Os. Górali and Os. Willowe belonging to the city council
Head	Municipal Social Care Centre, Os. Teatralne	Social aid in Nowa Huta
Member of allotment association	Mistrzejowice allotment association	Allotment association in Nowa Huta (Mistrzejowice allotments)
Head	Residents Board in block no. 36 (Os. Willowe)	Background to project
Head	Residents Board in block no. 3 (Os. Górali)	Background to project
Manager	Caretaker (Os. Oświecenia)	Background to project
Administrator	Os. Górali	Background to project

Notes

1 Although see Pickles (2010) for a discussion of the limits of neo-liberalism in East Central Europe and the former Soviet Union.
2 See *inter alia* Bridger and Pine (1998), Piirainen (1997), Ledeneva (1998), S. Clarke (2002), Humphrey (2002), Pickles (2002), Smith (2002a, c), Caldwell (2004a), Pavlovskaya (2004), Stenning (2005b), Round (2006a, b), Smith and Stenning (2006), Smith (2007), Smith and Rochovská (2007), Shevchenko (2009).
3 The Gini coefficient is a standard measure of the dispersion of income, where a result of 0 means that all incomes are equally distributed across a population, and a score of 1 would indicate that all income accrued to a single household.
4 Significant literatures draw attention to the ways in which the costs of transition are unevenly experienced according to gender (see, for example, Gal & Kligman, 2000a, b; Ashwin, 2000; Kiblitskaya, 2000; Kideckel, 2004; Kay, 2006), class (e.g. Crowley & Ost, 2001; Kideckel, 2002; Stenning, 2005c; Weiner, 2007) and generation (e.g. Hörschelmann, 2008; Round, 2006a; Zajicek et al., 2007).
5 For 2005, when the research was undertaken, unemployment in Kraków stood at 7% and 17.6% in Poland. In Slovakia, the unemployment rate at this time was 15.9% and in Bratislava 5.2%. Data on unemployment rates refer to registered persons and are derived from the Slovak and Polish Statistical Offices' websites. There may be some under-counting of unemployment as these data are not based on labour force survey estimates.
6 See Mercer Human Resources Consulting at www.mercerhr.com/pressrelease/ details.jhtml?idContent=1142150
7 This overtaking is more a result of Łódź's economic woes and population decline than of high levels of population growth in Kraków. This ranking also fails to take account of the Upper Silesian agglomeration, which is in fact Poland's largest urban area, with a population of some 3.2 million spread across a number of adjoining cities (OECD, 2008b: 51).
8 Data from www.citypopulation.de/Poland-Cities.html. Last accessed 03.07.09.

9   Data from Eurostat at http://epp.eurostat.ec.europa.eu/tgm/table.do?tab=tabl e&init=1&language=en&pcode=tgs00006&plugin=1. Last accessed 03.07.09.
10   Data from National Bank of Slovakia http://82.119.225.20/en/statistics/balance-of-payments-statistics/foreign-direct-investment. Last accessed 03.07.09.
11   Most studies, including those by the European Commission, use a measure of social exclusion set at 60% of equivalized national median income as defining an individual as being 'at risk' of poverty. The data for Nowa Huta and Petržalka are based on an 'at risk' of poverty level of 60% of the *regional* median, to reflect the relatively high costs of living in the two cities.
12   All data at neighbourhood level for Petržalka are derived from the 2001 census (ŠÚSR, 2001).
13   *Mrówkowiec* is Polish slang for a tower block, derived from the word for ant (mrówka), and implies an enormous block with not only multiple stories, but also multiple entrances and stairwells. The two blocks in Przy Arce have about 12 floors and 10 separate stairwells, totalling some 240 flats in each.
14   Households' wider consumption practices are explored in Stenning et al. (2009) and their related financial practices in Stenning et al. (2010).

CHAPTER TWO

1   Lange was a Pole working at the University of Chicago.
2   In employing Lenin's famous question, Sachs plays into the hands of those who critique his programmes as market Leninism (Glasman, 1994).
3   Debt write-off was a strategy that several other ECE countries were not in such a privileged position to pursue, as the current global economic crisis has made all too apparent (Smith & Swain, 2010).
4   Kolodko's advisers during this time included Mario Nuti (of the London Business School), Jerzy Hausner and Danuta Hübner, who was later to become Poland's first EU commissioner.
5   In 2003, Belka became responsible for economic policy in the Iraqi interim coalition administration, and since late 2008 has been Director of the IMF's European Department.
6   It was during this period of government that the notion of a flat tax of 15% for VAT and corporate and personal income tax was first introduced to Poland, a policy idea that was to return in later years and, as we show later, has been widespread across ECE.
7   Both leading parties, PiS and PO, had identified as right-wing, liberal, post-Solidarity parties prior to the election.
8   There is, however, one important counterweight to this agenda – in order to establish a working majority, Tusk had to bring the Polish People's Party (Polskie Stronnictwo Ludowe, PSL) into coalition. The PSL is a partially post-communist party with its roots in rural communities, and is generally seen as centre-left with an agenda of interventionism and slower privatization. PSL politicians hold the posts of both Minister of Economy and Minister of Labour and Social Policy in Tusk's government and, as a result of this, Tusk's programme has stronger elements of egalitarianism and interventionism than might be expected. Notwithstanding PO's expressed desires, there is no expectation of a major

overhaul of the welfare system and no likelihood of an immediate rolling out of a single 15% flat tax.

9   The first coalition government between 1998 and 2001 was more balanced in that it involved the social democratic party SMER.

10 Lying somewhere between May 5 and June 7, depending on the calculations used (Ódor, 2005), and according to the Hayek Foundation, 'Tax Freedom Day is … metaphorically the day when we finally start working and earning for ourselves, after having worked for the state in the previous period of the year' (see www.hayek.sk/en/modules.php?name=News&file=article&sid=49). The President of the Slovak Taxpayers Association is Jan Oravec, who is also President of the Hayek Foundation and of the Slovak Entrepreneurs Association, and the Association's Secretary General is Martin Chren, who is also Director of the Hayek Foundation.

11 The new system introduced in 2005 involves three 'pillars', including:
   - A pay-as-you-go pillar, involving a state system administered by the Social Insurance Agency, to 'protect' pensioners from poverty;
   - A funded pension pillar, which is voluntary for current workers. It is mandatory for those new to the labour market after 2005. Contributions are from workers and employers and are collected by the state Social Insurance Agency. The contributions are then transferred to one of several private asset management companies.
   - A voluntary private pension scheme based on personal pension plans.

12 Interview with leading figure, Hayek Foundation, Bratislava, 13 April 2005.

CHAPTER THREE

1   De Certeau marks out an important distinction between tactics and strategies in this process (see also Round et al., 2008).

2   For more on the ways in which household negotiations of neo-liberalization have been theorized using 'assets' and 'capitals', see DFID (2001) and, in the post-socialist context, Burawoy et al. (2000).

3   See also the discussion below on social reproduction.

4   See Smith and Stenning (2006) for further discussion of how debates over diverse economies connect to earlier discussions of the articulations of modes of production.

5   There is/was, however, a fine line between *załatwić* and *kombinować* in Polish, the latter having more dubious connotations of speculation and dealing. The border was policed by moral judgements of others' behaviour, which had either crossed this line or veered into blatant illegality (e.g. stealing from another person rather than the state).

CHAPTER FOUR

1   Average wages in financial services are higher in Bratislava than the national average, reflecting the predominance of high-end functions in the sector in the

capital, whereas in Kraków – even though average wages in the sector are higher than in others – they are lower than the national average. This reflects the existence of higher-end activities in financial services in other cities such as Warsaw.

2   There is a longer history of temporary employment in ECE connected to seasonal work in harvests and in production storming in enterprises to meet central plan targets. In Slovakia, much of this was organized through so-called *brigada* work in the construction of socialist work practices.

3   That is, contracts for the delivery of services rather than contracts of employment.

4   Named after the then Minister for Economy, Labour and Social Policy, Jerzy Hausner (see Chapter Two).

5   The analysis here draws on the period before the loss of power in 2006 of the neo-liberalizing Slovak government led by Mikuláš Dzurinda (see Chapter Two and Smith & Rochovská, 2007), which was the period during which the main fieldwork was undertaken. Since 2006, the new populist and more social democratic government has introduced a partial reform, not least increasing the minimum wage level. In Poland, despite repeated changes of government, there has been little substantive change in the sphere of labour market policy, as we discussed in Chapter Two. While these political changes have been important in the reconfiguration of the political economy of household social reproduction since 2006, given the time-frame of our research they did not have an impact on the research participants.

6   Mitra (2008) notes that the poverty rate among those working is lowest in services but it fails to account for the fact that the service sector has a very bifurcated labour market of highly paid jobs in producer services alongside low wage jobs in more basic service occupations. In the Polish context, CBOS (2008a) is one of the first pieces of research to draw attention to the possibility of in-work poverty, identifying a growing cohort of Poles in full-time, permanent employment who still find themselves living in poverty (i.e. below 60% of the median income).

7   A strict comparison between our survey-based unemployment level and the wider city-level unemployment rate is not possible due to the different survey and reporting methodologies. Rather, the data are used here as indicative.

8   Currency conversions in all chapters are based on a 2005 exchange rate. At that time, 1 euro equalled approximately PLN4 (Polish new złoty) and approximately SKK40 (Slovak koruna or crowns).

9   As we discuss in Chapter Seven, child benefits are not universal in Poland. The Pustelaks were only eligible for child benefit because Mr Pustelak's reported income fell below the social minimum.

10 Self-employment in Poland as a whole in 2005 stood at 14% and in Slovakia 15% (Eurostat, 2006a).

11 At the time of the household survey in 2005, in Nowa Huta, 11 working household members (out of a total of 304; 4%) reported having jobs outside Poland and in Petržalka 5 (out of a total of 326; 2%) had jobs outside Slovakia. However, interview evidence, especially in Nowa Huta, indicated greater levels of labour migration. In the Nowa Huta case, of the 34 households interviewed, there

were as many as 15 examples of household members working overseas, either at the time of interview or in the recent past and 13 households who could identify close family who had lived abroad for varying periods in recent months and years. The higher levels of migration identified in the interviews in part reflected the fact that this part of the research focused more on extended families than the questionnaire.

12 This discussion reflects that in Burawoy et al. (2000) who refer to state benefits as 'citizenship assets'.

13 Those earning over 130% have their pension payments suspended (ZUS, 2006: 30).

CHAPTER FIVE

1 The EU15 average was 65% at the time (Ball, 2007).

2 For more on the normalization of home ownership, see S. Smith (2008) and Gurney (1999).

3 Such growth rates were sustained through the years after EU accession but dropped dramatically in late 2008 and 2009 as the global financial crisis began to have an impact on ECE (see, for example, REAS, 2009).

4 In interview, 15 (out of 34) households acquired their first apartment in Nowa Huta through the steelworks or an allied enterprise, and of these five moved to live and work in Nowa Huta explicitly to acquire a family home more quickly.

5 Housing co-operatives represented a form of ownership developed in Poland in the 1960s and 1970s through which individuals could pool their resources and access state funds for construction to develop new housing beyond the mainstream state housing sector. By the late 1970s and through the 1980s, almost all new-build housing was developed by co-operatives and they had effectively been transformed into state housing companies. As such this sector was as affected by shortages and waiting lists as the wider state and enterprise housing sectors (Ciechocińska, 1990).

6 In Kraków as a whole in 2005, the average apartment size was 56.0 m² and the average space per person was 21.7 m² (Prezydent Miasta Krakowa, 2008: 231; NB data are not available for Nowa Huta). In Petržalka as a whole, average apartment size was smaller, at 42.1 m² (compared with 41.3 m² in Bratislava as a whole) and average space per person was 15.3 m² compared with 17.7 m² in Bratislava as a whole (ŠÚSR, 2001).

7 For example, in 2007, the market leader in DIY in Poland, Castorama (part of the UK's Kingfisher group), had total sales of £703 million (up from about £180 million in 2001/2; MacDonald, 2008). According to *Retail Week*: 'Kingfisher's two biggest stores globally by sales are Castoramas in Warsaw, each turning over about £50 million a year – about twice as much as a big B&Q in the UK.'

8 Thanks to Stefan Bouzarovski for his input on this issue.

9 Energy poverty implies that a household is unable to heat the home to the temperature required to sustain comfort and health and to perform the tasks of everyday life (Buzar, 2007).

10 The Pustelak family in Nowa Huta, for example, noted that the majority of residents in their block were 'connected on the side, simply for free'.

CHAPTER SIX

1 For example, Poland's near-disappearance from the map of Europe between 1795 and 1918 evokes a heightened attachment to land as the crucible of Polish national identity. In similar ways, the integration of what is today the Slovak Republic into the Austro-Hungarian Empire until the First World War and the dominance of landed Hungarian classes has meant that land and territory remain critical elements of Slovak national identity.

2 Flower production may also have a commercial element, entering a commodity economy of local sale, as one of our interviews in Nowa Huta demonstrated. In this case, an elderly woman worked with an allotment neighbour to grow flowers and sell them in two of Nowa Huta's markets, for a couple of złotys a bunch. Together, in season, they earn about 20 to 40 PLN (€5–10) a day, a significant supplement to their pension incomes.

3 In addition to those already mentioned, produce included peppers, beans, cucumbers, tomatoes, lettuce, onions, grapes, strawberries, raspberries, gooseberries, cranberries, blackcurrants, and, of course, potatoes.

4 Rearing rabbits on allotments was a major activity during the rationing of the late 1980s in Poland. One interviewee's father, for example, kept over 150 rabbits on his allotment throughout this period.

5 Interview with Ing. Stanislav Tokos, Department of Land Planning, City Council, Bratislava, 20 May 2006.

6 These include the controversial case of the development of the Gdańsk 2012 UEFA Cup stadium being constructed on one of that city's major allotment sites, a good example of how Poland's attempts to play a global game (in this case, literally) have had an impact on urban households' everyday economies.

7 Interview with allotment users, Petržalka, 23 October 2005.

8 Thanks to Judit Timár for further discussion of this issue.

9 *Pierogi* are small ravioli-like parcels which can be filled with meat, vegetables or potatoes. *Gołąbki* ('little pigeons') are cabbage leaves stuffed with rice, vegetables and meat.

10 *Bryndzové halušky* is a potato dumpling dish served in a sheep's cheese sauce and often accompanied by smoked bacon.

11 Other aspects of retail change and consumption practices are explored in Stenning et al. (2009).

12 For a sense of the scale of these chains, Żabka has over 1800 stores in Poland (and trades with the slogan 'Close, Quick and Convenient'); ABC is a chain of over 2500 franchises (it trades with the slogan 'The biggest chain of neighbourly shops'); Lewiatan is a franchise of over 2000 stores; and Groszek, also structured as a franchise, includes more than 900 stores in its network. Lewiatan and Groszek are now both owned by Emperia Holdings, a public-listed Polish

company. Local, Kraków chains such as Kefirek are also important. In Slovakia, locally owned chains are also present, notably that of Coop Jednota.

13   Tesco and other major retailers also pride themselves on sourcing many of their products domestically (Mesure, 2006). This means, of course, that the entry of global retailers into ECE markets has an impact on producers as well as consumers (FAO, 2005).

14   Many of the traders at Tomex are not Polish. Some are Ukrainian, some Romanian, and some of the clothes stalls are run by Vietnamese Poles. Signs at the entrance to Tomex list the rules of trade in Polish, Russian, Romanian and English.

15   See, for example, www.tesco.pl/promocje/gazetki/#, www.itesco.sk/products/list, www.biedronka.pl/index.php and www.carrefour.pl/page/pl/handlowy/hipermarkety/katalog/. Tesco Poland and Slovakia allow shoppers to subscribe to these promotional leaflets, receiving electronic versions a few days before their wider distribution.

16   The most extreme version of this was practised by an older man from Nowa Huta who spent no money on food, but spent his days going from supermarket to supermarket in search of free items, usually those approaching or past their sell-by date.

17   A *grosz* is the smaller unit of Polish currency. There are 100 grosze to the złoty.

18   For many, this food aid is the most visible evidence of Poland's integration within the European Union.

CHAPTER SEVEN

1   According to a study by the Ministry of Finance, tax revenue fell by approximately 0.5% of GDP between 2003 and 2004 following the introduction of the flat tax regime (Krajčír & Ódor, 2005). Using OECD data, Slovak tax revenue as a percentage of GDP fell from 33.4% in 2003 to 31.8% in 2004 and 29.8% in 2007, while the OECD average ranked between 35 and 36%, that for the Czech Republic ranged between 36% and 37% and that for Poland ranged between 32% and 33%. In 1998, Slovakia's tax revenue as a percentage of GDP was 37% (extracted from OECD Statistical Extracts Online, http://stats.oecd.org).

2   In contrasting examples, in Estonia and the Czech Republic claimants need only to have been employed for 12 of the previous 36 months.

3   The particular phenomenon of 'private maternalism' explicated by Glass and Fodor (2007) is discussed in more detail below.

4   A 2003 CBOS poll in Poland, cited in Ornacka and Szczepaniak-Wiecha (2005), noted that 70% of respondents live within close proximity of their close family; 72% see their parents at least once a week, with the corresponding figure for grandchildren 62%; adult children 60%; in-laws 47%; siblings 44%; and grandparents 36%.

5   Mrs Kielak and Mrs Modzelewska frequently use the verb '*załatwić*', which literally means 'to take care of' or 'to arrange'. It is a very important key word in Poland, and has been for decades, with a powerful and widely understood mean-

ing of 'to sort out' or 'facilitate'. It is often coupled with the word '*sprawy*', meaning business, affairs, or things, and to 'sort things out' (*załatwić sprawy*) is a common and often time-consuming activity. Wedel explores this in the context of 1980s Poland in *The Private Poland* (1986; see pp. 41–46 in particular; see also Chapter Three).

6   They met every season to 'stock take' and exchange unwanted clothes, so that clothes 'circulate' within the group.

7   In Petržalka, pensioner clubs filled the gap for older residents who could not draw on local social networks. Pensioner clubs also play an important role in Nowa Huta (Stenning, 2003, and see note 8).

8   In Nowa Huta, this kind of activity is also formalized through a pensioners' centre that facilitates a 'second-hand exchange market of goods collected, repaired and reconditioned by workers' (Stenning, 2003: 774).

9   Critically, Poland's ongoing social security reforms saw an end to all new early retirement entitlements from 2007 (Balcerzak-Paradowska et al., 2003: 223).

10   According to the Kraków City Council, 85% of all clients of social services in the city (MOPS) have had contact for at least two years. Over half have been engaged with social services for at least five years and one-third for more than ten years (Rada Miasta Krakowa, 2007).

11   In this context, it is interesting to note that one aspect of a pilot programme launched in 2001 to deal with some of the social, health, educational and economic problems confronted by Roma in Poland (Ministerstwo Spraw Wewnętrznych i Administracji, 2003) has focused on facilitating the provision of welfare support to Roma families. The Roma families amongst our interviewed households in Nowa Huta had both availed themselves of benefits within this scheme, and had more generally benefited considerably from improved contact with social services through the dedicated social worker assigned to the Roma community in Nowa Huta.

12   In Poland, unemployed single parents/mothers are eligible for guaranteed benefits equalling 88% of the social minimum (Balcerzak-Paradowska et al., 2003: 220). Since many of the single mothers in our research communities only had experience of employment in low-paid, insecure work, where pay was unlikely to be much above the social minimum, the income/benefits trade-off implied that it would not be worth returning to employment. Given, furthermore, the high costs and poor availability of childcare, for many single mothers, work simply did not pay. The presence of single-parent mothers was much less significant in Petržalka, although rules regulating alimony payments apply similarly to those in Poland.

13   The gravity of this situation was exacerbated by the fact that the number of alimony benefit claimants in Poland increased from 116,000 in 1990 to 436,000 in 2000, an increase at least in part explained by economic crises and the growth in unemployment which reduced the ability of fathers to meet their alimony obligations as well as the increased incidence of divorce (Krakowskie Centrum Praw Kobiet, 2005).

14   For more on these charities, see www.pkps.org.pl/, www.pck.pl/pages,11.html, and www.redcross.sk/co-robime/socialna-cinnosti/socialna-cinnost-sck/.

15   Establishing a charitable association was in itself a coping strategy for one inter-viewee. Mrs Idziak has, with friends, set up a charity called the Give Heart Association (Stowarzyszenie Podaruj Serce) with the aim of becoming a food aid distributor and of collecting money for medical treatments etc. and, on the way, benefiting themselves.

CHAPTER EIGHT

1   See www.pin.nowa-huta.net.
2   In the 2002 and 2006 parliamentary elections, voters in Petržalka returned the leading neo-liberal coalition party Slovak Democratic and Christian Union (SDKU) with more than double the national share of this party's vote (36% compared with 15% nationally in 2002, and 38% compared with 18% nationally in 2006). By contrast, in Nowa Huta, the majority of voters supported the pro-tectionist PiS in the 2005 presidential elections that took place during our field-work (www.prezydent2005.pkw.gov.pl/PZT/PL/WYN/W/126101.htm).

Bibliography

Alam, A., Murthi, M., Yemtsov, R., Murrugarra, E., Dudwick, N., Hamilton, E. & Tiongson, E. (2005) *Growth, Poverty and Inequality: Eastern Europe and the Former Soviet Union*. Washington, DC: World Bank.

Anderson, R. (2007) Growing incomes boost saving and borrowing, *The Financial Times*, Slovakia: Special Report, 20 February: 2.

Andrusz, G., Harloe, M. & Szelenyi, I. (eds) (1996) *Cities after Socialism: Urban and Regional Change and Conflict in Post-Socialist Societies*. Oxford: Blackwell.

Arnstberg, K.-O. and Borén, T. (eds) (2003) *Everyday Economy in Russia, Poland and Latvia*, Södertörn Academic Studies 16. Stockholm: Almqvist and Wiksell.

Ashwin, S. (ed.) (2000) *Gender, State and Society in Soviet and Post-Soviet Russia*. London: Routledge.

Bakardjieva, M. (2005) Domestication running wild: From the moral economy of the household to the mores of culture. In Berker, T., Hartmann, M., Punie, Y. & Ward, K. (eds) *Domestication of Media and Technologies*. Maidenhead: Open University Press, 62–79.

Bakker, I. (2007) Social reproduction and the constitution of a gendered political economy, *New Political Economy*, 12 (4): 541–556.

Balcerowicz, L. (1995) *Socialism, Capitalism, Transformation*. Budapest: Central European University Press.

Balcerowicz, L. (2000) Interview for PBS Commanding Heights, available at: www.pbs.org/wgbh/commandingheights/shared/minitext/int_leszekbalcerowicz.html. Last accessed 15.02.2008.

Balcerowicz, L. (2006) Losing Milton Friedman, a revolutionary muse of liberty, *Daily Star (Lebanon)*, 22 November. Reprinted at www.naomiklein.org/shock-doctrine/resources/part4/chapter9/balcerowicz. Last accessed 15.02.2008.

Balcerzak-Paradowska, B., Chłoń-Domińczak, A., Kotowska, I., Olejniczuk-Merta, A., Topińska, I. & Wóycicka, I. (2003) The gender dimensions of social security reform in Poland. In Fultz, E., Ruck, M. & Steinhilber, S. (eds) *The Gender Dimensions of Social Security Reform in Central and Eastern Europe*. Budapest: ILO Subregional Office for Central and Eastern Europe, 187–314.

Ball, M. (2007) *European Housing Review 2007*, RICS Research/Savills. Available at: www.rics.org/NR/rdonlyres/5B277011-8346-4111-9299-C7A6991B2090/0/ EuropeanHousingReviewfullreport.pdf. Last accessed 08.07.2009.

Barancová, H. (2006) EU adhesion of the Slovak Republic and the development of employment legislation, *Transition Studies Review*, 13 (1): 9–12.

Bardonne, L. & Guio, A.-C. (2005) In-work poverty: New commonly agreed indicators at the EU level, *Statistics in Focus: Population and Social Conditions*, No. 5. Luxembourg: European Communities.

Barnett, C. (2005) The consolations of 'neoliberalism', *Geoforum*, 36 (1): 7–12.

Bauman, Z. (1998) *Work, Consumerism and the New Poor*. Buckingham: Open University Press.

Beall, J. & Kanji, N. (1999) *Households, Livelihoods and Urban Poverty*, Urban Governance, Partnership and Poverty, Theme Paper 3, Department of Social Policy and Administration, London School of Economics.

Beatty, C. & Fothergill, S. (2002) Hidden unemployment among men, *Regional Studies*, 36 (8): 811–823.

Beck, U. (2000) *The Brave New World of Work*. Cambridge: Polity.

Begg, R. & Pickles, J. (1998) Institutions, social networks and ethnicity in the cultures of transition: industrial change, mass unemployment and regional transformation in Bulgaria. In Pickles, J. & Smith, A. (eds) *Theorising Transition: The Political Economy of Post-Socialist Transformations*. London: Routledge.

Belka, M. (2001) Lessons from the Polish transition. In Blazyca, G. & Rapacki, R. (eds) *Poland into the New Millennium*. Cheltenham: Edward Elgar, 13–32.

Bellows, A. (2004) One hundred years of allotment gardens in Poland, *Food and Foodways*, 12 (4): 247–276.

Bennett, T. & Watson, D. (2002) *Understanding Everyday Life*. Oxford: Blackwell Publishers.

Beynon, H. & Hudson, R. (1993) Place and space in contemporary Europe: Some lessons and reflections, *Antipode* 25 (3): 177–190.

Bieńkowska, A. (2008) Hope for the holidays, *Krakow Post*, www.krakowpost.com/ article/1197. Last accessed 08.07.2009.

Birdsall, K. (2000) 'Everyday crime' at the workplace: Covert earning schemes in Russia's new commercial sector. In Ledeneva, A. & Kurkchiyan, M. (eds) *Economic Crime in Russia*. London: Kluwer Law International, 145–162.

Blazyca, G. (1999) Polish socioeconomic development in the 1990s and scenarios for EU accession, *Europe–Asia Studies*, 51 (5): 799–819.

Blazyca, G. & Rapacki, R. (eds) (2001) *Poland into the New Millennium*. Cheltenham: Edward Elgar.

Blunt, A. (2005) Cultural geography: Cultural geographies of home, *Progress in Human Geography*, 29: 505–515.

Blunt, A. & Muzioł-Węcławowicz, A. (1998) Improved management of the existing stock: The case of Poland, *Housing Studies*, 13 (5): 697–711.

Blunt, A. & Varley, A. (2004) Geographies of home, *Cultural Geographies*, 11 (3): 3–6.

Bockmann, J. & Eyal, G. (2002) Eastern Europe as a laboratory for economic knowledge: The transnational roots of neoliberalism, *American Journal of Sociology*, 108 (2): 310–352.

Bodnár, J. (2001) *Fin-de-Millénaire Budapest: Metamorphoses of Urban Life.* Minneapolis: University of Minnesota Press.

Bodnár, J. & Böröcz, J. (1998) Housing advantages for the better connected? Institutional segmentation, settlement type and social network effects in Hungary's late state-socialist housing inequalities, *Social Forces,* 76 (4): 1275–1304.

Bohle, D. & Greskovits, B. (2007) Neoliberalism, embedded neoliberalism and neo-corporatism: Towards transnational capitalism in Central-Eastern Europe, *West European Politics,* 30 (3): 443–466.

Bohle, D. & Neunhöffer, G. (2005) Why is there no third way? The role of neoliberal ideology, networks and think tanks in combating market socialism and shaping transformation in Poland. In Plehwe, D. Walpen, B. & Neunhöffer, G. (eds) *Neoliberal Hegemony: A Global Critique.* London: Routledge, 89–104.

Bourdieu, P. (1977) *Outline of a Theory of Practice.* Cambridge: Cambridge University Press.

Bourdieu, P. (1984) *Distinction: A Social Critique of the Judgement of Taste.* London: Routledge.

Bourdieu, P. (1990) *The Logic of Practice.* Cambridge: Polity Press.

Bourdieu, P. (1998) The essence of neoliberalism, *Le Monde Diplomatique,* December, http://mondediplo.com/1998/12/08bourdieu. Last accessed 2.06.09.

Boym, S. (1994) *Common Places: Mythologies of Everyday Life in Russia.* Cambridge, MA: Harvard University Press.

Bradshaw, M. & Stenning A. (2001) The progress of economic transition in east central Europe. In Bachtler, J, Downes, R. & Gorzelak, G. (eds) *Transition, Cohesion and Regional Policy in Central and Eastern Europe.* Aldershot: Ashgate, 11–32.

Bradshaw, M. & Stenning, A. (eds) (2004) *East Central Europe and the Former Soviet Union: The Post-Socialist States.* Harlow: Pearson.

Brenner, N., Peck, J. & Theodore, N. (2010) Variegated neoliberalization: Geographies, modalities, pathways, *Global Networks,* 10 (2): 182–222.

Bridge, G. (2002) *The Neighbourhood and Social Networks,* ESRC Centre for Neighbourhood Research Paper 4.

Bridge, G. (2004) Pierre Bourdieu. In Hubbard, P., Kitchin, R. & Valentine, G. (eds) *Key Thinkers on Space and Place.* London: Sage, 59–64.

Bridger, S. & Pine, F. (eds) (1998) *Surviving Post-Socialism: Local Strategies and Regional Responses in Eastern Europe and the Former Soviet Union.* London: Routledge.

Bromley, R. & Thomas, C. (1993) The retail revolution, the carless shopper and disadvantage, *Transactions of the Institute of British Geographers,* 18 (2): 222–236.

Brook, A.-M. & Leibfritz, W. (2005) Slovakia's introduction of a flat tax as part of wider economic reforms, Working Paper No. 448, OECD, Economics Department.

Brown, D. (2007) Persistent unemployment and passive policies: Politics and institutional change in post-communist Poland, *Human Relations,* 60 (10): 1467–1491.

Buchowski, M. (2003) Coming to terms with capitalism: An example of a rural community in Poland, *Dialectical Anthropology,* 27 (1): 47–68.

Bukowski, A., Jabłońska, B., and Smagacz, M. (2006) *Zjawisko Wykluczenia Społecznego w Badaniach CASE,* Instytut Socjologii UJ and Miejski Ośrodek Wspierania Inicjatyw Społecznych: Kraków. Available at: www.krakow.pl/mowis/pliki/caseuj.pdf. Last accessed 6.11.08.

Burawoy, M. (1999) Afterword. In Burawoy, M. & Verdery, K. (eds) *Uncertain Transition: Ethnographies of Change in the Postsocialist World*. Oxford: Rowman and Littlefield, 301–311.

Burawoy, M. & Verdery, K. (eds) (1999) *Uncertain Transition: Ethnographies of Change in the Post-Socialist World*. Oxford: Rowman and Littlefield.

Burawoy, M., Krotov, P. & Lytkina, T. (2000) Involution and destitution in capitalist Russia, *Ethnography*, 1 (1): 43–65.

Burchell, B., Ladipo, D. & Wilkinson, F. (2002) *Job Insecurity and Work Intensification*, Routledge: London.

Burgermeister, J. (2004) Roma face starvation in the slums of Slovakia, *The Observer*, February 29.

Búriková, Z. (2004) Consuming socialism: Domesticated socialist shops in the Slovak village. In Cashin, A. & Jirsa, J. (eds) *Thinking Together: Proceedings of the IWM Junior Fellows' Conference Volume XVI*, IWM: Vienna. Available at: www.iwm. at/publ-jvc/jc–16-02.pdf. Last accessed 08.07.2009.

Burns, A. and Kowalski, P. (2004) *The Jobs Challenge in Poland*. Economic Department Working Paper 414. Paris: OECD.

Burrell, K. (2003) The political and social life of food in socialist Poland, *Anthropology of East Europe Review*, 21 (1). Available at: http://condor.depaul.edu/~rrotenbe/ aeer/V21n1/Burrell.pdf. Last accessed 08.07.2009.

Buzar, S. (2007) *Energy Poverty in Eastern Europe: Hidden Geographies of Deprivation*, Aldershot: Ashgate.

Caldwell, M. (2004a) *Not by Bread Alone: Social Support in the New Russia*. Berkeley: University of California Press.

Caldwell, M. (2004b) Domesticating the French fry: McDonald's and consumerism in Moscow, *Journal of Consumer Culture*, 4 (1): 5–26.

Carpenter, M. (1997) Slovakia and the triumph of nationalist-populism, *Communist and Post-Communist Studies*, 30 (2): 205–219.

Carter, F. (1994) *Trade and Urban Development in Poland: An Economic Geography of Cracow from its Origins to 1795*. Cambridge University Press.

Castree, N. (2006) From neoliberalism to neoliberalisation: consolations, confusions, and necessary illusions, *Environment and Planning A*, 38: 1–6.

Cazes, S. & Nesporova, A. (2003a) *Towards Excessive Job Insecurity in Transition Economies?* Geneva: ILO. Available at: www.ilo.org/public/english/employment/ strat/download/ep23.pdf. Last accessed 08.07.2009.

Cazes, S. & Nesporova, A. (2003b) *Labour Markets in Transition*. Geneva: ILO.

Cazes, S. & Nesporova, A. (2004) Labour markets in transition: balancing flexibility and security in Central and Eastern Europe, *Revue de l'OFCE*, April/Special Issue: 23–54. Available at: www.ofce.sciences-po.fr/pdf/revue/03–89bis.pdf. Last accessed 08.07.2009.

CBOS (2008a), *Pracujący Biedni*, BS/182/2008. Available at: www.cbos.pl/ SPISKOM.POL/2008/K_182_08.PDF. Last accessed 08.07.2009.

CBOS (2008b) *Zachowania Konsumenckie*, Centrum Badania Opinii Społecznej BS/117/2008. Available at: www.cbos.pl/SPISKOM.POL/2008/K_117_08.PDF. Last accessed 24.3.09.

Cellarius, B. (2004) *In the Land of Orpheus: Rural Livelihoods and Nature Conservation in Postsocialist Bulgaria*. Madison: University of Wisconsin Press.

Cerami, A. (2008) *Central Europe in Transition: Emerging Models of Welfare and Social Assistance*, MPRA Paper No. 8377. Available at: http://mpra.ub.uni-muenchen. de/8377/. Last accessed 5.11.08.

Chakrabarty, D. (2000) *Provincializing Europe: Postcolonial Thought and Historical Difference*. Princeton: Princeton University Press.

Chancellery of the Prime Minister (2002) *Information on the Polish Government Programme "Entrepreneurship–Development–Work" – A Strategy for the Economic Development of Poland*. Available at: www.kprm.gov.pl/english/english/s. php?id=909. Last accessed 22.05.09.

Chase, C. (1983) Symbolism of food shortage in current Polish politics, *Anthropological Quarterly*, 56 (2): 76–82.

Chelcea, L. (2002) The culture of shortage during state-socialism: Consumption practices in a Romanian village in the 1980s, *Cultural Studies*, 16 (1): 16–43.

Christie, H., Smith, S. & Munro, M. (2008) The emotional economy of housing, *Environment and Planning A*, 40: 2296–2312.

Ciechocińska, M. (1990) The social image of urban housing – dreams and realities: The case of Poland, *Journal of Urban Affairs*, 12 (2): 157–172.

Ciechocińska, M. (1993) Gender aspects of dismantling the command economy in Eastern Europe: The Polish case, *Geoforum*, 24 (1): 31–44.

Cienski, J. (2003) Cost-cutting budget seeks to claw back Polish deficit, *Financial Times*, 9 October 2003.

Cienski, J. (2004a) Poland shrinks from painful cure for ailing economy, *Financial Times*, 19 January 2004.

Cienski, J. (2004b) Poland's minority government scrabbles among the opposition to gain support for spending reforms, *Financial Times*, 12 February 2004.

Cienski, J. & Buckley, S. (2005) Hypermarkets 'not welcome' in Poland, *Financial Times*, 4 November.

Cienski, J. & Wagstyl, S. (2007a) FT Report – Poland 2007: High expectations of everyday life, *Financial Times*, 12 December.

Cienski, J. & Wagstyl, S. (2007b) Poland sets out agenda to free up business, *Financial Times*, 23 October.

Cienski, J. & Wagstyl, S. (2007c) Polish PM promises a 'machete' approach, *Financial Times*, 30 November.

Cirman, A. (2006) Housing tenure preferences in the postprivatisation period: The case of Slovenia, *Housing Studies*, 21 (1): 113–134.

Clapham, D. (1995) Privatisation and the East European housing model, *Urban Studies*, 32: 679–694.

Clark, E. & Soulsby, A. (1998) Organization-community embeddedness: The social impact of enterprise restructuring in the post-communist Czech Republic, *Human Relations*, 51 (1): 25–50.

Clarke, J. (2004) Dissolving the public realm? The logics and limits of neo-liberalism, *Journal of Social Policy*, 33 (1): 27–48.

Clarke, J. (2007) Subordinating the social? Neo-liberalism and the remaking of welfare capitalism, *Cultural Studies*, 21 (6): 974–987.

Clarke, S. (1999) *New Forms of Employment and Household Survival Strategies in Russia*. Coventry: ISITO/CCLS.

Clarke, S. (2002) *Making Ends Meet in Contemporary Russia: Secondary Employment, Subsidiary Agriculture and Social Networks.* Edward Elgar: Cheltenham.

Clarke, S., Varshavskaya, L., Alasheev, S. & Karelina, M. (2000) The myth of the urban peasant, *Work, Employment and Society,* 14 (3): 481–499.

Coe, N., Johns, J. & Ward, K. (2006) Flexibility in action: the temporary staffing industry in the Czech Republic and Poland, *Environment and Planning A,* 40 (6): 1391–1415.

Community Economies Collective (2001) Imagining and enacting noncapitalist futures, *Socialist Review,* 28 (3/4): 93–135.

Cook, A. (2010) The expatriate real estate complex: Creative destruction and the production of luxury in post-socialist Prague, *International Journal of Urban and Regional Research,* 34 (2).

Creed, G. (1998) *Domesticating Revolution: From Socialist Reform to Ambivalent Transition in a Bulgarian Village.* University Park: Penn State University Press.

Crewe, L. (2000) Geographies of retailing and consumption, *Progress in Human Geography,* 24 (2): 275–290.

Crow, G., Allan, G. & Summers, M. (2002) Neither busybodies nor nobodies: Managing proximity and distance in neighbourly relations, *Sociology,* 36 (1): 127–145.

Crowley, S. & Ost, D. (2001) *Workers after Workers' States: Labor and Politics in Postcommunist Eastern Europe.* Oxford, Rowman and Littlefield.

Czarzasty, J. (2007) Pay disputes in public health sector escalate, *EIROnline,* www.eurofound.europa.eu/eiro/2007/07/articles/pl0707019i.htm. Last accessed 26.5.09.

Danglová, O. (1998) The phenomenon of poverty in the Slovak countryside, *Human Affairs,* 8 (2): 193–200.

Davies, N. (1986) *Heart of Europe: A Short History of Poland.* Oxford: Oxford University Press.

Dawidson, K. (2005) Geographic impacts of the political: Dealing with nationalised housing in Romania, *Political Geography,* 24 (5): 545–567.

Day, M. (2005) Conservative twins set to dominate politics in Poland, *The Daily Telegraph,* 24 October.

De Boeck, F. (1998) Domesticating diamonds and dollars: Identity, expenditure and sharing in southwestern Zaire (1984–1997), *Development and Change,* 29 (4): 777–810.

de Certeau, M. (1984) *The Practice of Everyday Life.* Berkeley: University of California Press.

de Certeau, M., Giard, L. & Mayol, P. (1998) *The Practice of Everyday Life Volume 2: Living and Cooking.* Minneapolis: University of Minnesota Press.

Dempsey, J. (2007) Letter from Europe: Shaping the agenda of Poland's drift to the far right, *International Herald Tribune,* 26 July.

DFID (2001) *Sustainable Livelihoods Guidance Sheets.* Available at: www.livelihoods. org/info/info_guidancesheets.html. Last accessed 03.03.2009.

di Leonardo, M. (1987) The female world of cards and holidays: Women, families and the work of kinship, *Signs: Journal of Women in Culture and Society,* 12 (3): 440–453.

Domański, B. (1992) Social control over the milltown: Industrial paternalism under socialism and capitalism, *Tijdschrift Voor Economische en Sociale Geografie,* 83 (5): 353–360.

Domański, B. (1997) *Industrial Control over the Socialist Town*. Praeger: London.

Domański, H. (1990) Dynamics of labor market segmentation in Poland, 1982–1987, *Social Forces*, 69 (2): 423–38.

Domański, H. (2002) Is the East European "underclass" feminized? *Communist and Post-Communist Studies*, 35: 383–394.

Drahokoupil, J. (2007) Analysing the capitalist state in post-socialism: Towards the Porterian workfare postnational regime, *International Journal of Urban and Regional Research*, 31(2): 401–424.

du Gay, P. (1996) *Consumption and Identity at Work*. London: Sage.

Duncan, S. (2005) Mothering, class and rationality, *The Sociological Review*, 53 (1): 50–76.

Duncan, S. & Edward, R. (1997) Lone mothers and paid work: Rational economic man or gendered moral rationalities, *Feminist Economics*, 3 (2): 29–61.

Duncan, S. & Smith, D. (2002) Family geographies and gender cultures, *Social Policy and Society*, 1 (1): 21–34.

Dunford, M. & Smith, A. (2000) Catching up or falling behind? Economic performance and regional trajectories in the "new" Europe, *Economic Geography*, 76: 169–95.

Duszczyk, M. & Wiśniewski, J. (2006) The Polish pension system in comparative perspective, *European Papers on the New Welfare*, 4: 126–136.

Dyck, I. (2005) Feminist geography, the 'everyday', and local–global relations: Hidden spaces of place-making, *The Canadian Geographer*, 49 (3): 233–243.

Džambazovič, R. (2007) *Chudoba na Slovensku: diskurz, rozsah a profil chudoby*. Bratislava: Univerzita Komenského.

Dziennik Polski (2007) Ogródki na wagę złota, 13 June. Available at: www1.dziennik.krakow.pl/var/html/2007/06.13/pierwsza.pdf. Last accessed 24.10.08.

Eade, J., Drinkwater, S. and Garapich, M. (2006) *Class and Ethnicity: Polish Migrants in London*. ESRC End of Award Report. University of Surrey. Available at: www.surrey.ac.uk/Arts/CRONEM/polish/POLISH_FINAL_RESEARCH_REPORT_WEB.pdf. Last accessed 08.07.2009.

EBRD (1996) *Transition Report*. London: European Bank for Reconstruction and Development.

EC (European Commission) (2008) Annexes to the Commission staff working document accompanying the proposal for a Council Regulation amending Regulations (EC) No 1290/2005 on the financing of the common agricultural policy as regards food distribution to the most deprived persons in the Community. Impact assessment. COM (2008) 563. Available at: ec.europa.eu/agriculture/markets/freefood/impactannex-en.pdf. Last accessed 01.06.2009.

Economist, The (2005) The case for flat taxes, *The Economist*, 14 April.

Einhorn, B. (1993) *Cinderella Goes to the Market: Citizenship, Gender and Women's Movements in East Central Europe*. London: Verso.

EIROnline (2002) Temporary work under debate, 10 October. Available at: www.eurofound.europa.eu/eiro/2002/10/inbrief/pl0210104n.htm. Last accessed 08.07.2009.

EIROnline (2004) New labour market legislation adopted, 7 June. Available at: www.eurofound.europa.eu/eiro/2004/05/feature/pl0405105f.htm. Last accessed 08.07.2009.

England, K. & Ward, K. (eds) (2007) *Neoliberalization: States, Networks, Peoples*. Oxford: Blackwell Publishers.

Escobar, A. (2004) Development, violence and the new imperial order, *Development*, 47 (1): 15–21.

Eurostat (2006a) One in six workers self-employed, *Eurostat News Release* 133/2006, 5 October.

Eurostat (2006b) Regional unemployment rates in the EU25 ranged from 2.6% to 30.1% in 2005, *Eurostat News Release* 150/2006, 16 November.

Falt'an, L'. & Dodder, R. (1995) Privatizing the housing sector: The case of Slovakia, *Public Administration and Development*, 15 (4): 391–396.

Fankhauser, S. & Tepic, S. (2007) Can poor consumers pay for energy and water? An affordability analysis for transition countries, *Energy Policy*, 35: 1038–1049.

FAO (Food and Agriculture Organization) (2005) *Central and Eastern Europe: Impact of Food Retail Investments on the Food Chain*, FAO Investment Centre/EBRD Cooperation Programme, Report Series No. 7. Available at: ftp.fao.org/docrep/fao/008/af100e/af100e00.pdf. Last accessed 21.4.09.

Federation of Polish Food Banks (2008) *European Food Aid Programme*, www.bankizywnosci.pl/epead.html. Last accessed 7.11.08.

Ferge, Z. (1997) *And what if the state fades away? The civilizing process and the state*, IWM Working Paper 7, Vienna. Available at: www.iwm.at/publ-wp/wp–97-07.pdf. Last accessed 30.7.03.

Fisher, B. & Tronto, J. (1990) Towards a feminist theory of caring. In E. Abel & M. Nelson (eds) *Circles of Care: Work and Identity in Women's Lives*. Albany: State University of New York Press.

Fisher, S., Gould, J. & Haughton, T. (2007) Slovakia's neoliberal turn, *Europe–Asia Studies*, 59 (6): 977–998.

Fitzpatrick (2001) *Everyday Stalinism*. Oxford: Oxford University Press.

Forbes, S. (2003) Fact and comment, *Forbes.com*, 11 August. Available at: www.forbes.com/free_forbes/2003/0811/021.html. Last accessed 17.11.2005.

Förster, M. & Tóth, I. (2001) Child poverty and family transfers in the Czech Republic, Hungary and Poland, *Journal of European Social Policy*, 11 (4): 324–341.

Fraad, H. (2000) Exploitation in the labor of love. In Gibson-Graham, J.K., Resnick, S. & Wolff, R. (eds) *Class and its Others*. Minneapolis: University of Minnesota Press.

Fraad, H., Resnick, S. & Wolff, R. (1994) *Bringing It All Back Home*. London: Pluto Press.

Fraser, N. (2000) Rethinking recognition, *New Left Review*, 3: 107–120.

Friedman, M. & Friedman, R. (1990) *Free to Choose*. Harcourt.

Fultz, E. & Steinhilber, S. (2003) The gender dimensions of social security reform in the Czech Republic, Hungary, and Poland. In Fultz, E., Ruck, M. & Steinhilber, S. (eds) *The Gender Dimensions of Social Security Reform in Central and Eastern Europe*. Budapest: ILO Subregional Office for Central and Eastern Europe, 13–41.

Gal, S. & Kligman, G. (2000a) *The Politics of Gender after Socialism*. Princeton: Princeton University Press.

Gal, S. & Kligman, G. (eds) (2000b) *Reproducing Gender: Politics, Publics, and Everyday Life after Socialism*. Princeton: Princeton University Press.

Gardawski, J. (2002) Industrial relations and work in foreign hypermarket chains, *EIROnline*, 27 November. Available at: www.eurofound.europa.eu/eiro/2002/11/ feature/pl0211104f.htm. Last accessed 24.3.09.

Gardiner, M. (2000) *Critiques of Everyday Life: An Introduction*. London: Routledge.

GfK Slovakia and INCOMA (2006) Expanzia hypermarketov a obchodných centier aj nad'alej pokračuje. Tlačová správa spoločností GfK Slovakia a INCOMA Research k výsledkom štúdie 'Hypermarket & Shopping Center 2006', 26 April 2006, Bratislava.

Gibson, K. & Graham, J. (1992) Rethinking class in industrial geography, *Economic Geography*, 68 (2): 109–127.

Gibson-Graham, J.K. (1996) *The End of Capitalism (As We Knew It)*. Oxford: Blackwell.

Gibson-Graham, J.K. (2006) *A Post-Capitalist Politics*. Minneapolis: University of Minnesota Press.

Gilbert, M. (1998) "Race," space, and power: The survival strategies of working poor women, *Annals of the Association of American Geographers*, 88 (4): 595–621.

Glasman, M. (1994) The great deformation: Polanyi, Poland and the terrors of planned spontaneity, *New Left Review*, 205: 61–86.

Glass, C. & Fodor, E. (2007) From public to private maternalism? Gender and welfare in Poland and Hungary after 1989, *Social Politics: International Studies in Gender, State & Society*, 14 (3): 323–350.

Goliaš, P. & Kičina, R. (2005) Slovak tax reform: one year after, Inštitút pre Ekonomické a Sociálne Reformy, Bratislava. Available at: www.ineko.sk/ reformy2003/menu_dane_paper_golias.pdf. Last accessed 02.12. 2005.

Goliaš, P. & Kičina, R. (2007) Experience of the 2003–2004 Labour Market Reform in Slovakia, INEKO Bratislava, Institute for Economic and Social Reform. Available at: www.ineko.sk/file_download/240/Labour+market+reform.pdf. Last accessed 25.11.2008.

Golinowska, S. (2000), Bieda w świecie, w Europie i w Polsce. Miary i tendencje, *Kronika*, Instytut Lecha Wałęsy, 5: 62–67.

Gomułka, S. (1998) The Polish model of transformation and growth, *Economics of Transition*, 6 (1): 163–171.

Gowan, P. (1995) Neo-liberal theory and practice for Eastern Europe, *New Left Review*, 213: 3–60.

Grabher, G. & Stark, D. (eds) (1997) *Restructuring Networks in Post-Socialism: Legacies, Linkages and Localities*, Oxford: Oxford University Press.

Grime, K. (1999) The role of privatisation in post-socialist urban transition: Budapest, Kraków, Prague and Warsaw, *GeoJournal*, 49: 35–42.

Grossman, G. (1977) The "second economy" of the USSR, *Problems of Communism*, 26.

Gurney, C. (1999) Pride and prejudice: Discourses of normalisation in public and private accounts of home ownership, *Housing Studies*, 14 (2): 163–183.

Hall, P. & Soskice, D. (2001) *Varieties of Capitalism: The Institutional Foundations of Comparative Advantage*. Oxford: Oxford University Press.

Hann, C. (ed.) (2002) *Postsocialism: Ideals, Ideologies and Practices in Eurasia*. London: Routledge.

Hann, C., Humphrey, C. & Verdery, K. (2002) Introduction: Post-socialism as a topic of anthropological investigation. In C. Hann (ed.) *Postsocialism*. London: Routledge.

Haraszti, M. (1977) *A Worker in a Workers' State*. London: Penguin.

Hardy, J. & Rainnie, A. (1996) *Restructuring Krakow: Desperately Seeking Capitalism*. Mansell: London.

Hardy, J. & Stenning, A. (2002) Out with the old, in with the new? The changing experience of work for Polish women. In Smith, A., Rainnie A. & Swain, A. (eds) *Work, Employment and Transition*. London: Routledge, 99–116.

Hardy, J., Kozek, W. & Stenning, A. (2008) In the front line: Women, work and new spaces of labour politics in Poland, *Gender, Place and Culture*, 15 (2): 99–117.

Harvey, D. (2005) *A Brief History of Neoliberalism*. Oxford: Oxford University Press.

Haughton, T. (2001) HZDS: The ideology, organization and support base of Slovakia's most successful party, *Europe–Asia Studies*, 53 (5): 745–769.

Haughton, T. (2002) Vladimír Mečiar and his role in the 1994–8 Slovak coalition government, *Europe–Asia Studies*, 54 (8): 1319–1338.

Haughton, T. & Rybář, M. (2008) A change of direction: The 2006 parliamentary elections and party politics in Slovakia, *Journal of Communist Studies and Transition Politics*, 24 (2): 232–255.

Hayek, F. (1994) *The Road to Serfdom*. Chicago: Chicago University Press.

Hegedüs, J. & Tosics, I. (1992) Conclusion: Past tendencies and recent problems of the east European housing model. In Turner, B., Hegedüs, J. & Tosics, I. (eds), *The Reform of Housing in Eastern Europe and the Soviet Union*. London: Routledge, 318–334.

Hegedüs, J., Mayo, S. & Tosics, I. (1996) Transition of the housing sector in the east central European countries, *Review of Urban and Regional Development Studies*, 8: 101–136.

Heinen, J. & Wator, M. (2006) Child care in Poland before, during and after the transition: Still a women's business, *Social Politics: International Studies in Gender, State and Society*, 13 (2): 189–216.

Helms, G. & Cumbers, A. (2006) Regulating the new urban poor: Local labour market control in an old industrial city, *Space and Polity*, 10 (1): 67–86.

Hemment, J. (2003) Introduction to special issues: Ethnographies of postsocialism, *Anthropology of Eastern Europe Review*, 21 (2). Available at: http://condor. depaul.edu/~rrotenbe/ aeer/v21n2/HemmentEdNotesv21n2.pdf. Last accessed 5.12.07.

Highmore, B. (2002) Introduction: Questioning everyday life. In Highmore, B. (ed.) *The Everyday Life Reader*. London: Routledge, 1–34.

Hiscock, R., Kearns, A., Macintyre, S. & Ellaway, A. (2001) Ontological security and psychosocial benefits from the home: Qualitative evidence on issues of tenure, *Housing, Theory and Society*, 18 (1–2): 50–66.

Hochschild, A., with Machung, A. (2003) *The Second Shift*. Penguin: London.

Hopkins, P. & Pain, R. (2007) Geographies of age: Thinking relationally, *Area*, 39 (3): 287–294.

Hörschelmann, K. (2008) Transitions to work and the making of neo-liberal selves growing up in (former) East Germany. In Smith, A., Stenning, A. & Willis, K. (eds) *Social Justice and Neoliberalism: Global Perspectives*. London: Zed, 135–163.

Horváth, S. (2005) Everyday life in the first Hungarian socialist city, *International Labor and Working-Class History*, 68: 24–46.

Hraba, J. (1985) Consumer shortages in Poland: Looking beyond the queue into a world of making do, *The Sociological Quarterly*, 26 (3): 387–404.

Hryciuk, R. (2005) *Political Motherhood in Poland: The Emergence of Single-Mothers for the Alimony Fund Movement*, Paper presented at 'Women & Globalization' conference, Centre for Global Justice, Mexico. Available at: www.globaljusticecenter. org/papers2005/hryciuk.htm. Last accessed 6.11.08.

Hüfner, F. (2009) Adjusting housing policies in Slovakia in light of Euro adoption, OECD Economics Department Working Papers, No 682. Available at: www.olis. oecd.org/olis/2009doc.nsf/LinkTo/NT00000DD2/$FILE/JT03260698.pdf. Last accessed 30.6.09.

Humphrey, C. (2002) *The Unmaking of Soviet Life: Everyday Economies After Socialism*. Cornell University Press: Ithaca.

Hyclak, T. (1987) Worker self-management and economic reform in Poland, *International Journal of Social Economics*, 14 (7/8/9): 127–135.

Ira, V. (2003) The changing intra-urban structure of the Bratislava city and its perception, *Geografický časopis*, 55 (2): 91–105.

James, A., Martin, R. & Sunley, P. (2007) The rise of cultural economic geography. In Martin, R. & Sunley, P. (eds) *Critical Concepts in Economic Geography: Volume IV The Cultural Economy*. London: Routledge, 3–18.

Jarvis, H. (1999) The tangled webs we weave: Household strategies to co-ordinate home and work, *Work, Employment and Society*, 13 (2): 225–247.

Jarvis, H. (2005) Moving to London time: Household co-ordination and the infrastructure of everyday life, *Time and Society*, 14 (1): 133–154.

Jenkins, R. (2002) *Pierre Bourdieu*. London: Routledge.

Junghans, T. (2001) Marketing selves: Constructing civil society and self-hood in post-socialist Hungary, *Critique of Anthropology*, 21 (4): 383–400.

Jurajda, Š. & Mathernová, K. (2004) *How to Overhaul the Labor Market: Political Economy of Recent Czech and Slovak Reforms*. Washington, DC: World Bank.

Kaldor, M. (1996) Nation-states, European institutions and citizenship. In Einhorn, B., Kaldor, M. & Kavan, Z. (eds) *Citizenship and Democratic Control in Contemporary Europe*. Cheltenham: Elgar, 9–23.

Kalleberg, A. & Stark, D. (1993) Career strategies in capitalism and socialism: work values and job rewards in the United States and Hungary, *Social Forces* 72: 181–198.

Kaplan, A. & Ross, K. (1987) Introduction, *'Everyday Life': Yale French Studies*, 73: 1–4.

Katz, C. (1995) Major/minor: Theory, nature and politics, *Annals of the Association of American Geographers*, 85 (1): 164–168.

Katz, C. (2001) Vagabond capitalism and the necessity of social reproduction, *Antipode*, 33 (4): 709–728.

Kay, R. (2006) *Men in Contemporary Russia: The Fallen Heroes of Post-Soviet Change?* London: Ashgate.

Keane, M. & Prasad, E. (2002) Inequality, transfers, and growth: New evidence from the economic transition in Poland, *The Review of Economics and Statistics*, 84 (2): 324–341.

Kennedy, M. (2002) *Cultural Formations of Post-Communism*. London: University of Minnesota Press.

Kenney, P. (1997) *Rebuilding Poland: Workers and Communists, 1945–1950*. Ithaca: Cornell University Press.

Kenney, P. (1999) The gender of resistance in communist Poland, *The American Historical Review*, 104 (2): 399–425.

Kenney, P. (2003) *A Carnival of Revolution: Central Europe 1989*. Princeton: Princeton University Press.

Kiblitskaya, M. (2000) 'Once we were kings': Male experiences of loss of status at work in post-communist Russia. In S. Ashwin (ed.) *Gender, State and Society in Soviet and Post-Soviet Russia*. London: Routledge, 90–103

Kideckel, D. (2002) The unmaking of an east-central European working class. In Hann, C. (ed.) *Postsocialism: Ideals, Ideologies and Practices in Eurasia*. London: Routledge, 114–132.

Kideckel, D. (2004) Miners and wives in Romania's Jiu Valley: Perspectives on post-socialist class, gender, and social change, *Identities*, 11: 39–63.

Kideckel, D. (2008) *Getting By in Postsocialist Romania: Labor, The Body and Working-Class Culture*. Indiana University Press: Bloomington.

King, R. & Vullnetari, J. (2004) *Migration and Development in Albania*, Country Background Paper, Development Research Centre on Migration, Globalisation and Poverty, University of Sussex.

Kirschbaum, S. (2006) *A History of Slovakia*. London: Palgrave Macmillan.

Kleer, J. (1987) Small-scale agricultural production in urban areas in Poland, *Food and Nutrition Bulletin*, 9 (2). Available at: www.unu.edu/Unupress/food/8F092e/8F092E06.htm. Last accessed 09.07.2009.

Kochanowicz, J. (1997) Incomplete demise: Reflections on the welfare state in Poland after communism, *Social Research*, 64 (4): 1445–1469.

Kochanowicz, J. (2007) Right turn, *Eurozine*. Available at: www.eurozine.com/articles/2007-09-14-kochanowicz-en.html. Last accessed: 14.09.2007.

Kochanowicz, J., Kozarzewski, P. & Woodward, R. (2005) *Understanding Reform: The Case of Poland*, Centre for Social and Economic Research CASE Reports 59/2005.

Kofman, E. (2006) *Gendered Migration, Social Reproduction and Welfare Regimes: New Dialogues and Directions*. Paper presented at the ESRC seminar on Working Lives in Post Industrial Europe. Available at: www.izfg.unibe.ch/pdf/kofman.pdf. Last accessed 15.11.2008.

Kolarska-Bobińska, L. (ed.) (2000) *The Second Wave of Polish Reforms*, Warsaw: Instytut Spraw Publicznych.

Kolarska-Bobińska, L. and Rymsza, M. (2007) Social policy needed now, *Institute of Public Affairs: Analyses and Opinions*, 73 (May). Available at: http://isp.org.pl/files/7900876708702460011 82943638.pdf.

Kolodko, G. (1998) Economic neoliberalism became almost irrelevant…, *Transition*, 9 (3). Available at: www.worldbank.org/html/prddr/trans/june1998/kolodko.htm. Last accessed 09.07.2009.

Kolodko, G. (2005) Seven lessons the emerging markets can learn from Poland's transition. In Kolodko, G. (ed.) *The Polish Miracle: Lessons for the Emerging Markets*. Aldershot: Ashgate, 1–2.

Kolodko, G. & Nuti, D.M. (1997) *The Polish Alternative: Old Myths, Hard Facts and New Strategies in the Successful Transformation of the Polish Economy*, UNU/WIDER. Available at: www.tiger.edu.pl/kolodko/working/wider/WIDER_1997.pdf. Last accessed 09.07.2009.

Kovacheva, S. (2002) Bulgaria. In Wallace, C. (ed.) *Research Report #1: Critical Review of Literature.* Vienna: Institute for Advanced Studies, 155–185.

Kovács, Z. (1999) Cities from state socialism to global capitalism: An introduction, *GeoJournal*, 49: 1–6.

Kowalik, T. (2001) The ugly face of Polish success: Social aspects of transformation. In Blazyca, G. & Rapacki, R. (eds) *Poland into the New Millennium*. Edward Elgar: Cheltenham, 33–53.

Kowalik, T. (2006) Poland's sudden shift to the right: Some tentative remarks, Paper presented to 12th Workshop on Alternative Economic Policy in Europe, Brussels, 29 September–1 October. Available at: www.raumplanung.uni-dortmund.de/irpud/presom/fileadmin/docs/presom/external/12th_workshop/Kowalik.pdf. Last accessed 09.07.2009.

Kowalik, T. (2007) Blaski i cienie transformacji polskiej. In Kaltwasser, M., Majewska, E. & Szreder, K. (eds) *Futuryzm Miast Przemysłowych*. Kraków: ha!art, 267–279.

Krajčír, Z. & Ódor, Ľ. (2005) *Prvý rok daňovej reformy alebo 19% v akcii*, Ekonomická analýa 8, Inštitút finančnej politiky, Ministerstvo financií SR, Bratislava.

Krakowskie Centrum Praw Kobiet (2005) *Alimentare Znaczy Jeść*, Krakowskie Centrum Praw Kobiet/Stefan Batory Foundation: Kraków.

Kupiszewski, M. (2005) *Migration in Poland in the Period of Transition – the Adjustment to the Labour Market Change*, PIE Discussion Paper No. 266, Institute of Economic Research, Hitotsubashi University. Available at: www.ier.hit-u.ac.jp/pie/Japanese/discussionpaper/dp2004/dp266/text.pdf. Last accessed 10.4.08.

Kusá, Z. & Džambazovič, R. (eds) (2006) *Chudoba v Slovenskej spoločnosti a vzt'ah Slovenskej spoločnosti v chudobe*. Bratislava: Sociologický ústav SAV.

Lange, O. (1957) *Some Problems Relating to the Polish Road to Socialism*. Warsaw: Polonia.

Lange, O. (1994) *Economic Theory and Market Socialism*. Cheltenham: Edward Elgar.

Larner, W. (2000) Neo-liberalism: Policy, ideology, governmentality, *Studies in Political Economy*, 63, 5–25.

Larner, W. (2003) Neoliberalism? *Environment and Planning D: Society and Space*, 21 (5): 309–312.

Larner, W., Le Heron, R. & Lewis, N. (2007) Co-constituting 'After Neoliberalism?': Political projects and globalising governmentalities in Aotearoa New Zealand. In England, K. & Ward, K. (eds) *Neo-Liberalization: States, Networks, People*. Oxford: Blackwell, 223–247.

Ledeneva, A. (1998) *Russia's Economy of Favours: Blat, Networking and Informal Exchange*. Cambridge: Cambridge University Press.

Lee, R. (2000) Shelter from the storm? Geographies of regard in the worlds of horticultural consumption and production, *Geoforum*, 31: 137–157.

Lee, R. (2006) The ordinary economy: Tangled up in values and geography, *Transactions of the Institute of British Geographers*, 31 (4): 413–432.

Lee, R., Leyshon, A. & Smith, A. (2008) Rethinking economies/economic geographies, *Geoforum*, 39: 1111–1115.

Leitner, H., Sheppard, E. & Peck, J. (2007) Squaring up to neoliberalism. In Leitner, H., Peck, J. & Sheppard, E. (eds) *Contesting Neoliberalism: Urban Frontiers*. New York: Guilford, 311–327.

Leyshon, A. & Lee, R. (2003) Introduction: Alternative economic geographies. In Leyshon, A., Lee, R. & Williams, C. (eds) *Alternative Economic Geographies*. London: Sage, 1–26.

Leyshon, A., Lee, R. & Williams, C. (eds) (2003) *Alternative Economic Geographies*. London: Sage.

Lie, M. & Sørensen, K. (eds) (1996) *Making Technologies Our Own? Domesticating Technology into Everyday Life*. Oslo: Scandinavian University Press.

Lipton, D. & Sachs, J. (1990) Creating a market economy in eastern Europe: The case of Poland, *Brookings Papers on Economic Activity*, 1: 75–147.

Lokshin, M., Harris, K. & Popkin, B. (2000) Single mothers in Russia: Household strategies for coping with poverty, *World Development*, 28 (12): 2183–2198.

Lomnitz, L. & Sheinbaum, D. (2002) *Trust, Social Networks and the Informal Economy in Post-Socialist Societies: A Comparative Analysis*, Honesty and Trust: Theory and Experience in the Light of Post-Socialist Transformation, Workshop 2: Formal and Informal Cooperation, Budapest, 22 November.

Lovei, L., Gurenko, E., Haney, M., O'Keefe, P. & Shkaratan, M. (2000) *Maintaining Utility Services for the Poor: Policies and Practices in Central and Eastern Europe and the Former Soviet Union*. World Bank: Washington DC.

Lux, M. (2000) Social housing in the Czech Republic, Poland and Slovakia, *European Journal of Housing Policy*, 1 (2): 189–209.

Lux, M. (2003) Efficiency and effectiveness of housing policies in the Central and Eastern Europe countries, *European Journal of Housing Policy*, 3 (3): 243–265.

MacDonald, G. (2008) DIY: Kingfisher's pole position, *Retail Week*, 6 November. Available at: www.retail-week.com/News/home/2008/11/diy_kingfishers_pole_position.html. Last accessed 09.07.2009.

Machnicka, M. (2005) *Hypermarket Revolution: Poland Goes Compact*. Warsaw: PMR Publications.

Marcuse, P. (1996) Privatization and its discontents: Property rights in land and housing in the transition in Eastern Europe. In Andrusz, G., Harloe, M. & Szelenyi, I. (eds) *Cities After Socialism: Urban and regional change and conflict in post-socialist societies*. Oxford: Blackwell, 119–191.

Markham, M. (2003) *Poland: Housing Challenge in a Time of Transition*, A Paper Prepared for HUT 264M. Available at: www.housingfinance.org/pdfstorage/Europe_Poland_HousingChallengeInATimeOfTransition.pdf. Last accessed 09.07.2009.

Marston, S. (2003) A long way from home: Domesticating the social production of scale. In McMaster, R. & Sheppard, E. (eds) *Scale and Geographic Inquiry: Nature, Society, Method*. Blackwell: Oxford, 170–191.

Massey, D. (1993) Power-geometry and a progressive sense of place. In Bird, J., Curtis, B., Putnam, T., Robertson, G. & Tickner, L. (eds) *Mapping the Futures: Local Cultures, Global Change*. London: Routledge, 59–70.

Matlovič, R. (2004) The transitive image of the town and its intra-urban structures in the era of post-communist transformation and globalisation, *Sociology – Slovak Sociological Review*, 36 (2): 137–158.

May, J., Cloke, P. & Johnsen, S. (2005) Re-phasing neoliberalism: New Labour and Britain's crisis of street homelessness, *Antipode*, 37 (4): 703–730.

McCarthy, J. (2006) Cracks in the levee: Katrina, environmental politics, and neoliberal hegemony, Paper presented at the Annual Conference of the AAG, Chicago, USA, 7–11 March.

McDowell, L (2003) *Redundant Masculinities?* Oxford: Blackwell.

McKie, L., Gregory, S. & Bowlby, S. (2004) *Caringscapes: Experiences of Caring and Working*, Research Briefing 13, Centre for Research on Families and Relationships. Available at: www.crfr.ac.uk/reports/rb13caringscapes.pdf. Last accessed 09.07.2009.

McLaughlin, D. (2005) Polish 'moral revolution' targets Tesco, *The Guardian*, 13 November. Available at: www.guardian.co.uk/business/2005/nov/13/supermarkets. internationalnews. Last accessed 24.3.09.

McMenamin, I. & Timonen, V. (2002) Poland's health care reform: Politics, markets and informal payments, *Journal of Social Policy*, 31 (1): 103–118.

Medgyesi, M. (2002) Hungary. In Wallace, C. (ed.) *Research Report #1: Critical Review of Literature*. Vienna: Institute for Advanced Studies, 137–154.

Merrifield, A. (2002) *Metromarxism: A Marxist Tale of the City*. London: Routledge.

Mesežnikov, G. & Gyárfášová, O. (2008) *National Populism in Slovakia*. Bratislava: Institute for Public Affairs.

Mesure, S. (2006) Tesco increases its presence in Poland, *The Independent*, 18 July. Available at: www.independent.co.uk/news/business/news/tesco-increases-its-presence-in-poland-408407.html. Last accessed 20.05.09.

Meurs, M. (1998) Imagined and imagining equality in East Central Europe: Gender and ethnic differences in the economic transformation of Bulgaria. In Pickles, J. & Smith, A. (eds) *Theorising Transition*. London: Routledge, 330–346.

Meurs, M. (2002) Economic strategies of surviving postsocialism: Changing household economies and gender divisions of labour in the Bulgarian transition. In Rainnie, A., Smith, A. & Swain, A. (eds) *Work, Employment and Transition: Restructuring Livelihoods in Post-Communism*. London: Routledge, 213–226.

Michalak, W. (2001) Retail in Poland: An assessment of changing market and foreign investment conditions, *Canadian Journal of Regional Science/Revue Canadienne des Sciences Régionales*, 24 (3): 485–503.

Michálek, A. (2004) Chudoba na lokálnej úrovni (centrá chudoby na Slovensku), *Geografický časopis*, 56: 1–23.

Michálek, A. (2005) Koncentrácia a atribúty chudoby na Slovansku na lokálnej úrovni, *Geografický časopis*, 57: 3–22.

Milanovic, B (1999) Explaining the increase in inequality during transition, *Economics of Transition*, 7: 299–341.

Millard, F. (2006) Poland's politics and the travails of transition after 2001, *Europe–Asia Studies*, 58 (7): 1007–1031.

Millard, F. (2007) The 2005 parliamentary and presidential elections in Poland, *Electoral Studies*, 26: 210–215.

Miller, D., Jackson, P., Thrift, N., Holbrook, B. & Rowlands, N. (1998) *Shopping, Place and Identity*. London: Routledge.

Ministerstwo Spraw Wewnętrznych i Administracji (2003) *Program na rzecz społeczności romskiej w Polsce*. Available at: www.mswia.gov.pl/portal/pl/185/2982/Tresc_Programu. html. Last accessed 30.10.2008.

Ministry of the Economy, Labour and Social Policy (2004) *Plan for the Rationalisation of Social Expenditures*. Warsaw: Ministry of the Economy, Labour and Social Policy.

Miškolci, A. & Mládek, J. (1994) The basic characters of population structure of Petržalka, *Acta Facultatis Rerum Naturalium Universitas Comenianae, Geographica*, 34: 83–94.

Mitchell, K. (2006) Neoliberal governmentality in the European Union: Education, training, and technologies of citizenship, *Environment and Planning D: Society and Space*, 24 (3): 389–407.

Mitchell, K., Marston, S. & Katz, C. (2003) Life's work: An introduction, review and critique, *Antipode*, 35 (3): 415–442.

Mitchell, T. (2002) *Rule of Experts: Egypt, Techno-Politics, Modernity*. Berkeley: California University Press.

Mitchell, T. (2005) The work of economics: How a discipline makes its world, *European Journal of Sociology*, 45 (2): 297–320.

Mitchell, T. (2008) Rethinking economy, *Geoforum*, 39: 1116–1121.

Mitra, P. (2008) *Innovation, Inclusion and Integration: From Transition to Convergence in Eastern Europe and the Former Soviet Union*. Washington, DC: World Bank.

Mládek, J. (1994) Petržalka – development and transformation of urban structure, *Acta Facultatis Rerum Naturalium Universitas Comenianae, Geographica*, 34: 3–12.

Mládek, J., Kovalovská, V. & Chovancová, J. (1998) Petržalka – demografické, najmä migračné špecifiká mladej urbánnej štruktúry, *Geografický časopis*, 50 (2): 109–137.

Moran, J. (2005) *Reading the Everyday*. Abingdon: Routledge.

Morley, D. (2003) What's 'home' got to do with it? Contradictory dynamics in the domestication of technology and the dislocation of domesticity, *European Journal of Cultural Studies*, 6 (4): 435–485.

Muller, K (2002) From the state to the market? Pension reform paths in central-eastern Europe and the former Soviet Union, *Social Policy and Administration*, 36 (2): 156–175.

Murphy, J. (2008) Studying practice: Ontological, epistemological, and methodological reflections, paper presented in *Researching Practice in the Space Economy: Possibilities and Limitations*, Annual Conference of the AAG, Boston, USA, 15–19 April.

Myant, M. (1993) *Transforming Socialist Economies: The Case of Poland and Czechoslovakia*. Aldershot: Elgar.

Myers, G. (2006) The unauthorized city: Late colonial Lusaka and postcolonial geography, *Singapore Journal of Tropical Geography*, 27 (3): 289–308.

Nafus, D. (2006) Post-socialism and notions of context in St Petersburg, *Journal of the Royal Anthropological Institute*, 12: 607–624.

Nagar, R., Lawson, V., McDowell, L. & Hanson, S. (2002) Locating globalization: Feminist (re)readings of the subjects and spaces of globalization, *Economic Geography*, 78 (3): 257–284.

Neilsen, E. & Simonsen, K. (2003) Scaling from 'below': Practices, strategies and urban spaces, *European Planning Studies*, 11 (8): 911–927.

Nemec, J. (2005) Reforms of Health Care Delivery in Slovakia and Measurement of Their Impacts: Quality of Hospital Services and Quality of Financial Management in Hospitals. Available at: www.spa.msu.ru/e-journal/9/91_3.php. Last accessed 09.07.2009.

Nölke, A. & Vliegenthart, A. (2009) Enlarging the varieties of capitalism: The emergence of dependent market economies in east central Europe, *World Politics*, 61 (4): 670–702.

Ódor, Ľ. (2005) Skutočný deň daňovej slobody, Institute of Financial Policy, Ministry of Finance of the Slovak Republic. Available at: www.finance.gov.sk/Default.aspx?CatID=4360. Last accessed 2.12.05.

OECD (2006) *OECD Employment Outlook 2006*. Available at: www.oecd.org/docum ent/23/0,2340,en_2825_495670_36786071_1_1_1_1,00.html. Last accessed 09.07.2009.

OECD (2007) *Economic Survey of the Slovak Republic 2007*, OECD Policy Brief. Paris: Organization for Economic Cooperation and Development.

OECD (2008a) *OECD Territorial Review: Poland*. Paris: Organization for Economic Cooperation and Development.

OECD (2008b) *Economic Survey of Poland 2008*, OECD Policy Brief. Paris: Organization for Economic Cooperation and Development.

Offe, C. (1996) *Modernity and the State*. Cambridge: Polity Press.

Olech, P. (2008) *Poland – National Report 2008: Housing and Homelessness*, European Observatory on Homelessness, FEANTSA. Available at: www.feantsa.org/files/Housing_Annual_Theme/National_Reports/Poland_housing_homelessness_EN.pdf. Last accessed 09.07.2009.

Ong, A. (2006) *Neoliberalism as Exception: Mutations in Citizenship and Sovereignty*. Durham: Duke University Press.

Ornacka, K. & Szczepaniak-Wiecha, I. (2005) The contemporary family in Poland: New trends and phenomena, *Journal of Family and Economic Issues*, 26 (2): 195–224.

Ost, D. (2005) *The Defeat of Solidarity: Anger and Politics in Postcommunist Europe*. New York: Cornell University Press.

Owusu, M., 1997. Domesticating democracy: Culture, civil society, and constitutionalism in Africa, *Comparative Studies in Society and History* 39 (1): 120–152.

Pailhé, A. (2003) Labour market segmentation in central Europe during the first years of transition, *Labour*, 17 (1): 127–152.

Painter, J. (2000) Pierre Bourdieu. In Crang, M. & Thrift, N. (eds) *Thinking Space*. London: Routledge, 239–259.

Pavlovskaya, M. (2004) Other transitions: Multiple economies of Moscow households in the 1990s, *Annals of the Association of American Geographers*, 94 (2): 329–351.

Pawlik, W. (1992) Intimate commerce. In Wedel, J. (ed.) *The Unplanned Society: Poland during and after Communism*. New York: Columbia University Press, 78–94.

Peck, J (1996) *Work Place*. New York: Guildford Press.

Peck, J. (2004) Geography and public policy: Constructions of neoliberalism, *Progress in Human Geography*, 28 (3): 392–405.

Peck, J. (2008) Re-making laissez faire, *Progress in Human Geography*, 32 (1): 3–48.

Peck, J. & Theodore, N. (2000) 'Work first': Workfare and the regulation of contingent labour markets, *Cambridge Journal of Economics*, 24: 119–138.

Peck, J. & Theodore, N. (2001) Contingent Chicago: Restructuring the spaces of temporary labor, *International Journal of Urban and Regional Research*, 25 (3): 471–496.

Peck, J. & Theodore, N. (2007) Variegated capitalism, *Progress in Human Geography*, 31: 731–772.

Peck, J. & Tickell, A. (2002) Neoliberalizing space. In Brenner, N. & Theodore, N. (eds) *Spaces of Neoliberalism*. Oxford: Blackwell Publishers, 33–57.

Perren, K., Arber, S. & Davidson, K. (2004) Neighbouring in later life: The influence of socio-economic resources, gender and household composition on neighbourly relationships, *Sociology*, 38 (5): 965–984.

Phillips, J. (2007) *Care*. Cambridge: Polity.

Piacentini, M., Hibbert, S. & Al-Dajani, H. (2001) Diversity in deprivation: Exploring the grocery shopping behavior of disadvantaged consumers, *International Review of Retail, Distribution and Consumer Research*, 11: 141–158.

Pichler-Milanovich, N. (1994) The role of housing policy in the transformation process of Central-East European cities, *Urban Studies*, 31 (7): 1097–1115.

Pichler-Milanovich, N. (2001) Urban housing markets in central and eastern Europe: Convergence, divergence or policy collapse, *European Journal of Housing Policy*, 1 (2): 145–187.

Pickles, J. (2002) Gulag Europe? Mass unemployment, new firm creation, and tight labour markets in the Bulgarian apparel industry. In Rainnie, A., Smith, A. & Swain, A. (eds) *Work, Employment and Transition*. London: Routledge, 246–272.

Pickles, J. (2004a) *A History of Spaces: Cartographic Reason, Mapping and the Geo-Coded World*. London: Routledge.

Pickles, J. (2004b) Disseminated economies and the new economic geographies of post-socialism: notes on the way to an installation, paper presented at the ESRC workshop on *Rethinking "Economy" in Post-Socialism*, Queen Mary, University of London, September.

Pickles, J. (2010) The spirit of post-socialism: Common spaces and the production of diversity, *European Urban and Regional Studies*, 17 (2): 127–140.

Pickles, J. & Smith, A. (eds) (1998) *Theorising Transition: The Political Economy of Post-Communist Transformations*. London: Routledge.

Pickup, F. & White, A. (2003) Livelihoods in postcommunist Russia: Urban/rural comparisons, *Work, Employment and Society*, 17 (3): 419–434.

Piirainen, T. (1997) *Towards a New Social Order in Russia: Transforming Structures and Everyday Life*. Aldershot: Ashgate.

Pine, F (1998) Dealing with fragmentation: The consequences of privatisation in rural central and southern Poland. In Bridger, S. & Pine, F. (eds) *Surviving Post-Socialism*. London: Routledge, 106–123.

Pine, F. (2002) Retreat to the household? Gendered domains in post-socialist Poland. In Hann, C. (ed) *Postsocialism: ideals, ideologies and practices in Eurasia*. London: Routledge, 95–113.

Pittaway, M. (2005) Creating and domesticating Hungary's socialist industrial landscape: From Dunapentele to Sztálinváros, 1950–1958, *Historical Archaeology*, 39 (3): 75–93.

Poirine, B. (1997) A theory of remittances as an implicit family loan arrangement, *World Development*, 25 (4): 589–611.

Polski Związek Działkowców (2008) Co to jest PZD? www.pzd.pl/strona.php?4. Last accessed 24.10.08.

Południkiewicz, J. (2005) Accessible housing programs in Poland and European experiences in this area, *Bulletin: Shaping the New Social Policy in Poland*, www.barka.org.pl/equal_inndex_eng.htm. Last accessed 09.07.2009.

Popke, J. (2006) Geography and ethics: Everyday mediations through care and consumption, *Progress in Human Geography*, 30 (4): 504–512.

Popov, V. (2000) Shock therapy versus gradualism: The end of the debate, *Comparative Economic Studies*, 42: 1–57.

Popov, V. (2007) Shock therapy *versus* gradualism reconsidered: Lessons from transition economies after 15 years of reforms, *Comparative Economic Studies*, 49: 1–31.

Pounds, N., Dziewon´ski, K., Kortus, B., and Vlassenbroeck, W. (1985) The growth of Cracow and Nowa Huta. In Cochrane, A., Hamnett, C. & McDowell, L., (eds), *City, Economy and Society: A Comparative Reader*. London: Harper & Row, 16–25.

Prezydent Miasta Krakowa (2008) *Raport o Stanie Miasto 2007*. Available at: www.bip.krakow.pl/?sub_dok_id=22035. Last accessed 09.07.2009.

Priemus, H. & Mandič, S. (2000) Rental housing in Central and Eastern Europe as no man's land, *Journal of Housing and the Built Environment*, 15 (3): 205–215.

Rada Miasta Krakowa (2007) *Strategia Rozwiązywania Problemów Społecznych Krakowa, na lata 2007–2013: Diagnoza*. Kraków City Council: Kraków.

Rainnie, A. & Hardy, J. (1995) Desperately seeking capitalism: Solidarity and Polish industrial relations in the 1990s, *Industrial Relations Journal*, 26 (4): 267–279.

Rainnie, A., Smith, A. & Swain, A. (2002a) Employment and work restructuring in "transition". In Rainnie, A., Smith, A. & Swain, A. (eds) *Work, Employment and Transition: Restructuring Livelihoods in 'Post-Communist' Eastern Europe*. London: Routledge, 9–34.

Rainnie, A., Smith, A. & Swain, A. (eds) (2002b) *Work, Employment and Transition: Restructuring Livelihoods in 'Post-Communist' Eastern Europe*. London: Routledge.

Rankin, K. (2003) Anthropologies and geographies of globalization, *Progress in Human Geography*, 27 (6): 708–734.

Rashid, M., Rutkowski, J. & Fretwell, D. (2005) Labor markets. In Barr, N. (ed.) *Labor Markets and Social Policy in Central and Eastern Europe*. Washington, DC: World Bank, pp.59–87.

Ratajczyk, A. (2009) Poland shines amid global crisis, *Warsaw Voice*, 29 April. Available at: www.warsawvoice.pl/view/20165. Last accessed 11.06.09.

Read, R. (2007) Labour and love: Competing constructions of 'care' in a Czech nursing home, *Critique of Anthropology*, 27 (2): 203–222.

Read, R. & Thelen, T. (2007) Introduction: Social security and care after socialism: Reconfigurations of public and private, *Focaal*, 50: 3–18.

REAS (2009) *Residential Market in Poland: Spring 2009*, Warsaw. Available at: www.residentialadvisors.eu/index.php?pid=202&fileid=947. Last accessed 09.07.2009.

Reckwitz, A. (2002) Toward a theory of social practices: A development in culturalist theorizing, *European Journal of Social Theory* 5 (2): 243–263.

Rochovská, A. (2004) *Vybrané aspekty chudoby na Slovensku s bližším zretel'om na ženy*. Unpublished PhD thesis, Comenius University.

Rose, N. (1999) *Governing the Soul*. London: Free Association Books.

Rose, R. (2000) Uses of social capital in Russia: Modern, pre-modern and anti-modern, *Post-Soviet Affairs*, 16 (1): 33–57.

Round, J. (2006a) The economic marginalization of post-Soviet Russia's elderly population and the failure of state ageing policy: A case study of Magadan city, *Oxford Development Studies*, 34 (4): 441–456.

Round, J. (2006b) Marginalized for a lifetime: The everyday experiences of gulag survivors in post-Soviet Magadan, *Geografiska Annaler B*, 87 (1): 15–34.

Round, J., Williams, C. & Rogers, P. (2008) Everyday tactics and spaces of power: The role of informal economies in post-soviet Ukraine, *Social and Cultural Geography*, 9 (2): 171–185.

Royal Institute of Chartered Surveyors (2007) *European Housing Review 2007*. London: RICS.

Ruddick, S. (2004) Domesticating monsters: Cartographies of difference and the emancipatory city. In L. Lees (ed.) *The Emancipatory City: Paradoxes and Possibilities*. London: Sage, 23–39.

Rulyova, N. (2007) Domesticating the Western format on Russian TV: Subversive glocalisation in the game show, *Pole Chudes* (*The Field of Miracles*), *Europe–Asia Studies*, 59 (8): 1367–1386.

Rybak, A. & McAndrew, F. (2006) How do we decide whom our friends are? Defining levels of friendship in Poland and the United States, *Journal of Social Psychology*, 146 (2): 147–163.

Sachs, J. (1990) What is to be done? *The Economist*, January 13: 19–24.

Sachs, J. (2000) Interview for PBS Commanding Heights, available at: www.pbs.org/wgbh/commandingheights/shared/pdf/int_jeffreysachs.pdf. Last accessed 15.02.2008.

Sachs, J. & Lipton, D. (1990) Poland's economic reform, *Foreign Affairs*, 69 (3): 47–66.

Sadecki, J. (1994) Nowy czas Nowej Huty, *Rzeczpospolita*, 22 July: 3.

Sailer-Fliege, U. (1999) Characteristics of post-socialist urban transformation in East Central Europe, *GeoJournal*, 49: 7–16.

Saxonberg, S. & Sirovátka, T. (2006) Failing family policy in post-communist central Europe, *Journal of Comparative Policy Analysis*, 8 (2): 185–202.

Saxonberg, S. & Szelewa, D. (2007) The continuing legacy of the communist legacy? The development of family policies in Poland and the Czech Republic, *Social Politics: International Studies in Gender, State and Society*, 14 (3): 351–379.

Schatzki, T. (1996) *Social Practices: A Wittgensteinian Approach to Human Activity and the Social*. Cambridge: Cambridge University Press.

Schatzki, T. (1998) The nature of social reality, *Philosophy and Phenomenological Research*, 49 (2): 239–260.

Schatzki, T. (2002) *The Site of the Social: A Philosophical Account of the Constitution of Social Life and Change*. Pennsylvania: Penn State Press.

Schatzki, T., Knorr, C., Karin, D. & von Savigny, E. (eds) (2001) *The Practice Turn in Contemporary Theory*. London: Routledge.

Schmigotzki, B. (2004) *The Polish Housing Market: A Concise Description of the Current Status, Problems and Investment Perspectives*, IWO (Housing Initiative for Eastern Europe).

Schrooten, M. (2005) *Bringing Home the Money: What Determines Worker's Remittances to Transition Countries?* The Institute of Economic Research Discussion Paper Series A, No.466, Hitotsubashi University, Tokyo. Available at: www.ier.hit-u.ac. jp/Common/publication/DP/DP466.pdf. Last accessed 20.08.07.

Seabright, P. (ed.) (2000) *The Vanishing Rouble: Barter Networks and Non-Monetary Transactions in Post-Soviet Societies*. Cambridge: Cambridge University Press.

Seeth, H., Chachnov, S., Surinov, A. & von Braun, J. (1998) Russian poverty: Muddling through economic transition with garden plots, *World Development*, 26 (9): 1611–1623.

Sennett, R. (1998) *The Corrosion of Character*. London: Norton.

Sevenhjuisen, S. (2000) Caring in the Third Way: The relation between obligation, responsibility and care in Third Way discourse, *Critical Social Policy*, 20 (1): 5–37.

Shevchenko, O. (2009) *Crisis and the Everyday in Postsocialist Moscow*. Bloomington: Indiana University Press.

Shields, S. (2007) Too much shock, not enough therapy: Transnational capital and the social implications of Poland's ongoing transition to a market, *Competition and Change*, 11 (2): 155–178.

Siemieńska, R. (1967) Niektóre aspekty adaptacji ludnosci wiejskiej do zycia w Nowej Hucie. In Nowakowski, S. (ed.) *Procesy Urbanizacyjne w Powojennej Polsce*. Warsaw: PWN.

Sik, E. (1988) Reciprocal exchange of labour in Hungary. In Pahl, R. (ed.) *On Work: Historical, Comparative and Theoretical Approaches*. Oxford: Blackwell, 527–547.

Sik, E. (1994) From the multicolored to the black-and-white economy: The Hungarian second economy and the transformation, *International Journal of Urban and Regional Research*, 18 (1): 46–70.

Sik, E. (1995) *Network Capital in Capitalist, Communist and Post-Communist Societies*, Working Paper No 212, Kellogg Institute for International Studies, University of Notre Dame.

Silk, J. (1998) Caring at a distance, *Philosophy and Geography*, 1 (2): 165–182.

Silverstone, R. (2005) Domesticating domestication: Reflections on the life of a concept. In Berker, T., Hartmann, M., Punie, Y. & Ward, K. (eds) *Domestication of Media and Technologies*. Maidenhead: Open University Press, 229–248.

Simonsen, K. (2001) Space, culture and economy: A question of practice, *Geografiska Annaler*, 83B (1): 41–53.

Simonsen, K. (2007) Practice, spatiality and embodied emotions: An outline of a geography of practice, *Human Affairs*, 17: 168–181.

Slay, B. (2000) The Polish economic transition: Outcome and lessons, *Communist and Post-Communist Studies*, 33: 49–70.

Slovak Embassy (2004) *Health Care Reform: Summary: Main Principles and Objectives of the Health Reform*, Slovak Embassy, Washington, DC. Available at: www. slovakembassy-us.org/text/Healthcarereform.pdf. Last accessed 03.03.2008.

Slovak Ministry of Labour, Social Affairs and Family (2004) *National Action Plan on Social Inclusion 2004–2006*. Bratislava: Slovak Ministry of Labour, Social Affairs and Family.

Sme (2006) *Prieskum: Tretina nemá na lieky*, 24 April.

Smith, A. (1994) Uneven development and the restructuring of the armaments industry in Slovakia, *Transactions of the Institute of British Geographers*, 19: 404–424.

Smith, A. (1998) *Reconstructing the Regional Economy: Industrial Transformation and Regional Development in Slovakia*. Cheltenham: Edward Elgar.

Smith, A. (2000) Employment restructuring and household survival in 'postcommunist transition': Rethinking economic practices in Eastern Europe, *Environment and Planning A*, 32 (10): 1759–1780.

Smith, A. (2002a) Culture/economy and spaces of economic practice: Positioning households in post-communism, *Transactions of the Institute of British Geographers*, 27 (2): 232–250.

Smith, A. (2002b) Imagining geographies of the "new Europe": Geo-economic power and the new European architecture of integration, *Political Geography*, 21: 647–70.

Smith, A. (2002c) Economic practices and household economies in Slovakia: Rethinking 'survival' in austerity. In Rainnie, A., Smith, A. & Swain, A. (eds) *Work, Employment and Transition: Restructuring Livelihoods in 'Post-Communist' Eastern Europe*. London: Routledge, 227–245.

Smith, A. (2007) Articulating neo-liberalism: diverse economies and everyday life in "post-socialist" cities. In Leitner, H., Peck, J. & Sheppard, E. (eds) *Contesting Neoliberalism: Urban Frontiers*. New York: Guilford, 204–222.

Smith, A. & Pickles, J. (1998) Introduction: Theorising transition and the political economy of transformation. In Pickles, J. & Smith, A. (eds) *Theorising Transition: The Political Economy of Post-Communist Transformations*. London: Routledge, 1–22.

Smith, A. & Rochovská, A. (2007) Domesticating neo-liberalism: Everyday lives and the geographies of post-socialist transformations, *Geoforum*, 38 (6): 1163–1178.

Smith, A. & Stenning, A. (2006) Beyond household economies: Articulations and spaces of economic practice in post-socialism, *Progress in Human Geography*, 30 (2): 190–213.

Smith, A. & Swain, A. (2010) The global economic crisis, Eastern Europe, and the Former Soviet Union: models of development and the contradictions of internationalization, *Eurasian Geographies and Economics*, 51 (1): 1–34.

Smith, A., Stenning, A. & Willis, K. (eds) (2008a) *Social Justice and Neoliberalism: Global Perspectives*. London: Zed Books.

Smith, A., Stenning, A., Rochovská, A. & Świątek, D. (2008b) The emergence of a working poor: Labour markets, neoliberalisation and diverse economies in post-socialist cities, *Antipode*, 40 (2): 283–311.

Smith, D. (1996) The socialist city. In G. Andrusz, M. Harloe & I. Szelenyi (eds) *Cities after Socialism: Urban and Regional Change and Conflict in Post-Socialist Societies*. Oxford: Blackwell, 70–99.

Smith, J. & Jehlička, P. (2007) Stories around food, politics and change in Poland and the Czech Republic, *Transactions of the Institute of British Geographers*, 32: 395–410.

Smith, S. (2008) Owner-occupation: At home with a hybrid of money and materials, *Environment and Planning A*, 40: 520–535.

Smolar, A. (2006) Poland: Radicals in power, *Eurozine*, available at: www.eurozine. com/articles/2006-09-28-smolar-en.html. Last accessed 09.07.2009.

Smollet, E. (1989) The economy of jars: Kindred relationships in Bulgaria – an exploration, *Ethnologie Europa*, 19 (2): 125–140.

Soja, M. (1986) Functioning of the Lenin Steel Works in Cracow in the light of selected spatial links, *Zeszyty Naukowe Uniwersytetu Jagiellońskiego – Prace Geograficzne*, 66: 61–92.

Soja, M. (1990) Social and spatial aspects of location and functioning of the Lenin Steel Works in Cracow, *Zeszyty Naukowe Uniwersytetu Jagiellońskiego – Prace Geograficzne*, 104: 90–98.

Sokol, M. (2007) *Case Study: Bratislava/Slovakia: Benchmarking and Fostering Transformative Use of ICT in EU Regions*, WPI Case Study Report for TRANSFORM.

Sokolowski, S. W. (2001) *Civil Society and the Professions in Eastern Europe: Social Change and Organizational Innovation in Poland*. Kluwer: New York.

Speak, S. & Graham, S. (2000) Service not included: Marginalised neighbourhoods, private service disinvestment, and compound social exclusion, *Environment and Planning A*, 31: 1985–2001.

Stack, C. (1974) *All Our Kin*. Basic Books: New York.

Staeheli, L. & Brown, M. (2003) Where has welfare gone? Introductory remarks on the geographies of care and welfare, *Environment and Planning A*, 35 (5): 771–777.

Stanková, M. (2009) Winter fills up homeless shelters, *The Slovak Spectator*, 12 January.

Stark, D. (1996) Recombinant property in East European capitalism, *American Journal of Sociology*, 101 (4): 993–1027.

Stark, D. & Bruszt, L. (1998) *Postsocialist Pathways: Transforming Politics and Property in East Central Europe*. Cambridge: Cambridge University Press.

Steele, J. (2005) Poland's disenchanted killed off 'New Europe', *The Guardian*, 28 October. Available at: www.guardian.co.uk/politics/2005/oct/28/eu.world. Last accessed 09.07.2009.

Stenning, A. (1999) Marketisation and democratisation in the Russian Federation: The case of Novosibirsk, *Political Geography*, 18 (5): 591–617.

Stenning, A (2000) Placing (post-)socialism: The making and remaking of Nowa Huta, Poland, *European Urban and Regional Studies*, 7 (2): 99–118.

Stenning, A. (2003) Shaping the economic landscapes of postsocialism? Labour, workplace and community in Nowa Huta, Poland, *Antipode*, 35: 761–780.

Stenning, A. (2004) Urban change and the localities. In Bradshaw, M. & Stenning, A. (eds) *East Central Europe and the Former Soviet Union: The Post-Socialist States*. London: Prentice Hall, 87–108.

Stenning, A (2005a) Re-placing work: Economic transformations and the shape of a community in post-socialist Poland, *Work, Employment and Society*, 19 (2): 235–259.

Stenning, A. (2005b) Post-socialism and the changing geographies of the everyday in Poland, *Transactions of the Institute of British Geographers*, 30 (1): 113–127.

Stenning, A. (2005c) Where is the post-socialist working class? Working class lives in the spaces of (post-)socialism, *Sociology*, 39 (5): 983–999.

Stenning, A. (2010) Work, place and community in socialism and post-socialism. In McGrath-Champ, S., Herod, A. & Rainnie, A. (eds) *Handbook of Employment and Society: Working Space*. Cheltenham: Edward Elgar, 197–212.

Stenning, A. & Bradshaw, M. (1999) Globalisation and transformation: The changing geography of the post-socialist world. In J. Bryson, N. Henry, D. Keeble & R. Martin (eds) *The Economic Geography Reader*. Chichester: Wiley, 97–107.

Stenning, A. & Hardy, J. (2005) Public sector reform and women's work in Poland: 'Working for juice, coffee and cheap cosmetics!' *Gender, Work, Organisation*, 12 (6): 503–526.

Stenning, A. & Hörschelmann, K. (2008) History, geography and difference in the post-socialist world; or do we still need post-socialism? *Antipode*, 40: 312–335.

Stenning, A., Smith, A., Rochovská, A. & Świątek, D. (2009) *Consumption Practices and the Remaking of Retail Space in Post-Socialist Cities*. Paper presented in School of Geography, University of Leeds, 23.04.09.

Stenning, A., Smith, A., Rochovská, A. & Świątek, D. (2010) Credit, debt, and everyday financial practices: Low-income households in two post-socialist cities, *Economic Geography*, 86 (2): 119–145.

Stenning, A., Świątek, D., Smith, A. & Rochovská, A. (2007) Social exclusion and household economic practices in Nowa Huta, *Geographia Polonica*, 80 (1): 7–24.

Stephens, M. (2005) A critical analysis of housing finance reform in a 'super' home-ownership state: The case of Armenia, *Urban Studies*, 42 (10): 1795–1815.

Stewart, M. (2002) Deprivation, the Roma and the 'underclass'. In Hann, C. (ed.) *Postsocialism: Ideals, Ideologies and Practices in Eurasia*. London: Routledge, 133–155.

Stiglitz, J. (2002) *Globalization and its Discontents*. Penguin: London.

Surdej, A. (2004) *Managing Labor Market Reforms: Case Study of Poland*, World Bank, Washington. Background paper prepared for World Bank Development Report 2005. Available at: http://siteresources.worldbank.org/INTWDR2005/Resources/bp_poland_labor_market_reform.pdf. Last accessed 09.07.2009.

ŠÚSR (2001) *Sčitanie domov a bytov*. ŠÚSR: Bratislava: Štatistický úrad Slovenskej republiky.

Svašek, M. (2008) *Postsocialism: Politics and Emotions in Central and Eastern Europe*. Oxford: Berghahn Books.

Swain, A. (2006) Soft capitalism and a hard industry: Virtualism, the 'transition industry' and the restructuring of the Ukrainian coal industry, *Transactions of the Institute of British Geographers*, 31: 208–223.

Swain, N. (1994) Czechoslovak agriculture prior to system change, *Centre for Central and Eastern European Studies Working Paper* No. 28, Rural Transition Series, University of Liverpool.

Swain, N. (2001) Traditions of household farming and gardening in Central Europe, *Centre for Central and Eastern European Studies Working Paper* No. 51, Rural Transition Series, University of Liverpool.

Sýkora, L. (1999) Processes of socio-spatial differentiation in post-communist Prague, *Housing Studies*, 14 (5): 677–699.

Sýkora, L. (2000) The geography of post-communist cities: Research agenda for 2000+, *Acta Facultatis Rerum Naturalium Universitatis Comeianae, Geographica*, Supplementum No. 2/II: 269–278.

Synak, B. (1990) The Polish family: Stability, change and conflict, *Journal of Aging Studies*, 4 (4): 333–344.

Szaleniec, M. (2008) *Poland's Grocery Market at a Time of Crisis*. Warsaw: PMR Publications.

Szczerbiak, A. (2007) 'Social Poland' defeats 'Liberal Poland'? The September–October 2005 Polish parliamentary and presidential elections, *Journal of Communist and Post-Communist Studies*, 23 (2): 203–232.

Szelényi, I. (1983) *Urban Inequalities Under State Socialism*. Oxford: Oxford University Press.

Szelényi, I. (1996) Cities under socialism – and after. In Andrusz, G. et al. (eds) *Cities After Socialism*. Oxford: Blackwell, 286–317.

Tarkowska, E. (1996) Unequal distribution of time: A new dimension of social differentiation in Poland, *Polish Sociological Review*, 2 (114): 163–174.

Tarkowska, E. (1999) *Social History of Poverty in Central Europe*, SOCO Project Paper 69. Vienna: IWM.

Tarkowska, E. (2000) Zróżnicowanie biedy: wiek i płeć. In Domański, H., Ostrowska, A. & Rychard, A. (eds) *Jak żyją Polacy?* IFiS PAN: Warsaw, 259–280.

Tchorek, K. (2008) Tesco outposts facing Polish revolt, *The Guardian*, 4 February. Available at: www.guardian.co.uk/business/2008/feb/04/tesco.poland. Last accessed 24.3.09.

Tezy Tuska (2008) *Gazeta Wyborcza*, 24 February. Available at: www.gazetawyborcza. pl/1,76842,4958825.html. Last accessed 25.2.2008.

Thrift, N. & Olds, K. (1997) Refiguring the economic in economic geography, *Progress in Human Geography*, 20 (3): 311–337.

Tickell, A. & Peck, J. (2003) Making global rules: Globalization or neoliberalization? In Peck, J. & Yeung, H. (eds) *Remaking the Global Economy: Economic and Geographical Perspectives*. London: Sage, 163–181.

Timár, J. (1998) Recent changes and governmental problems in urban-rural fringes in the Great Hungarian Plain. In Barlow, M., Lengyel, I. & Welch, R. (eds) *Local Development and Public Administration in Transition*. József Attila University, Szeged: 150–157.

Torsello, D. (2003) *Trust, Property and Social Change in a Southern Slovakian Village*. Münster: Lit Verlag.

Tusk, D. (2007) Exposé [Maiden Speech] of the Prime Minister, 23 November, Warsaw, available at: www.kprm.gov.pl/english/s.php?id=1413. Last accessed 09.07.2009.

tvn24.pl (2008) Przeydent wetuje Palikota, 25 November. Available at: www.tvn24. pl/1,1574606,prezydent-wetuje-palikota,wiadomosc.html. Last accessed 27.11.08.

Tymowska, K. (2001) Health care under transformation in Poland, *Health Policy*, 56: 85–98.

Uchman, R. & Adamski, J. (2003) How to meet the market rules and social goals for housing? Local government and housing in Poland. In Lux, M. (ed.) *Housing Policy: An End or a New Beginning?* DFID-LGI Local Government Policy Partnership Programme, 120–181.

UNECE (1999) *Country Profiles on the Housing Sector: Slovakia*. Geneva: United Nations Economic Commission for Europe. Available at: www.unece.org/hlm/prgm/cph/countries/slovakia. Last accessed 09.07.2009.

UNICEF Innocenti Research Centre (2005) *TransMonee 2005: Statistical Tables*. Florence: UNICEF, Innocenti Research Centre.

Územný plan hlavného mesta Slovenskej republiky (2007), available at: www.bratislava.sk/vismo/dokumenty2.asp?id_org=700000&id=80478&p1=51737. Last accessed 09.07.2009.

van Hoven, B. & Hörschelmann, K. (2005) *Spaces of Masculinities*. London: Routledge.

van Kempen, R., Dekker, K., Hall, S. & Tosics, I. (eds) (2005) *Restructuring Large Housing Estates in Europe*. Bristol: Policy Press.

Vanderbeck, R. (2007) Intergenerational geographies: Age relations, segregation and reengagements, *Geography Compass*, 1: 200–221.

Vann, E. (2005) Domesticating consumer goods in the global economy: Examples from Vietnam and Russia, *Ethnos*, 70 (4): 465–488.

Vašečka, M., Jurásková, M. & Nicholson, T. (eds) (2003) *Čačipen pal o Roma: A Global Report on Roma in Slovakia*. Bratislava: Institute of Public Affairs.

Voicu, M., Voicu., B. & Strapcova, K. (2008) Housework and gender inequality in European countries, *European Sociological Review*, 25 (3): 365–377.

von Mises, L. (1996) *Human Action: A Treatise on Economics*. Fox and Wilkes.

Wagstyl, S. (2005) Jerzy Hausner: Academic stays rooted in reality, *Financial Times*, 6 May.

Waite, L. (2008) A place and space for a critical geography of precarity? *Geography Compass*, 3 (1): 412–433.

Walkerdine, V (2003) Reclassifying upward mobility: Femininity and the neo-liberal subject, *Gender and Education*, 15 (3): 237–248.

Wallace, C. (2002) Household strategies: Their conceptual relevance and analytical scope in social research, *Sociology*, 36 (2): 275–292.

Ward, K. (2005) The bald guy just ate an orange: Domestication, work and home. In Berker, T., Hartmann, M., Punie, Y. & Ward, K. (eds) *Domestication of Media and Technologies*. Maidenhead: Open University Press, 145–164.

Ward, K. & England, K. (2007) Introduction: Reading neoliberalization. In England, K. & Ward, K. (eds) *Neoliberalization: States, Networks, Peoples*. Oxford: Blackwell, 1–22.

Ward, K., Fagan, C., McDowell, L., Perrons, D. & Ray, K. (2007) Living and working in urban working class communities, *Geoforum*, 38: 312–325.

Warr, D. (2005) Social networks in a 'discredited' neighbourhood, *Journal of Sociology*, 41 (3): 285–308.

Warsaw Business Journal (2008) President vetoes bill to reclassify urban agricultural land, 26 November. Available at: www.wbj.pl/article-43478-president-vetoes-bill-to-reclassify-urban-agricultural-land.html. Last accessed 27.11.08.

Warsaw Voice (2007) No end to strikes, 20 June. Available at: www.warsawvoice.pl/view/15126. Last accessed 26.5.09.

Warsaw Voice (2008) Surplus food for European Union's poorest, 29 November. Available at: www.warsawvoice.pl/view/19330. Last accessed 5.12.08.

Warzywoda-Kruszyńska, W. (ed.) (1999) *(Żyć) Na Marginesie Wielkiego Miasta*, Instytut Socjologii, Uniwersytet Łódzki, Łódź.

Washington Post (2009) Editorial: Polish economics, 23 April 2009. Available at: www.washingtontimes.com/news/2009/apr/23/polish-economics/. Last accessed 11.06.09.

Wedel, J. (1986) *The Private Poland: An Anthropologist's Look at Everyday Life.* New York: Facts on File.

Wedel, J. (ed.) (1992) *The Unplanned Society: Poland During and After Communism.* Columbia University Press: New York.

Weiner, E. (2005) No (wo)man's land: The post-socialist purgatory of Czech female factory workers, *Social Problems,* 52 (4): 572–592.

Weiner, E. (2007) *Market Dream: Gender, Class and Capitalism in the Czech Republic.* Ann Arbor: University of Michigan Press.

Wellman, B. & Wortley, S. (1990) Different strokes from different folks: Community ties and social support, *American Journal of Sociology,* 96 (3): 558–588.

Wheelock, J. & Oughton, E. (1996) The household as a focus for research, *Journal of Economic Issues,* 30 (1): 143–159.

Wierzbicka, A. (1997) *Understanding Cultures through their Key Words.* Oxford: Oxford University Press.

Williams, C. & Round, J. (2007) Re-thinking the nature of the informal economy: Some lessons from Ukraine, *International Journal and Urban and Regional Research* 31 (2): 425–441.

Williams, P. & Hubbard, P. (2001) Who is disadvantaged? Retail change and social exclusion, *International Review of Retail, Distribution and Consumer Research,* 11: 267–286.

Williamson, J. (1990) What Washington means by policy reform. In Williamson, J. (ed.) *Latin American Adjustment: How Much Has Happened?* Washington: Institute for International Economics. Available at www.iie.com/publications/papers/paper. cfm?researchid=486. Last accessed 20.11.09.

Wills, J. (2001) Community unionism and trade union renewal in the UK: moving beyond the fragments at last? *Transactions of the Institute of British Geographers,* 26, 465–483.

Wolch, J. (1989) The shadow state: Transformations in the voluntary sector. In Wolch, J. & Dear, M. (eds) *The Power of Geography: How Territory Shapes Social Life.* Boston: Unwin Hyman, 197–221.

World Bank (2009) *Global Crisis Pushing Almost 35 Million People Back into Poverty and Vulnerability in Europe and Central Asia,* 24 April. Available at: http://go.world-bank.org/WENCL94N30. Last accessed 11.06.09.

Wrigley, N. (2000) The globalization of retail capital. In Clark, G.L., Gertler, M.J. & Feldman, M.P. (eds) *The Oxford Handbook of Economic Geography.* Oxford: Oxford University Press, 292–313.

Wygnańska, J. (2006) *Statistical Update Poland 2006,* European Observatory on Homelessness, FEANTSA. Available at: www.bezdomnosc.edu.pl/images/PLIKI/ Raporty/polish_stats_update_2006_final.pdf. Last accessed 09.07.2009.

Yemtsov, R. (2007) *Housing Privatization and Household Wealth in Transition,* UNU-WIDER Research Paper No. 2007/02. Available at: www.wider.unu.edu/publications/ working-papers/research-papers/2007/en_GB/rp2007-02/_files/7809182701656 7108/default/rp2007-02.pdf. Last accessed 09.07.2009.

Young, M. & Willmott, P. ([1957]2007) *Family and Kinship in East London.* London: Penguin.

Yurchak, A. 2003: Russian neoliberal: The entrepreneurial ethic and the spirit of "true careerism", *The Russian Review*, 62: 72–90.

Zajicek, A., Calasanti, T. & Zajicek, E. (2007) Pension reforms and old people in Poland: An age, class and gender lens, *Aging Studies*, 21: 55–68.

Zapletalová, J. (2003) The role of self-government in housing development in Slovakia. In Lux, M. (ed.) *Housing Policy: An End or a New Beginning?* Open Society Institute, pp. 293–351.

Žižek, S. (2006) A plea for ethical violence. Paper given at the Lunchtime Lecture Series on Violence, Birkbeck College, University of London, May.

Žižek, S. (2008) *Violence: Six Sideways Reflections*. London: Profile Books.

ZUS (2006) *Social Insurance in Poland*. Warsaw: Zakład Ubezpieczeń Społecznych. Available at: www.zus.pl/files/english.pdf. Last accessed 16.02.07.

Index

acts of resistance 60, 220–1
agency, household economies 63, 223
agriculture 146
alimony benefits 212
allotments 145, 146–58
armaments industry 50
assets
  family networks 197
  housing 126–32
  income-generating 107–8, 132
  land 158
  practices 63–4, 221–2
  violence of neo-liberalism 230

Balcerowicz, Leszek 40, 41, 42–6,
    47, 49
Balcerowicz Plan 40–5
Ball, M. 117–18
Barnett, C. 37
Belka, Marek 45, 46, 49
Bellows, A. 148
benefit payments *see* welfare sector
black economy *see* informal economies
Bockman, J. 38
Bourdieu, P. 59, 63–4
Bratislava 11
  care 179–218
  foreign investment 13
  history 12–13
  housing 118–43

labour markets 21, 22, 23, 85–111
land and food 145–74
population growth 16, 17
see also Petržalka
Brown, D. 46

Caldwell, M. 73–4
capital, forms of 63–4
capitalism
  everyday economic practices 65–8,
    72, 220, 226–7
  neo-liberal theory 1–3, 33–9
  transition to from communism *see*
    post-socialism
car ownership 169–71
care 6–7, 31–2, 175–218
  changing landscapes of 177–9,
    215–16
  charities 213, 215
  definition 175–6
  domestic work 182–8
  exploitative practices 220–1
  family networks 105, 176, 181,
    188–97, 205–6, 212–13, 216–18
  family structures 179–81
  friendship networks 189, 197–206,
    216, 217
  policy ideas 236
  problems with accessing 214–15,
    236

care (cont'd)
    state assistance 177–9, 186, 191,
        206–13, 216
    trade unions 213–14
    violence of neo-liberalism 230–1
Caritas 213, 215
case study cities 10–28
    research method 28–30
    see also Nowa Huta; Petržalka
casualized labour 84, 95–6, 100, 187
Catholic Church 178, 233
Chakrabarty, D. 66–7
charities 171–2, 213, 215
child benefits 208–10
children
    care of 187, 191–2, 216
    household structures 18–19,
        180–1
    neighbour networks 203
Clarke, Simon 148
class 82, 86
    food provisioning 148–9
    neo-liberalism 34–6, 229–30
colonial practice 73
commodified sector, food 161–9,
    173–4
communism–capitalism transition
    see post-socialism
community development
    neo-liberal subjectivities 228
    violence of neo-liberalism 229
Community Economies Collective 65,
    67–8
community financial institutions
    236
comparative neo-liberalisms 232–4
complexity of economic
    practices 225–7
consumers
    disadvantaged 169–72
    shopping practices 161–9, 171,
        173–4
consumption 7, 145, 153, 155, 159–67,
    172–3
credit unions 236
Creed, G. 3, 72, 219
Czechoslovakia 49–50

De Boeck, F. 73
de Certeau, M. 60, 62, 75, 221
demographic shifts 17, 117
disadvantaged consumers 169–72
diverse economies 64–8, 225–7
do-it-yourself (DIY) 129
domestic labour 182–8
domesticating neo-liberalism 1–32
    everyday economic practices 58–72,
        219–25
        domestication 3–4, 72–7
        post-socialism see post-socialism
            below
        social reproduction 77–9
    political responses 235–7
    post-socialism 4–10
        care 175–218
        comparative neo-liberalisms 232–4
        diverse economies of 225–7
        domestic economic policies 38–40
        domestication 73–4
        economic practices 68–72, 219–25
        food provisioning 144–74
        housing 112–43
        neo-liberal subjectivities 227–9
        Polish economic policy 39–49,
            55–7, 178, 232–4
        political contestation 235–6
        Slovak economic policy 39–40,
            49–57, 178, 232–4
        tempering of neo-liberalism 236–7
        violence of neo-liberalism 229–32
        work 81–111
Dywizjonu 303 20, 26–7, 122–3, 124,
    203
Dzurinda, Mikuláš 51, 56, 85

economic crisis, global 237
economic history 12
economic practices, everyday 58–79
    see also household economic practices
economies of generosity 227–8
education assistance 208–10
education–employment transition 95
education levels 17, 19, 20, 21, 22
elderly care 185, 204–5, 216
employment 6–7, 31, 81–111

care and 185–6, 187, 191–2, 216–17
changing labour markets 86–90
exploitative practices 220
food provisioning 152, 154–5, 167,
    171, 174
housing 135–6
in-work poverty 86, 90–7, 228, 236
income inequality 8–10
informal 97, 98–108
labour migration 101–3
multiple jobs 70, 103–4
policy ideas 236
Polish economic policy 46, 47, 48–9,
    56, 85, 178
retraining/reskilling 94
Slovak economic policy 51–2, 53–4,
    55, 56, 85, 178
energy liberalization 139, 141
England, K. 35
ethnicity 231–2
European Union (EU)
    accession to 5–6, 39, 51, 231–2
    food aid 171–2, 213
    house prices 118
    labour markets 85, 101–3
    poverty 7–8
everyday economic practices 58–72
    domestication 3–4, 72–7
    social reproduction 77–9
    see also household economic
        practices
exchange networks 69–71, 190, 226
    see also social networks
exploitative practices 220–1
extended families 188–96
Eyal, G. 38

family benefits 208
family life 7
    see also household economic
        practices
family networks
    care 105, 176, 181, 188–97, 205–6,
        212–13, 216–18
    housing 127–8
    work 105
family structures 179–81

feminism
    conceptualizing the household 76
    social reproduction 78–9
feminization, labour markets 93–4
financial institutions 236
Fodor, E. 191, 192
food aid 171–2, 213
food provisioning 6–7, 31, 144–74
    culinary practices 161
    disadvantaged consumers 169–72
    domestic processing 160–1
    domestic production 145–57,
        158–60
    flows of products 158–61
    food consumption practices 161–9,
        171, 173–4
    household expenditure 169, 170
    income-generating activity 107–8
    land development 157–8
    retail sector 161–9, 173–4
    social networks 154–5, 158–61, 166,
        168
    survival strategies 70, 71, 148
free markets see markets
Friedman, Milton 40, 49
friendship networks 189, 197–206,
    216, 217

garden plots 146–57
gender divisions
    care 177, 178–9, 182–6, 190–1, 192,
        205–6, 211, 217–18, 230–1
    conceptualizing the household 76
    exploitative practices 220–1
    food provisioning 149, 151, 171
    labour markets 83–4, 93–4, 185–6,
        192
    securing social assistance 211
    social reproduction 78, 79
    violence of neo-liberalism 230–1
generation differentials
    care 184, 190–2
    exploitative practices 220–1
    food provisioning 149, 151, 171
    housing 117, 121, 126, 132
    labour markets 83–4, 94
    violence of neo-liberalism 230, 231

generations, relationships between 76, 190, 231
  see also grandparents
generosity, economies of 227–8
Gessayova 21, 22–3, 121–2, 123, 203
Gibson-Graham, J.K. 65, 227
Gilowska, Zyta 47
Glass, C. 191, 192
global economic crisis 237
Gomulka, Stanislaw 41, 44
Górali 20, 25, 122, 124, 199–200, 202, 203
grandparents 189, 191–3, 197, 212–13, 216
grey economy *see* informal economies
grocery markets 161–9, 173–4

Haanova 21, 22, 122, 123, 202–3
Harvey, D. 33, 35
Hausner Plan 46, 49, 85, 178
Havel, Václav 50
Hayek, F. 40
Hayek Foundation 53
health sector 1–2, 48, 54, 185
Highmore, B. 63
homelessness 132–3
household economic practices 6–10, 30–2, 58, 59, 219–25
  assets 63–4
  care 175–218
  comparative neo-liberalisms 232–4
  conceptualizing the household 75–7
  diversification/diversity 69–72, 225–7
  housing 112–43
  income-generating assets 107–8, 132
  land and food 6–7, 31, 70, 71, 107–8, 132, 144–74
  neo-liberal subjectivities 227–9
  political contestation 235–6
  research method 28–30
  social reproduction *see* social reproduction
  survival strategies 7, 58, 76, 148, 176
  violence of neo-liberalism 229–32
  work 81–111
household structures 18–19, 179–81

housework 182–8
housing 6–7, 10, 31, 112–43
  capitalizing on 126–32
  care and 217
  case study districts 13–17, 18, 20, 21, 22–7, 119–43
  comparative neo-liberalisms 233–4
  costs 138–41
  demographic shifts 117
  illegal occupation 133–4
  labour markets 135–6
  land development 158
  living space 125–6, 132
  maintenance 116, 129–30
  management structures 116, 130
  means of acquisition 119–21, 125, 140–1, 142, 158
  mobility 124–5, 140–1, 221
  mortgage finance 117–18, 132
  negotiating crises in 132–8
  neighbourhood differences 121–7, 131
  non-residential space as 137, 158
  policy ideas 236
  prices 118–19, 121, 122, 132, 142–3
  privatization 115–16, 118–19, 121, 142–3
  sharing 135–7, 139–40
  shortages 114–15, 132
  social 116–17, 133–4, 138, 142–3, 236
  social differentiation 131, 138
housing benefits 116–17, 137–8, 210
Hubbard, P. 169
hypermarkets 162–5, 167–8, 169, 171

iceberg metaphor, capitalism 65, 66
ill-health 185, 192
illegal employment 98–101
illegal occupation of housing 133–4
income benefits 206–13, 236
income inequality 8–10
  allotment ownership 149, 150
  Balcerowicz Plan 44
  Slovak pension policy 53
  wage polarization 83, 86
  see also inequality

individualism, economic 38
individualizing subjectivities 34–5, 227
industrial decline 82
industrial development 12, 13–16
inequality 7, 8–10, 221–4
    access to social services 211–12
    allotment ownership 149, 150
    case study districts 18, 19
    diversity of household
        economies 225–7
    global economic crisis 237
    housing 115, 130–2
    neo-liberal subjectivities 227–9
    neo-liberalism 34–6, 44
    Polish economic policy 44, 45–6, 56
    political responses 235–7
    Slovak economic policy 52–5, 56
    violence of neo-liberalism 229–32
    wage polarization 83, 86
informal economies 53–4, 69–71,
    97–108
information for household
    economies 223
infrastructural geographies 224
intergenerational relationships 76, 190,
    231
    see also grandparents
internal/external dichotomy 74–5
International Monetary Fund
    (IMF) 43
internationalization 5, 43, 47
    food provisioning 144–5, 162–4,
        173–4
interviews
    key informants 250–7
    research method 29–30
    summary information 239–40

Jarvis, H. 224
Jenkins, R. 61

Kaczyński twins 47
Kaldor, M. 235
Kideckel, D. 235
kinship and family networks
    care 105, 176, 181, 188–97, 212–13,
        216–18

housing 127–8
    work 105
Klaus, Václav 50
knowledge, household economies 223
Kochanowicz, R. 41, 42–3, 47
Kolodko, Grzegorz 44, 45, 46
Komárek, Valtr 50
Kowalik, Tadeusz 44
Kraków
    care 179–218
    history 11–12
    housing 118–43
    labour markets 16, 20, 25, 26,
        85–111
    land and food 145–74
    population growth 16, 17
    see also Nowa Huta
Kuroń, Jacek 44

labour markets 7, 31, 81–97, 108–11
    age differentials 83–4, 94
    care 185–6, 187, 191–2, 216–17
    casualization 84, 95–6, 100
    changing 86–90
    exploitative practices 220
    food provisioning 152, 154–5, 171,
        174
    gender differentials 83–4
    housing and 135–6
    in-work poverty 86, 90–7, 228, 236
    markers of inequality 222
    policy ideas 236
    Polish economic policy 49, 85
    segmentation 83, 86, 90–7
    Slovak economic policy 51–2,
        55, 85
    social reproduction 78–9
    wage polarization 83, 86
labour migration 101–3
land 31
    case study districts 17–18
    food and 144–74
        domestic production 145–57,
            158–60
        flows of 158–61
        land development 157–8
        retail sector 161–9

land (cont'd)
   social networks 154–5, 158–61,
     166, 168
   income-generating 107–8, 132
   in rainbow economy 70
learning, household economies 223
Ledeneva, A. 69, 70
leisure, land for 153–5
liberal economists, Poland 40–1, 42–3
liberalization 5
   energy prices 139, 141
   Polish economic policy 43, 48
Lipton, David 41–2
local/global dichotomy 74–5, 224
Lomnitz, L. 69
Lúky-sever 21, 23, 122, 123, 124,
    202, 203

McDonald's 73–4
Marcinkiewicz, Kazimierz 47
market socialism 42
markets 33–4, 35–7, 38–9
   alternative 226–7
   care 177
   Community Economies Collective's
    theory 67–8
   DIY 129–30
   everyday economic practices 60,
    220, 226–7
   food 145, 161–9, 173–4
   housing 112–13, 114, 224
    capitalizing on 128–32
    exclusion from 132–8
    privatization 115–16, 118–19,
     142–3
   informal economies 69–71
   land 145, 157–8
   Polish economic policy 43, 44, 47,
    48, 55–6, 232
   Slovak economic policy 50–2, 54,
    55–6, 232
Marxism 78–9
means testing 208
Mečiar, Vladimir 50–1, 55
Meurs, M. 148
migration, labour 101–3
Mikloš, Ivan 51

Mitchell, T. 38
moral rationalities 62
Morley, D. 75
mortgage finance 117–18, 132
mother–daughter relationships 190
multicoloured economies 68–70
multinational retailers 144–5, 162–4,
   173–4
Myers, G. 73

neighbour networks 189, 197–206, 217
neighbourhoods, practices and 62
neighbourhoods studied 10–28, 233–4
   research method 28–30
Neilsen, E. 63
neo-liberalism 1–3, 33–57, 60, 71–2
   post-socialism 1–2, 4–10, 38–40
    in everyday life see household
     economic practices
    Polish economic policy 39–49,
     55–7, 178, 232–4
    political contestation 1–2, 235–6
    Slovak economic policy 39–40,
     49–57, 178, 232–4
    tempering 236–7
   subjectivities 34–5, 227–9
   violence of 229–32
nested geographies 62, 75, 224
networks, household 77
   see also social networks
networks of exchange 69–71, 190, 226
   see also social networks
Nowa Huta 13–16, 79–80, 219–25
   care 179–218
   comparative neo-liberalisms 232–4
   diversity of practices 225–7
   food 145–8, 149–74
   household structures 18–19, 179–81
   housing 13–16, 18, 20, 23–7,
    119–43, 233–4
   income-generating assets 107–8, 132
   land and food 17–18, 145–74
   map 14
   neighbourhoods 20, 23–8, 233–4
   neo-liberal subjectivities 227–9
   population growth 16, 17
   poverty 18–19, 90–7

research method 28–30
violence of neo-liberalism 230–1
work 16, 20, 25, 26, 108–11
  in-work poverty 90–7
  informal and illegal 97–108
  labour market change 86–90
  labour migration 101–3
  unemployment 20, 90
nurses, white protests 1–2

Ost, D. 42, 45
Oświecenia 20, 27–8, 123, 124, 125,
  203
Owusu, M. 73

PEAD (Programme Européen d'Aide
  aux plus Demunis) 171–2, 213
pensions 49, 53, 106–7, 206–8, 212–13
Petržalka 13, 16–17, 79–80, 219–25
  care 179–218
  comparative neo-liberalisms 232–4
  diversity of practices 225–7
  food 145–8, 149–74
  household structures 19, 179–81
  housing 16–17, 21, 22–3, 119–43
  income-generating assets 107–8
  land and food 145–74
  map 15
  neighbourhoods 19–23, 234
  neo-liberal subjectivities 227–9
  population growth 16, 17
  poverty 18, 19, 90–7
  research method 28–30
  violence of neo-liberalism 230–2
  work 21, 22, 23, 108–11
    in-work poverty 90–7, 228
    informal and illegal 97–108
    labour market change 86–90
    labour migration 101–3
    unemployment 21, 22, 23, 90
Phillips, J. 175–6
Piacentini, M. 169
Pichler-Milanovich, N. 115
Pinera, José 49, 53
planning, household economies 223
Poland
  care 175–218

housing 114–43
Kraków 11–12
  see also Nowa Huta
land and food 144–74
neo-liberalization 1–4, 6–10, 39–49,
  55–7, 232–4
population growth 16, 17
turn away from neo-liberalism 237
work 46, 47, 48–9, 56, 81–111, 178
Polish Social Welfare Committee 213
political protests 1–2, 235–6
population growth 16, 17
post-colonial practice 73
post-socialism 1–2, 4–10, 34–5
  care 175–218
  comparative neo-liberalisms 232–4
  conceptualizing the household 76
  diverse economies of 225–7
  domestic economic policies 38–40
  domestication 73–4
  economic practices 68–72, 219–25
  food provisioning 144–74
  housing 112–43
  neo-liberal subjectivities 227–9
  Polish economic policy 39–49, 55–7,
    178, 232–4
  political contestation 235–6
  Slovak economic policy 39–40,
    49–57, 178, 232–4
  tempering of neo-liberalism 236–7
  violence of neo-liberalism 229–32
  work 81–111
poverty 7–8, 9–10, 221–2
  care 185, 192–3, 196, 197, 199–200,
    201, 203, 206–15, 217
  case study districts 18–19
  global economic crisis 237
  housing 117, 138–41
  housing ownership 128–9
  in-work 86, 90–7, 228, 236
  land and food 152, 153, 155–6,
    159–60, 169–72
  neo-liberal subjectivities 227–9
  Polish economic policy 44, 56
  political protest 235
  political responses 235–7
  Slovak economic policy 53–4, 55, 56

poverty (cont'd)
  sources of assistance 206–15, 217,
    228
  survival strategies 7, 58, 69–71, 76,
    148, 176
power 63, 76
practices 58–64, 223
  see also household economic practices
privatization 5, 34
  care 175
  food retail sector 162
  housing 115–16, 118–19, 121,
    142–3
  Polish economic policy 43, 45, 48,
    49
  Slovak economic policy 50–1, 54, 55
proactive practices 223, 227
Przy Arce 20, 26, 122–3, 124, 203
public transport 152, 171

rainbow economies 68–70
Rankin, K. 63
reciprocity, networks 196–7, 206
Red Cross 213
redundancy 7
remittance income 101–3
research method 19, 28–30
  key informants 250–7
  summary interview
    information 239–40
resistance, acts of 60, 220–1
retail sector 145, 161–9, 173–4
Roma community 1, 2, 194–5, 231–2
Rostowski, Jacek 41, 48
Rulyova, N. 74

Sachs, Jeffrey 41–2, 43
scale, spatiality of practices 62–3
Schatzki, T. 60–1, 62
school assistance 208–10
Seeth, H. 148
self-employment 101
self-provisioning 145–57, 158–61
service sector 82, 86
  food retail 161–9, 173–4
sex discrimination see gender divisions
Sheinbaum, D. 69

Shields, S. 46
shock therapy
  Poland 43–5
  Slovakia 50
shopping practices 161–9, 171, 173–4
sibling relationships 193–4, 197
Sik, E. 68, 76
Silverstone, R. 74, 75
Simonsen, K. 59–60, 61–2, 63, 64, 223
skills
  employment 94
  household economies 223
Slovakia
  Bratislava 11, 12–13
    see also Petržalka
  care 175–218
  housing 114–43
  land and food 144–74
  neo-liberalization 1, 2–4, 6–10,
    39–40, 49–57, 232–4
  population growth 16, 17
  turn away from neo-liberalism 237
  work 51–2, 53–4, 55, 56, 81–111,
    178
social benefits see welfare sector
social exclusion 18–19, 28–30, 222
social housing 116–17, 133–4, 138,
    142–3, 236
social market economy 50
social networks
  care 176–7, 179, 188–206, 212–13,
    216–18
  housing 127–9, 140–1, 224, 233–4
  land and food 154–5, 158–61, 166,
    168
  work 105–6
social policy
  Polish economic reform 44–7, 48–9,
    56, 178
  Slovak economic reform 51–2, 53–5,
    56, 178
  turn from neo-liberalism 237
social protests 1–2, 235
social relations, neo-liberalism 37
social reproduction 2–3, 7, 30–2, 77–9,
    219–20, 221–2
  care 186, 188–93, 218

food provisioning 172–3, 174
fragility 222
household structure–poverty
    link 18–19
neighbourhoods studied 19–28
neo-liberal subjectivities 228
policies to enhance 236
research method 28–30
violence of neo-liberalism 229,
    230–1
work 86–9, 110
social services 211–12
social wage 86–8, 97, 216–17
social welfare *see* welfare sector
socialism *see* state socialism
Solidarity 41, 42–3, 44–6, 233
spaces of domestication 73–5, 234
spatiality of practices 61–3
squatting 133–4
stabilization 5, 43
state benefits *see* welfare sector
state role, neo-liberalism 34
state socialism 68–70, 71–2, 225
    care 177, 216
    Czechoslovakia 50
    domestication 3, 38–9, 69, 72
    food provisioning 146–8, 161–2
    housing 112, 114, 119, 131, 142
    life after *see* post-socialism
    Poland 40–2
    work 81–2, 86–90
steelworks, Nowa Huta 13–16
    employment 88, 97
    housing 119–20, 125, 233
    welfare 213–14
subaltern acts of resistance 60, 220–1
subjectivities, neo-liberal 34–5, 227–9
supermarkets 162–5, 167–8
survival strategies 7, 58, 69–71, 76,
    148, 176
Szczerbiak, A. 47
Szejnfeld, Adam 48

tax policies 45–6, 47, 52
temporary work agencies 96
trade unions 41, 42–3, 213–14
transnational migration 101–3

transport 152, 169–71
Tusk, Donald 47–8, 49, 237

unemployment 7, 31, 81, 84–5
    age differentials 84, 94
    case study districts 20, 21, 22, 23, 90
    labour market segmentation 94,
        95–7
    Polish economic policy 46, 47, 48–9,
        56, 85, 178
    Slovak economic policy 51–2, 53,
        56, 85, 178
    social networks 105
    state benefits 84–5, 90, 99, 178, 207,
        208, 210
utility costs 138–9, 141

violence of neo-liberalism 229–32
von Mises, L. 40

wage inequality *see* income inequality
Ward, K. 35
Washington Consensus 5
weapons production 50
welfare sector
    care 177–9, 186, 191
        forms of support 206–13, 216,
            236
    housing benefits 116–17, 137–8, 210
    policy ideas 236
    Polish economic policy 44, 46, 48–9,
        85, 178
    post-socialist survival strategies 71
    Slovak economic policy 1, 2, 53–4,
        55, 85, 178
    work–benefits links 84–5, 90, 99,
        106–7, 178, 210
Wellman, B. 176
white protests 1–2
Williams, P. 169
Willowe 20, 23–5, 122, 124, 202, 203
women
    care 177, 178–9, 182–6, 190, 192,
        205–6, 211, 217–18, 230–1
    exploitative practices 220–1
    labour markets 83–4, 93–4, 185–6,
        192

women (*cont'd*)
  securing social assistance 211
  shopping 171
  violence of neo-liberalism 230–1
work 6–7, 31, 81–111
  care 185–6, 187, 191–2, 216–17
  changing labour markets 86–90
  exploitative practices 220
  food provisioning 152, 154–5, 167,
    171, 174
  in-work poverty 86, 90–7, 228, 236
  income inequality 8–10
  informal 97, 98–108
  labour migration 101–3
  markers of inequality 222
  multiple jobs 70, 103–4

  policy ideas 236
  Polish economic policy 46, 47, 48–9,
    56, 85, 178
  Slovak economic policy 51–2, 53–4,
    55, 56, 85, 178
  social networks 105–6
  social reproduction 78–9
worker self-management 42
World Bank
  EU labour markets 85
  global economic crisis 237
  housing 115
  Polish neo-liberalization 43
Wortley, S. 176

Yemtsov, R. 115